THE MODERN NEW TESTAMENT

The Modern New Testament from the Aramaic

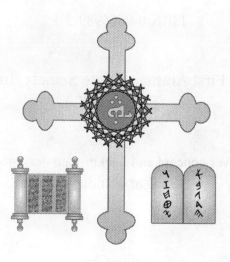

Translated by
Dr. George M. Lamsa

The Aramaic Bible Society, Inc.
P.O. Box 212145, Martinez, GA 30907
Telephone: 770/784-9062 Telephone/Fax: 770/385-7216
website : www.aramaicbiblesociety.org

ISBN:0-9675989-3-1

First Aramaic Bible Society, Inc.
Edition 2004

Cover concept and background designed by
dmahar@snet.net

Printed by:

Lightning Source Inc.
1246 Heil Quaker Blvd.
La Vergne, TN 37086

This Edition Dedicated To

Those who believe that the resurrection of Jesus Christ, the Messiah, portends their own resurrection or reincarnation, if not in three days as it was with Jesus, then surely within a lifetime.

Without the doctrine of reincarnation, Christianity rests with the occult. When First Century Christianity is restored we will come to know that Jesus Christ was indeed resurrected. Then the best ideas and instincts of the East and West will merge and advance the truth to be found in each. This, we believe, was indeed the theology that underlined the mission of Dr. George M. Lamsa, Dan MacDougald, Jr., Edgar Cayce and a host of others who lived on this earth in our time.

Robert E. Allen, Jr.
August, 2002

The Lord's Prayer

IN

ARAMAIC

The language which Christ Spoke

ENGLISH TRANSLATION	ARAMAIC	PRONUNCIATION
Our Father in Heaven		A-voon de-vesh-ma-ya
Hollowed Be Thy Name		Nith-ka-dash smakh
Thy Kingdom Come		Tai-thai mal-koo-thakh
Thy Will Be Done.		Neh-wey sev-ya-nakh
as in Heaven so on Earth		Ai-ken-na de-vesh-ma-ya
Give Us Bread for Our Needs		Up ber-ah, hav-lan
from Day to Day		Lakh-ma de-soon-ka-nan
Forgive Us Our Offences, as We		Yo-ma-na wush-vok-lan
Have Forgiven Our Offenders		khoe-baine ai-ken-na de-up
Do Not Let Us Enter into		khnan sh-vak-n el-kha-ya-ven
Temptation		Ula ta-e-lun el-nis-yoe-na
Deliver Us from Evil		Il-la pes-on min-bee-sha
For Thine Is the Kingdom		Mit-thil de-de-lakh-ee
... and the Power		Mal-koo-tha oo-khay-la
... and the Glory		Oo-tish-boakh-ta
For Ever and Ever "Amen"		El-a-lum all-meen A-men

vi

Aramaic-English Interlinear

Matthew 6:9-13

9 Our-Father | who(is)in-heaven | holy-may-be | your-name

10 come-may | Kingdom-your | be-it-let | Will-your

like (or "as") | of-in--heaven | also | earth-the-in

11 Give | to-us | bread-the | of-our-need | today

12 And-forgive | to-us | our-debts | as | also | we

we-forgive | our-debtors | **13** And-not | bring-us | into-temptation

but | deliver-us | from | the-evil | because | yours

are | the-kingdom | and-the-power | and-the-glory

to-age | upon-age

TABLE OF CONTENTS

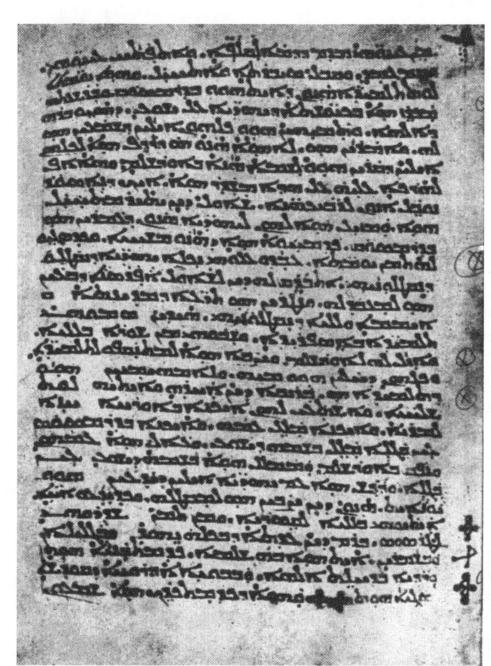

Through the courtesy of William M. Mortimer, Esq., and Harrison B. McCawley, Esq.
Showing portion of Ancient Aramaic (Syriac) New Testament Manuscript
(circ. early 6th century, A.D.)

INTRODUCTION

EASTERN TEXT

NEW TESTAMENT

Owing to church controversies which began in the fifth century A. D. with the rise of Islam, the ancient Christians of the Near East were lost to the rest of Christendom. Their Bible Texts and other sacred literature were, for many centuries, not known to the Western world. A few decades before the World War, contacts were made with the section of the ancient Church in the East which had survived many persecutions and privations since the thirteenth century A.D. Since the war and the opening of Mesopotamia by Great Britain, people who had been given up as lost have been brought to light together with new documents and new facts. European as well as American scholars are aware of the importance of the Aramaic language and the survival of the people who speak it.

PESHITTA

The original Eastern text of both the New and Old Testaments is called *Peshitta* which means simple, true and straight. The Peshitta text with which European and American scholars have been familiar is that of Monophysite Christians. This is clearly seen from the facsimiles reproduced in books and portions of the New Testament printed in Europe.

The Peshitta New Testament is an ancient and the only authoritative document of the New Testament in use among the Syriac Aramaic speaking people of Palestine, Syria, Mount Lebanon, Mesopotamia, Persia and Malabar (South India) from the first century A.D. to the present day. The terms Aramaic and Syriac are interchangeable in English. It is also the root from which Hebrew sprang. Peshitta is the authorized text of the Scriptures and had its origin in the lands from which Christianity sprang and it is written in the language in which Our Blessed Lord, His disciples and the early Christians spoke and wrote. These facts are known to all Biblical scholars. Even those who have made translations from the Greek, frankly admit that Jesus spoke Aramaic and his teachings were handed down in that language. Peshitta is still the text of more than a million Maronites, Chaldean Roman Catholics in the Near East, the Jacobites, the Malkites and the Assyrian Christians. These people are the remnant of the ancient churches of Galilee, Jerusalem, Damascus, Antioch and Edessa. Both the Peshitta Old and New Testaments were also used by the Armenians until the fifth century when a translation into the Armenian language was made.

The name Peshitta was given to this ancient text of the Scriptures in order to distinguish it from the revised Aramaic (Syriac) text of the Scriptures which had undergone slight revision and which is known as the *Philoxenian* version made in 508 which was further revised by Thomas of Harkela in 616. The three manuscripts from which this translation was made antedate the Philoxenian version by not less than three hundred years. They are from the ancient, original sources. The revisions were introduced into the East by the Monophysite bishops in the fifth and sixth centuries A. D. under the influence of the Greek Church when the Byzantine Empire had spread in Syria, Edessa and other cities west of the Euphrates River. Byzantine emperors, especially Justinian and Heraclius, made every attempt to heal the breach that had divided the church at Ephesus and Chalcidon. Amendments and revisions of the Scriptures were necessary if the dreams of the Byzantine emperors for a united Christianity were to be realized. This unity was essential because of Persian ascendancy in the Euphrates valley, and the weakening of the Roman position owing to the divisions of Christianity.

While all these rival churches in the East fought and bitterly denounced one another, since the Council of Ephesus in 431 A. D., they agree on the originality and antiquity of Peshitta. It is impossible to believe that after the split, one of the hostile sects would have accepted its New Testament from another. Other books containing doctrines and dogmas written after the Council of Ephesus by a member of one sect are rejected by other sects. On the other hand, Peshitta, being the first and only text of the Scriptures preceding all other Christian literature, is claimed and highly revered by all ancient churches in the East. These claims are strongly supported by history, geography, testimonies of the early fathers and unbroken traditions.

There is no mention of any translation of the New Testament being made into Aramaic from any language in the ten Christian Councils which took place in the Persian Empire, third and fourth centuries A. D. The Council of Beth-Lapeth deliberated on the acceptance of the *Book of Revelation* which is not included in the Peshitta canon and which was not accepted by Eastern Christians for many centuries. The Council of Seleucia (410 A. D.) makes no mention of any New Testament revision or translation or the need for such a work. Why should the greatest event in the history of the Church in the East be ignored by the writers and historians in the East? Armenians and other peoples celebrate the date of their Bible translations.

The Christians in Palestine and Syria were the first to embrace Christianity. They must have had Gospels in Aramaic in order to preach to Greeks and other people. Gospels were in circulation before St. Paul's conversion. They were written ten or fifteen years after the Crucifixion. They were the recordings of the eyewitnesses who had traveled with Jesus and who could record most of the teachings of their Lord. Papias tells us that Matthew wrote in the language of the Hebrews, that is Aramaic. This is supported by the testimonies of the early fathers and historians.

Rev. Carl Sumner Knopf, Ph. D., Dean of the School of Religion and Professor of Biblical Literature and Archaeology at the University of Southern California, confirms the Semitic background of the New Testament, the Eastern customs and the importance of the Aramaic language. He says:

"Papias said that Matthew wrote in the Hebrew language. Hebrew was dead by that time, but there was a Jewish vernacular, Aramaic, closely related to ancient Hebrew, and used by Jesus and His disciples. Sections of Matthew's gospel point quite definitely to a Greek rendering of a previous Aramaic original - just as though Jesus' sayings had been jotted down by an Aramaic speaking Jew whose notebook was later incorporated in a wonderful new gospel that shows Jesus as the long-expected Messiah, teaching God's truth to needy humanity." Page 33, *Comrades of the Way* —The Methodist Book Concern.

RABBULA

The theory that the Peshitta New Testament was revised by Rabbula, a Monophysite bishop, was advanced about forty years ago by the late Dr. F. Crawford Burkitt of Cambridge, England. At that time, he was just beginning his Aramaic studies. Dr. Burkitt's thesis on the subject was conjectural and he said so. If Dr. Burkitt's logic were correct, then the Peshitta would agree with Greek texts but Peshitta does not agree with Greek texts.

Rabbula was probably the 15th bishop of the ancient See of Edessa. His predecessors must have had the Scriptures in Aramaic. We know that the first fifteen bishops of Jerusalem were all Semites and they spoke and worshipped in Aramaic. Christian Churches in Palestine and Syria were organized very early. St Paul, prior to his conversion to Christianity, was a persecutor of the Church in Judea and Syria, Acts 9:2.

Rabbula was only a bishop. He could not have made a revision of the New Testament without the proper authority from the head of the Church in the East who at that time was the patriarch Yawalaha whose See was in Seleucia, the Persian Capital. On the other hand, Rabbula made no claims to a revision of the New Testament in Aramaic.

DIATESSARON

What Rabbula did was this: He suppressed the *Diatessaron* or, as it is called in Aramaic, *Damkhalty*, which is a single narrative of the four Gospels compiled by Tatian, an Assyrian, from Aramaic sources of the New Testament about 150 A. D., and substituted for it *Damparshey*, a lectionary containing the four Gospels of the Peshitta text. This pertained to Rabbula's own diocese but meant nothing to the rest of the Church where the *Diatessaron* was never heard of and where the copies of the four Gospels had been in common use before the birth of Tatian and still are to the present day.

The *Diatessaron* was compiled for a single reason, to facilitate the circulation of the Gospels by condensing to a single narrative. Paper was unknown and parchment was expensive and hard to procure at the time. Tatian's work, even though a radical departure from the accepted canon, made it possible for poor priests and deacons to own copies of the four Gospels as a single narrative yet containing the complete teachings and works of our Lord. Nevertheless, in the eyes of many bishops and conservative Christians, this was a departure from the ancient tradition and they would not tolerate this radical change in the four Gospels handed down by the Apostles.

On the other hand, Rabbula was a Monophysite. He was bitterly opposed to the doctrines of the Church in the East. He demanded that Theodore's writings be condemned, as he had condemned those of Nestorius. Since Rabbula's acts and his teachings were condemned by the majority of Christians in the East, it would have been impossible for them to accept a New Testament revision made by him. Moreover, there was no need for such an undertaking. The New Testament Scriptures in Aramaic were widely circulated centuries before Rabbula's birth. Edessa, Rabbula's diocese, is close to Antioch where the Apostles established their headquarters after they were driven out of Jerusalem. It was Christianized in the early part of the first century A. D. (Eus. 11.107.) It was easy to get texts from Antioch to Edessa.

The originality of the Peshitta New Testament text is strongly supported by even earlier evidence. Aphraates quoted it; St. Ephraim, about 360, wrote a commentary on it; and the doctrine of Addi, placed it at the apostolic times.

Aside from the historical and geographical support, the Peshitta New Testament text varies considerably from the Greek and Latin versions which were made later for the use of new converts to Christianity. There are hundreds of passages where the meaning is different from that of the Greek version. The style of writing is purely Aramaic and the idioms are Eastern. Neither does Peshitta agree with recent New Testament translations made from Greek into Aramaic.

The New Testament revisions in the Monophysite text had no effect on the main body of the Church in the East under the Persian Empire. The Church rejected the doctrines advanced at the Council of Ephesus and bitterly opposed the spread of Greek and Monophysite doctrines. Neither were these revisions used in Monophysite Churches. They were only used privately by bishops and scholars as Greek sources of the Scriptures to facilitate their work in achieving unity between the Imperial Byzantine Church and the Monophysites in Syria and Egypt. Then again, Persia, an enemy of the Byzantine empire, for political reasons was strongly opposed to the introduction of Greek doctrines among the Christians in the East. The Persian kings issued decrees to imprison and expel priests and bishops found to be sympathetic to the Byzantine Church.

Such were the political and religious conditions which isolated the Christians in the East from the rest of the Christians in the Byzantine Empire and the rest of the Christian world. This isolation continued through Arab, Mongol and Turkish rule from the sixth to the thirteenth century. As the result of this continued isolation, the Biblical customs and manners and the Aramaic language remained unchanged and the Scriptures escaped additions and revisions.

Asahel Grant, M.D., the first American missionary to discover the Assyrians, writes in his book, *The Nestorians, or the Lost Tribes*: "The Nestorians have preserved the Scriptures in manuscript with great care and purity." He puts the date of Peshitta New Testament in the early part of the second century A. D.

The Christians in the Persian Empire, because of continuous warfare between Persia and Rome, did not participate in the Councils which took place in the Roman Empire, and therefore, escaped the introduction of new doctrines and dogmas which might make necessary Scriptural revisions. Until the coming of American and English missionaries in the early part of the nineteenth century, the Assyrian Christians were not aware of the religious and political changes which had taken place in the Byzantine Empire and the rest of the Western World. They had not even heard of Martin Luther, The Reformation, or the discovery of America. The news that others had escaped the fury of Genghis Khan and Tameriane was a surprise to them.

THE PAULINE EPISTLES

The Pauline Epistles were letters written by Paul to small Christian congregations in Asia Minor, Greece and Rome. These early Christians were mostly Jews of the Dispersion, men and women of Hebrew origin.

Paul on his journeys always spoke in the Jewish synagogues. His first converts were Hebrews. Then came Arameans as in the case of Timothy and Titus. Their fathers were Aramean and their mothers were Jewish.

Paul emphasizes Hebrew law and history. He refers to Abraham, Isaac and Jacob as our fathers. In his letters and teaching he appeals to the Jewish people to accept Jesus as the promised Messiah. Paul's mission was first to his own people. When they refused to listen to him, he shook his garment and went out among the Gentiles. Acts 18:6.

Paul was educated in Jewish law in Jerusalem. He was a member of the Jewish Council. His native language was western Aramaic but he acquired his education through Hebrew and Chaldean or Palestinian Aramaic, the language which was spoken in Judea. He defended himself when on trial in the Hebrew tongue. Acts 22:2. Paul was converted, healed and baptized in Damascus. Acts 9:17,18.

Very early the Epistles were translated into Greek for the use of converts who spoke Greek. Later they were translated into all tongues.

ARAMAIC

Leshana Aramaya, the Aramaic tongue, is the name of an ancient language spoken in Syria and Mesopotamia and later in Palestine. It was the mother tongue of the New Testament writers. The term Aramaic is derived from Aram, the youngest son of Shem. Gen. 10:22. After Abraham had left his home and kindred in Ur-Chaldea, he sojourned in Haran for many years and from thence he departed to Palestine. His son, Isaac, married Rebekah, sister of Laban, an Aramean. Years later, Isaac sent Jacob to Padan-aram where he married two of his uncle's daughters. "And Jacob obeyed his father and his mother, and was gone to Padan-aram." Gen. 28:7. Nahor, the brother of

Abraham, is called the father of Aram. The descendants of this brother are termed Arameans. In Deut. 26:5 Jacob is called "a wandering Aramean." Thus Hebrews and Arameans of western Syria were closely related.

According to the Old Testament, Aramaic was the language before the division of languages in the land of Shinar. Gen. 11:2. During the Assyrian and Babylonian rule, Aramaic came to be the *lingua franka* of western Asia. It was the vernacular of the Assyrians, Chaldeans and Syrians and, owing to the Assyrian conquest of the Kingdom of Israel and the settlement of the Assyrians and Babylonians in Samaria and Galilee, Aramaic became the vernacular of Northern Palestine in 721 B. C. (2 King 17:6, 24.) Then in 586 B. C., Nebuchadnezzar took Jerusalem and carried Judah into captivity. During the captivity, Hebrew was replaced by Eastern Aramaic, that is, Chaldean. Thus the Chaldean or Eastern Aramaic which is also known as Palestinian Aramaic, became the language of the Jews until 900 A. D. when Aramaic as the vernacular tongue was replaced by Arabic in Palestine and Syria after the conquest of Palestine and Syria by the Arabs in the sixth century.

Nevertheless, Aramaic continued to be the language of Christian and Jewish Scriptures and it is still spoken in Iraq and Syria to the present day. In the New Testament, Aramaic is known as the Hebrew language, which means the Aramaic spoken by the Hebrews. Hebrew and Aramaic are related languages.

Dr. Philip K. Hitti, noted historian and Professor of Semitic languages at Princeton University, in his book *The History of the Arabs*, Macmillan & Co., Ltd., London uses Aramaic and Syriac terms interchangeably and states that Aramaic is still a living language. He says on page 353 "In country places and on their farms these dhimmis clung to their ancient cultural patterns and preserved their native languages: Aramaic and Syriac in Syria and Al-`Iraq, Iranian in Persia and Coptic in Egypt." And on page 361 "In Al-`Iraq and Syria the transition from one Semitic tongue, the Aramaic, to another, the Arabic, was of course easier. In the out-of-the-way places, however, such as the Lebanons with their preponderant Christian population, the native Syriac put up a desperate fight and has lingered until modern times. Indeed Syriac is still spoken in Ma'lula and two other villages in Anti-Lebanon. With its disappearance, Aramaic has left in the colloquial Arabic unmistakable traces noticeable in vocabulary, accent and grammatical structure."

ARAMAIC DIALECTS

Aramaic has two main dialects, the Eastern and Western. Greek has several dialects as Doric, Ionic, Æolic and Attic. The Greek spoken in Athens is the dialect in which most of the Greek literature has been handed down. Western Aramaic is spoken in Syria and Eastern Aramaic in Mesopotamia. Eastern Aramaic is sub-divided into two dialects, the Northern spoken in Assyria and the Southern spoken in Babylon. After the Babylonian conquest, Southern or Chaldean Aramaic became the language of Judea. The Aramaic of Edessa in which the Old Testament was written is the purest of all dialects and it became the literary language of both the Eastern and Western Arameans and is so to the present day. The difference in these dialects is chiefly in accent and idioms. The language of sacred literature is the same.

THE CHALDEAN AND GALILEAN ARAMAIC

Chaldean Aramaic came to be the vernacular of Judea during the exile. Northern Aramaic was the language of Galilee since the fall of Samaria 722 B.C. This was the dialect spoken in Galilee during the time of Our Lord Jesus Christ and His disciples. Like other Easterners, Jesus spoke several dialects. Nevertheless, on several occasions, the Jews were unable to understand Him as in the case of Nicodemus. "Born again" is a Northern Aramaic or Galilean idiom which means to become like a child. Nicodemus took it literally just as we often take idioms of a foreign language literally. Then again, Peter was betrayed by his Galilean speech. "Surely thou art one of them: for thou art a Galilean, and thy speech agreeth thereto." Mark 14:70.

It was natural for the disciples and their converts to record the teaching of their Master in their own Aramaic dialect for the use of the people in Galilee and Syria where Jesus had lived and started his preaching. There was no reason to write the Gospels in a dialect other than their own Galilean dialect.

The disciples used their own language to write to Christians in Syria. Acts 15:23. The Jewish priests sent an Epistle to the Jews in Damascus by the hand of Paul. This Epistle was written in Chaldean Aramaic, the language the Jews spoke. Acts 9:2.

The pure Chaldean Aramaic which the Jews had brought from Babylon had been to some extent amalgamated with Hebrew. This difference is noticed by comparing the Book of Daniel which was written in Aramaic 450 B. C. with the Talmud.

SYRIAC

Syriac is the Greek term wrongly used for the Aramaic spoken in Syria. It is derived from the name of the country, Syria. The Greeks called the Arameans by the name of the country.

European and American scholars, when referring to Aramaic spoken in Mesopotamia and Syria, use the term Syriac. However, the term Syriac is seldom understood in the East. It was introduced by Greeks and later by European missionaries. Native writers still use the name Aramaic when referring to the language. The use of both terms has created considerable confusion among western people. Some readers are wrongly led to believe that Syriac and Aramaic are two separate languages. This is not so. Syriac is a western term for Aramaic. The Eastern text of the Old Testament, when referring to the language, uses the term *Leshana Aramaya*. The edict of the Persian Artaxeries was written and interpreted in the Aramaic. Ezra 4:7.

ARAMAIC SCRIPT

The Aramaic script varies according to the nature of the work. The Scriptures are chiefly written in Estrangelo characters. Assyrian liturgical books are written in what is known as the ordinary Aramaic script or Nestorian characters. The Jacobite liturgical books are written in Jacobite characters. These character differences came into use in the fifth century after the division of the Church for the purpose of distinguishing between the various sects. These differences were slight modifications in the formation of certain characters. The number of characters, the construction and the spelling, however, are the same. The Gospels might have been first written in plain Aramaic script or in square Assyrian characters. The present Hebrew script is known as Assyrian script and it was used by the Jews since the fifth century B. C.

IN CONCLUSION

One thing which has impressed the readers of these manuscripts is the care with which they were produced. There is hardly a word of variance. Eastern scribes always copy Scriptures carefully. Time is immaterial to them when copying the Word of God.

Sir Frederick Kenyon, Curator at the British Museum, in his book *Textual Criticism of the New Testament*, speaks highly of the accuracy and antiqulty of Peshitta MSS.

This translation is made from ancient MSS., fascimile pages of which are reproduced in this volume. The story of the woman caught in adultery, II Peter, II and III John, Jude and the Book of Revelation are translated from printed texts. Aramaic MSS. were used for these printed texts and they contain these portions of the Scriptures which are not found in the ancient Peshitta texts. These added portions were not accepted by the Christians in the East in the early centuries.

According to Aramaic MSS., the order of Peshitta differs from that of King James. The Epistles of the Apostles, James, Peter and John, follow after the Book of Acts and the Pauline Epistles follow them. In this translation, the order of the King James version has been retained.

I have accomplished this work with the help of God and by diligent care. I know Aramaic and I speak it. English is my adopted tongue. I am indebted to all who have so generously helped me to make this work possible. I pray God this translation will benefit Christians everywhere and will help them toward a better understanding of the greatest and most inspiring book of all ages. After all, sincere faith in Jesus Christ has its own reward and devotion to Christ is the principle of all Christianity. Help to understanding is where we look for it in faith and devotion.

George M. Lamsa

WORDS WITH MANY MEANINGS

The following list of Aramaic words further illustrates the difficulties of the early translators from the Aramaic into Greek, at a time when questions of punctuation, accentuation and paragraphing were unknown. This is especially true of Aramaic, which is the richest and most expressive language of the Semitic group, but having a small vocabulary when compared with the Greek and Latin. This limitation of words made necessary the use of the same words with various shades of meanings. This is because Aramaic is one of the world's most ancient languages.

Translators are well aware of these grammatical difficulties, particularly in a language like Aramaic where a single dot above or under a letter radically changes the meaning of a word. These tiny dots are made by scribes, who are not authors but mere copyists, hired for this purpose by rich and by learned men. But owing to the humidity of the climate and the nature of the ink, blots appear on the pages when pressed against each other. Again because of exposure of a manuscript and its careless handling, flies alight on the pages and leave marks. Furthermore as the lines are crowded for lack of space, a dot placed above one letter may read as though it were placed under a letter in the previous line.

Some Aramaic words are written and pronounced alike, but their meaning differs according to the context. In other cases the differences are indicated by dots which alter the pronunciation. In yet other instances, if the translator does not speak the language from which he translates the meaning and usage of some words must be left to his knowledge and judgment.

WORDS WITH MANY MEANINGS

ܪܘܚܐ Rokha {
Spirit
Wind
Temper
Pride
Rheuma-
tism
}

ܒܪܬܐ Barta {
Daughter
Egg
}

ܓܡܠܐ Gamla {
Large
rope
Camel
Beam
}

ܥܠ Al {
Enter
On
By
Attack
Upon
Because
}

ܐܬܪܐ Athra {
Country
Place
Chance
Land
Region
}

ܡܠܐܟܐ Mal-akha {
Angel
Mes-
senger
}

ܒܪܢܫܐ Barn-asha {
Son of
man
Man-
kind
Human
being
Man
}

ܫܠܡ Shlem {
Finished
Fulfilled
In peace
Accom-
plished
}

ܛܥܐ Taa {
Forsake
Mislead
Lost
Deceive
}

ܫܥܐ Shaa {
Hour
Time
Turn
}

ܓܡܝܪܐ Gmira {
Complete
Perfect
Finished
Compre-
hensive
True
}

ܥܠܡܐ Alma {
World
People
}

ܡܫܝܚܐ Mshikha {
Christ
Anointed
}

ܫܡܝܐ Shmaya {
Universe
Heaven
Sky
}

ܡܫܚܐ Mishkha {
Oil
Butter
}

WORDS WITH MANY MEANINGS

ܕܝܘܢܐ Dewana
- Insane
- Crazy
- Lunatic

ܫܒܩ Shbak
- Reserve
- Keep
- Spare
- Leave
- Forgive
- Allow
- Permit

ܫܕܢܐ Shedana
- Insane
- Crazy
- Lunatic

ܕܝܘܐ Dewa
- Wildman
- Devil

ܡܐܢܐ Maney
- Vessels
- Utensils
- Goods or Merchandise

Words spelled alike but pronounced differently, and with different meanings.

ܓܪܒܐ Garbey / ܓܪܒܐ Garva
- Leper
- Muslin, Sheepskin

ܐܡܗܬܐ Amhatha / ܐܡܗܬܐ Aemhatha
- Maidservants
- Mothers

ܚܡܪܐ Khamra / ܚܡܪܐ Khmara
- Wine
- Donkey

ܟܟܪܐ Kakra / ܟܪܟܐ Karkha
- Talent
- Province

ܥܒܕܐ Avda / Avada
- Servant
- Work

ܡܠܟܐ Malka / ܡܠܟܐ Milka
- King
- Council

ܣܦܪܐ Sapra / Sepra
- Scribe
- Book, Reading

ܥܘܠܐ Awla / ܥܘܠܐ Awela
- Iniquity
- Baby

ܣܗܪܐ Sahra / ܣܗܕܐ Sahda
- Moon
- Witness

Portion of Psalm 7 from the Syriac manuscript Codex Ambrosianus.

The Modern New Testament

From the Aramaic

by

Dr. George M. Lamsa

**Bible Translator, Interpreter and Scholar on Customs,
Habits and Culture of the People in the Time of Jesus**

The Names of the Books of
THE NEW TESTAMENT
Arranged in the Order of the Peshitta Canon

Writings Attributed to
The Original Apostles

Writings Attributed to
The Apostle Paul

Matthew	3	Romans	239
Mark	45	I Corinthians	257
Luke	71	II Corinthians	275
John	115	Galatians	287
The Acts	149	Ephesians	293
James	193	Philippians	299
I Peter	199	Colossians	305
II Peter	205*	I Thessalonians	309
I John	209	II Thessalonians	313
II John	214*	I Timothy	317
III John	215*	II Timothy	323
Jude	216*	Titus	327
Revelation	218*	Philemon	329
		Hebrews	331

* = the writing was missing from the earliest versions of the NT Peshitta, and added later to the canon. With the exception of those writings, the order of material arranged and presented in this volume follows the canonical order of the oldest Peshitta versions, an arrangement still in use with some later manuscripts (i.e., the Khabouris Manuscript).

Significant differences between this translation and the Authorized King James Version are indicated by verse references at the foot of each page for comparison.

The Syriac titles and conclusions at the beginning and end of each New Testament book are found in the Aramaic texts, as recorded in *Syriac New Testament and Psalms*, published by the United Bible Societies. Some translations missing in Lamsa's version have been supplied here from previous English translations (e.g., Murdock, Etheridge) of the Syriac Peshitta, as noted.

D.J.Mahar, *Editor*
March 26, 2004

THE GOSPEL ACCORDING TO
ST. MATTHEW

❖ ܐܘܢܓܠܝܘܢ ܩܕܝܫܐ ܕܡܬܝ ❖

CHAPTER 1

*T*HE book of the genealogy of Jesus Christ, the son of David, the son of Abraham.

2 Abraham begot Isaac; Isaac begot Jacob; Jacob begot Judah and his brothers;

3 Judah begot Perez and Zerah of his wife Tamar; Perez begot Hezron; Hezron begot Aram;

4 Aram begot Aminadab; Aminadab begot Nahson; Nahson begot Salmon;

5 Salmon begot Boaz of his wife Rahab; Boaz begot Obed of his wife Ruth; Obed begot Jesse;

6 Jesse begot David the king; David the king begot Solomon of the wife of Uriah;

7 Solomon begot Rehoboam; Rehoboam begot Abijah; Abijah begot Asa;

8 Asa begot Jehoshaphat; Jehoshaphat begot Joram; Joram begot Uzziah;

9 Uzziah begot Jotham; Jotham begot Ahaz; Ahaz begot Hezekiah;

10 Hezekiah begot Manasseh; Manasseh begot Amon; Amon begot Josiah;

11 Josiah begot Jechoniah and his brothers, about the captivity of Babylon.

12 And after the captivity of Babylon, Jechoniah begot Shealtiel; Shealtiel begot Zerubbabel;

13 Zerubbabel begot Abiud; Abiud begot Eliakim; Eliakim begot Azor;

14 Azor begot Sadoc; Sadoc begot Achim; Achim begot Eliud;

15 Eliud begot Eleazar; Eleazar begot Matthan; Matthan begot Jacob;

16 Jacob begot Joseph the husband of Mary, of whom was born Jesus, who is called Christ.

17 ¶ Therefore all the generations, from Abraham down to David, are fourteen generations; and from David down to the Babylonian captivity, fourteen generations; and from the Babylonian captivity down to Christ, fourteen generations.

18 ¶ The birth of Jesus Christ was in this manner. While Mary his mother was acquired for a price for Joseph, before they came together, she was found with child of the Holy Spirit.

19 But Joseph her husband was a pious man, and did not wish to make it public; so he was thinking of divorcing her secretly.

20 While he was considering this, the angel of the Lord appeared to him in a dream, and said to him, O, Joseph, son of David, do not be afraid to take your wife Mary, because he that is to be born of her is of the Holy Spirit.

21 She will give birth to a son, and you will call his name Jesus; for he shall save his people from their sins.

22 ¶ All this happened, that what was spoken from the Lord by the prophet might be fulfilled,

23 Behold, a virgin will conceive and give birth to a son, and they shall call his name Immanuel, which is interpreted, Our God is with us.

24 When Joseph rose up from his sleep, he did just as the angel of the Lord commanded him, and he took his wife.

25 And he did not know her until she gave birth to her first-born son; and she called his name Jesus.

Cf. dif. verses 1:3, 5-6, 18-20, 23, 25.

CHAPTER 2

W HEN Jesus was born in Bethlehem of Judah, in the days of Herod the king, there came Magi from the East to Jerusalem.

2 And they were saying, Where is the King of the Jews, who has been born? For we have seen his star in the East, so we have come to worship him.

3 But when Herod the king heard it, he trembled, and all Jerusalem with him.

4 So he gathered together all the high priests and the scribes of the people, and he kept asking them, where the Christ would be born?

5 They said, In Bethlehem of Judah, for thus it is written in the book of the prophet:

6 Even you, Bethlehem of Judah, you are not insignificant in the eyes of the kings of Judah, for from you shall come out a king, who will shepherd my people Israel.

7 Then Herod called the Magi secretly, and he learned from them at what time the star appeared to them.

8 And he sent them to Bethlehem, and said to them, Go and enquire very carefully concerning the boy, and when you have found him, come back and let me know, so that I also may go and worship him.

9 When they had heard from the king, they went away; and behold, the same star that they had seen in the east was going before them, until it came and stood just above the place where the infant boy was.

10 When they saw the star, they rejoiced exceedingly.

11 And they entered the house, and they saw the infant boy with Mary, his mother; and they threw themselves down and worshipped him; and they opened their treasures and offered to him gifts - gold and frankincense, and myrrh.

12 And they saw in a dream not to return to Herod, so they departed to their own country by another way.

13 When they had gone, the angel of the Lord appeared to Joseph in a dream, and said to him, Arise, take the infant boy and his mother, and escape to Egypt, and stay there until I tell you, for Herod is ready to demand the child so as to destroy him.

14 Then Joseph rose up, took the infant boy and his mother in the night, and escaped to Egypt.

15 And he remained there until the death of Herod, so that what was said from the Lord by the prophet, might be fulfilled, I have called my son from Egypt.

16 ¶ When Herod saw that he was insulted by the Magi, he was greatly enraged, so he sent forth and had all the infant boys in Bethlehem and in its suburbs killed, from two years old and down, according to the time that he had enquired from the Magi.

17 Then was fulfilled what was said by the prophet Jeremiah who said,

18 A voice was heard in Ramah, weeping and wailing exceedingly, Rachel weeping for her sons, and she would not be comforted, because they could not be brought back.

19 ¶ When King Herod died, the angel of the Lord appeared in a dream to Joseph in Egypt.

20 And he said to him, Arise, take the boy and his mother, and go to the land of Israel, for those who were seeking the boy's life are dead.

21 So Joseph rose up, took the boy and his mother, and he came to the land of Israel.

22 But when he heard that Archelaus had become king over Judaea, in the place of his father Herod, he was afraid to go there; and it was revealed to him in a dream to go to the land of Galilee.

23 And he came and dwelt in a city called Nazareth, so that what was said by the prophet, might be fulfilled, He shall be called a Nazarene.

CHAPTER 3

*I*N those days came John the Baptist; and he was preaching in the wilderness of Judaea,

2 Saying, Repent; for the kingdom of heaven is near.

3 For it was he of whom it was said by the prophet Isaiah, The voice which cries in the wilderness, Prepare the way of the Lord, and straighten his highways.

4 Now the same John's clothes were made of camel's hair, and he had leathern belts around his waist, and his food was locusts and wild honey.

5 Then there went out to him, Jerusalem and all of Judaea, and the whole country around Jordan.

6 And they were baptized by him in the river Jordan, as they confessed their sins.

7 But when he saw a great many of the Pharisees and Sadducees who were coming to be baptized, he said to them, O offspring of scorpions, who has warned you to escape from the anger which is to come?

8 Bring forth therefore fruits which are worthy of repentance;

9 And do not think and say within yourselves, We have Abraham as our father; for I say to you that God can raise up children for Abraham from these stones.

10 Behold, the axe is already placed at the root of the trees; therefore, every tree which bears not good fruits shall be cut down and dropped in the fire.

11 I am just baptizing you with water for repentance; but he who is coming after me is greater than I, the one even whose shoes I am not worthy to remove; he will baptize you with the Holy Spirit and with fire.

12 Whose shovel is in his hand, and he purifies his threshings; the wheat he gathers into his barns, and the straw he burns up in the unquenchable fire.

13 ¶ Then Jesus came from Galilee to the Jordan to John, to be baptized by him.

14 But John tried to stop him, and said, I need to be baptized by you, and yet have you come to me?

15 But Jesus answered and said to him, Permit now, for this is necessary for us so that all righteousness may be fulfilled; and then he permitted him.

16 ¶ When Jesus was baptized, he immediately came out of the water; and the heavens were opened to him, and he saw the Spirit of God descending like a dove, and coming upon him;

17 And behold, a voice from heaven, which said, This is my beloved Son, with whom I am pleased.

CHAPTER 4

*T*HEN Jesus was carried away by the Holy Spirit into the wilderness, to be tempted by the adversary.

2 So he fasted forty days and forty nights; but at last he was hungry.

3 And the tempter drew near and said to him, If you are the Son of God, tell these stones to become bread.

4 But he answered and said, It is written, that it is not by bread alone that man can live, but by every word which comes from the mouth of God.

5 Then the adversary took him to the holy city, and he made him to stand up on the pinnacle of the temple.

6 And he said to him, If you are the Son of God, throw yourself down; for it is written, that he will command his angels concerning you, and they will bear you up on their hands, so that even your foot may not strike a stone.

7 Jesus said to him, Again it is written, that you shall not try out the Lord your God.

8 Again the adversary took him to a very high mountain, and he showed him all the

kingdoms of the world and their glory.

9 And he said to him, All of these I will give to you, if you will fall down and worship me.

10 Then Jesus said to him, Go away, Satan, for it is written, You shall worship the Lord your God, and him only shall you serve.

11 Then the adversary left him alone; and behold the angels drew near and ministered unto him.

12 ¶ Now when Jesus heard that John was delivered up, he departed to Galilee.

13 And he left Nazareth, and came and settled in Capernaum, by the seaside, within the borders of Zabulon and of Napthali.

14 So that it might be fulfilled, which was said by the prophet Isaiah, who said,

15 O land of Zabulon, O land of Napthali, the way to the sea, across the Jordan, Galilee of the Gentiles!

16 The people who dwelt in darkness saw a great light, and those who settled in the country and in the midst of the shadows of death, light shone on them.

17 ¶ From that time Jesus began to preach and to say, Repent, for the kingdom of heaven is coming near.

18 And while he was walking by the shore of the sea of Galilee, he saw two brothers, Simon who was called Peter and his brother Andrew, who were casting nets into the sea, for they were fishermen.

19 And Jesus said to them, Come after me, and I will make you to become fishers of men.

20 So they immediately left their nets and went after him.

21 And when he left that place he saw two other brothers, James the son of Zebedee and his brother John, in a ship with Zebedee their father, repairing their nets; and Jesus called them.

22 So they immediately left the ship and their father, and followed him.

23 ¶ And Jesus travelled throughout Galilee, teaching in their synagogues, and preaching the good news of the kingdom, and healing every kind of disease and sickness among the people.

24 And his fame was heard throughout Syria; so they brought to him all who were badly afflicted with divers sickness, and those who were tormented with pains, and the insane, and the epileptics, and the cripples; and he healed them.

25 So large crowds followed him from Galilee, and from the ten cities, and from Jerusalem and from Judaea, and from across the Jordan.

CHAPTER 5

*W*HEN Jesus saw the crowds, he went up to the mountain; and as he sat down, his disciples drew near to him.

2 And he opened his mouth and taught them, and he said,

3 Blessed are the poor in pride, for theirs is the kingdom of heaven.

4 Blessed are they who mourn, for they shall be comforted.

5 Blessed are the meek, for they shall inherit the earth.

6 Blessed are those who hunger and thirst for justice, for they shall be well satisfied.

7 Blessed are the merciful, for to them shall be mercy.

8 Blessed are those who are pure in their hearts, for they shall see God.

9 Blessed are the peacemakers, for they shall be called sons of God.

10 Blessed are those who are persecuted for the sake of justice, for theirs is the kingdom of heaven.

11 ¶ Blessed are you, when they reproach you and persecute you, and speak against you every kind of bad word, falsely, for my sake,

12 Then be glad and rejoice, for your reward is increased in heaven; for in this very manner they persecuted the prophets who were before you.

13 ¶ You are indeed the salt of the earth; but if the salt should lose its savor, with what could it be salted? It would not be worth anything, but to be thrown outside and to be trodden down by men.

14 You are indeed the light of the world; a city that is built upon a mountain cannot be hidden.

15 Nor do they light a lamp and put it under a basket, but on a lamp holder, so it gives light to all who are in the house.

16 Let your light thus shine before men, so that they may see your good works and glorify your Father in heaven.

17 ¶ Do not expect that I have come to weaken the law or the prophets; I have not come to weaken, but to fulfil.

18 For truly I tell you, Until heaven and earth pass away, not even one yoth * or a dash shall pass away from the law until all of it is fulfilled.

19 Whoever therefore tries to weaken even one of these smallest commandments, and teaches men so, he shall be regarded as small in the kingdom of heaven; but anyone who observes and teaches them, he shall be regarded as great in the kingdom of heaven.

20 For I say to you, that unless your righteousness exceeds that of the scribes and Pharisees, you shall not enter the kingdom of heaven.

21 ¶ You have heard that it was said to those who were before you, You shall not kill, and whoever kills is guilty before the court.

22 But I say to you, that whoever becomes angry with his brother for no reason, is guilty before the court: and whoever should say to his brother, Raca (which means, I spit on you) is guilty before the congregation; and whoever says to his brother, you are a nurse maid, is condemned to hell fire.

23 If it should happen therefore that while you are presenting your offering upon the altar, and right there you remember that your brother has any grievance against you,

24 Leave your offering there upon the altar, and first go and make peace with your brother, and then come back and present your offering.

25 Try to get reconciled with your accuser promptly, while you are going on the road with him; for your accuser might surrender you to the judge, and the judge would commit you to the jailer, and you will be cast into prison.

26 Truly I say to you, that you would never come out thence until you had paid the last cent.

27 ¶ You have heard that it is said, You shall not commit adultery.

28 But I say to you, that whoever looks at a woman with the desire to covet her, has already committed adultery with her in his heart.

29 If your right eye should cause you to stumble, pluck it out and throw it away from you; for it is better for you to lose one of your members, and not all your body fall into hell.

30 And if your right hand should cause you to stumble, cut it off and throw it away from you; for it is better for you to lose one of your members, and not all your body fall into hell.

31 It has been said that whoever divorces his wife, must give her the divorce papers.

32 But I say to you, that whoever divorces his wife, except for fornication, causes her to commit adultery; and whoever marries a woman who is separated but not divorced, commits adultery.

* Mt. 5:18 - Yoth is the smallest letter in Aramaic and Hebrew.

Cf.dif. vv. 5:12, 17, 19, 22-25, 31-32.

33 ¶ Again you have heard it was said to them who were before you, that you shall not lie in your oaths, but entrust your oaths to the Lord.

34 But I say to you, never swear; neither by heaven, because it is God's throne;

35 Nor by the earth, for it is a stool under his feet; nor by Jerusalem, for it is the city of a great king.

36 Neither shall you swear by your own head, because you cannot create in it a single black or white hair.

37 But let your words be yes, yes, and no, no; for anything which adds to these is a deception.

38 ¶ You have heard that it is said, An eye for an eye, and a tooth for a tooth.

39 But I say to you, that you should not resist evil; but whoever strikes you on your right cheek, turn to him the other also.

40 And if anyone wishes to sue you at the court and take away your shirt, let him have your robe also.

41 Whoever compels you to carry a burden for a mile, go with him two.

42 Whoever asks from you, give him; and whoever wishes to borrow from you, do not refuse him.

43 ¶ You have heard that it is said, Be kind to your friend, and hate your enemy.

44 But I say to you, Love your enemies, and bless anyone who curses you, and do good to anyone who hates you, and pray for them who carry you away by force and persecute you,

45 So that you may become sons of your Father who is in heaven, who causes his sun to shine upon the good and upon the bad, and who pours down his rain upon the just and upon the unjust.

46 For if you love only those who love you, what reward will you have? Do not even the publicans do the same thing?

47 And if you salute only your brothers, what is it more that you do? Do not even the publicans do the same thing?

48 Therefore, you become perfect, just as your Father in heaven is perfect.

CHAPTER 6

BE careful concerning your alms, not to do them in the presence of men, merely that they may see them; otherwise you have no reward with your Father in heaven.

2 Therefore when you give alms, do not blow a trumpet before you, just as the hypocrites do in the synagogues and in the market places, so that they may be glorified by men. Truly I say to you, that they have already received their reward.

3 But when you give alms, let not your left hand know what your right hand is doing;

4 So that your alms may be done secretly, and your Father who sees in secret, shall himself reward you openly.

5 ¶ And when you pray, do not be like the hypocrites, who like to pray, standing in the synagogues and at the street corners, so that they may be seen by men. Truly I say to you, that they have already received their reward.

6 But you, when you pray, enter into your inner chamber, and lock your door, and pray to your Father who is in secret, and your Father who sees in secret he himself shall reward you openly.

7 And when you pray, do not repeat your words like the pagans, for they think that because of much talking they will be heard.

8 Therefore, do not be like them, for your Father knows what you need, before you ask him.

9 ¶ Therefore pray in this manner: Our Father in heaven, hallowed be thy name.

10 Thy kingdom come. Thy will be done, as in heaven so on earth.

11 Give us bread for our needs from day to day.

12 And forgive us our offences, as we have forgiven our offenders;

13 And do not let us enter into temptation, but deliver us from error. Because thine is the kingdom and the power and the glory for ever and ever. Amen.

14 For if you forgive men their faults, your Father in heaven will also forgive you.

15 But if you do not forgive men, neither will your Father forgive even your faults.

16 ¶ When you fast, do not look sad like the hypocrites; for they disfigure their faces, so that they may appear to men that they are fasting. Truly I say to you, that they have already received their reward.

17 But you, when you fast, wash your face and anoint your head;

18 So that it may not appear to men that you are fasting, but to your Father who is in secret; and your Father who sees in secret, he will reward you.

19 ¶ Do not lay up for yourselves treasures buried in the ground, a place where rust and moth destroy, and where thieves break through and steal.

20 But lay up for yourselves a treasure in heaven, where neither rust nor moth destroy, and where thieves do not break through and steal.

21 For where your treasure is, there also is your heart.

22 The eye is the lamp of the body; if therefore your eye be clear, your whole body is also lighted.

23 But if your eye is diseased, your whole body will be dark. If therefore the light that is in you is darkness, how much more will be your darkness.

24 ¶ No man can serve two masters; for either he will hate the one, and like the other; or he will honor one, and despise the other. You cannot serve God and mammon (wealth).

25 For this reason, I say to you, Do not worry for your life, what you will eat, and what you will drink, nor for your body, what you will wear. Behold, is not life much more important than food, and the body than clothing?

26 Watch the birds of the sky, for they do not sow, neither do they harvest, nor gather into barns, and yet your Father in heaven feeds them. Are you not much more important than they?

27 Who is among you who by worrying can add one cubit to his stature?

28 Why do you worry about clothing? Observe the wild flowers, how they grow; they do not get tired out, nor do they spin.

29 But I say to you, that not even Solomon with all of his glory was covered like one of them.

30 Now if God clothes in such fashion the grass of the field, which today is and tomorrow falls into the fireplace, is he not much more to you, O you of little faith?

31 Therefore do not worry or say, What will we eat, or what will we drink, or with what will we be clothed?

32 For worldly people seek after all these things. Your Father in heaven knows that all of these things are also necessary for you.

33 But you seek first the kingdom of God and his righteousness, and all of these things shall be added to you.

34 Therefore do not worry for tomorrow; for tomorrow will look after its own. Sufficient for each day, is its own trouble.

CHAPTER 7

*J*UDGE not, that you may not be judged.
2 For with the same judgment that you judge, you will be judged, and with the same measure with which you measure, it will be measured to you.

3 Why do you see the splinter which is in your brother's eye, and do not feel the beam which is in your own eye?

4 Or how can you say to your brother, let me take out the splinter from your eye, and behold there is a cross beam in your own eye?

5 O hypocrites, first take out the beam from your own eye, and then you will see clearly to get out the splinter from your brother's eye.

6 ¶Do not give holy things to the dogs; and do not throw your pearls before the swine, for they might tread them with their feet, and then turn and rend you.

7 ¶ Ask, and it shall be given to you; seek, and you shall find; knock and it shall be opened to you.

8 For whoever asks, receives; and he who seeks, finds; and to him who knocks, the door is opened.

9 Or who is the man among you, who when his son asks him for bread, why, will he hand him a stone?

10 Or if he should ask him for fish, why, will he hand him a snake?

11 If therefore you who err, know how to give good gifts to your sons, how much more will your Father in heaven give good things to those who ask him?

12 Whatever you wish men to do for you, do likewise also for them; for this is the law and the prophets.

13 Enter in through the narrow door, for wide is the door, and broad is the road which carries to destruction, and many are those who travel on it.

14 O how narrow is the door, and how difficult is the road which carries to life, and few are those who are found on it.

15 ¶ Be careful of false prophets who come to you in lamb's clothing, but within they are ravening wolves.

16 You will know them by their fruits. Why, do they gather grapes from thorns, or figs from thistles?

17 So every good tree bears good fruits; but a bad tree bears bad fruits.

18 A good tree cannot bear bad fruits, neither can a bad tree bear good fruits.

19 Any tree which does not bear good fruits will be cut down and cast into the fire.

20 Thus by their fruits you will know them.

21 ¶ It is not everyone who merely says to me, My Lord, my Lord, will enter into the kingdom of heaven, but he who does the will of my Father in heaven.

22 A great many will say to me in that day, My Lord, my Lord, did we not prophesy in your name, and in your name cast out devils, and in your name do many wonders?

23 Then I will declare to them, I have never known you; keep away from me, O you that work iniquity.

24 ¶ Therefore whoever hears these words of mine, and does them, he is like a wise man, who built his house upon a rock.

25 And the rain came down, and the rivers overflowed, and the winds blew, and they beat upon that house; but it did not fall down, because its foundations were laid upon a rock.

26 And whoever hears these words of mine, and does them not, is like a foolish man, who built his house upon sand.

27 And the rain came down, and the rivers overflowed, and the winds blew, and they beat upon that house; and it fell down, and its fall was very great.

28 ¶And it happened when Jesus finished these words, the crowds were stunned at his teaching.

29 For he taught them as one who had the power, and not like their own scribes and Pharisees.

CHAPTER 8

WHEN he came down from the mountain, large crowds followed him.

2 And behold a leper came and worshipped him, and said, My Lord, if you wish, you can cleanse me.

3 And Jesus stretched out his hand and touched him, and he said, I do wish, be cleansed. And in that hour his leprosy was cleansed.

4 Jesus then said to him, Look here, why are you telling it to men? go first and show yourself to the priests, and offer an offering as Moses has commanded, for a testimonial to them.

5 ¶ When Jesus entered Capernaum, a centurion approached him, and appealed to him,

6 Saying, My Lord, my boy is lying in the house, paralyzed, and suffering greatly.

7 Jesus said to him, I will come and heal him.

8 The centurion then answered and said, My Lord, I am not good enough that you should enter under the shadow of my roof; but just say a word, and my boy will be healed.

9 For I am also a man in government service, and there are soldiers under my command; and I say to this one, Go, and he goes; and to the other, Come, and he comes; and to my servant, Do this, and he does it.

10 When Jesus heard it, he was amazed, and he said to those who accompanied him, Truly I say to you, that not even in Israel have I found such faith as this.

11 And I say to you, that a great many will come from the east and from the west, and sit down with Abraham and Isaac and Jacob in the kingdom of heaven.

12 But the sons of the kingdom will be put out in the outer darkness; there shall be weeping and gnashing of teeth.

13 So Jesus said to the centurion, Go, let it be done to you according to your belief. And his boy was healed in that very hour.

14 ¶ And Jesus came to the Simon's house, and he saw his mother-in-law laid up and sick with fever.

15 And he touched her hand, and the fever left her, and she got up and waited on them.

16 ¶ Now when evening came, they brought to him a great many lunatics, and he cured them just by a word; and he healed all who were badly afflicted.

17 So that what was spoken by the prophet Isaiah, might be fulfilled, who said, He will take our afflictions and bear our sickness.

18 ¶ When Jesus saw large crowds surrounding him, he gave orders to go to the crossing place. 19 And a scribe drew near and said to him, O my teacher, I will follow you wherever you go.

20 Jesus said to him, The foxes have holes, and the fowls of the sky a sheltering place, but the Son of man has no place even to lay his head.

21 Another of his disciples said to him, My Lord, permit me first to go and bury my father.

22 But Jesus said to him, Come after me, and let the dead bury their own dead.

23 ¶ And when Jesus went up into the boat, his disciples went with him.

24 And behold the sea became very rough, so that the boat was almost covered by the waves; but Jesus was asleep.

25 And his disciples came near and woke him up, and said to him, Our Lord, save us, we are perishing.

26 Jesus said to them, Why are you fearful, O you of little faith? Then he got up and rebuked the wind and the sea, and there was a great calm.

27 But the men were surprised, saying, Who is this man, that even the winds and the sea obey him?

28 ¶ And when Jesus came to the port on the other side, to the country of the Gadarenes, he was met by two lunatics,* who were just coming out of the cemetery. They were exceedingly vicious so that no man would dare to pass by that road.

29 And they cried aloud saying, What business have we together, Jesus, "son of God"? Have you come here to torment us before the time?

30 Now there was near by them a large herd of swine feeding.

31 And the lunatics kept asking him, saying, If you are going to heal us, permit us to attack # the herd of swine.

32 Jesus said to them, Go. And immediately they left and attacked the swine, and the whole herd went straight over the cliff, and fell into the sea, and were drowned in the water.

33 And they who fed them ran away and went to the city, and reported everything that happened, and about the lunatics.

34 So all the city went out to meet Jesus; and when they saw him, they urged him to depart from their borders.

CHAPTER 9

SO he went up into the boat, and crossed over and came to his own city.

2 And they brought to him a paralytic, lying on a quilt-bed; and Jesus saw their faith, and he said to the paralytic, Have courage, my son; your sins have been forgiven.

3 Some of the scribes said among themselves, This man blasphemes.

4 But Jesus knew their thoughts; so he said to them, Why do you think evil in your hearts?

5 For which is easier to say, Your sins have been forgiven, or to say, Arise and walk?

6 But that you might know that the Son of man has authority on earth to forgive sins, then he said to the paralytic, Arise, take up your quilt-bed, and go to your home.

7 And he rose up and went to his home.

8 But when the crowds saw it, they were frightened, and they glorified God, because he had given such power as this to men.

9 ¶ And as Jesus passed from that place, he saw a man whose name was Matthew, sitting in the custom house, and he said to him, Follow me; and he got up and went after him.

10 And while they were guests in the house, a great many publicans and sinners came, and they sat as guests with Jesus and with his disciples.

11 And when the Pharisees saw it, they said to his disciples, Why does your master eat with publicans and sinners?

12 But when Jesus heard it, he said to them, Those who are well need no doctor, but those who are seriously sick.

13 Go and learn what this means, I want mercy and not sacrifice; for I came not to invite righteous men, but sinners.

14 ¶ Then the disciples of John came up to him, and said, Why do we and the Pharisees fast a great deal, and your disciples never fast?

15 Jesus said to them, Is it possible for those at the wedding feast to fast as long as the bridegroom is with them? But the days are coming, when the bridegroom will be taken from them, and then they will fast.

16 No man puts a new patch on an old garment, so as not to weaken that garment, and make the hole larger.

---

* Mt.8:28 - Aramaic *Devana* means lunatic or insane; those suffering from mental diseases were supposed to be possessed of devils or evil spirits.

Mt.8:31 - Aramaic *al* means to attack, to chase, to enter.

Cf.dif. vv. 8:28-29, 31, 33; 9:2, 8, 12, 14, 16.

17 Neither do they pour new wine into worn out skins, so as not to rend the skins, and spill the wine, and the wine runs out, and the skins are ruined; but they pour new wine into new skins, and both of them are well preserved.

18 ¶ While he was speaking these things with them, a leader of the synagogue came near and worshipped him; and he said, My daughter has just died, but come and put your hand on her and she will live.

19 And Jesus and his disciples rose up and went with him.

20 ¶ And behold a woman who had had the hemorrhage for twelve years, came up from behind him, and she touched the edge of his cloak;

21 For she was saying to herself, If I can only touch his garment, I will be healed.

22 And Jesus turned around and saw her and said to her, Have courage, my daughter, your faith has healed you; and the woman was healed in that very hour.

23 ¶ So Jesus arrived at the house of the synagogue leader, and saw the singers and the excited crowds.

24 And he said to them, That is enough; for the little girl is not dead, but she is asleep; and they laughed at him.

25 But when he had put the people out, he went in and held her by her hand, and the little girl got up.

26 And this news spread all over that country.

27 ¶ And as Jesus passed from there, he was delayed by two blind men, who were crying out and saying, Have mercy on us, O son of David.

28 And when he came into the house, the same blind men came up to him. Jesus said to them, Do you believe that I can do this? They said to him, Yes, our Lord.

29 Then he touched their eyes and said, Let

it be to you according to your faith.

30 And immediately their eyes were opened; and Jesus charged them and said, See that no one knows it.

31 But they went out and spread the news all over that country.

32 ¶ And when Jesus went out, they brought to him a dumb man who was demented.

33 And as soon as he was restored, the dumb man spoke, and the people were amazed and said, Such a thing has never been seen in Israel.

34 But the Pharisees said, He is casting out devils by the help of the prince of devils.

35 And Jesus travelled in all the cities and villages, teaching in their synagogues, and preaching the gospel of the kingdom, and healing every kind of sickness and disease.

36 ¶ When Jesus saw the multitudes, he had compassion on them, because they were tired out and scattered, like sheep which have no shepherd.

37 So he said to his disciples, The harvest is great, and the laborers are few;

38 Therefore urge the owner of the harvest to bring more laborers to his harvest.

CHAPTER 10

AND he called his twelve disciples, and gave them power over the unclean spirits, to cast them out, and to heal every kind of disease and sickness.

2 The names of the twelve apostles are these: The first of them Simon who is called Peter, and Andrew his brother; James the son of Zebedee, and John his brother;

3 Philip and Bartholomew, Thomas and Matthew the publican, James the son of Alphaeus, and Lebbaeus surnamed Thaddaeus;

4 Simon the Zealot, and Judas of Iscariot, who betrayed him.

5 These twelve Jesus sent out, and charged

Jesus sends the twelve apostles.

them and said, Keep away from pagan practices, and do not enter a Samaritan city;

6 But above all, go to the sheep which are lost from the house of Israel.

7 And as you go, preach and say, that the kingdom of heaven is near.

8 Heal the sick, cleanse the lepers, cast out demons; freely you have received, freely give.

9 Do not accumulate gold, nor silver, nor brass in your purses;

10 Nor a bag for the journey, nor two shirts and shoes, nor a staff; for a laborer is at least worthy of his food.

11 Whatever city or town you enter, ask who is trustworthy in it, and remain there until you leave.

12 And when you enter into the house, salute the family.

13 And if the family is trustworthy, your salutation of peace shall come upon it; but if it is not trustworthy, your salutation shall return to you.

14 Whoever will not welcome you, and will not listen to your words, when you leave the house or the village, shake off the sand from your feet.

15 Truly I say to you, that it will be easier for the land of Sodom and Gomorrah on the day of judgment than for that city.

16 ¶ Behold, I am sending you like lambs among the wolves; therefore be wise as serpents, and pure as doves.

17 But be careful of men; for they will deliver you up to the courts, and they will scourge you in their synagogues;

18 And they will bring you before the presence of governors and kings for my sake, as a testimony to them and to the Gentiles.

19 But when they deliver you up, do not worry as to how or what you will speak; for it will be given to you in that very hour what you are to speak.

20 For it is not you who speak, but the Spirit of your Father, which speaks through you.

21 Brother will deliver up his own brother to death, and father his son; and children will rise up against their parents and put them to death.

22 And you will be hated by everybody because of my name; but he who endures until the end shall live.

23 When they persecute you in this city, escape to another; for truly I say to you, that you shall not finish converting all the cities of the house of Israel, until the Son of man returns.

24 No disciple is more important than his teacher, and no servant than his master.

25 It is enough for a disciple to be like his teacher, and for a servant to be like his master. If then, they have called the master of the house Beelzebub, how much more those of his household.

26 Therefore do not be afraid of them; for there is nothing covered that will not be uncovered, and hidden that will not be known.

27 What I tell you in the dark, tell it in the daylight; and what you hear with your ears, preach on the house tops.

28 Do not be afraid of those who kill the body, but who cannot kill the soul; but above all, be afraid of him who can destroy both the soul and the body in hell.

29 Are not two sparrows sold for a penny? And yet not one of them will fall on the ground without your Father's will.

30 But so far as you are concerned, even the hairs of your head are all numbered.

31 Therefore fear not; you are much more important than many sparrows.

32 Everyone therefore who will acknowledge me before men, I will also acknowledge him before my Father in heaven.

33 But whoever will deny me before men, I will also deny him before my Father in heaven.

Cf.dif. vv. 10:5-6, 9-11, 15-16, 23-24, 30, 32.

34 ¶ Do not expect that I have come to bring peace on earth; I have not come to bring peace but a sword.

35 For I have come to set a man against his father, and a daughter against her mother, and a daughter-in-law against her mother-in-law.

36 And a man's enemies will be the members of his own household.

37 Whoever loves father or mother more than me is not worthy of me; and whoever loves son or daughter more than me is not worthy of me.

38 And whoever does not take up his cross and follow me is not worthy of me.

39 He who is concerned about his life shall lose it; and he who loses his life for my sake shall find it.

40 Whoever receives you, receives me; and whoever receives me, receives him who sent me.

41 He who receives a prophet in the name of a prophet, shall receive a prophet's reward; and whoever receives a righteous man in the name of a righteous man, shall receive a righteous man's reward.

42 Anyone who gives a drink to one of these little ones, if only a cup of cold water, in the name of a disciple, truly I say to you, he shall never lose his reward.

CHAPTER 11

WHEN Jesus had finished commanding his twelve disciples, he departed from that place to teach and to preach in their cities.

2 But when John heard in prison of the works of Christ, he sent by his disciples,

3 And said to him, Are you the one who is to come, or are we to expect another?

4 Jesus answered and said, Go and describe to John the things which you see and hear.

5 The blind see, and the lame walk, and the lepers are cleansed, and the deaf hear , and the dead rise up, and the poor are given hope.

6 And blessed is he who does not stumble on account of me.

7 ¶ When they went away, Jesus began to speak to the people concerning John, What did you go out to the wilderness to see? A reed which is shaken by the wind?

8 If not so, what did you go out to see? A man dressed in fine clothes? Behold those who wear fine clothes are in kings' houses.

9 And if not so, What then did you go out to see? A prophet? Yes, I tell you, and much more than a prophet.

10 For this is he of whom it is written, Behold, I send my messenger before your face, to prepare the way before you.

11 ¶ Truly I say to you, that among those who are born of women, there has never risen one who is greater than John the Baptist; and yet even the least person in the kingdom of heaven is greater than he.

12 From the days of John the Baptist until now, the kingdom of heaven has been administered by force, and only those in power control it.

13 For all the prophets and the law prophesied until John.

14 And if you wish, accept it, that he is Elijah who was to come.

15 He who has ears to hear, let him hear.

16 ¶ But to whom shall I liken this generation? It is like boys who sit in the street and call to their friends.

17 And say, We have sung to you, but you would not dance; and we have wailed to you but you did not mourn.

18 For John came, neither eating nor drinking, and they said he is crazy.

19 The Son of man came, eating and drinking, and they said, Behold, a glutton and a wine-bibber, and a friend of publicans and sinners. And yet wisdom is justified by its works.

20 ¶ Then Jesus began to reproach the cities in which his many works were done, and

Cf.dif. vv. 10:39; 11:2, 5-6, 11-12, 16, 18-19.

which did not repent. And he said,

21　Woe to you, Chorazin! woe to you, Bethsaida! for if in Tyre and Sidon had been done the works which were done in you, they might have repented in sackcloth and ashes.

22　But I say to you, It will be easier for Tyre and Sidon in the day of judgment, than for you.

23　And you, Capernaum, which have exalted yourself up to heaven, shall be brought down to Sheol; for if in Sodom had been done the works which were done in you, it would be standing to this day.

24　But I say to you, It will be easier for the land of Sodom in the judgment day, than for you.

25　¶ At that time, Jesus answered and said, I thank you, O my Father, Lord of heaven and earth, because you have hidden these things from the wise and the men of understanding, and you have revealed them to children.

26　O yes, my Father, for such was your will.

27　Everything has been delivered to me by my Father, and no man knows the Son except the Father, nor does any man know the Father but the Son, and he to whomever the Son wishes to reveal.

28　¶ Come to me, all you who are tired out and carrying burdens, and I will give you rest.

29　Take my yoke upon you, and learn from me, for I am genial and meek in my heart, and you will find rest to your souls.

30　For my yoke is very pleasant, and my burden is light.

CHAPTER 12

AT that time, Jesus walked on the sabbath through the wheat fields; and his disciples became hungry, and they began to pluck ears of wheat and eat.

2　But when the Pharisees saw them, they said to him, Behold, your disciples are do-ing what is unlawful to do on the sabbath.

3　But he said to them, Have you not read what David did, when he and those who were with him were hungry?

4　How he entered into the house of God, and did eat bread that was on the table of the Lord, that which was not lawful for him to eat, nor for those who were with him, but only for the priests?

5　Or, have you not read in the book of law, that the priests in the temple disregard the sabbath, and yet are blameless?

6　But I say to you, that there is one here, who is greater than the temple.

7　But if you only knew what it means, I want mercy and not sacrifice, you would not condemn those who are blameless.

8　For the Son of man is Lord of the sabbath.

9　¶ And Jesus departed from thence and came to their synagogue.

10　And there was a man there whose hand was withered. And they questioned him, saying, Is it lawful to heal on the sabbath? that they might accuse him.

11　He said to them, Who is the man among you who has only one sheep, and if it should fall into a pit on the sabbath, would he not take hold of it and lift it up?

12　How much more important is a man than a sheep? It is therefore lawful to do good on the sabbath.

13　Then he said to the man, Stretch out your hand. And he stretched out his hand, and it was restored like the other.

14　¶ And the Pharisees went out, and they took counsel concerning him, so as to do away with him.

15　But Jesus knew of it, and departed from thence; and a great many people followed him, and he healed them all.

16　And he charged them not to say where he was,

17　So that what was said by the prophet Isaiah might be fulfilled, who said,

18 Behold my servant with whom I am pleased, my beloved one, in whom my soul rejoices; I will put my Spirit upon him, and he will preach justice to the peoples.

19 He will not argue, nor will he cry aloud; and no man will hear his voice in the street.

20 He will not break even a bruised reed, and he will not extinguish a flickering lamp, until he brings justice to victory;

21 And in his name will the peoples find hope.

22 ¶ Then they brought near to him a lunatic, who was also dumb and blind; and he healed him, so that the dumb and blind man could speak and see.

23 All the people were amazed and said, Perhaps this man is the son of David?

24 But when the Pharisees heard of it, they said, This man does not cast out demons, except by Beelzebub, the prince of demons.

25 But Jesus knew their thoughts, and said to them, Every kingdom which is divided against itself, will be destroyed; and every house or city that is divided against itself, will not stand.

26 And if Satan cast out Satan. he is divided against himself; how then will his kingdom stand?

27 So if I cast out demons by Beelzebub, by what do your sons cast them out? for this reason they will be your judges.

28 And if I cast out devils by the Spirit of God, then the kingdom of God has come near to you.

29 Or, how can a man enter into a strong man's house and plunder his goods, except he first bind the strong man, and then he plunders his house?

30 ¶ He who is not with me is against me; and he who does not gather with me, shall be dispersed.

31 Therefore I say to you, that all sins and blasphemies will be forgiven to men; but the blasphemy against the Spirit shall not be forgiven to men.

32 And whoever speaks a word against the Son of man, will be forgiven; but whoever speaks against the Holy Spirit shall not be forgiven, neither in this world nor in the world to come.

33 Either produce like a good tree with good fruits, or produce like a bad tree with bad fruits; for a tree is known by its fruits.

34 O generation of scorpions, how can you speak good things when you are bad? For the mouth speaks from the fullness of the heart.

35 A good man brings out good things from good treasures, and a bad man brings out bad things from bad treasures.

36 For I say to you, that for every foolish word which men speak, they will have to answer for it on the day of judgment.

37 For by your words you shall be justified, and by your words you shall be found guilty.

38 ¶ Then some of the men of the scribes and Pharisees answered and said to him, Teacher, we would like to see a sign from you.

39 But he answered and said to them, An evil and adulterous generation wants a sign; and no sign will be given to it, except the sign of the prophet Jonah.

40 For as Jonah was in the whale's belly three days and three nights, so the Son of man will be in the heart of the earth, three days and three nights.

41 Even the men of Nineveh will rise up in judgment with this generation, and find it guilty; for they repented through the preaching of Jonah, and behold, a greater than Jonah is here.

42 The queen of the south will rise up in judgment with this generation, and find it guilty; for she came from the far ends of the earth that she might hear Solomon's wisdom,

Cf.dif. vv. 12:18, 20-21, 30, 33, 42.

and behold a greater than Solomon is here.

43 When an unclean spirit goes out of a man, it travels in places where there is no water, and seeks rest, and does not find it.

44 Then it says, I will return to my own house from whence I came out; so it comes back and finds it empty, warm, and well furnished.

45 Then it goes away and brings with it seven other spirits worse than itself, and they enter and live in it; and the end of that man becomes worse than at first. Such will happen to this evil generation.

46 ¶ While he was speaking to the people, his mother and his brothers came and stood outside, and wanted to speak with him.

47 Then a man said to him, Behold your mother and your brothers are standing outside, and they want to speak with you.

48 But he answered and said to him who told him, Who is my mother and who are my brothers? 49 And he pointed his hand to his disciples and said, Behold my mother, and behold my brothers.

50 For whoever does the will of my Father in heaven, he is my brother and my sister and my mother.

CHAPTER 13

*T*HAT same day Jesus went out of the house, and sat by the seaside.

2 And many people gathered around him, so that he had to go up and sit in a boat, and all the people stood on the seashore.

3 And he spoke many things to them in parables, and said, Behold the sower went out to sow;

4 And when he had sown, some seed fell on the roadside, and the fowls came and ate it.

5 Other fell upon the rock, where there was not sufficient soil; and it sprang up earlier because the ground was not deep enough;

6 But when the sun shone, it was scorched, and because it had no root, it dried up;

7 And other fell among thistles, and the thistles sprung up and choked it.

8 And other fell in good soil, and bore fruit, some one hundred, and some sixty, and some thirty.

9 He who has ears to hear, let him hear.

10 ¶ Then his disciples drew near to him and said, Why do you speak to them in parables?

11 He answered and said to them, Because to you it is granted to know the mystery of the kingdom of heaven, but it is not granted to them.

12 For to him who has, shall be given and it shall increase to him; but to him who has not, even that which he has shall be taken away from him.

13 This is the reason I speak to them in figures, because they see and yet cannot perceive; and they hear and yet do not listen, nor do they understand.

14 And in them is fulfilled the prophecy of Isaiah who said, Hearing you will hear, but you will not understand; and seeing you will see, but you will not know.

15 For the heart of this people has become hardened, and their ears hear heavily, and their eyes are dull; so that they cannot see with their eyes, and hear with their ears, and understand with their hearts; let them return, and I will heal them.

16 But as for you, blessed are your eyes for they see; and your ears for they hear.

17 For truly I say to you, a great many prophets and righteous men have longed to see what you see, and did not see it; and to hear what you hear, and did not hear it.

18 ¶ Now you listen to the parable of the seed.

19 Whoever hears the word of the kingdom and does not understand it, the evil one comes and snatches away the word which has been sown in his heart. This is that which was sown on the roadside.

20 That which was sown upon the rock, this is he who hears the word, and immediately

Cf.dif. vv. 12:44;   13:5, 12-13, 15, 18-19.

accepts it with joy;

21 But it has no root in him, except for a while; and when trouble or persecution comes because of the word, he immediately stumbles.

22 That which was sown among thistles, this is he who hears the word, but worldly thoughts and the deception caused by riches choke the word, and it becomes fruitless.

23 That which was sown upon good soil, this is he who hears my word, and understands it, so he bears fruit and produces some one hundred, and some sixty, and some thirty.

24 ¶ He related another parable to them, and said, The kingdom of heaven is like a man who sowed good seed in his field.

25 And when the men slept, his enemy came and sowed tares among the wheat, and went away.

26 But when the blade sprang up and bore fruit, then the tares also appeared.

27 So the servants of the landowner came and said to him, Our lord, behold, did you not sow good seed in your field; whence did the tares come into it?

28 He said to them, An enemy did this; his servants then said to him, Do you want us to go and pick them out?

29 But he said to them, It might happen that while you were picking out the tares, you might uproot with them also the wheat.

30 Let them both grow together until the harvest; and at the harvest season, I will say to the reapers, Pick out first the tares, and bind them into bundles to be burned; but gather the wheat into my barns.

31 ¶ He related another parable to them, and said, The kingdom of heaven is like a grain of mustard seed, which a man took and sowed in his field.

32 It is the smallest of all seeds; but when it is grown, it is larger than all of the herbs; and it becomes a tree, so that the fowls of the sky come and nest in its branches.

33 ¶ He told them another parable. The kingdom of heaven is like the leaven, which a woman took and buried in three measures of flour, until it was all leavened.

34 ¶ Jesus spoke all these things to the people in parables; and without parables he did not speak to them.

35 So that it might be fulfilled which was said by the prophet, who said, I will open my mouth in parables, and I will bring out secrets hidden before the foundation of the world.

36 Then Jesus left the multitudes and came into the house; and his disciples came up to him, and said, Explain to us the parable of the tares and the field.

37 He answered and said to them, He who sowed good seed is the Son of man.

38 The field is the world; the good seed are the sons of the kingdom; but the tares are the sons of evil.

39 The enemy who sowed them is Satan; the harvest is the end of the world; and the reapers are the angels.

40 Therefore, just as the tares are picked out and burned in the fire, so shall it be at the end of the world.

41 The Son of man will send his angels, and they will pick out from his kingdom all things which cause stumbling, and all workers of iniquity.

42 And they will throw them into the furnace of fire; there shall be weeping and gnashing of teeth.

43 Then the righteous ones shall shine as the sun in the kingdom of their Father. He who has ears to hear, let him hear.

44 ¶ Again, the kingdom of heaven is like a treasure which is hidden in the field, which a man discovered and hid, and because of his joy, he went and sold everything he had, and bought that field.

Cf.dif. vv. 13:20-23, 29, 35, 41.

45 Again, the kingdom of heaven is like a merchant, who was seeking good pearls.

46 And when he had found one costly pearl, he went and sold everything he had, and bought it.

47 Again, the kingdom of heaven is like a net which was thrown into the sea, and it gathered fish of every kind.

48 When it was filled, they drew it to the shore, and sat down and sorted them; the good ones they put into bags, and the bad they threw away.

49 So will it be at the end of the world; the angels will go out and separate the bad from among the righteous,

50 And they will throw them into the furnace of fire; there shall be weeping and gnashing of teeth.

51 ¶ Jesus said to them, Have you understood all of these things? They said to him, Yes, our Lord.

52 He said to them, Therefore every scribe who is converted to the kingdom of heaven, is like a man who is a householder, who brings out new and old things from his treasures.

53 ¶ When Jesus had finished these parables, he departed thence.

54 And he came to his own city; and he taught them in their synagogues, in such a way, that they were amazed and said, Where did he get this wisdom and these wonders?

55 Is he not the carpenter's son? Is not his mother called Mary? and his brothers, James and Joses and Simon and Judah?

56 Are not all his sisters with us? Where did he get all these things?

57 And they were perplexed about him. But Jesus said to them, No prophet is insulted, except in his own city and in his own house.

58 And he did not perform many miracles there, because of their unbelief.

CHAPTER 14

AT that time Herod the tetrarch heard the news about Jesus.

2 And he said to his servants, This man is John the Baptist; he has risen from the dead; this is why great miracles are wrought by him.

3 ¶ For Herod had arrested John, and bound him, and put him in prison, because of Herodias, his brother Philip's wife.

4 For John had said to him, It is unlawful to have her as your wife.

5 So Herod wanted to kill him, but he was afraid of the people, because they accepted him as a prophet.

6 When Herod's birthday came, the daughter of Herodias danced before the guests, and it pleased Herod.

7 He therefore swore to her with oaths, that he would give her anything that she asked.

8 And she, because she was instructed by her mother, said, Give me right here on a tray the head of John the Baptist.

9 And the king was very sorry; but because of the oaths and the guests, he commanded that it be given to her.

10 So he sent and had John beheaded in the prison.

11 And his head was brought in on a tray, and given to the girl; and she took it to her mother.

12 Then his disciples came and took up his body and buried it, and they came and informed Jesus.

13 ¶ When Jesus heard it, he departed thence by boat, alone to a desert place; and when the people heard of it, they followed him by land from the cities.

14 And Jesus went out and saw large crowds, and he had pity for them, and healed their sick.

15 ¶ When it was evening, his disciples came to him, and they said to him, This is a lonely place, and it is getting late; dismiss the people so that the men may go to the villages and buy food for themselves.

16 But he said to them, It is not necessary for them to go; you give them something to eat.

17 They said to him, We have nothing here, except five loaves of bread and two fish.

18 Jesus said to them, Bring them here to me.

19 And he ordered the people to sit down on the ground, and he took the five loaves of bread and the two fish, and he looked up to heaven and he blessed them, and he broke them, and gave them to his disciples, and the disciples placed them before the people.

20 So they all ate, and were satisfied; and they took up the fragments which were left over, twelve full baskets.

21 And the men who ate were five thousand, not counting the women and children.

22 ¶ And immediately he urged his disciples to go up into the boat, in advance of him to the crossing place, while he dismissed the people.

23 And when he had dismissed the people, he went up to the mountain alone to pray; and when darkness fell he was still there alone.

24 But the boat was many miles away from the land, tossed by the waves, for the wind was against it.

25 And in the fourth watch of the night, Jesus came to them, walking on * the water.

26 And his disciples saw him walking on the water, and they were scared, and they said, It is a false vision; and they cried out because of their fear.

27 But Jesus spoke to them at once and said, Have courage; it is I; do not be afraid.

28 And Peter answered and said to him, My Lord, if it is you, command me to come to you on the water.

29 Jesus said to him, Come. So Peter went down from the boat, and walked on the water, to come to Jesus.

30 But when he saw that the wind was severe, he was afraid, and began to sink, and he raised his voice and said, My Lord, save me.

31 And our Lord immediately stretched out his hand and grasped him; and he said to him, O you of little faith, why did you doubt?

32 And when they went up into the boat, the wind quieted down.

33 And they who were in the boat came and worshipped him; and they said, Truly you are the Son of God.

34 ¶ And they rowed and came to the land of Gennesaret.

35 And the men of that country recognized him, and they sent word to all the villages around them; so they brought to him all who were seriously sick.

36 And they besought him, that they might touch even the edge of his robe; and those who touched it were healed.

CHAPTER 15

*T*HEN Pharisees and scribes from Jerusalem came up to Jesus, saying,

2 Why do your disciples disregard the tradition of the elders, and they do not wash their hands when they eat food?

3 Jesus answered and said to them, Why do you also disregard the commandment of God on account of your tradition.

4 For God said, Honor your father and your mother, and whoever curses his father and

---

* Mt.14:25 - The Aramaic on or by. There was no crossing at this time, for the boat was at a distance from its starting point.

Cf.dif. vv. 14:15, 22, 24, 26, 31, 35.

his mother, let him be put to death.

5 But you say, Whoever says to a father or to a mother, Whatever you may be benefited from me is Corban (my offering), he need not honor his father or his mother.

6 So you have rendered useless the word of God for the sake of your tradition.

7 O you hypocrites, the prophet Isaiah well prophesied concerning you and said,

8 This people honor me with their lips, but their heart is far away from me.

9 And they worship me in vain, when they teach the doctrines of the commandments of men.

10 ¶ Then he called the people and said to them, Listen and understand.

11 It is not what enters into the mouth which defiles man; but what goes out of the mouth, that is what defiles man.

12 Then his disciples came up and said to him, Do you know that the Pharisees who heard this saying were offended?

13 But he answered and said to them, Every plant that my heavenly Father did not plant, shall be uprooted.

14 Leave them alone; they are blind guides of the blind. And if the blind lead around the blind, both will fall into a pit.

15 And Simon Peter answered and said to him, My Lord, explain this parable to us.

16 And he said to them, Even yet do you not understand?

17 Do you not know that what enters into the mouth goes into the stomach, and thence, through the intestines, is cast out?

18 But what comes out of the mouth comes out from the heart; and that is what defiles man.

19 For from the heart come out evil thoughts, such as fornication, murder, adultery, theft, false witness, blasphemy.

20 It is these that defile man; but if a man should eat when his hands are unwashed, he will not be defiled.

21 ¶ And Jesus went out from thence, and he came to the border of Tyre and Sidon.

22 And behold, a Canaanite woman from these borders, came out crying aloud, and saying, Have mercy on me, O my Lord, son of David; my daughter is seriously afflicted with insanity.

23 But he did not answer her. And his disciples came up to him and urged him, saying, Dismiss her, for she keeps crying aloud after us.

24 And he answered and said to them, I am not sent, except to the sheep which went astray from the house of Israel.

25 But she came and worshipped him, and said, My Lord, help me.

26 Jesus said to her, It is not right to take the children's bread and throw it to the dogs.

27 But she said Yes, my Lord, even the dogs eat of the crumbs which fall from the master's tray, and they live.

28 Then Jesus said to her, O woman, your faith is great; let it be to you as you wish; and her daughter was healed from that very hour.

29 ¶ And Jesus departed from thence, and he came toward the sea of Galilee; and he went up to a mountain and sat down there.

30 And a great many people came to him, who had with them the lame, blind, dumb, maimed, and many others; and they laid them down at the feet of Jesus, and he healed them.

31 So that the people wondered, to see the dumb speaking, and the maimed healed, and the lame walking, and the blind seeing; and they praised the God of Israel.

32 ¶ Jesus then called his disciples and said to them, I have compassion for this people, for they have remained with me three days, and they have nothing to eat; and if I dismiss them fasting, they might faint on the way; but this I do not wish to do.

33 His disciples said to him, Where can we get bread in this desolate place to feed all this people?

34 Jesus said to them, How many loaves of bread have you? They said to him, Seven, and a few small fish.

35 So he ordered the people to sit on the ground.

36 Then he took the seven loaves of bread and the fish, and gave thanks, and he broke them, and gave to his disciples, and the disciples gave them to the people.

37 And all of them did eat and were satisfied; and they took up of the fragments that were left over, seven full baskets.

38 And those who did eat were four thousand men, besides women and children.

39 And when he had dismissed the people, he went up to the boat and came to the border of Magadan.

CHAPTER 16

AND the Pharisees and Sadducees came up to him to tempt him; and they asked him to show them a sign from heaven.

2 But he answered and said to them, When it is evening, you say, It is clear, for the sky is red.

3 And in the morning you say, It is a winter day, for the sky is red and cloudy. O hypocrites, you know how to judge the face of the sky, but the signs of the present time you are not able to distinguish.

4 A wicked and adulterous generation wants a sign; and no sign shall be given to it, except the sign of the prophet Jonah. And he left them and went away.

5 When his disciples came to the crossing place, they had forgotten to take bread with them.

6 He said to them, Look out and beware of the leaven of the Pharisees and of the Sadducees.

7 And they were reasoning among themselves and saying, It is because we have not brought bread.

8 But Jesus knew it and said to them, What are you thinking among yourselves, O you of little faith; is it because you have not brought bread?

9 Do you not yet understand? Do you not remember the five loaves of bread of the five thousand, and how many baskets you took up?

10 Neither the seven loaves of bread of the four thousand, and how many baskets you took up?

11 How is it that you did not understand that I was not talking to you about the bread, but to beware of the leaven of the Pharisees and of the Sadducees?

12 Then they understood, that he did not say that they should beware of the leaven of the bread, but of the teaching of the Pharisees and the Sadducees.

13 ¶ When Jesus came to the country of Caesarea of Philippi, he asked his disciples saying, What do the men say concerning me, that I am merely a son of man?

14 They said, There are some who say John the Baptist, others Elijah, and still others Jeremiah, or one of the prophets:

15 He said to them, Who do you say that I am?

16 Simon Peter answered and said, You are the Christ, the Son of the living God.

17 Jesus answered and said to him, Blessed are you, Simon son of Jonah, for flesh and blood did not reveal it to you, but my Father in heaven.

18 I tell you also that you are a stone, and upon this stone I will build my church; and the doors of Sheol shall not shut in on it.

19 I will give you the keys of the kingdom of heaven; and whatever you bind on earth shall be bound in heaven, and whatever you

Cf.dif. vv. 16:3, 5, 13, 17, 18.

release on earth shall be released in heaven.

20 Then he charged his disciples not to tell any man that he is the Christ.

21 ¶ From that time Jesus began to make known to his disciples, that he will shortly have to go to Jerusalem, and suffer a great deal from the elders, and the high priests and scribes, and be killed, and rise up on the third day.

22 So Peter took him aside and began to rebuke him, and he said, Far be it from you, my Lord, that this should happen to you.

23 But he turned, and said to Peter, Get behind me, Satan, you are a stumbling-block to me; for you are not thinking of the things of God, but of men.

24 ¶ Then Jesus said to his disciples, He who wishes to come after me, let him deny himself, and take up his cross and follow me.

25 For whoever wishes to save his life shall lose it; and whoever loses his life for my sake shall find it.

26 For how will a man be benefited, if he should gain the whole world and lose his own soul? Or what shall a man give in exchange for his soul?

27 For the Son of man will come in the glory of his Father with his holy angels; and then he will reward each man according to his works.

28 Truly I say to you, There are men who stand here, who will not taste death, until they see the Son of man coming in his kingdom.

CHAPTER 17

AND after six days Jesus took Peter and James and his brother John, and brought them up to a high mountain alone.

2 And Jesus was transfigured before them, and his face shone like the sun, and his clothes turned white like light.

3 And there appeared to them Moses and Elijah, as they were talking with him.

4 Then Peter answered and said to Jesus, My Lord, it is better for us to remain here; and if you wish, we will make three shelters here, one for you, and one for Moses, and one for Elijah.

5 And while he was speaking, behold, a bright cloud overshadowed them, and a voice came out of the cloud saying, This is my beloved Son, I am pleased with him; hear him.

6 When the disciples heard it, they threw themselves on their faces, and they were greatly frightened.

7 And Jesus came near them and touched them, and said, Arise, do not be afraid.

8 And they raised up their eyes, and they saw no man, except Jesus alone.

9 And as they were going down from the mountain, Jesus commanded them, and said to them, Do not speak of this vision in the presence of anyone, until the Son of man rises from the dead.

10 And his disciples asked him, and said, Why then do the scribes say that Elijah must come first?

11 Jesus answered and said to them, Elijah will come first, so that everything might be fulfilled.

12 But I say to you, Elijah has already come, and they did not know him, and they did to him whatever they pleased. Thus also the Son of man is bound to suffer from them.

13 Then the disciples understood that what he had told them was about John the Baptist.

14 ¶ And when they came to the people, a man approached him and knelt on his knees, and said to him,

15 My Lord, have mercy on me; my son is an epileptic and has become worse; he often falls into the fire, and often into the water.

Cf.dif. vv. 16:21-23;   17:11, 15.

16 And I brought him to your disciples, but they were not able to heal him.

17 Jesus answered and said, O faithless and crooked generation, how long shall I be with you? and how long shall I preach to you? bring him here to me.

18 And Jesus rebuked him, and the demon went out of him; and the boy was healed from that very hour.

19 Then the disciples came up to Jesus when he was alone, and said to him, Why could we not heal him?

20 Jesus said to them, Because of your unbelief; for truly I say to you, If there is faith in you even as a grain of mustard, you will say to this mountain, move away from here, and it will move away; and nothing would prevail over you.

21 Nevertheless this kind does not come out, except by fasting and prayer.

22 ¶ While they were returning through Galilee, Jesus said to them, The Son of man will shortly be delivered into the hands of men;

23 And they will kill him, and on the third day he will rise up. And they were very much grieved.

24 ¶ And when they came to Capernaum, those who collect two coins of silver as head-tax came to Peter and said to him, Would not your master give his two coins?

25 He said to them, Yes. And when Peter entered the house, Jesus anticipated and said to him, What do you think, Simon? from whom do the kings of the earth collect custom duties and head- tax? from their sons, or from strangers?

26 Simon said to him, From strangers. Jesus said to him, Then the sons are free.

27 But so as not to offend them, go to the sea, and throw out a hook, and the first fish which comes up, open its mouth and you will find a coin; take it and give it for me and for you.

CHAPTER 18

AT that very hour the disciples came up to Jesus and said, Who is greatest in the kingdom of heaven?

2 So Jesus called a little boy, and made him to stand up in the midst of them,

3 And he said, Truly I say to you, Unless you change and become like little boys, you shall not enter into the kingdom of heaven.

4 Whoever therefore will humble himself like this little boy, shall be great in the kingdom of heaven.

5 And he who will welcome one like this little boy, in my name, welcomes me.

6 And whoever misleads one of these little ones who believe in me, it would be better for him that an ass' millstone were hanged on his neck and he were sunk in the depths of the sea.

7 ¶ Woe to the world because of offences! Offences are bound to come; but woe to the man by whose hand the offences come!

8 If your hand or your foot offends you, cut it off and throw it away from you; for it is much better for you to go through life lamed or maimed, rather than having two hands or two feet, and fall into the everlasting fire.

9 And if your eye offends you, remove it and throw it away from you; it is better for you to go through life with one eye, rather than having two eyes and fall into the gehenna of fire.

10 See to it that you do not despise one of these little ones; for I say to you, their angels always see the face of my Father in heaven.

11 For the Son of man has come to save what was lost.

12 What do you think? If a man should have a hundred sheep, and one of them is lost, would he not leave the ninety and nine on the mountain, and go in search of the one which is lost?

Cf.dif. vv. 17:17-18, 20, 22-25; 18:6, 8, 12.

13 And if he should find it, truly I say to you, he rejoices over it more than over the ninety and nine which were not lost.

14 Even so, your Father in heaven does not want one of these little ones to be lost.

15 ¶ Now then, if your brother is at fault with you, go and rebuke him alone; if he listens to you, then you have won your brother.

16 But if he will not listen to you, take one or two with you, because at the mouth of two or three witnesses every word is sustained.

17 And if he will not listen to them, tell the congregation; and if he will not listen to the congregation, then regard him as a publican and a heathen.

18 Truly I say to you, Whatever you bind on earth will be bound in heaven, and whatever you release on earth will be released in heaven.

19 Again I say to you, that if two of you are worthy on earth, anything that they would ask, it will be done for them by my Father in heaven.

20 For wherever two or three are gathered in my name, I am there among them.

21 ¶ Then Peter came up and said to him, My Lord, if my brother is at fault with me, how many times should I forgive him? up to seven times?

22 Jesus said to him, I do not say to you up to seven times, but up to seventy times seven.

23 ¶ Therefore the kingdom of heaven is likened to a king who wanted to take an accounting from his servants.

24 And when he began to take the accounting, they brought to him one who owed ten thousand talents.

25 And as he could not pay, his lord commanded him to be sold, together with his wife and children, and all that he had, so that he could pay.

26 The servant then fell down, worshipped him, and said, My lord, have patience with me, and I will pay you everything.

27 Then the master of that servant had pity, so he released him, and cancelled his debt.

28 But that servant went out, and found one of his fellow-servants, who owed him one hundred cents; and he seized him, and tried to choke him, saying to him, Give me what you owe me.

29 So his fellow-servant fell down at his feet, and begged him and said, Have patience with me, and I will pay you.

30 But he was not willing; and he went and had him put into prison, until he should pay him what he owed him.

31 When their fellow-servants saw what had happened, they were very sorry, and they came and informed their master of everything that had happened.

32 Then his master called him and said to him, O wicked servant, I cancelled all your debt because you begged me.

33 Was it not right for you to have mercy on your fellow-servant, just as I had mercy on you?

34 So his master was angry, and delivered him to the scourgers, until he should pay everything he owed him.

35 So will my Father in heaven do to you, if you do not forgive each man his brother's fault from your heart.

CHAPTER 19

WHEN Jesus had finished these sayings, he departed from Galilee, and came to the border of Judaea, at the crossing of the Jordan.

2 And a great many people followed him, and he healed them there.

3 ¶ And the Pharisees came up to him and were tempting him and saying, Is it lawful for a man to divorce his wife for any cause?

4 But he answered and said to them, Have you not read, that he who made from the beginning, made them male and female?

Cf. dif. vv. 18:15, 17, 19, 27, 28, 34-35;　19:1, 3.

5 And he said, Because of this, a man shall leave his father and his mother, and shall be joined to his wife, and the two shall be one flesh.

6 Henceforth they are not two, but one body; therefore what God has joined together, man must not separate.

7 They said to him, Why then did Moses command to give a letter of separation and then divorce her?

8 He said to them, Moses, considering the hardness of your heart, gave you permission to divorce your wives; but from the beginning it was not so.

9 But I say to you, Whoever leaves his wife without a charge of adultery and marries another commits adultery; and he who marries a woman thus separated commits adultery.

10 ¶ His disciples said to him, If there is so much scandal between man and woman, it is not worthwhile to marry.

11 He said to them, This saying does not apply to every man, but to whom it is needed.

12 For there are eunuchs who were born this way from their mother's womb; and there are eunuchs who were made eunuchs by men; and there are eunuchs who made themselves eunuchs for the sake of the kingdom of heaven. To him who can grasp, this is enough.

13 ¶ Then they brought little boys to him, that he may lay his hand on them and pray; and his disciples rebuked them.

14 But Jesus said to them, Allow the little boys to come to me, and do not stop them; for the kingdom of heaven is for such as these.

15 And he laid his hand on them, and went away from thence.

16 ¶ Then a man came up and said to him, O good * Teacher, what is the best that I should do to have life eternal?

17 He said to him, Why do you call me good? There is no one who is good except the one God; but if you want to enter into life, obey the commandments.

18 He said to him, Which ones? And Jesus said to him, You shall not kill; You shall not commit adultery; You shall not steal; You shall not bear false witness;

19 Honor your father and your mother; and, Love your neighbor as yourself.

20 The young man said to him, I have obeyed all these from my boyhood, what do I lack?

21 Jesus said to him. If you wish to be perfect, go and sell your possessions and give them to the poor, and you will have a treasure in heaven; then follow me.

22 When the young man heard this word, he went away sad, for he had great possessions.

23 ¶ Jesus then said to his disciples, Truly I say to you, It is difficult for a rich man to enter into the kingdom of heaven.

24 Again I say to you, It is easier for a rope to go through the eye of a needle, than for a rich man to enter into the kingdom of God.

25 When the disciples heard it, they were exceedingly astonished, saying, Who then can be saved?

26 Jesus looked at them and said, For men this is impossible, but for God everything is possible.

27 ¶ Then Peter answered and said to him, Behold, we have left everything and followed you; what will we have?

28 Jesus said to them, Truly I say to you, that in the new world when the Son of man shall sit on the throne of his glory, you who

---

* Mt. 19:16 - Aramaic *tava* means wonderful.
# Mt. 19:24 - The Aramaic word *gamla* means rope and camel.
Cf.dif. vv. 19:6-7, 9-12, 21, 24, 28.

27

have come after me shall also sit on twelve chairs, and you shall judge the twelve tribes of Israel.

29 And every man who leaves houses, or brothers, or sisters, or father, or mother, or wife, or children, or fields, for my name's sake, shall receive a hundredfold, and shall inherit everlasting life.

30 But many who are first shall be last, and the last first.

CHAPTER 20

*F*OR the kingdom of heaven is like a man, who is a householder, who went out early in the morning to hire laborers for his vineyard.

2 He bargained with the laborers for a penny a day, and sent them to his vineyard.

3 And he went out at the third hour, and saw others standing idle in the market place.

4 And he said to them, You also go to the vineyard, and I will give you what is right. And they went.

5 And he went out again at the sixth and at the ninth hour, and did the same.

6 And towards the eleventh hour he went out and found others standing idle, and he said to them, Why do you stand all day idle?

7 They said to him, Because no man has hired us. He said to them, You also go to the vineyard, and you will receive what is right.

8 When evening came, the owner of the vineyard said to his steward, Call the laborers and pay them their wages; and begin from the last ones to the first.

9 When those of the eleventh hour came, they each received a penny.

10 But when the first ones came, they expected to receive more; but they also got each one a penny.

11 And when they received it, they murmured against the householder,

12 Saying, These last ones have worked only one hour, and you have made them equal with us who have borne the weight of the day and its heat.

13 He answered and said to one of them, My friend, I am not doing you an injustice; did you not bargain with me for a penny?

14 Take what is yours and go away; I wish to give to this last one the same as to you.

15 Have I no right to do what I wish with mine own? Or are you jealous because I am generous?

16 Even so the last shall be first, and the first last; for many are called, but few are chosen.

17 ¶ Now Jesus was ready to go up to Jerusalem; and he took his twelve disciples apart on the road, and he said to them,

18 Behold, we are going up to Jerusalem, and the Son of man will be delivered to the high priests and the scribes, and they will condemn him to death.

19 And they will deliver him to the Gentiles and they will mock him, and scourge him, and crucify him; and on the third day he will rise up.

20 ¶ Then the mother of the sons of Zebedee came up to him, together with her sons; and she worshipped him, and requested something of him.

21 He said to her, What do you wish? She said to him, Command that these two sons of mine sit, one at your right and one at your left, in your kingdom.

22 Jesus answered and said, You do not know what you are asking. Can you drink the cup that I am ready to drink, or be baptized with the baptism with which I am to be baptized? They said to him, We can.

23 He said to them, Indeed my cup you shall drink, and the baptism with which I am to be baptized, you too shall be baptized with; but to sit at my right hand and at my left, that is not mine to give, but it is for those for whom it is prepared by my Father.

Cf.dif. vv. 20:2, 13, 15.

24 When the ten heard it, they were angry at the two brothers.

25 And Jesus called them and said, You know that the princes of the people are also their owners; and their officials rule over them.

26 Let not this be so among you; but whoever wishes to be great among you, let him be a minister to you;

27 And whoever wishes to be first among you, let him be a servant to you;

28 Just as the Son of man did not come to be ministered to, but to minister, and to give his life as a salvation for the sake of many.

29 ¶ And when Jesus went out of Jericho a large crowd followed him.

30 And behold, two blind men were sitting by the roadside, and when they heard that Jesus was passing by, they cried aloud, saying, Have mercy upon us, O Lord, son of David.

31 But the people rebuked them to keep quiet; but they cried louder, saying, Our Lord, have mercy upon us, son of David.

32 And Jesus stopped and called them, and he said, What do you wish me to do for you?

33 They said to him, Our Lord, that our eyes may be opened.

34 And Jesus had mercy upon them, so he touched their eyes; and immediately their eyes were opened, and they followed him.

CHAPTER 21

WHEN he came near to Jerusalem, he came to Bethphage on the side of the Mount of Olives. Jesus then sent two of his disciples,

2 And he said to them, Go to that village which is in front of you, and straightway you will find an ass which is tied up, and a colt with her; untie them and bring them to me.

3 And if any man should say anything to you, tell him that our Lord needs them; and he will immediately send them here.

4 All this happened, so that what was said by the prophet, might be fulfilled, who said,

5 Tell the daughter of Zion, Behold your king is coming to you, meek, and riding upon an ass, and upon a colt, the foal of an ass.

6 And the disciples went and did as Jesus had commanded them.

7 And they brought the ass and the colt, and they put their garments on the colt, and Jesus rode on it.

8 And a great many people spread their garments on the road; and others cut down branches from the trees and spread them on the road.

9 And the people who were going before him and coming after him, were shouting and saying, Hosanna to the son of David; Blessed is he who comes in the name of the Lord; Hosanna in the highest.

10 When he entered Jerusalem, the whole city was stirred up, and they were saying, Who is this man?

11 And the people were saying. This is the prophet, Jesus, from Nazareth in Galilee.

12 ¶ And Jesus entered into the temple of God, and put out all who were buying and selling in the temple, and he overturned the trays of the money-changers and the stands of those who sold doves.

13 And he said to them, It is written, My house shall be called the house of prayer; but you have made it a bandits' cave.

14 And in the temple they brought to him the blind and the lame, and he healed them.

15 But when the high priests and the Pharisees saw the wonders that he did, and the boys who were crying aloud in the temple, and saying, Hosanna to the son of David, they were displeased.

16 And they said to him, Do you hear what they are saying? Jesus said to them, Yes; have you never read, From the mouth of little children and of boys you made praise?

Cf.dif. vv. 20:25; 21:1, 7, 10, 12, 14, 16.

17 ¶ And he left them, and went outside of the city to Bethany, and he lodged there.

18 In the morning, as he returned to the city, he became hungry.

19 And he saw a fig tree on the roadside, and he came to it and found nothing on it except leaves; and he said to it, Let there be no fruit on you again for ever. And shortly the fig tree withered.

20 When the disciples saw it, they were amazed and said, How is it that the fig tree has withered so soon?

21 Jesus answered and said to them, Truly I say to you, If you have faith, and do not doubt, you will perform a deed not only like this of the fig tree, but should you say even to this mountain, Be removed and fall into the sea, it shall be done.

22 And everything that you will ask in prayer and believe, you shall receive.

23 ¶ When Jesus came to the temple, the high priests and the elders of the people came up to him, while he was teaching, and said to him, By what authority do you do these things? and who gave you this authority?

24 Jesus answered and said to them, I will also ask you a word, and if you tell me, I will then tell you by what authority I do these things.

25 Whence is the baptism of John? Is it from heaven, or from men? And they reasoned with themselves, saying, If we should say from heaven, he will say to us, Why then did you not believe him?

26 And if we should say, from men, we are afraid of the people, for all of them regard John as a prophet.

27 So they answered and said to him, We do not know. Jesus said to them, Neither will I tell you by what authority I do these things.

28 ¶ What do you think? A man had two sons, and he came to the first one and said to him, My son, go and work today in the vineyard.

29 He answered and said, I do not want to, but later he regretted and went.

30 And he came to the other one and said to him likewise. And he answered and said, Here am I, my Lord, and yet he did not go.

31 Which of these two did the will of his father? They said to him, The first one. Jesus said to them, Truly I say to you, that even the publicans and the harlots will precede you into the kingdom of God.

32 For John came to you in a righteousness way, and you did not believe him; but the publicans and the harlots believed him; but you, even though you saw, did not repent, so that later you may believe him.

33 ¶ Hear another parable. There was a man who was a householder, and he planted a vineyard, and fenced it, and he dug in it a winepress, and built a tower, and then he leased it to laborers, and went away on a journey.

34 And when the fruit season was at hand, he sent his servants to the laborers, that they might send him of the fruits of his vineyard.

35 And the laborers seized his servants, and some were beaten, and some were stoned, and some were killed.

36 Again he sent other servants, many more than the first; and they did likewise to them.

37 At last he sent his son to them, saying, They might feel ashamed before my son.

38 But when the laborers saw the son, they said among themselves, This is the heir; come, let us kill him and retain his inheritance.

39 So they seized him, and took him out of the vineyard, and killed him.

40 When therefore the owner of the vineyard comes, what will he do to those laborers?

41 They said to him, He will destroy them severely, and lease his vineyard to other laborers, who will give him fruits in their seasons.

Cf.dif. vv. 21:37-38.

42 Jesus said to them, Have you never read in the scripture, The stone which the builders rejected, the same became the cornerstone; this was from the Lord, and it is a marvel in our eyes?

43 Therefore I say to you, that the kingdom of God will be taken away from you, and will be given to a people who bear fruits.

44 And whoever falls on this stone will be broken, and on whomever it falls it will scatter him.

45 ¶ When the high priests and Pharisees heard his parables, they understood that he was speaking against them.

46 So they wanted to arrest him, but they were afraid of the people, because they regarded him as a prophet.

CHAPTER 22

AND Jesus answered again by parables, and said,

2 The kingdom of heaven is like a king who gave a marriage-feast for his son.

3 And he sent his servants to call those who were invited to the marriage-feast, but they would not come.

4 Again he sent other servants and said, Tell those who are invited, Behold my supper is ready, and my oxen and fatlings are killed, and everything is prepared; come to the marriage-feast.

5 But they sneered at it, and went away, one to his field, another to his business;

6 And the rest seized his servants and insulted them, and killed them.

7 When the king heard it he was angry; and he sent out his armies and destroyed those murderers, and burned their city.

8 Then he said to his servants, Now the marriage-feast is ready, and those who were invited were unworthy.

9 Go, therefore, to the main roads, and whomever you may find, invite them to the marriage- feast.

10 So the servants went out to the roads and gathered together every one they could find, bad and good; and the wedding-house was filled with guests.

11 When the king entered to see the guests, he saw there a man who was not wearing wedding garments.

12 And he said to him, My friend, how did you enter here, when you do not have wedding garments? And he was speechless.

13 Then the king said to the servants, Bind his hands and his feet and take him out into darkness; there shall be weeping and gnashing of teeth.

14 For many are invited, and few are chosen.

15 ¶ Then the Pharisees went away and took counsel how to trap him by a word.

16 So they sent to him their disciples together with the Herodians, and they said to him, Teacher, we know that you are true, and you teach the way of God justly; and you do not favor any man, for you do not discriminate between men.

17 Tell us, therefore, what do you think? Is it lawful to pay head-tax to Caesar, or not?

18 But Jesus knew their evil, and said, Why do you tempt me, O hypocrites?

19 Show me the head-tax penny. And they brought to him a penny.

20 And Jesus said to them, Whose is this image and inscription?

21 They said, Caesar's. He said to them, Give therefore to Caesar what is Caesar's, and to God what is God's.

22 And when they heard it, they were amazed; and they left him and went away.

23 ¶ That same day the Sadducees came and said to him, There is no resurrection of the dead; and they asked him,

24 And said to him, Teacher, Moses has told us, If a man die without sons, let his brother take his wife, and raise up offspring for his brother.

Cf.dif. vv. 21:42, 44;   22:3, 6, 8, 10, 15-17, 19, 23.

25 Now there were with us seven brothers; the first married and died, and because he had no sons, he left his wife to his brother.

26 Likewise the second, also the third, up to the seventh.

27 And after them all the woman also died.

28 Therefore at the resurrection, to which of these seven will she be a wife? for they all married her.

29 Jesus answered, and said to them, You err, because you do not understand the scriptures nor the power of God.

30 For at the resurrection of the dead, they neither marry women, nor are women given to men in marriage, but they are like the angels of God in heaven.

31 But concerning the resurrection of the dead, have you not read what was said to you by God, saying,

32 I am the God of Abraham, the God of Isaac, the God of Jacob? And yet God is not the God of the dead, but of the living.

33 And when the people heard it, they were amazed at his teaching.

34 ¶ But when the Pharisees heard that he had silenced the Sadducees, they gathered together.

35 And one of them who knew the law, asked him, testing him,

36 Teacher, which is the greatest commandment in the law?

37 Jesus said to him, Love the Lord your God with all your heart, and with all your soul, and with all your power, and with all your mind.

38 This is the greatest and the first commandment.

39 And the second is like to it, Love your neighbor as yourself.

40 On these two commandments hang the law and the prophets.

41 ¶ While the Pharisees were gathered together, Jesus asked them,

42 And he said, What do you say concerning the Christ? whose son is he? They said to him, son of David.

43 He said to them, How is it then that David through the Spirit calls him Lord? For he said,

44 The Lord said to my Lord, Sit at my right hand, until I put your enemies under your feet.

45 If David then calls him Lord, how can he be his son?

46 And no man was able to answer him, and from that day no man dared to question him.

CHAPTER 23

*T*HEN Jesus spoke with the people and with his disciples.

2 And he said to them, The scribes and the Pharisees sit on the chair of Moses.

3 Therefore whatever they tell you to obey, obey and do it, but do not do according to their works; for they say and do not.

4 And they bind heavy burdens, and put them on men's shoulders, but they themselves are not willing to touch them, even with their finger.

5 And all their works they do, just to be seen by men; for they widen the fringes of their garments, and they lengthen the ends of their robes,

6 And they like the chief places at feasts, and the front seats in the synagogues,

7 And the greetings in the streets, and to be called by men, Rabbi.

8 But you do not be called, Rabbi; for one is your Master, and all you are brethren.

9 And call no one on earth, father, for one is your Father in heaven.

10 Nor be called leaders, for one is your leader, the Christ.

11 But he who is greatest among you, let him be your minister.

12 For whoever exalts himself shall be humbled; and whoever humbles himself shall be exalted.

13 ¶ Woe to you, scribes and Pharisees, hypocrites! for you embezzle the property of widows, with the pretense that you make long prayers; because of this you shall receive a greater judgment.*

14 Woe to you, scribes and Pharisees, hypocrites! for you have shut off the kingdom of heaven against men; for you do not enter into it yourselves, and do not permit those who would enter.

15 Woe to you, scribes and Pharisees, hypocrites! for you traverse sea and land to make one proselyte; and when he becomes one, you make him the son of hell twice more than yourselves.

16 Woe to you, blind guides, for you say, Whoever swears by the temple, it is nothing; but whoever swears by the gold which is in the temple, he is guilty!

17 O you fools and blind! for which is greater, the gold or the temple that sanctifies the gold?

18 And whoever swears by the altar, it is nothing; but whoever swears by the offering that is on it, he is guilty.

19 O you fools and blind! for which is greater, the offering, or the altar that sanctifies the offering?

20 Therefore he who swears by the altar, he swears by it and by everything that is on it.

21 And whoever swears by the temple, swears by it and by him who dwells in it.

22 And he who swears by heaven, swears by the throne of God, and by him who sits on it.

23 Woe to you, scribes and Pharisees, hypocrites! for you take tithes on mint, dill, and cummin, and you have overlooked the more important matters of the law, such as justice, mercy, and trustworthiness. These were necessary for you to have done, and the same by no means to have left undone.

24 O blind guides, who strain at gnats and swallow camels!

25 Woe to you, scribes and Pharisees, hypocrites! you clean the outside of the cup and of the dish, but inside they are full of extortion and iniquity.

26 Blind Pharisees! clean first the inside of the cup and of the dish, so that their outside may also be clean.

27 Woe to you, scribes and Pharisees, hypocrites! for you are like tombs painted white, which look beautiful from the outside, but inside are full of dead bones and all kinds of corruption.

28 Even so, from the outside you appear to men to be righteous, but from within you are full of iniquity and hypocrisy.

29 Woe to you, scribes and Pharisees, hypocrites! for you build the tombs of the prophets, and you decorate the graves of the righteous;

30 And you say, If we had been living in the days of our forefathers, we would not have been partakers with them in the blood of the prophets.

31 Now you testify concerning yourselves, that you are the children of those who killed the prophets.

32 You also fill up the measure of your fathers.

33 O you serpents, and seed of scorpions! how can you flee from the judgment of hell?

34 ¶ Because of this, I am sending to you prophets and wise men and scribes; some of them you will kill and crucify; and some you will scourge in your synagogues, and pursue them from city to city;

---

* Mt.23:13 - The order of verses 13 and 14 is reversed in the Eastern Version.

Cf.dif. vv. 23:13, 23, 26, 33.

35 So that all the blood of the righteous shed on the ground may come on you, from the blood of Abel the righteous down to the blood of Zachariah, son of Barachiah, whom you killed between the temple and the altar.

36 Truly I say to you, All of these things shall come upon this generation.

37 O Jerusalem, Jerusalem, murderess of the prophets, and stoner of those who are sent to her! how often I wanted to gather together your children, just as a hen gathers her chickens under her wings, and yet you would not!

38 Behold, your house will be left to you desolate.

39 For I say to you, from now you will not see me until you say, Blessed is he who comes in the name of the Lord.

CHAPTER 24

*A*ND Jesus went out of the temple to go away; and his disciples came up to him, and were showing him the building of the temple.

2 But he said to them, Behold, do you not see all of these? truly I say to you, Not a stone shall be left here upon a stone, which will not be torn down.

3 ¶ While Jesus sat on the Mount of Olives, his disciples came up talking among themselves, and they said to him, Tell us when these things will happen, and what is the sign of your coming, and of the end of the world?

4 Jesus answered and said to them, Be careful that no man deceives you.

5 For many will come in my name, and say, I am the Christ, and they will deceive many.

6 You are bound to hear of revolutions and rumors of wars; look out and do not be disturbed; for all of these things must come to pass, but the end is not yet.

7 For nation will rise against nation, and kingdom against kingdom; and there will be

famines and plagues and earthquakes, in different places.

8 But all these things are just the beginning of travail.

9 Then they will deliver you over to be oppressed, and they will kill you; and you will be hated by all nations for my name's sake.

10 Then many will stumble, and they will hate one another, and betray one another.

11 And many false prophets will rise, and will mislead a great many.

12 And because of the growth of iniquity, the love of many will become cold.

13 But he who has patience to the end, he will be saved.

14 And this gospel of the kingdom shall be preached throughout the world as a testimony to all the nations; then the end will come.

15 When you see the sign of the refuse of desolation, as spoken by the prophet Daniel, accumulating in the holy place, whoever reads will understand it.

16 Then let those who are in Judaea, flee to the mountain,

17 And he who is on the roof, let him not come down to take things out of his house.

18 And he who is in the field, let him not return back to take his clothes.

19 But woe to those who are with child, and to those who give suck in those days!

20 Pray that your flight may not be in winter, nor on the sabbath.

21 For then will be great suffering, such as has never happened from the beginning of the world until now, and never will be again.

22 And if those days were not shortened, no flesh would live; but for the sake of the chosen ones those days will be shortened.

23 Then if any man should say to you, Behold, here is the Christ, or there, do not believe it.

24 For there will rise false Christs and lying prophets, and they will show signs and great

wonders, so as to mislead, if possible, even the chosen ones.

25 Behold, I have told you in advance.

26 Therefore, if they should say to you, Behold, he is in the desert, do not go out; or, behold, he is in the room, do not believe it.

27 For just as the lightning comes out from the east, and is seen even in the west, so will be the coming of the Son of man.

28 For wherever the corpse is, there will the eagles gather.

29 ¶ Immediately after the suffering of those days, the sun will be darkened, and the moon will not give her light, and the stars will fall from the sky, and the powers of the universe will be shaken.

30 Then the sign of the Son of man will appear in the sky; and then all the generations of the earth will mourn, and they will see the Son of man coming on the clouds of the sky, with an army and great glory.

31 And he will send his angels with a large trumpet, and they will gather his chosen ones from the four winds, from one end of the universe to the other.

32 From the fig tree learn a parable. As soon as its branches become tender and bring forth leaves, you know that summer is coming.

33 So even you, when you see all these things, know that it has arrived at the door.

34 Truly I say to you, that this generation will not pass away, until all these things happen.

35 Even heaven and earth will pass away, but my words shall not pass away.

36 ¶ But concerning that day and that hour, no man knows, not even the angels of heaven, but the Father alone.

37 Just as in the days of Noah, so will be the coming of the Son of man.

38 For as the people before the flood were eating and drinking, marrying and giving in marriage, until the day Noah entered into the ark,

39 And they knew nothing until the flood came and carried them all away; such will be the coming of the Son of man.

40 Then two men will be in the field, one will be taken away and the other left.

41 Two women will be grinding at the hand-mill, one will be taken and the other left.

42 ¶ Be alert, therefore, for you do not know at what hour your Lord will come.

43 But know this much, that if the master of the house knew at what watch of the night the thief comes, he would keep awake and would not let his house be plundered.

44 For this reason, you also be ready, for the Son of man will come at an hour when you do not expect him.

45 Who then is the faithful and wise servant, whom his Lord has appointed over his household, to give them food in due time?

46 Blessed is that servant, when his Lord comes and finds him so doing.

47 Truly I say to you, he will appoint him over all that he has.

48 But if a bad servant should say in his heart, My lord will delay his coming,

49 And he begins to beat his fellow servants, and to eat and drink with drunkards,

50 The Lord of that servant will come on a day when he does not expect, and at an hour that he does not know.

51 And he will severely scourge him, and give him a portion like that of the hypocrites; there will be weeping and gnashing of teeth.

CHAPTER 25

*T*HEN the kingdom of heaven will be like ten virgins, who took their lamps, and went out to greet the bridegroom and the bride.

2 Five of them were wise, and five were foolish.

Cf.dif. vv. 24:26-27, 30-31, 43-44, 51; 25:1.

3 And the foolish ones took their lamps, but took no oil with them.

4 But the wise ones took oil in the vessels with their lamps.

5 As the bridegroom was delayed, they all slumbered and slept.

6 And at midnight there was a cry, Behold, the bridegroom is coming; go out to greet him.

7 Then all the virgins got up and fixed their lamps.

8 And the foolish ones said to the wise ones, Give us some of your oil, for our lamps are going out.

9 Then the wise ones answered and said, Why, there would not be enough for us and for you; go to those who sell and buy for yourselves.

10 And while they went to buy, the bridegroom came; and those who were ready entered with him into the wedding house, and the door was locked.

11 Afterward the other virgins also came and said, Our lord, our lord, open to us.

12 But he answered and said to them, Truly I say to you, I do not know you.

13 Be alert, therefore, for you do not know, that day nor the hour.

14 ¶ It is just like a man who went on a journey, who called his servants and put his wealth in their charge.

15 To one he gave five talents, to one two, to another one; to each one according to his ability; and immediately he went on a journey.

16 The one who received five talents then went and traded with them, and he earned five others.

17 Likewise the second one, he gained by trading gained two others.

18 But he who received one, went and dug in the ground, and hid his lord's money.

19 After a long time, the lord of those servants returned, and took an accounting from them.

20 Then the one who received five talents came up, and offered five others, and he said, My lord, you gave me five talents; behold, I have gained five others to them.

21 His lord said to him, Well done, good and reliable servant; you have been faithful over a little, I will appoint you over much; enter into your master's joy.

22 Then the one with the two talents came and he said, My lord, you gave me two talents, behold I have gained two others to them.

23 His lord said to him, Well done, good and reliable servant, you have been faithful over a little, I will appoint you over much; enter into your master's joy.

24 Then the one who received one talent also came up, and he said, My lord, I knew that you are a hard man, and you reap where you did not sow, and gather where you did not scatter.

25 So I was afraid, and I went and hid your talent in the ground; here it is, it is your own one.

26 His lord answered and said to him, O wicked and lazy servant, you knew me that I reap where I did not sow, and I gather where I did not scatter.

27 You should then have put my money in the exchange, and when I returned I would have demanded my own with interest.

28 Therefore take away the talent from him, and give it to the one who has ten talents.

29 For to him who has, it shall he given, and it shall increase to him; but he who has not, even that which he has shall be taken away from him.

30 And the idle servant they threw into the outer darkness; there will be weeping and gnashing of teeth.

         Cf.dif. vv. 25:8, 5, 10, 13-14, 21, 25, 27, 29-30.

31 ¶ When the Son of man comes in his glory, and all his holy angels with him, then he will sit upon the throne of his glory.

32 And all nations will gather before him; and he will separate them one from another, just as a shepherd separates the sheep from the goats;

33 And he will set the sheep at his right, and the goats at his left.

34 Then the King will say to those at his right, Come, you blessed of my Father, inherit the kingdom which has been prepared for you from the foundation of the world.

35 For I was hungry, and you gave me to eat; I was thirsty, and you gave me to drink; I was a stranger and you took me in;

36 I was naked, and you covered me; I was sick, and you visited me; I was in prison, and you came to me.

37 Then the righteous will say to him, Our Lord, when did we see you hungry, and feed you? or thirsty and gave you drink?

38 And when did we see you a stranger, and took you in? Or that you were naked, and covered you?

39 And when did we see you sick, or in the prison, and come to you?

40 The king then will answer and say to them, Truly I tell you, Inasmuch as you have done it to one of these least brethren, you did it to me.

41 Then he will also say to those at his left, Go away from me, you cursed, to the everlasting fire, which is prepared for the adversary and his angels.

42 For I was hungry, and you did not give me to eat; I was thirsty, and you did not give me to drink;

43 I was a stranger, and you did not take me in; I was naked, and you did not cover me; I was sick and in prison and you did not visit me.

44 Then they also will answer and say, Our lord, when did we see you hungry, or thirsty, or a stranger, or naked, or sick or in the prison, and did not minister to you?

45 Then he will answer and say to them, Truly I say to you, Inasmuch as you did not do it to one of these least ones, you also did not do it to me.

46 And these shall go into everlasting torment, and the righteous into eternal life.

CHAPTER 26

WHEN Jesus had finished all these sayings, he said to his disciples,

2 You know that after two days will be the passover, and the Son of man will be betrayed to be crucified.

3 Then the high priests and the scribes and the elders of the people assembled in the court yard of the high priest, who is called Caiaphas.

4 And they took counsel concerning Jesus, to arrest him by a snare and kill him.

5 And they said, Not on the feast day, so as not to cause a riot among the people.

6 ¶ And when Jesus was at Bethany, in the house of Simon the leper,

7 A woman came up to him with an alabaster vessel of precious perfume, and she poured it upon the head of Jesus, while he was reclining.

8 When his disciples saw it, they were displeased, and said, Why is this loss?

9 For it could have been sold for a great deal, and given to the poor.

10 But Jesus understood it and said to them, Why are you troubling the woman? She has done a good work to me.

11 For you always have the poor with you, but you will not have me always.

12 But this one who poured the perfume on my body, did it as for my burial.

Cf.dif. vv. 26:2-4, 7, 12.

13 And truly I say to you, Wherever this my gospel is preached throughout the world, what she has done will also be told as a memorial to her.

14 ¶ Then one of the twelve, called Judas of Iscariot, went to the high priests;

15 And he said to them, What are you willing to give me, and I will deliver him to you? And they promised him thirty pieces of silver.

16 And from that time he sought an opportunity to betray him.

17 ¶ On the first day of unleavened bread, the disciples came up to Jesus and said to him, Where do you wish that we may prepare the passover for you to eat?

18 And he said to them, Go into the city to a certain man, and say to him, Our Master says, My time has come, I will observe the passover with my disciples at your house.

19 And his disciples did as Jesus had commanded them; and they prepared the passover.

20 And when it was evening, he was reclining with his twelve disciples.

21 And while they were eating he said, Truly I say to you, that one of you will betray me.

22 And they felt very sad, and began to say to him one by one, Why, is it I, my Lord?

23 And he answered and said, He who dips his hand with me in the dish, he will betray me.

24 The Son of man is going through, just as it is written concerning him; but woe to the man by whose hand the Son of man is betrayed! it would have been far better for that man never to have been born.

25 Then Judas the traitor answered and said, Master, perhaps it is I? Jesus said to him, You say that.

26 ¶ While they were eating, Jesus took bread and blessed it, and he broke it, and gave it to his disciples, and he said, Take, eat; this is my body.

27 Then he took the cup and gave thanks, and gave it to them and said, Take, drink of it, all of you.

28 This is my blood of the new covenant which is shed for many for the remission of sins.

29 But I say to you, from now on I shall not drink from this fruit of the vine, until the day when I drink it anew with you in the kingdom of God.

30 And they offered praise, and went out to the Mount of Olives.

31 ¶ Then Jesus said to them, All of you will deny me this night; for it is written, I will smite the shepherd, and the sheep of his flock will be scattered.

32 But after I am risen, I will be in Galilee before you.

33 Peter answered and said to him, Even if every man should deny you, I will never deny you.

34 Jesus said to him, Truly I say to you, that in this very night, before the cock crows, you will deny me three times.

35 Peter said to him, Even if I must die with you, I will never deny you. All the disciples said likewise.

36 ¶ Then Jesus came with them to a place which is called Gethsemane, and he said to his disciples, Sit down here, while I go to pray.

37 And he took Peter and the two sons of Zebedee, and he began to be sorrowful and oppressed.

38 He said to them, My soul is sorrowful even to death; wait for me here, and watch with me.

39 And he went a little further and fell on his face, and prayed saying, O my Father, if it be possible, let this cup pass from me; but let it be, not as I will, but as you.

40 Then he came to his disciples and found them sleeping, and he said to Peter, So, you

Cf.dif. vv. 26:18, 20, 22, 24-25, 27, 29-30.

were not able to watch with me even for one hour?

41 Awake and pray, that you may not enter into temptation; the spirit indeed is ready, but the body is weak.

42 He went away again the second time and prayed and said, O my Father, if this cup cannot pass, and if I have to drink it, let it be according to your will.

43 He came again and found them sleeping, for their eyes were heavy.

44 And he left them and went away again and prayed the third time, and he said the same word.

45 Then he came to his disciples and said to them, Sleep from now on and get your rest; behold, the hour has come, and the Son of man will be delivered into the hands of sinners.

46 Arise, let us go; behold, he who is to deliver me has arrived.

47 ¶ While he was speaking, behold, Judas the traitor, one of the twelve, came and with him a large crowd with swords and staves, from the high priests and the elders of the people.

48 Now Judas the traitor had given them a sign, saying, He whom I kiss, it is he, arrest him.

49 And immediately he came up to Jesus and said, Peace, Master; and he kissed him.

50 Jesus said to him, Is it for this that you have come, my friend? Then they came near and laid hands on Jesus, and arrested him.

51 And behold, one of those who were with Jesus stretched out his hand and drew a sword, and struck it at the servant of the high priest, and cut off his ear.

52 Then Jesus said to him, Return the sword to its place; for all who take swords will die by swords.

53 Or do you think that I cannot ask of my Father, and he will now raise up for me more than twelve legions of angels?

54 How then could the scriptures be fulfilled, that it must be so?

55 At that very hour Jesus said to the people, Have you come out with swords and staves to arrest me like a bandit? I sat with you every day, teaching in the temple, and you did not arrest me.

56 But this has happened so that the scriptures of the prophets might be fulfilled. Then all the disciples left him, and fled.

57 ¶ And those who had arrested Jesus took him to Caiaphas the high priest, where the scribes and the elders had assembled.

58 But Simon Peter followed him afar off, up to the courtyard of the high priest, and he went inside and sat with the soldiers, to see the end.

59 Now the high priests and the elders and the whole council were seeking witnesses against Jesus, so that they might put him to death.

60 But they could not find any; then there came a great many false witnesses; but at the end two came forward,

61 And said, This man said, I can tear down the temple of God, and build it in three days.

62 And the high priest stood up and said to him, You are not answering anything. What is it that these men testify against you?

63 But Jesus was silent. Then the high priest answered and said to him, I adjure you by the living God, to tell us if you are the Christ, the Son of God?

64 Jesus said to him, You say that. But I say to you that from henceforth you will see the Son of man sitting at the right hand of the power, and coming upon the clouds of the sky.

65 The high priest then rent his clothes and said, Behold, he is blaspheming; why therefore do we need witnesses? behold, you have now heard his blasphemy.

66 What else do you want? They answered and said, He is guilty of death.

Cf.dif. vv. 26:42, 49-50, 53,55, 59-60, 62, 64, 66.

67 Then they spat in his face, and struck him on his head, and others beat him,

68 Saying, O Christ, prophesy to us; who smote you?

69 ¶ Now Peter sat outside in the courtyard; and a maidservant came up to him, and said to him, You also were with Jesus the Nazarene.

70 But he denied it before all of them, and said, I do not understand what you are saying.

71 And as he was going to the porch, another one saw him, and she said to them, This man was also there with Jesus the Nazarene.

72 Again he denied it with oaths, I do not know the man.

73 After a while, those who were standing came up, and said to Peter, Truly you also are one of them, for even your speech proves it.

74 Then he began to curse and to swear, I do not know the man. At that very hour the cock crowed.

75 And Peter remembered the word of Jesus, which he had said to him, Before the cock crows, you will deny me three times. And he went outside and wept bitterly.

CHAPTER 27

WHEN it was morning, the high priests and the elders of the people took counsel concerning Jesus, how to put him to death.

2 So they bound him, and took him and delivered him to Pilate the governor.

3 ¶ Then Judas the traitor, when he saw that Jesus was convicted, repented, and went away and brought back the same thirty pieces of silver to the high priests and the elders.

4 And he said, I have sinned, because I have betrayed innocent blood. But they said to him, What is that to us? You know better.

5 Then he threw the silver in the temple, and departed; and he went and hanged himself.

6 The high priests took the silver and said, It is not lawful to put it in the house of offerings, because it is the price of blood.

7 And they took counsel, and bought with it the potter's field, for a cemetery for strangers.

8 On this account that field was called The field of blood, to this day.

9 ¶ Then what was spoken by the prophet was fulfilled, who said, I took the thirty pieces of silver, the costly price which was bargained with the children of Israel.

10 And I gave them for the potter's field, as the Lord commanded me.

11 And Jesus stood before the governor; and the governor asked him and said to him, Are you the King of the Jews? Jesus said to him, You say that.

12 And while the chief priests and elders were accusing him, he gave no answer.

13 Then Pilate said to him, Do you not hear how much they testify against you?

14 But he did not answer him, not even a word; and because of this Pilate marvelled greatly.

15 Now on every feast day it was the custom of the governor to release one prisoner to the people, anyone whom they wanted.

16 They had a well-known prisoner, called Bar-Abbas, who was bound.

17 When they were gathered together, Pilate said to them, Whom do you want me to release to you? Bar-Abbas, or Jesus who is called the Christ?

18 For Pilate knew that because of envy they had delivered him.

19 ¶ When the governor was sitting on his judgment seat, his wife sent to him and said to him, Have nothing to do with that righteous man; for today I have suffered a great deal in my dream because of him.

20 But the high priests and the elders urged the people to ask for Bar-Abbas, and to destroy Jesus.

21 And the governor answered and said to them, Which of these two do you want me to release to you? They said, Bar-Abbas.

22 Pilate said to them, What shall I then do with Jesus who is called the Christ? They all said, Let him be crucified.

23 Pilate said to them, What evil has he done? But they cried out the more and said, Let him be crucified.

24 ¶ Now when Pilate saw that he was gaining nothing, but that instead confusion was increasing, he took water and washed his hands before the people, and said, I am innocent of the blood of this righteous man; do as you please.

25 All the people then answered and said, Let his blood be on us and on our children.

26 ¶ Then he released to them Bar-Abbas, and had Jesus scourged with whips, and delivered to be crucified.

27 Then the soldiers of the governor took Jesus into the Praetorium, and the whole company gathered around him.

28 And they removed his clothes and put on him a scarlet robe.

29 And they wove a crown of thorns and put it on his head, and a reed in his right hand; and they knelt on their knees before him, and they were mocking him and saying, Hail, King of the Jews!

30 And they spat in his face, and took the reed and struck him on his head.

31 And when they had mocked him, they took off the robe from him and put on him his own clothes, and took him away to be crucified.

32 And as they were going out, they found a man of Cyrene, whose name was Simon, whom they compelled to carry his cross.

33 ¶ And they came to a place which is called Golgotha, which is interpreted The Skull.

34 And they gave him to drink vinegar mixed with gall; and he tasted it, but he would not drink.

35 ¶ And when they had crucified him, they divided his clothes by casting lots.

36 And they were sitting there and watching him.

37 And they placed above his head in writing the reason for his death: THIS IS JESUS THE KING OF THE JEWS.

38 ¶ And there were crucified with him two bandits, one on his right and one on his left.

39 And those who passed by blasphemed against him, nodding their heads,

40 And saying, O you who can tear down the temple and build it in three days, deliver yourself, if you are the Son of God, and come down from the cross.

41 The high priests likewise were mocking, together with the scribes, the elders and the Pharisees.

42 And they were saying, He saved others, but he cannot save himself. If he is the King of Israel, let him now come down from the cross, so that we may see and believe in him.

43 He trusted in God; let him save him now, if he is pleased with him; for he said, I am God's Son.

44 The bandits also, who were crucified with him were reproaching him.

45 Now from the sixth hour, there was darkness over all the land, until the ninth hour.

46 And about the ninth hour, Jesus cried out with a loud voice and said, Eli, Eli, lmana shabachthani! which means, My God, my God, for this I was kept! *

47 Some of the men who were standing by, when they heard it, said, This man has called for Elijah.

48 And immediately one of them ran and took a sponge and filled it with vinegar, and put it on a reed, and gave him to drink.

49 But the rest said, Hush, let us see if Elijah will come to save him.

50 ¶ But Jesus again cried out with a loud voice, and gave up his breath.

Cf.dif. vv. 27:24, 26-27, 37, 39, 44, 46, 49-50.

51 And immediately the door curtains of the temple were rent in two, from the top to the bottom; and the earth quaked, and the rocks split;

52 And the tombs were opened; and the bodies of a great many saints who were sleeping in death rose up,

53 And they went out; and after his resurrection, they entered into the holy city, and appeared to a great many.

54 ¶ When the centurion and those who were with him watching Jesus, saw the earthquake and all that happened, they were very much frightened, and they said, Truly this man was the Son of God.

55 There were also many women there, who were looking from afar, those who had followed Jesus from Galilee, and who used to minister to him.

56 One of them was Mary of Magdala; and Mary the mother of James and Joses, and the mother of the sons of Zebedee.

57 ¶ When evening came, there came a rich man of Arimathaea, whose name was Joseph, who was also a disciple of Jesus.

58 He went to Pilate and asked for the body of Jesus. And Pilate commanded that the body should be given to him.

59 So Joseph took the body, and wrapped it in a shroud of fine linen,

60 And laid it in his own new tomb which was hewn in a rock; and they rolled a large stone, and

placed it against the door of the tomb, and went away.

61 And there were there Mary of Magdala and the other Mary, who were sitting opposite the tomb.

62 ¶ The next day, which is after Friday, the high priests and the Pharisees together came to Pilate,

63 And they said to him, Our lord, we have just remembered that that deceiver used to say when he was alive, After three days I will rise again.

64 Now, therefore, command that precautions be taken at the tomb for three days. It is probable that his disciples may come and steal him at night, and then say to the people, He has risen from the dead; and the last deception will be worse than the first.

65 Pilate said to them, You have guards; go and take precautions as best you know.

66 So they went and kept a watch at the tomb, and together with the guards they sealed the stone.

CHAPTER 28

*I*N the evening of the sabbath day, when the first day of the week began, there came Mary of Magdala and the other Mary, to see the tomb.

2 And behold, a great earthquake took place; for the angel of the Lord came down from heaven, and went up and rolled away the stone from the door, and sat on it.

3 His appearance was like lightning, and his garments white as snow.

4 And for fear of him the guards who were watching trembled, and became as if they were dead.

5 But the angel answered and said to the women, You need not be afraid; for I know that you are seeking Jesus who was crucified.

6 He is not here, for he has risen, just as he had said. Come in, see the place where our Lord was laid.

7 And go quickly, and tell his disciples that he has risen from the dead; and behold, he will be before you to Galilee; there you will see him; behold, I have told you.

---

* Mt.27:46 - This was my destiny for which I was born.

8 And they went away hurriedly from the tomb with fear and with great joy, running to tell his disciples.

9 And behold, Jesus met them, and said to them, Peace be to you. And they came up and laid hold of his feet, and worshipped him.

10 Then Jesus said to them, Do not be afraid; but go and tell my brethren to go to Galilee, and there they shall see me.

11 ¶ When they were going, some of the guards came into the city, and told the high priests everything that had happened.

12 So they gathered with the elders and took counsel; and they gave money, not a small sum, to the guards,

13 Telling them, Say that his disciples came by night and stole him while we were sleeping.

14 And if this should be heard by the governor, we will appeal to him, and declare that you are blameless.

15 So they took the money, and did as they were instructed; and this word went out among the Jews, until this day.

16 ¶ The eleven disciples then went to Galilee to a mountain, where Jesus had promised to meet them.

17 And when they saw him, they worshipped him; but some of them were doubtful.

18 And Jesus came up and spoke with them, and said to them, All power in heaven and on earth has been given to me. Just as my Father has sent me I am also sending you.

19 Go, therefore, and convert all nations; and baptize them in the name of the Father and of the Son and of the Holy Spirit;

20 And teach them to obey everything that I have commanded you; and, behold, I am with you all the days , to the end of the world. Amen.

Completion of the Holy Gospel as published by Matthew; and which he published in Hebrew, in the land of the Palestineans. *

,ܝܬܡ݁ܝ ܟܗܘܪܘܒ ܗܝܢܐ ܒܐܘܝܠܘܐ ܡܠܫ ܀
܀ ܟܝܘܦܘܠܐܦ ܕܘܐ݁ܪܝܒܐ ܠܠܗܘܬ ܟܘܝܠܐ

___

* As translated by James Murdock, *The New Testament, A Literal Translation from the Syriac Peschito Version* (Robert Carter & Bros., 1851).

THE GOSPEL ACCORDING TO

ST. MARK

❖ ܦܘܩܪܝܘܢ ܐܘܢܓܠܝܘܢ ܩܕܝܫ ܕܡܪܩܘܣ ❖

CHAPTER 1

*T*HE beginning of the gospel of Jesus Christ, the Son of God.

2 As it is written in Isaiah the prophet, Behold I send my messenger before your face, that he may prepare your way,

3 The voice that cries in the wilderness, Make ready the way of the Lord, and straighten his high ways.

4 John was in the wilderness, baptizing and preaching the baptism of repentance for the forgiveness of sins,

5 And the whole province of Judaea went out to him, and all the people of Jerusalem; and he baptized them in the river Jordan, when they confessed their sins.

6 ¶ John wore a dress of camel's hair, with a girdle of leather fastened around his loins; and his food was locusts and wild honey.

7 And he preached saying, Behold, there is coming after me one who is mightier than myself, even the strings of whose shoes I am not good enough to bend down and untie.

8 I have baptized you with water; but he will baptize you with the Holy Spirit.

9 ¶ And it came to pass in those days, Jesus came from Nazareth of Galilee, and was baptized in the Jordan by John.

10 And immediately, as he went up out of the water, he saw the sky was clear open, and the Spirit as a dove came down upon him.

11 And a voice came from heaven, You are my beloved Son, I am pleased with you.

12 And immediately the Spirit drove him out into the wilderness.

13 And he was there in the wilderness forty days, being tried out by Satan; and he was with the wild beasts; and the angels ministered to him.

14 ¶ But after John was delivered up, Jesus came to Galilee, preaching the gospel of the kingdom of God,

15 And saying, The time has come to an end, and the kingdom of God is at hand; repent and believe in the gospel.

16 While he walked along the sea of Galilee, he saw Simon and Andrew his brother throwing their nets into the sea; for they were fishermen.

17 And Jesus said to them, Come after me, and I will make you fishers of men.

18 And straightway they left their nets, and went after him.

19 And when he went a little further, he saw James the son of Zebedee and his brother John; they also were in a boat mending their nets.

20 And he called them; and immediately they left their father Zebedee with the hired men, and went after him.

21 When they entered into Capernaum, straightway he taught on the sabbaths in their synagogues.

22 And they were amazed at his teaching; for he taught them as one with an authority, and not like their scribes.

23 ¶ And there was in their synagogue a man who had in him an unclean spirit; and he cried out,

24 And said, Jesus of Nazareth, what have we in common? Have you come to destroy us? I know you, who you are, "Holy One of God."

25 And Jesus rebuked him and said, Be silent, and come out of him.

26 And the unclean spirit threw him down, and cried out in a loud voice, and left him.

27 And they were all astonished, and kept asking one another saying, What does this mean? and what is this new teaching, that with such a power he commands even unclean spirits and they obey him?

28 And his fame immediately spread throughout the country of Galilee.

29 Then they went out of the synagogue, and came to the house of Simon and Andrew, together with James and John.

30 And Simon's mother-in-law was laid up with fever; and they spoke to him about her.

31 And he went and held her hand, and lifted her up; and immediately the fever left her, and she ministered to them.

32 In the evening towards sunset, they brought to him all who were seriously sick, and the insane.

33 And the whole city was gathered at the door.

34 And he healed many who were seriously sick with divers diseases, and he restored many who were insane; and he did not allow the insane to speak because some of them were his acquaintances.

35 And in the morning he rose up very early and went away to a lonely place, and there prayed.

36 And Simon and those who were with him were looking for him.

37 And when they found him, they said to him, Everyone wants you.

38 He said to them, Let us walk to the neighboring towns and cities, so that I may preach there also; because I came for this.

39 And he preached in all their synagogues throughout Galilee, and cast out demons.

40 And there came to him a leper, who fell down at his feet, and begged him, saying, If you will, you can make me clean.

41 And Jesus had mercy on him, and stretched out his hand and touched him, and said, I am willing; be clean.

42 And in that hour his leprosy disappeared from him, and he became clean.

43 And Jesus rebuked him and put him out,

44 And said to him, Look here, why are you telling it to the people? but go away, show yourself to the priests, and offer an offering for the sake of your cleansing, according to what Moses commanded, as their testimonial.

45 But when he went out, he began to publish it still more, and to spread the word, so that Jesus was no longer able to enter the city openly, but he remained outside in a lonely place; and yet they came to him from every place.

CHAPTER 2

AND Jesus entered again into Capernaum for a few days; and when they heard that he was in a house,

2 A great many gathered together so that it was impossible to hold them, not even in front of the entrance; so he spoke a few words to them.

3 And they came to him, and brought to him a paralyzed man, carried between four men.

4 But as they were unable to come near him because of the crowd, they went up to the roof and uncovered it over the place where Jesus was; and they lowered the quilt-bed in which the paralyzed man lay.

5 When Jesus saw their faith, he said to the paralytic, My son, your sins are forgiven.

6 Now some of the scribes and Pharisees were sitting there, and they reasoned in their hearts,

7 Why does this man speak blasphemy? Who can forgive sins except God only?

8 But Jesus perceived in his spirit that they were reasoning among themselves, and he said to them, Why do you reason these things in your heart?

9 Which is the easier, to say to the paralytic, Your sins are forgiven; or to say, Rise, take up your quilt-bed and walk?

10 But that you may know that the Son of man has power on earth to forgive sins, he said to the paralytic,

11 I tell you, Rise, take up your quilt-bed, and go to your house.

12 And immediately he rose, and took up his quilt-bed and went out before the eyes of them all; and they were all amazed, and gave glory to God, saying, We have never seen anything like it.

13 ¶ And he went out again by the seaside, and all the people kept coming to him, and he taught them.

14 And as he passed by, he saw Levi the son of Alphaeus, sitting at the custom house, and he said to him, Follow me; and he got up and followed him.

15 And it happened that while he was a guest at his house, a great many publicans and sinners were also guests with Jesus and his disciples; for there were many, and they followed him.

16 And when the scribes and the Pharisees saw him eating with the publicans and sinners, they said to his disciples, Why does he eat and drink with publicans and sinners?

17 When Jesus heard it, he said to them, Those who are healthy need no doctor, but those who are seriously sick; I came not to call the righteous, but the sinners.

18 The disciples of John and of the Pharisees were fasting; and they came and said to him, Why do the disciples of John and of the Pharisees fast, and your own disciples do not fast?

19 Jesus said to them, Why, can the sons of the wedding feast fast as long as the bridegroom is with them? No!

20 But the days will come when the bridegroom is taken away from them, then in that day they will fast.

21 No man puts a new patch and sews it on a worn out garment, so that the new patch may not weaken the old, and the hole become larger.

22 And no man pours new wine into old wine-skins, so that the wine may not rend the skins and the skins be ruined, and the wine run out; but they pour new wine into new wine-skins.

23 And it happened that while Jesus was going through the wheat fields on the sabbath, his disciples walked and pulled up the ears of wheat.

24 And the Pharisees said to him, Look what they are doing on the sabbath! that which is unlawful.

25 Jesus said to them, Have you not read what David did, when he was in need and hungry, he and those who were with him?

26 How he entered into the house of God when Abiathar was the chief priest, and ate the bread which was on the table of the Lord, which was not lawful to be eaten except by the priests, and he gave it also to those who were with him?

27 And he said to them, The sabbath was created for the sake of man, and not man for the sake of the sabbath.

28 The Son of man therefore is the Lord also of the sabbath.

CHAPTER 3

*J*ESUS entered again into the synagogue, and there was there a man whose hand was withered.

2 And they watched him if he would heal him on the sabbath, that they might accuse him.

3 And he said to the man whose hand was withered, Stand up in the midst.

4 Then he said to them also, Is it lawful to do good or evil on the sabbath, to save a life or to destroy it? But they were silent.

5 And he looked at them with anger, sad because of the hardness of their hearts; and he said to the man, Stretch out your hand, and he stretched it out; and his hand was restored.

6 ¶ And the Pharisees immediately went out with the Herodians, and they took counsel concerning him how to do away with him.

7 So Jesus went to the sea with his disciples; and a great many people from Galilee followed him, and from Judaea,

8 And from Jerusalem, and from Idumaea, and from around the Jordan, and from Tyre and from Sidon; large crowds, who had heard all that he was doing, came to him.

9 And he said to his disciples to bring the boat near to him, because of the crowds, so that they might not press on him.

10 For he was healing so many, that others pushed toward him so as to touch him.

11 And those who were afflicted with unclean spirits, when they saw him, fell down before him, and cried saying, You are indeed the Son of God.

12 And he cautioned them a great deal, not to make him known.

13 ¶ And he went up to the mountain, and called those he wanted; and they came to him.

14 And he chose twelve to be with him, that he might send them to preach,

15 And to have power to heal the sick, and cast out devils.

16 And Simon he surnamed Peter.

17 And James the son of Zebedee, and John the brother of James, he surnamed B'nai Rakhshi, which means sons of thunder,

18 And Andrew, and Philip, and Bartholomew, and Matthew, and Thomas, and James the son of Alphaeus, and Thaddaeus, and Simon the Zealot,

19 And Judas of Iscariot, who betrayed him. And they came into the house.

20 And the people gathered again, so that they could not find bread to eat.

21 And his relatives heard it, and went out to arrest him, for they said, He has lost his mind.

22 ¶ And the scribes who had come down from Jerusalem said, Beelzebub is with him, and, By the prince of demons he is casting out demons.

23 And Jesus called them, and said to them in parables, How can Satan cast out Satan?

24 If a kingdom is divided against itself, that kingdom cannot stand.

25 And if a household is divided against itself, that household cannot stand.

26 And if Satan rises up against himself and is divided, he cannot stand, but that is his end.

27 No man can enter into a strong man's house and plunder his goods, unless he first bind the strong man; and then he plunders his house.

28 Truly I say to you, that all sins and blasphemies which men blaspheme, shall be forgiven to them.

29 But he who blasphemes against the Holy Spirit, shall never be forgiven, but is guilty before the everlasting judgment.

30 Because they had said, He has an unclean spirit.

31 ¶ Then there came his mother and his brothers, and stood outside, and they sent in to call him.

32 But the people were sitting around him; and they said to him, Behold, your mother and your brothers are outside, asking for you.

33 And he answered and said to them, Who is my mother, and who are my brothers?

34 And he looked at those who sat near him and said, Behold my mother, and behold my brothers.

35 For whoever does the will of God, is my brother and my sister and my mother.

CHAPTER 4

AGAIN he began to teach by the sea side; and many people gathered unto him, so that he went up and sat in a boat in the sea; and all the people stood on the land by the sea.

2 And he taught them much by parables, and in his teaching he said,

3 Listen; Behold, a sower went out to sow.

4 And when he had sown, some fell on the roadside, and the fowls came and ate it.

5 Other fell upon the rock, where there was not sufficient soil; and it sprung up earlier because the ground was not deep enough;

6 But when the sun shone, it was scorched, and because it had no root, it dried up.

7 And other fell among thistles, and the thistles sprung up and choked it, and it bore no fruit.

8 But other fell in good soil, and it sprung up and grew and bore fruit, some thirty, and some sixty, and some one hundred.

9 And he said, He who has ears to hear, let him hear.

10 When they were alone by themselves, those who were with him together with the twelve asked him about that parable.

11 And Jesus said to them, To you is given to know the mystery of the kingdom of God, but to the outsiders everything has to be explained by parables.

12 For seeing they see, and yet do not perceive; and hearing they hear, and yet do not understand; if they return, their sins would be forgiven.

13 And he said to them, Do you not know this parable? how then will you know all the parables?

14 ¶ The sower who sowed, sowed the word.

15 Those on the roadside are those in whom the word is sown; and when they have heard it, Satan comes immediately and takes away the word which is sown in their hearts.

16 And those which were sown upon the rock, are those who when they have heard the word, immediately receive it with joy;

17 And they have no root in themselves, but last for a while; and when trouble or persecution comes because of the word, they soon stumble.

18 And those which were sown among thistles are those who have heard the word,

19 And the thoughts of this world, and the deception of wealth, and the lusts of other things, enter in and choke the word, and bear no fruit.

20 And those which were sown in good soil, are those who hear the word, and receive it and bear fruit, one thirty, and one sixty, and one a hundred.

21 ¶ And he said to them, Is a lamp brought and put under a basket or under a bed? Is it not put on a lampholder?

22 For there is nothing hidden which will not be uncovered; and nothing in secret which will not be revealed.

23 If any man has ears to hear, let him hear.

24 ¶ And he said to them, Take heed what you hear; with what measure you measure it will be measured to you; and increase especially to them who hear.

25 For he who has, to him will be given; and he who has not, even that which he has will be taken away from him.

26 ¶ And he said, Such is the kingdom of God, like a man who casts seed in the ground.

27 And he sleeps and rises up night and day, and the seed springs up and grows, while he is not aware of it.

28 For the earth causes it to yield fruit; and yet first it becomes a blade of grass, then an ear, and at last a full grain in the ear.

Cf.dif. vv. 4:1, 5, 8, 11-12, 21, 24, 27.

29 But when the fruit is ripe, then immediately comes the sickle, because the harvest is ready.

30 ¶ And he said, To what shall we compare the kingdom of God? and with what parable shall we picture it?

31 It is just like a grain of mustard seed, which, when it is sown in the earth, is the smallest of all the seeds on earth.

32 But when it is sown, it springs up and becomes greater than all the herbs, and puts forth large branches, so that the birds can settle under their shadow.

33 ¶ Jesus talked to them with parables as these, such parables as they were able to hear.

34 And without parables he did not speak to them; but to his disciples, among themselves, he explained everything.

35 On that day, at evening, he said to them, Let us cross over to the landing place.

36 And they left the people, and took him away while he was in the boat. And there were other boats with them.

37 And there arose a heavy storm and wind, and the waves kept falling into the boat, so that the boat was nearly filled up.

38 But Jesus was sleeping on a blanket in the stern of the boat; and they came and roused him and said to him, Teacher, do you not care that we are perishing?

39 So he got up, and rebuked the wind, and said to the sea, Peace, be still. And the wind quieted down, and there was a great calm.

40 And he said to them, Why are you so fearful? and why do you have no faith?

And they were exceedingly afraid, and said to each other, Oh, who is this, that even the wind and the sea obey him?

CHAPTER 5

AND they reached the port on the other side of the sea, in the country of the Gadarenes.

2 And as he went out of the boat, he was met by a man from the cemetery, who had an unclean spirit.

3 He lived in the cemetery, and no man could bind him in chains;

4 Because whenever he was bound with fetters and chains, he broke the chains and cut the fetters, and no man could control him.

5 And always, night and day, he was in the cemetery and in the mountains, crying aloud and cutting himself with stones.

6 When he saw Jesus from afar, he ran and worshipped him,

7 And he cried with a loud voice and said, What have we got together, Jesus, Son of the most high God? I adjure you by God, not to torment me.

8 For he said to him, Get out of the man, O you unclean spirit.

9 And he asked him, What is your name? And he said to him, Our name is Legion, because we are many.

10 And he begged him much that he would not send him out of the country.

11 Now there was there, near the mountain a large herd of swine feeding.

12 And the lunatics begged him saying, Send us to the swine, that we may attack * them.

13 And he permitted them. And the lunatics went out, and attacked the swine; and the herd ran to the steep rocks, and fell into the sea; they were about two thousand, and they were drowned in the water.

14 And those who fed them, fled, and told it in the city and also in the villages. So they went out to see what had happened.

* Mk. 5:12 - The same Aramaic word *al* means to attack and to enter. If it meant "enter into" it would have read *al bekhaw*.

    Cf.dif. vv. 4:29, 35, 37-38;   5:1, 4, 7, 10, 12, 13.

15 And they came to Jesus, and saw the lunatic, * clothed and well behaved, and sitting down; even the one who once had the legion within him; and they were afraid.

16 And those who saw it told them just how it happened to the lunatic and also to the swine.

17 So they began to urge him to leave their border.

18 As he went up to the boat, the lunatic begged him to remain with him.

19 And he would not permit him, but said to him, Go to your home, to your own people, and tell them what the Lord has done for you, and had mercy on you.

20 And he went away, and began to preach in the ten cities about what Jesus had done for him; and they were all surprised.

21 ¶ When Jesus crossed in the boat to the other side, large crowds again gathered around him, while he was by the sea.

22 And there came one of the leaders of the synagogue, whose name was Jairus; and when he saw him, he fell at his feet,

23 And he beseeched him much and said to him, My daughter is very seriously ill; come and lay your hand on her, and she will be healed, and live.

24 So Jesus went with him; and a large multitude followed him, and they pressed on him.

25 And there was a woman who had had the hemorrhage for twelve years,

26 Who had suffered much at the hands of many doctors, and had spent everything she had, and was not helped at all, but rather became worse.

27 When she heard concerning Jesus, she came through the dense crowd from behind him, and touched his cloak.

28 For she said, If I can only touch his cloak, I will live.

29 And immediately the hemorrhage was dried up; and she felt in her body that she was healed of her disease.

30 Jesus instantly knew that some power had gone out of him; so he turned around to the people and said, Who touched my garments?

31 His disciples said to him, You see the people pressing on you, and yet you say, Who touched me?

32 And he was looking round to see who had done this.

33 But the woman, frightened and trembling, because she knew what had happened to her, came and fell before him and told him the whole truth.

34 He said to her, My daughter, your faith has healed you; go in peace, and be healed of your disease.

35 While he was still talking, some men came from the house of the leader of the synagogue, saying, Your daughter is dead; why do you trouble the Teacher?

36 Jesus heard the word which they spoke, and he said to the leader of the synagogue, Fear not, only believe.

37 And he did not permit any man to go with him, except Simon Peter, and James, and John the brother of James.

38 And they came to the house of the leader of the synagogue, and he saw them in a tumult, weeping and wailing.

39 So he entered and said to them, Why are you excited and crying? The little girl is not dead, but she is asleep.

40 And they laughed at him. But Jesus put them all out, and took the little girl's father and mother and those who were with him, and he entered where the little girl was laid.

41 And he took the little girl by her hand, and said to her, Talitha, koomi, which means, Little girl, rise up.

---

* Mk. 5:15 - Mark here refers to one lunatic who conversed with Jesus and then he mentions lunatics in ver. 12. There were doubtless many. Cf. Matt. 8:28.

Cf.dif. vv. 5:15, 18, 20-21, 25, 30, 39.

42 And immediately the little girl got up and walked; for she was twelve years old. And they were astonished with a great astonishment.

43 But he commanded them that no man should know this; and he told them to give her something to eat.

CHAPTER 6

*A*ND Jesus went out from thence, and came to his city; and his disciples followed him.

2 When the sabbath came, he began to teach in the synagogue, and many who heard him were surprised, and said, Whence did he receive all this? and what wisdom is this which is given to him, that wonders like these are wrought by his hands?

3 Is he not the carpenter, the son of Mary, and the brother of James and Joses and Judas and Simon? and behold, are not his sisters here with us? And they denounced him.

4 And Jesus said to them, There is no prophet who is insulted, except in his own city, and among his own brothers, and in his own house.

5 And he could not perform even a single miracle there, except that he laid his hand on a few sick people and healed them.

6 And he wondered at their lack of faith. And he travelled in the villages teaching.

7 ¶ Then he called his twelve, and began to send them two by two; and he gave them power over the unclean spirits, to cast them out.

8 And he commanded them not to take anything for the journey, except a staff only; no bag, no bread, no copper money in their purses;

9 But to wear sandals, and not to wear two shirts.

10 And he said to them, Whatever house you enter, stay there until you leave that place.

11 And whoever will not receive you, nor hear you, when you leave that place, shake off the sand under your feet as a testimony to them. Truly I say to you, It will be easier for Sodom and Gomorrah in the day of judgment than for that city.

12 ¶ And they went out and preached that they should repent.

13 And they cast out many demons, and anointed with oil many who were sick, and they were healed.

14 ¶ And Herod the king heard about Jesus, for his name was known to him; and he said, John the Baptist has risen from the dead; this is why miracles are worked by him.

15 Others said, He is Elijah. And yet others, He is a prophet, just like one of the prophets.

16 But when Herod heard it, he said, John, whom I beheaded; it is he who has risen from the dead.

17 ¶ For this same Herod had sent out and arrested John, and cast him in prison, because of Herodias, wife of his brother Philip, whom he had married.

18 For John had said to Herod, It is not lawful for you to marry your brother's wife.

19 But Herodias was bitter towards him, and wanted to kill him; but she could not.

20 For Herod was afraid of John, because he knew that he was a righteous and holy man, and he guarded him; and he heard that he was doing a great many things, and he heard him gladly.

21 Then came a state day, when Herod on his birthday gave a banquet to his officials, and captains, and the leading men of Galilee.

22 And the daughter of Herodias entered in and danced, and she pleased Herod and the guests who were with him; and the king said to the little girl, Ask me whatever you wish, and I will give it to you.

Cf.dif. vv. 6:1, 3-4, 8, 15, 20-21.

23 And he swore to her, Whatever you ask me, I will give you, as much as half of my kingdom.

24 She went out and said to her mother, What shall I ask him? She said to her, The head of John the Baptist.

25 And immediately she entered cautiously to the king, and said to him, I do wish in this very hour that you may give me on a tray the head of John the Baptist.

26 And the king was exceedingly sorry; but because of the oaths, and because of the guests, he did not wish to refuse her.

27 So the king immediately sent the executioner, and commanded to bring the head of John. And he went and beheaded John in the prison,

28 And brought it on a tray and gave it to the girl; and the girl gave it to her mother.

29 And when his disciples heard of it, they came and took up his body and buried it in a grave.

30 ¶ And the apostles gathered together unto Jesus, and told him everything they had done, and what they had taught.

31 And he said to them, Come, let us go to the wilderness all alone, and rest awhile; for there were many coming and going, and they had no chance even to eat.

32 So they went away in a boat to a desert place by themselves.

33 And many people saw them when they were leaving, and they knew them, and from all the cities they hurried by land and reached the place before him.

34 And when Jesus went out he saw large crowds, and he had compassion on them, because they were like sheep without a shepherd; and he began to teach them a great many things.

35 ¶ And when it was getting late, his disciples came up to him and said to him, This is a desert place, and it is getting late;

36 Dismiss them, so that they may go away to the farms and villages around us, and buy bread for themselves; for they have nothing to eat.

37 He said to them, You give them to eat. They said to him, Shall we go and buy two hundred penny's worth of bread, and give it to them to eat?

38 He said to them, Go and see how many loaves of bread you have got here. And when they found out, they said to him, Five loaves of bread and two fish.

39 And he commanded them to make everyone sit down in groups on the grass.

40 So they sat down in groups, by hundreds and by fifties.

41 Then he took the five loaves of bread and the two fish, and he looked up to heaven, and he blessed and broke the loaves of bread, and gave them to his disciples to place before them; and they divided the two fish among them all.

42 And they all ate and were satisfied.

43 And they took up the fragments of bread, twelve full baskets, and also of the fish.

44 And those who ate the bread were five thousand men.

45 ¶ And immediately he urged his disciples to go up into the boat, and go in advance of him to the port at Bethsaida, while he dismissed the people.

46 And when he had dismissed them, he went up to the mountain to pray.

47 When evening came, the boat was in the midst of the sea, and he was alone on the land.

48 And he saw them struggling as they were rowing, for the wind was against them; and in the fourth watch of the night, Jesus came to them, walking on the water, and he wanted to pass by them.

49 But when they saw him walking on the water, they thought it was a false vision, and they cried out;

Cf.dif. vv. 6:25, 33, 36, 45, 49.

50 For they all saw him and were frightened. And immediately he spoke to them and said, Have courage, it is I, do not be afraid.

51 And he went up to them into the boat, and the wind quieted down; and they marvelled exceedingly, and were astonished in themselves.

52 For they did not understand the miracle of the loaves of bread, because their hearts were confused.

53 ¶ And when they had crossed to the port, they came to the land of Gennesaret.

54 And when they went out of the boat, the people of that place immediately knew him.

55 And they came running throughout that land; and began to bring those who were seriously sick, carrying them in quilt-beds, where they heard he was.

56 And wherever he entered into villages and cities, they laid the sick in the streets, and begged him even to touch the edge of his robe; and all who touched him were healed.

CHAPTER 7

*T*HEN there gathered unto him Pharisees and scribes, who had come from Jerusalem.

2 And they saw some of his disciples eating bread with their hands unwashed; and they reproached them.

3 For all the Jews, even the Pharisees, unless their hands are washed carefully would not eat, because they strictly observe the tradition of the elders.

4 Even the things from the market, if they are not washed, they would not eat them. And there are a great many other things, which they have accepted to obey, such as the washing of cups and pots, and copper utensils, and the bedding of dead men.

5 And the scribes and Pharisees asked him, Why do your disciples not walk according to the tradition of the elders, but eat bread with their hands unwashed?

6 He said to them, The prophet Isaiah well prophesied about you, O hypocrites, as it is written, This people honor me with their lips, but their heart is far away from me.

7 And they worship me in vain, when they teach the doctrines of the commandments of men.

8 For you have ignored the commandment of God, and you observe the tradition of men, such as the washing of cups and pots, and a great many other things like these.

9 He said to them, Well you do injustice to the commandment of God so as to sustain your own tradition.

10 For Moses said, Honor your father and your mother; and he who curses father or mother, let him be put to death.

11 But you say, If a man may say to his father or his mother, What is left over is Corban (my offering);

12 And yet you do not let him do anything for his father or mother.

13 So you dishonor the word of God for the sake of the tradition which you have established; and you do a great many like these.

14 ¶ Then Jesus called all the people and said to them, Hear me, all of you, and understand.

15 There is nothing outside of a man, if it should enter into him, which can defile him; but what goes out of him, that defiles the man.

16 Who has ears to hear, let him hear.

17 When Jesus entered into the house because of the people, his disciples asked him concerning that parable.

18 And he said to them, So even you are puzzled. Do you not know that whatever enters into a man from outside cannot defile him?

19 Because it does not enter into his heart, but into his stomach, and then is thrown out through the intestines, thereby purifying the food.

Cf.dif. vv. 6:52-53;   7:2, 4, 7, 9, 11, 18-19.

20 It is what goes out of man which defiles the man.

21 For from within, from the heart of men go out evil thoughts, such as fornication, adultery, theft, murder,

22 Extortion, wickedness, deceit, lust, an evil eye, blasphemy, pride, foolishness;

23 All these evils go out from within, and they defile the man.

24 ¶ Jesus moved away from thence, and came to the borders of Tyre and Sidon, and he entered into a house, and did not want any one to know about him. And yet he could not hide himself.

25 For immediately a woman heard about him, whose daughter had an unclean spirit; and she came and fell at his feet.

26 But the woman was a heathen, from Phoenicia in Syria; and she besought him to cast out the demon from her daughter.

27 And Jesus said to her, Let the children be first filled; for it is not right to take the children's bread and throw it to the dogs.

28 But she answered and said to him, Yes, my Lord; even the dogs eat the children's crumbs under the trays.

29 Jesus said to her, Go your way; just because of this word, the demon has gone out of your daughter.

30 So she went to her house, and found her daughter lying in bed, and the demon gone out of her.

31 ¶ Again Jesus went out from the border of Tyre and Sidon, and came to the sea of Galilee, to the border of the ten cities.

32 And they brought to him a deaf and dumb man; and they asked him to lay his hand on him.

33 So he drew him aside from the people, and put his fingers into his ears, then he spat, and touched his tongue;

34 And he looked up to heaven, and sighed, and he said to him, Ethpatakh, which means, Be opened.

35 And in that very hour his ears were opened, and the knot of his tongue was loosened, and he spoke plainly.

36 And he warned them not to tell this to any man; but the more he warned them, so much the more they published it.

37 And they were greatly astonished, saying, He does everything so well. He makes the deaf hear, and the dumb to speak.

CHAPTER 8

IN those days, when there was a large multitude, and they had nothing to eat, he called his disciples and said to them,

2 I have pity for this people, for they have remained with me three days, and they have nothing to eat;

3 And if I dismiss them to their homes, while they are fasting, they will faint on the way, for some of them have come from a distance.

4 His disciples said to him, How can any man here in this lonely place, feed all of these with bread?

5 And he asked them, How many loaves have you? They said to him, Seven.

6 So he commanded the people to sit on the ground; and he took the seven loaves of bread, and he blessed them, and broke them, and gave them to his disciples to set before them; and they set them before the people.

7 And there were a few fishes; he blessed them also, and commanded to set them before them.

8 So they ate and were satisfied, and they took up seven baskets of fragments which were left over.

9 The men who ate were about four thousand; and he dismissed them.

10 ¶ And immediately he went up into the boat with his disciples, and he came to the country of Dalmanutha.

11 And the Pharisees came out and began to question him, and they asked him for a sign from heaven, so as to test him.

Cf.dif. vv. 7:26, 31, 35; 8:10.

12 And he sighed in his spirit and said, Why does this generation want a sign? truly I say to you, No sign will be given to this generation.

13 And he left them, and went up into the boat, and departed from that port.

14 ¶ And they had forgotten to take bread; except one loaf they had none with them in the boat.

15 And he commanded them and said to them, Look out, and beware of the leaven of the Pharisees and of the leaven of Herod.

16 They were reasoning among themselves and saying, It is because we have no bread.

17 But Jesus knew it and said to them, What are you thinking, because you have no bread? Do you not even yet know, and do you not understand? Is your heart still hard?

18 You have eyes, and yet do you not see? You have ears, and yet do you not hear? And do you not remember?

19 When I broke the five loaves of bread for the five thousand, how many full baskets of fragments did you take up? They said to him, Twelve.

20 He said to them, And when the seven for the four thousand, how many baskets full of fragments did you take up? They said, Seven.

21 He said to them, How is it then that even yet you cannot understand?

22 ¶ And he came to Bethsaida; and they brought to him a blind man, and they besought him to touch him.

23 And he took the blind man by the hand and brought him outside the town; and he spat on his eyes, and put his hands on him, and asked him what he saw.

24 And he looked and said, I see men like trees, walking.

25 Again he put his hands over his eyes, and he was restored, and saw everything clearly.

26 And he sent him to his house, saying, Do not enter even into the town, nor tell it to anyone in the town.

27 ¶ And Jesus went out, and his disciples, to the towns of Caesarea of Philippi; and on the road he asked his disciples and said to them, What do men say about me, that I am?

28 They said, John the Baptist; and others, Elijah; and yet others, One of the prophets.

29 Jesus said to them, But you, who do you say I am? Simon Peter answered and said to him, You are the Christ, the Son of the living God.

30 And he warned them not to tell any man about him.

31 ¶ Then he began to teach them, that the Son of man will have to suffer a great deal, and be rejected by the elders, and the high priests, and the scribes, and be killed, and rise again on the third day.

32 And he spoke that word openly. So Peter took him aside and began to rebuke him.

33 But he turned around and looked on his disciples, and he rebuked Simon, and said, Get behind me, Satan; for you are not thinking the things of God, but of men.

34 And Jesus called the people together with his disciples, and said to them, He who wishes to come after me, let him deny himself, and take up his cross, and follow me.

35 For whoever wishes to save his life will lose it; and whoever loses his life for my sake and the sake of my Gospel, he will save it.

36 For how could a man be benefited, if he should gain the whole world and lose his life?

37 Or what could a man give in exchange for his life?

38 Whoever, therefore, is ashamed of me and of my words in this sinful and adulterous generation, the Son of man will also be ashamed of him, when he comes in the glory of his Father with his holy angels.

CHAPTER 9

AND he said to them, Truly I say to you, that there are men standing here, who shall not taste death, till they see that the kingdom of God has come with power.

2 ¶ And six days after, Jesus took Peter, and James, and John, and brought them up to a high mountain alone; and he was transfigured before their eyes.

3 His clothes shone, and became white like snow, in such a manner that men on earth cannot make white.

4 And there appeared to them Moses and Elijah, talking with Jesus.

5 And Peter said to him, Teacher, it is better for us to remain here; and let us make three shelters, one for you, and one for Moses, and one for Elijah.

6 For he did not know what he was saying, for they were in fear.

7 And there was a cloud overshadowing them, and a voice out of the cloud said, This is my beloved Son; hear him.

8 And suddenly, when the disciples looked around, they saw no man, except Jesus alone with them.

9 And as they came down from the mountain, he commanded them not to tell any man what they had seen, until the Son of man has risen from the dead.

10 So they kept that saying to themselves, and they wanted to know what "risen from the dead" means.

11 ¶ And they asked him, saying, Why then do the scribes say that Elijah must first come?

12 He said to them, Elijah does come first, to prepare everything; and as it is written concerning the Son of man, that he will suffer much and be rejected.

13 But I say to you, that Elijah has also come, and they did with him whatever they pleased, as it is written of him.

14 ¶ And when he came to his disciples, he saw a large crowd with them, and the scribes debating with them.

15 And immediately all the people saw him, and were greatly surprised, and they ran to greet him.

16 And he asked the scribes, What do you debate with them?

17 One of the multitude answered and said, Teacher, I brought my son to you, for he has a spirit of dumbness.

18 And whenever it seizes him, it troubles him; and he foams, and gnashes his teeth, and gets worn out. And I asked your disciples to cast it out, but they could not.

19 Jesus answered and said to him, O faithless generation, how long shall I be with you? and how long shall I preach to you? bring him to me.

20 And they brought the boy to Jesus; and when the spirit seized him, it immediately troubled him; and he fell on the ground, gasping and foaming.

21 So Jesus asked his father, How long has he been like this? He said to him, From his childhood.

22 And many times it has thrown him into the fire and into the water to destroy him; but whatever you can do, help me, and have mercy on me.

23 Jesus said to him, If you can believe, everything is possible to him who believes.

24 And immediately the father of the boy cried out weeping, and said, I do believe, help my little belief.

25 When Jesus saw that people were running and gathering to him, he rebuked the unclean spirit, and said to it, O deaf and dumb spirit, I command you, come out of him, and do not enter him again.

26 And the epileptic cried out much, and was tortured, and the spirit went out; then the boy became as if dead, so that many could say, He is dead.

Cf.dif. vv. 9:3, 6, 12, 16-20, 24, 26.

27 Then Jesus took him by the hand, and lifted him up.

28 When Jesus entered the house, his disciples asked him privately, Why could we not cast it out?

29 He said to them, This kind cannot be cast out by anything, except by fasting and prayer.

30 And when they went out from thence, they passed through Galilee; and he did not want any man to know about him.

31 For he taught his disciples, and said to them, The Son of man will be delivered into the hands of men, and they will kill him; and after he is killed, he will rise on the third day.

32 But they did not understand the saying, and they were afraid to ask him.

33 ¶ And they came to Capernaum; and when they entered the house, he asked them, What were you reasoning among yourselves on the road?

34 But they kept silent, for on the road they had argued with one another, which was the greatest of them.

35 And Jesus sat down, and he called the twelve and said to them, He who wishes to be first, let him be the last of every man, and the minister of every man.

36 And he took a little boy, and made him to stand in the midst; then he took him in his arms, and said to them,

37 Whoever receives a boy like this in my name, he receives me; and he who receives me, does not receive me, but him who has sent me.

38 ¶ John said to him, Teacher, we saw a man casting out demons in your name; and we forbade him, because he did not follow us.

39 Jesus said to them, Do not forbid him; for there is no man who performs miracles in my name, who will hastily speak evil of me.

40 Therefore, he who is not against you is for you.

41 For whoever gives you to drink even a cup of water only, because you represent the name of Christ, truly I say to you that his reward shall not be lost.

42 And whoever shall cause one of these little ones who believe in me to stumble, it were better for him that an ass' mill stone were hanged on his neck and then he were thrown into the sea.

43 If your hand offends you, cut it off; it is much better for you to go through life maimed, than to have two hands and go to Gehenna,

44 Where their worm does not die, and their fire does not quench.

45 And if your foot offends you, cut it off; it is much better for you to go through life lame, than to have two feet, and fall into Gehenna,

46 Where their worm does not die, and their fire does not quench.

47 And if your eye offends you, remove it; it is better for you to enter the kingdom of God with one eye, than to have two eyes and fall into the Gehenna of fire,

48 Where their worm does not die, and their fire does not quench.

49 For everything will be salted on fire, and every sacrifice will be salted with salt.

50 O how good is salt; but if the salt should lose its savor, with what could it be salted? Let there be salt in you, and be in peace with one another.

CHAPTER 10

AND he departed from thence, and came to the border of Judaea, at the crossing of the Jordan; and a great many people went to him there, and he taught them again, as he was accustomed to do.

2 ¶ And the Pharisees came up to him, tempting him and asking, Is it lawful for a man to desert his wife?

3 He said to them, What did Moses command you?

Cf.dif. vv. 9:30, 35, 39-41, 50;   10:1-2.

4 They said, Moses gave us permission to write a letter of separation, and then to divorce.

5 Jesus answered and said to them, It was because of the hardness of your heart, that he wrote for you this particular law.

6 But from the very beginning God made them male and female.

7 For this reason a man shall leave his father and his mother and follow his wife.

8 And both shall be one flesh; henceforth they are not two, but one flesh.

9 What therefore God has joined, let no man separate.

10 ¶ And his disciples again asked him about this in the house.

11 And he said to them, Whoever divorces his wife and marries another, commits adultery.

12 And if a woman divorces her husband, and marries another, she commits adultery.

13 ¶ And they brought little boys to him, that he might touch them; but his disciples rebuked those who brought them.

14 But when Jesus saw it, he was displeased, and he said to them, Allow the little boys to come to me, and do not forbid them; for the kingdom of God is for such as these.

15 Truly I say to you, Whoever does not receive the kingdom of God like a little boy shall not enter it.

16 Then he took them in his arms, and put his hand on them, and blessed them.

17 ¶ While he was on the way, a man came ran up and fell on his knees and he asked him, saying, O good Teacher, what shall I do to inherit life eternal?

18 Jesus said to him, Why do you call me good? There is no one who is good, except the one God.

19 You know the commandments, Do not commit adultery, Do not steal, Do not murder, Do not bear false witness, Do not oppress, Honor your father and mother.

20 But he answered and said to him, Teacher, all of these I have obeyed from my boyhood.

21 Then Jesus looked at him and loved him, and he said to him, You lack one thing; go, sell everything you have, and give it to the poor, and you shall have a treasure in heaven; and take up your cross and follow me.

22 But he felt sad because of this saying, and he went away depressed; for he had great wealth.

23 Then Jesus looked at his disciples and said to them, How hard it is for those who have wealth, to enter into the kingdom of God!

24 But the disciples were surprised at his words. And Jesus answered again and said to them, My sons, how hard it is for those who trust in their wealth, to enter into the kingdom of God!

25 It is easier for a rope to enter through the eye of a needle, than for a rich man to enter into the kingdom of God.

26 But they were the more surprised, saying among themselves, Who then can be saved?

27 Jesus looked at them, and said to them, With men this is impossible, but not with God; for everything is possible with God.

28 Then Peter began to say, Behold, we have left everything and followed you.

29 Jesus answered and said, Truly I say to you, There is no man who leaves houses, or brothers, or sisters, or father, or mother, or wife, or children, or fields, for my sake and for the sake of my gospel,

30 Who shall not receive now, in this time, an hundredfold, houses, and brothers and sisters, and maidservants, and children, and fields, and other worldly pursuits, and in the world to come life everlasting.

31 Many who are first shall be last, and the last first.

32 ¶ While they were going up on their way to Jerusalem, Jesus was ahead of them; and

Cf.dif. vv. 10:4, 13, 19, 24-25, 30, 32.

they were amazed; and they followed him with fear. And he took his twelve aside, and began to tell them what was surely to happen to him.

33 Behold, we are going up to Jerusalem, and the Son of man will be delivered to the high priests and the scribes, and they will condemn him to death, and deliver him to the Gentiles.

34 And they will mock him, and scourge him, and spit in his face, and kill him; and on the third day he will rise up.

35 ¶ And James and John, the sons of Zebedee, came up to him and said to him, Teacher, we wish you would do for us whatever we ask.

36 He said to them, What do you wish me to do for you?

37 They said to him, Grant us to sit, one at your right and one at your left, in your glory.

38 He said to them, You do not know what you are asking; can you drink the cup which I drink? and be baptized with the baptism with which I am to be baptized?

39 They said to him, We can. Jesus said to them, The cup which I shall drink, you will drink too; and with the baptism with which I am baptized, you will be baptized too;

40 But to sit at my right and at my left, that is not mine to give; except to those for whom it is prepared.

41 When the ten heard it, they began to murmur at James and John.

42 Jesus called them and said to them, You know that those who consider themselves princes of the people, are their owners too; and their officials rule over them.

43 Let not this be so among you; but he who wishes to be great among you, let him be a minister to you.

44 And anyone of you who wishes to be first, let him be a servant of every man.

45 For also the Son of man did not come to be ministered to, but to minister, and to give

his life as a salvation for the sake of many.

46 ¶ And they came to Jericho; and when Jesus went out of Jericho with his disciples and a large crowd, a blind man, Timaeus, the son of Timaeus, sat by the roadside begging.

47 When he heard that it was Jesus of Nazareth, he began to cry aloud and say, O son of David, have mercy on me.

48 And many rebuked him to keep quiet, but he cried out the more, saying, O son of David, have mercy on me.

49 Then Jesus stopped and commanded to call him. So they called the blind man, and said to him, Have courage, rise; he is calling you.

50 And the blind man threw off his robe, and he got up, and went to Jesus.

51 Jesus said to him, What do you wish me to do for you? The blind man said to him, Master, that I may see.

52 And Jesus said to him, See; your faith has healed you. And immediately he saw, and went on the way.

CHAPTER 11

WHEN he came near to Jerusalem, towards Bethphage and Bethany at the Mount of Olives, he sent two of his disciples,

2 And he said to them, Go to the village in front of us; and as soon as you enter it, you will find a colt which is tied up, on which no man of the sons of men has ever ridden; untie it and bring it.

3 And if any man should say to you, Why are you doing this? say to him that our Lord needs it; and immediately he will send it here.

4 So they went and found the colt tied by the door, outside, in the street. And as they were untying it,

5 Some of the men who stood there said to them, What are you doing, are you untying the colt?

6 And they said to them as Jesus had in-

Cf.dif. vv. 10:32, 41-42, 45, 52;   11:2, 4-6.

structed them; and they permitted them.

7 And they brought the colt to Jesus, and they put their garments on it, and Jesus rode on it.

8 And many spread their garments on the road; and others cut down branches from the trees, and spread them on the road.

9 And those who were in front of him, and those who were behind him, were crying and saying, Hosanna; Blessed is he who comes in the name of the Lord;

10 And blessed is the kingdom of our father David, which comes; Hosanna in the highest.

11 ¶ And Jesus entered Jerusalem, into the temple; and he saw everything, and when evening came, he went out to Bethany with the twelve.

12 ¶ And the next day, when they went out of Bethany, he became hungry.

13 And he saw a fig tree in the distance, which had leaves on it. So he came to it to see if he could find anything on it; and when he came he found nothing on it except leaves; for it was not yet time for the figs.

14 And he said to it, From now and forever, let no man eat of your fruit. And his disciples heard it.

15 ¶ And they came to Jerusalem; and Jesus entered into the temple of God, and began to cast out those who were buying and selling in the temple; and he overturned the trays of the money-changers and the stands of those who sold doves;

16 And he would not allow any man to bring goods into the temple.

17 And he taught them and said to them, Is it not written, My house shall be called the house of prayer for all the peoples? But you have made it a bandits' cave.

18 And the high priests and the scribes heard it, and they sought how to do away with him; for they were afraid of him, because all the people were amazed at his teaching.

19 And when evening came, they went outside of the city.

20 ¶ And in the morning, as they were passing, they saw the fig tree withered from its roots.

21 And Simon remembered, and said to him, Master, behold, the fig tree which you cursed has withered.

22 Jesus answered and said to them, If you have faith in God,

23 Truly I say to you, Whoever should say to this mountain, Remove and fall into the sea, and does not doubt in his heart, but believes that what he says will be done, whatever he says will be done to him.

24 Therefore I say to you, Anything you pray for and ask, believe that you will receive it, and it will be done for you.

25 And when you stand up to pray, forgive whatever you have against any man, so that your Father in heaven will forgive you your trespasses.

26 But if you will not forgive, even your Father in heaven will not forgive you your trespasses.

27 ¶ And they came again to Jerusalem; and while he was walking in the temple, the high priests, and the scribes, and the elders came to him.

28 And they said to him, By what authority do you do these things? and who gave you this authority to do these things?

29 Jesus said to them, I will also ask you a word to tell me, and then I will tell you by what authority I do these things.

30 Whence is the baptism of John, from heaven, or from men? Tell me.

31 And they reasoned among themselves and said, If we should say to him, from heaven, he will say to us, Why then did you not believe him?

32 And if we should say, from men, there is the fear of the people, for all of them regard John as a true prophet.

33 So they answered and said to Jesus, We do not know. He said to them, I will also not tell you by what authority I do these things.

CHAPTER 12

AND he began to speak to them in parables. A man planted a vineyard, and fenced it all around, and he dug in it a wine-press, and built a tower in it, and then he leased it to laborers, and went on a journey.

2 And in due season he sent his servant to the laborers, to receive some of the fruits of the vineyard.

3 But they beat him, and sent him away empty.

4 And again he sent to them another servant; they stoned him also, and wounded him, and sent him away in disgrace.

5 And again he sent another, but they killed him; and he sent many other servants, some of them they beat, and some they killed.

6 But finally, he had a very beloved son, and he sent him to them last of all, for he said, They might feel ashamed before my son.

7 But the laborers said among themselves, This is the heir; come, let us kill him, and the inheritance will be ours.

8 And they took and killed him, and threw him outside of the vineyard.

9 What then will the owner of the vineyard do? He will come and destroy those laborers, and give the vineyard to others.

10 Have you not read this scripture, The stone which the builders rejected, the same became the corner-stone?

11 This was from the Lord, and it is a wonder in our eyes.

12 ¶ They wanted to seize him, but they were afraid of the people; for they knew that he spoke this parable against them; and they left him and went away.

13 ¶ And they sent to him some men of the scribes and of the Herodians, that they might trap him by a word.

14 They came and asked him, Master, we know that you are true, and you do not favor any man; for you are impartial, and you teach the way of God in truth. Is it lawful to give head-tax to Caesar or not?

15 Shall we give or shall we not give? But he knew their scheme, and said to them, Why do you tempt me? Bring me a penny, that I may see it.

16 And they brought it to him. He said to them, Whose is this image and inscription? They said, Caesar's.

17 Jesus said to them, Give to Caesar what is Caesar's, and to God what is God's. And they were amazed at him.

18 ¶ Then the Sadducees came to him, those who say there is no resurrection; and they asked him, saying,

19 Teacher, Moses wrote to us, that if a man's brother die, and leave a wife, and leave no children, his brother should take his wife, and raise up offspring for his brother.

20 Now there were seven brothers; the first one took a wife and died, and left no offspring.

21 Then the second one married her, and he died; he also left no offspring; and likewise the third one.

22 So all seven of them married her, and left no offspring. And after them all the woman also died.

23 Therefore at the resurrection, whose wife will she be? for all seven had married her.

24 Jesus said to them, Do you not err, because you do not understand the scriptures, nor the power of God?

25 For when they rise from the dead, they neither marry women, nor are women given in marriage to men; but they are like the angels in heaven.

                               Cf. dif. vv. 11:33;   12:4, 6, 13-15, 25.

26 Now concerning the rising of the dead, have you not read in the book of Moses, how God said to him from the bush, I am the God of Abraham and the God of Isaac and the God of Jacob? 27 And yet he was not the God of the dead, but of the living. You therefore greatly err.

28 ¶ And one of the scribes came near and heard them debating, and he saw that he gave them a good answer. So he asked him, Which is the first commandment of all?

29 Jesus said to him, The first of all commandments is, Hear, O Israel, the Lord our God is one Lord;

30 And you must love the Lord your God with all your heart, and with all your soul, and with all your mind, and with all your power; this is the first commandment.

31 And the second is like to it, You must love your neighbor as yourself. There is no other commandment greater than these.

32 The scribe said to him, Well, Teacher, you have said the truth, that he is one, and there is no other beside him;

33 And that a man should love him with all the heart, and with all the mind, and with all the soul, and with all the power, and love his neighbor as himself; this is far more important than all burnt offerings and sacrifices.

34 When Jesus saw that he replied wisely, he answered and said to him, You are not far from the kingdom of God. And no man dared again to question him.

35 ¶ And Jesus answered and said, as he taught in the temple, How do the scribes say that Christ is the son of David?

36 For David himself said through the Holy Spirit, The Lord said to my Lord, Sit on my right hand, until I put your enemies a stool under your feet.

37 Now therefore David himself calls him my Lord, and how can he be his son? And all the people heard him with pleasure.

38 ¶ And in his teaching he said to them, Beware of the scribes, who like to walk in long robes, and love to be saluted in the streets,

39 And the front seats in the synagogues, and the head places at banquets;

40 Those who embezzle the property of widows, with the pretense of making long prayers. They shall receive greater judgment.

41 ¶ And when Jesus sat towards the treasury, he watched how the people cast their alms into the treasury; and many rich men were casting in a great deal.

42 And there came a poor widow, and she cast in two coins, which are farthings.

43 And Jesus called his disciples, and said to them, Truly I say to you, that this poor widow has cast in the treasury more than all the men who are casting;

44 For all of them cast of their abundance; but she of her poverty cast everything she had, even all of her possessions.

CHAPTER 13

WHEN JESUS went out of the temple, one of his disciples said to him, Teacher, behold, look at those stones and those buildings.

2 Jesus said to him, Do you see these great buildings? Not a stone shall be left here upon another stone, which shall not be torn down.

3 ¶ While Jesus sat on the Mount of Olives, towards the temple, Peter and James and John and Andrew asked him alone,

4 Tell us when these things will happen, and what is the sign when all these things are about to be fulfilled?

5 Then Jesus began to tell them; Be careful that no man deceive you.

6 For many will come in my name, and say, I am he; and they will deceive many.

7 And when you hear of wars and rumors of revolutions, do not be afraid; for this is bound to happen, but the end is not yet.

Cf. dif. vv. 12: 27-28, 32, 36-38, 40-41, 44; 13:7.

8 For nation will rise against nation, and kingdom against kingdom; and there will be earthquakes in different places, and there will be famines and uprisings. These things are just the beginning of travail.

9 Look out for yourselves; for they will deliver you to the judges, and they will scourge you in their synagogues; and you will stand before kings and governors for my sake, and as a testimony to them.

10 But my gospel must first be preached among all nations.

11 When they bring you up to deliver you, do not worry beforehand what you will speak; and do not think of anything except what is given you in that very hour; speak that; for it is not you that speak, but the Holy Spirit.

12 A brother will deliver his brother to death, and a father his son; and the children will rise up against their parents, and put them to death.

13 And you will be hated by all men because of my name; but he who has patience to the end, will be saved.

14 But when you see the sign of the refuse of desolation, as spoken by the prophet Daniel, accumulating where it should not be, whoever reads can understand it. Then let those who are in Judaea flee to the mountain;

15 And he who is on the roof, let him not come down, and not enter to take anything out of his house;

16 And he who is in the field, let him not return to take his clothes.

17 But woe to those who are with child, and to those who give suck in those days!

18 Pray that your flight may not be in winter.

19 For in those days there will be suffering, such as has never been from the beginning of the creation, which God created until now, and never will be again.

20 And if the Lord had not shortened those days, no flesh would live; but for the sake of the chosen ones, which he chose, he shortened those days.

21 Then if any man should say to you, Behold, here is the Christ; or, behold, there; do not believe it.

22 For there will rise false Christs, and lying prophets, and they will show signs and wonders, and mislead, if possible, even the chosen ones.

23 But you be careful; behold, I have told you everything in advance.

24 ¶ But in those days, after that suffering, the sun will be darkened, and the moon will not give her light,

25 And the stars will fall down from the sky, and the powers of the universe will be shaken.

26 Then they will see the Son of man coming in the clouds, with a great army and with glory.

27 Then he will send his angels, and gather his chosen ones from the four winds, from the utmost part of the earth to the utmost part of heaven.

28 From the fig tree learn a parable. When its branches become tender and bring forth leaves, you know that summer is coming.

29 So even you, when you see all these things happen, understand that it is near the door.

30 Truly I say to you that this generation will not pass away, until all these things happen.

31 Heaven and earth will pass away, but my words shall not pass away.

32 But concerning that day and that hour, no man knows, not even the angels of heaven, neither the Son, except the Father.

33 Look out, be alert and pray; for you do not know when the time is.

34 It is just like a man who went on a journey, and left his house, and gave authority to his servants, and to each man his work, and he commanded the porter to keep awake.

Cf. dif. vv. 13:8-11, 14, 22, 25, 34.

35 Be alert therefore, for you do not know when the owner of the house will come, in the evening, or at midnight, or at the cockcrow, or in the morning.

36 He might come suddenly, and find you asleep.

37 What I say to you I say to all of you: Be alert.

CHAPTER 14

AFTER two days, the passover of unleavened bread was to come; and the high priests and the scribes were seeking how to seize him by craft and kill him.

2 And they said, Not during the feast, for it may cause a riot among the people.

3 ¶ When he was in Bethany, in the house of Simon the leper, while he reclined, there came a woman who had with her an alabaster vessel of perfume of pure nard, of good quality and very expensive; and she opened it, and poured it upon the head of Jesus.

4 But there were some men of the disciples who were displeased within themselves, and said, Why was this perfume wasted?

5 For it could have been sold for more than three hundred pennies and given to the poor. So they annoyed her.

6 Jesus said, Leave her alone; why do you trouble her? She has done a good work to me.

7 For you always have the poor with you, and when you wish, you can do good to them; but I am not always with you.

8 But this one has done it with what she had; she anointed my body in advance as for the burial.

9 And truly I say to you, Wherever this my gospel is preached throughout the world, what she has done will also be told as a memorial to her.

10 Then Judas of Iscariot, one of the twelve, went to the high priests, to deliver Jesus to them.

11 When they heard it, they were glad, and promised to give him money. So he sought an opportunity to deliver him.

12 ¶ On the first day of unleavened bread, on which the Jews sacrifice the passover, his disciples said to him, Where do you wish that we go and prepare the passover for you to eat?

13 And he sent two of his disciples, and said to them, Go to the city, and behold you will meet a man carrying a vessel of water; follow him.

14 And wherever he enters, say to the owner of the house, Our master says, Where is the guestchamber, where I may eat the passover with my disciples?

15 And he will show you a large upper room furnished and prepared; there make ready for us.

16 And his disciples went out and came to the city, and they found just as he had told them; and they prepared the passover.

17 ¶ And when it was evening, he came with his twelve.

18 And when they were reclining and eating, Jesus said, Truly I say to you, One of you who eats with me, he will betray me.

19 They began to feel troubled, and said to him one by one, Why, is it I?

20 But he said to them, One of the twelve who dips with me in the dish.

21 The Son of man will go, as it is written of him; but woe to the man by whose hand the Son of man is betrayed! It would have been far better for that man never to have been born.

22 ¶ While they were eating, Jesus took bread, and blessed it, and he broke it, and gave it to them, and he said to them, Take it; this is my body.

23 And he took the cup, and gave thanks, and he blessed it and gave it to them, and they all drank of it.

Cf.dif. vv. 13:36; 14:1, 3, 5, 8-9, 12, 18-19, 22.

24 And he said to them, This is my blood of the new covenant, which is shed for the sake of many.

25 Truly I say to you, I shall not drink again of the fruit of the vine, until that day in which I drink it new in the kingdom of God.

26 ¶ And they offered praise, and went out to the Mount of Olives.

27 Then Jesus said to them, All of you will deny me this night; for it is written, I will smite the shepherd, and his sheep will scatter.

28 But when I am risen, I will be in Galilee before you.

29 Peter said to him, Even if all of them should deny you, but not I.

30 Jesus said to him, Truly I say to you, that you, today, in this night, before the cock crows twice, will deny me three times.

31 But he kept telling him still more, Even if I must die with you, I will never deny you, O my Lord. All the disciples said also, like him.

32 ¶ And they came to a place, which is called Gethsemane; and he said to his disciples, Sit down here, while I pray.

33 And he took with him Peter and James and John, and he began to be sorrowful and oppressed.

34 And he said to them, My soul is sorrowful even to death; wait for me and keep awake.

35 And he went a little aside, and fell on the ground, and prayed, that if it were possible, the hour might pass away from him.

36 And he said, *Abba, Ave,* O Father, my Father, you can do everything; make this cup pass away from me; but not according to my will, but yours.

37 And he came and found them sleeping, and he said to Peter, Simon, are you sleeping? Could you not keep awake even for one hour?

38 Awake and pray, that you may not enter into temptation; the spirit indeed is willing and ready, but the body is weak.

39 He went away again and prayed, and he said the same word.

40 And he returned again, and came and found them sleeping, because their eyes were heavy; and they did not know what to say to him.

41 Then he came the third time, and said to them, From now on sleep and get rest; the end has arrived and the hour has come; and behold, the Son of man will be delivered into the hands of sinners.

42 Arise, let us go; behold, he who is to deliver me is near.

43 ¶ While he was speaking, Judas of Iscariot, one of the twelve, came and many other people, with swords and staves, from the high priests and the scribes and the elders.

44 And the traitor who was to do the delivering gave them a sign, and he said, He whom I kiss, it is he; seize him carefully, and take him away.

45 And immediately he drew near and said to him, My teacher, my teacher; and he kissed him.

46 And they laid hands on him and arrested him.

47 But one of those who stood by drew a sword, and struck it at the servant of the high priest, and cut off his ear.

48 And Jesus answered and said to them, Have you come out against me as against a bandit, with swords and staves to arrest me?

49 I was with you every day teaching in the temple, and you did not arrest me; but this has happened so that the scriptures might be fulfilled.

50 Then his disciples left him and fled.

51 And a young man was following him, naked, with a loin cloth around him; and they seized him.

Cf.dif. vv. 14: 26-27, 29,31, 34, 36, 38, 41, 44-45, 51.

52 But he left the loin cloth, and fled naked.

53 ¶ And they took Jesus to Caiaphas the high priest; and there gathered to him all the high priests and the scribes and the elders.

54 But Simon followed him afar off, up to the courtyard of the high priest; and he sat with the servants, warming himself before the fire.

55 The high priests and the whole council were seeking testimony against Jesus so that they might put him to death; but they could not find it.

56 For even though many testified against him, their testimonies were not worthy.

57 Then some men, who were false witnesses, stood up against him, and said,

58 We heard him say, I will tear down this temple which is made with hands, and in three days I will build another which is not made with hands.

59 But even this testimony was not worthy.

60 Then the high priest stood up in the midst, and asked Jesus, and said, Do you not answer? What do these testify against you?

61 But Jesus was silent, and made no answer. Again the high priest asked him, and said, Are you the Christ, the Son of the Blessed One?

62 Jesus said to him, I am; and you will see the Son of man sitting at the right hand of power, and coming upon the clouds of the sky.

63 Then the high priest tore his robe, and said, Why therefore do we need witnesses?

64 Behold, you have heard blasphemy from his own mouth; what do you think? And they all decided that he is guilty of death.

65 Then some of the men began to spit in his face, and to cover his face, and to strike him on his head, saying, Prophesy; and the soldiers smote him on his cheeks.

66 ¶ And when Simon was below in the courtyard, there came a young maidservant of the high priest;

67 And she saw him warming himself, and looked at him, and said to him, You also were with Jesus the Nazarene.

68 But he denied it and said, I do not understand what you are saying. Then he went out to the porch, and the cock crowed.

69 And the same young maid saw him, and began to say to those who stood by, This one also is one of them.

70 But he denied it again. And a little later, those who stood by said to Peter, Truly you are one of them, for you also are a Galilean, and even your speech is like theirs.

71 And he began to curse and to swear, I do not know this man of whom you speak.

72 At that very hour the cock crowed the second time. And Simon remembered the word that Jesus said to him, Before the cock crows twice you will deny me thrice. And then he began to weep.

CHAPTER 15

AND immediately in the morning the high priests took counsel together with the elders and the scribes and with the whole council; and they bound Jesus and took him away, and delivered him to Pilate the governor.

2 And Pilate asked him, Are you the King of the Jews? He answered and said to him, You say that.

3 And the high priests accused him of many things.

4 Then Pilate asked again and said to him, Do you not answer? see, how many are testifying against you.

5 But Jesus gave no answer, so that Pilate marvelled.

Cf.dif. vv. 14:56-57, 59, 63-65;   15:2, 4.

6 ¶ Now it was the custom on every feast to release to them one prisoner, whom they asked for.

7 There was one called Bar-Abbas, who was bound with those who made insurrection, and who had committed murder during the insurrection.

8 And the people cried out, and began to ask, to do for them according to the custom.

9 Pilate answered and said, Are you willing that I release to you the King of the Jews?

10 For Pilate knew that the high priests had delivered him because of envy.

11 But the high priests incited the people the more, that he should release Bar-Abbas to them.

12 Pilate said to them, What then do you wish me to do to this man whom you call "the King of the Jews"?

13 And they cried out again, Crucify him!

14 Then Pilate said to them, What evil has he done? but they cried aloud the more, Crucify him!

15 Now Pilate wanted to do the will of the people; so he released Bar-Abbas to them, and he delivered to them Jesus, scourged, to be crucified.

16 Then the soldiers took him to the inner courtyard, which is the Praetorium; and they called together the whole company.

17 And they dressed him in purple, and wove a crown of thorns and put it on him.

18 And they began to salute him, Hail, O King of the Jews.

19 And they stuck him on his head with a reed, and spat on his face, and knelt on their knees and worshipped him.

20 And when they had mocked him, they took off the purple, and put on him his own clothes, and took him out to crucify him.

21 ¶ And they compelled one who was passing by, Simon the Cyrenian, who was coming from the field, the father of Alexander and Rufus, to carry his cross.

22 And they brought him to Golgotha, a place which is interpreted The Skull.

23 And they gave him to drink wine mixed with myrrh; but he would not take it.

24 And when they had crucified him, they divided his clothes, and cast lots on them, what each man should take.

25 It was the third hour when they crucified him.

26 And the reason for his death was inscribed in writing, THIS IS THE KING OF THE JEWS.

27 And they crucified with him two bandits, one on his right and one on his left.

28 And the scripture was fulfilled which said, He was reckoned with the wicked.

29 ¶ Even those who passed by blasphemed against him, nodding their heads and saying, O destroyer of the temple and builder of it in three days,

30 Deliver yourself and come down from the cross.

31 The high priests likewise were laughing among themselves, with the scribes, and saying, He saved others; but he cannot save himself.

32 "O Christ, the King of Israel!" let him now come down from the cross, so that we may see and believe in him. Even those who were crucified with him reproached him.

33 And when the sixth hour was come, there was darkness over all the land, until the ninth hour.

34 And at the ninth hour, Jesus cried out with a loud voice, and said, Eli, Eli, Lmana, shabachthani! which means, My God, my God, for this I was kept!

35 Some of the men who were standing by, when they heard it, said, He called for Elijah.

36 And one ran and filled a sponge with vinegar, and tied it on a reed to give him a drink; and he said, Hush, let us see if Elijah will come to take him down.

Cf.dif. vv. 15:6, 8, 11, 15, 22-23, 26, 28-29, 31-32, 34.

37 But Jesus cried with a loud voice, and the end came.

38 And the door curtains of the temple were rent in two, from the top to the bottom.

39 ¶ And when the centurion, who stood by near him, saw that he cried out in this manner and passed away, he said, Truly this man was the Son of God.

40 There were also women who were looking from afar, Mary of Magdala, and Mary the mother of James the young and of Joses, and Salome;

41 Who had followed him, when he was in Galilee, and ministered to him; and many other women who had come up with him to Jerusalem.

42 ¶ And when it was Friday evening, which is before the sabbath,

43 There came Joseph of Arimathaea, an honorable counsellor, who was also waiting for the kingdom of God; and he dared and went to Pilate, and asked for the body of Jesus.

44 But Pilate marvelled that he was already dead. So he called the centurion and asked him if he had died before the time.

45 And when he learned it, he gave the body to Joseph.

46 And Joseph bought linen, and took him down and wrapped him in it, and laid him in a tomb which was hewn in a rock; and he rolled a stone against the door of the tomb.

47 But Mary of Magdala and Mary the mother of Joses, saw where he was laid.

CHAPTER 16

WHEN the sabbath had passed, Mary of Magdala and Mary the mother of James, and Salome, bought spices, that they might come and anoint him.

2 Early in the morning, on the first day of the week, they came to the tomb, as the sun was just rising.

3 And they said among themselves, Who will roll away the stone from the door of the tomb for us?

4 And they looked and saw that the stone was rolled away, for it was very large.

5 And they entered the tomb, and saw a young man, sitting on the right, covered in a white robe; and they were astonished.

6 But he said to them, Do not be afraid. You seek Jesus the Nazarene, who was crucified; he has risen; he is not here; behold the place where he was laid.

7 But go away and tell his disciples, and Peter, that he will be before you in Galilee; there you will see him, just as he has told you.

8 And when they heard it, they fled and went out of the tomb, for they were seized with amazement and trembling; and they said nothing to any man, for they were frightened.

9 ¶ Now he rose early on the first day of the week, and appeared first to Mary of Magdala, from whom he had cast seven demons.

10 And she went and brought glad tidings to those who were with him, who now were mourning and weeping.

11 And when they heard them saying that he was alive, and had appeared to them, they did not believe them. *

12 ¶ After these things he appeared to two of them in another manner, as they were walking and going to a village.

13 And they went and told the rest; but they did not believe them also.

14 ¶ At last he appeared to the eleven while they were reclining, and he upbraided them for their little faith and the dulness of their hearts, because they had not believed those who saw him risen.

15 ¶ And he said to them, Go to all the world, and preach my gospel to the whole creation.

16 He who believes and is baptized shall be saved; and he who does not believe shall be condemned.

17 And wonders will follow those who be-

Cf.dif. vv. 15:37-39, 42-44;   16:5, 8, 10- 11, 14-15, 17.

lieve these things. In my name they will cast out demons; and they will speak with new tongues;

18 And they will pick up snakes; and if they should drink any poison of death, it will not harm them; and they will lay their hands on the sick, and they will be healed.

19 ¶ Then our Lord Jesus, after he had spoken to them, ascended to heaven, and sat on the right hand of God.

20 And they went out, and preached in every place; and our Lord helped them, and he strengthened their words by the miracles which they performed.

Completion of the Holy Gospel, the announcement of Mark;
which he uttered and proclaimed in Latin at Rome.

ܘܩܘܒܕܗ ܐܗܘܠܢܐ ܟܪܘܙ ܐܘܢܓܠܝܘܢ ܫܠܡ ܀

܀ ܟܪܡܝܗܒ ܬܐܟܪܘܙܘܬܗ ܐܠܟܐܗܪ

---

* Mk. 16:11 - All three women returned from the tomb and brought the news, but Mary of Magdala was the chief speaker.

THE GOSPEL ACCORDING TO
ST. LUKE

✣ ܐܘܢܓܠܝܘܢ ܩܕܝܫܐ ܟܪܘܙܘܬܐ ܕܠܘܩܐ ✣

CHAPTER 1

SINCE many have desired to have in writing the story of those works, with which we are familiar,

2 According to what was handed down to us by those who from the beginning were eyewitnesses and ministers of that very word,

3 And since these were seen by me also because I was near and considered them all very carefully, I will therefore write to you everything in its order, most honorable Theophilus,

4 So that you may know the truth of the words, by which you were made a convert.

5 ¶ There was in the days of Herod, king of Judaea, a priest whose name was Zacharias, of the order of ministry of the house of Abijah; and his wife was of the daughters of Aaron, and her name was Elizabeth.

6 They were both righteous before God, and walked in all his commandments, and in the righteousness of the Lord without blame.

7 But they had no son, because Elizabeth was barren, and they were both well on in years.

8 And it happened, while he was ministering in the order of his ministry before God,

9 According to the custom of the priesthood, his turn came to burn incense; so he entered the temple of the Lord.

10 And all the congregation of the people prayed outside, at the time of incense.

11 And the angel of the Lord appeared to Zacharias, standing on the right of the altar of incense.

12 And when Zacharias saw him he became dumbfounded, and fear came upon him.

13 And the angel said to him, Fear not, Zacharias; for your prayer has been heard, and your wife Elizabeth will bear you a son, and you will call his name John.

14 And you will have joy and gladness; and a great many will rejoice at his birth.

15 For he will be great before the Lord, and he will not drink wine and strong drink; and he will be filled with the Holy Spirit, while he is still in the womb of his mother.

16 And many Israelites he will cause to turn to the Lord their God.

17 And he will go before them with the spirit and the power of Elijah, to turn the hearts of parents to their children, and those who are disobedient to the wisdom of the righteous; and he will prepare a true people for the Lord.

18 And Zacharias said to the angel, How will I understand this? for I am an old man, and my wife is well on in years.

19 And the angel answered, saying to him, I am Gabriel, who stand in the presence of God; and I am sent to speak to you, and to bring you these glad tidings.

20 From henceforth you will be dumb, and not able to speak, till the day these things happen, because you did not believe these my words which are to be fulfilled in their time.

21 Now the people stood waiting for Zacharias, and wondered because he remained so long in the temple.

22 When Zacharias came out, he could not speak with them; and they understood that he had seen a vision in the temple; and he made signs to them with his eyes, but remained dumb.

Cf.dif. vv. 1:1-9, 22.

23 And when the days of his ministry were finished, he went to his house.

24 And it happened after those days, his wife Elizabeth conceived, and hid herself for five months; and she said,

25 The Lord has done these things to me in the days that he has been mindful of me, to remove my reproach among men.

26 ¶ Now in the sixth month the angel Gabriel was sent from God to Galilee, to a city called Nazareth,

27 To a virgin who was acquired for a price for a man named Joseph, of the house of David; and the name of the virgin was Mary.

28 And the angel went in and said to her, Peace be to you, O full of grace; our Lord is with you, O blessed one among women.

29 When she saw him, she was disturbed at his word, and wondered what kind of salutation this could be.

30 And the angel said to her, Fear not, Mary; for you have found grace with God.

31 For behold, you will conceive and give birth to a son, and you will call his name Jesus.

32 He will be great, and he will be called the Son of the Highest; and the Lord God will give him the throne of his father David.

33 And he will rule over the house of Jacob for ever; and there will be no limit to his kingdom.

34 Then Mary said to the angel, How can this be, for no man has known me.

35 The angel answered and said to her, The Holy Spirit will come, and the power of the Highest will rest upon you; therefore the one who is to be born of you is holy, and he will be called the Son of God.

36 And behold, Elizabeth your kinswoman has also conceived a son in her old age; and yet this is the sixth month with her, who is called barren.

37 For nothing is impossible for God.

38 Mary said, Here I am, a handmaid of the Lord; let it be to me according to your word. And the angel went away from her.

39 ¶ In those days, Mary rose up, and went hurriedly to a mountain, to a city of Judaea.

40 And she entered the house of Zacharias, and saluted Elizabeth.

41 And when Elizabeth heard the salutation of Mary, the babe leaped in her womb; and Elizabeth was filled with the Holy Spirit.

42 And she cried in a loud voice, and said to Mary, Blessed are you among women, and blessed is the fruit of your womb.

43 How does this happen to me, that the mother of my Lord should come to me?

44 For behold, when the voice of your salutation fell on my ears, the babe in my womb leaped with great joy.

45 And blessed is she who believed; for there will be a fulfillment of the things which were spoken to her from the Lord.

46 And Mary said, My soul magnifies the Lord,

47 And my spirit rejoices in God my Saviour.

48 For he has regarded the meekness of his handmaid; for behold, from henceforth, all generations shall envy me.

49 For he who is mighty has done great things to me; holy is his name.

50 And his mercy is for centuries and generations, upon those who fear him.

51 He has brought victory with his arm; he has scattered the proud in the imagination of their heart.

52 He has put down the mighty from their seats, and he has lifted up the meek.

53 He has filled the hungry with good things; and dismissed the rich empty.

54 He has helped his servant Israel, and has remembered his mercy,

55 Just as he spoke with our forefathers, with Abraham, and with his seed for ever.

Cf.dif. vv. 1:27-29, 33, 35, 44-45, 50, 52, 54.

56 ¶ Mary stayed with Elizabeth about three months, and then returned to her own home.

57 ¶ Now the time came for Elizabeth to be delivered, and she gave birth to a son.

58 And when her neighbors and relatives heard that God had increased his mercy to her, they rejoiced with her.

59 And it happened on the eighth day, they came to circumcise the boy; and they would have called him Zacharias, after the name of his father.

60 And his mother answered and said to them, Not so; but he should be called John.

61 And they said to her, There is no man in your family, who is called by this name.

62 Then they made signs to his father, what he wanted to call him.

63 And he asked for a tablet and wrote, saying, John is his name. And every one was surprised.

64 And immediately his mouth and his tongue were opened, and he spoke and blessed God.

65 And fear came on all their neighbors; and these things were spoken throughout the mountain of Judaea.

66 And all who heard it reasoned in their hearts, saying, What a boy he will be! And the hand of the Lord was with him.

67 ¶ And his father Zacharias was filled with the Holy Spirit, and prophesied, and said,

68 Blessed is the Lord, the God of Israel; for he has visited his people and wrought a salvation for them.

69 And he has raised up a horn of salvation for us in the house of his servant David;

70 Just as he spoke by the mouth of his holy prophets who have been for ages,

71 That he would save us from our enemies, and from the hand of all who hate us.

72 He has shown mercy to our fathers, and he has remembered his holy covenants;

73 And the oaths which he swore to Abraham our father,

74 To grant to us, that we may be saved from the hand of our enemies, and serve before him without fear,

75 In justice and righteousness all our days.

76 And you, boy, will be called the prophet of the Highest; for you will go before the face of the Lord, to prepare his way;

77 To give knowledge of life to his people by the forgiveness of their sins,

78 Through the mercy and kindness of our God; whereby we shall be visited by a ray from above,

79 To give light to those who sit in darkness and in the shadow of death, to guide our feet into the way of peace.

80 The boy grew and became strong in spirit; and he was in the desert until the day of his appearance to Israel.

CHAPTER 2

*A*ND it happened in those days that there went out a decree from Caesar Augustus, to take a census of all the people in his empire.

2 This first census took place during the governorship of Quirinius in Syria.

3 And every man went to be registered in his own city.

4 Joseph also went up from Nazareth, a city of Galilee, to Judaea, to the city of David, which is called Bethlehem; because he was of the house and family of David;

5 With his acquired wife Mary, while she was with child, that they might be registered there.

6 And it came to pass while they were there, that her days of deliverance were to be fulfilled.

7 And she gave birth to her first-born son; and she wrapped him in swaddling clothes, and laid him in a manger; because they had no place where they were lodging.

Cf.dif. vv. 1:58-59, 63, 66, 68, 70, 72, 78;   2:1-3, 5, 7.

8 ¶ Now there were shepherds in that region, where they were staying, and they were watching their flocks at night.

9 And behold, the angel of God came to them, and the glory of the Lord shone on them; and they were seized with a great fear.

10 And the angel said to them, Do not be afraid; for behold, I bring you glad tidings of great joy, which will be to all the world.

11 For today is born to you in the city of David, a Saviour, who is the Lord Christ.

12 And this is a sign for you; You will find a babe wrapped in swaddling clothes, and laid in a manger.

13 And suddenly there appeared with the angel, many hosts of heaven, praising God, and saying,

14 Glory to God in the highest, and on earth peace and good hope for men.

15 ¶ And it happened, when the angels departed from them and went to heaven, the shepherds spoke to one another, saying, Let us go to Bethlehem, and see this thing that has happened, as the Lord has shown to us.

16 And they came very hurriedly, and found Mary, and Joseph, and the babe laid in the manger.

17 When they saw it, they made known the word which was spoken to them concerning the boy.

18 And all who heard it were amazed at the things which were spoken by the shepherds.

19 But Mary treasured all these things, and dwelt on them in her heart.

20 And the shepherds returned, glorifying and praising God for all that they had seen and heard, as it was spoken to them.

21 ¶ And when eight days were fulfilled to circumcise the child, his name was called Jesus; because he was named by the angel before he was conceived in the womb.

22 ¶ And when the days for their purification were fulfilled, according to the law of Moses, they brought him up to Jerusalem, to present him to the Lord;

23 As it is written in the law of the Lord, Every male that opens the womb shall be called holy to the Lord;

24 And to offer a sacrifice, as it is said in the law of the Lord, A pair of turtledoves, or two young pigeons.

25 Now there was a man in Jerusalem, whose name was Simon; and this man was pious and righteous, waiting for the consolation of Israel; and the Holy Spirit was upon him.

26 And it was said to him by the Holy Spirit, that he would not see death, until he sees the Anointed of the Lord.

27 This man was led by the Spirit to the temple; and when the parents brought in the boy Jesus, to do for him according to what is commanded in the law,

28 He received him in his arms, and blessed God, and said,

29 Now dismiss thy servant, O my Lord, in peace, according to your word;

30 For behold, mine eyes have already seen your mercies,

31 Which you have prepared before the face of all peoples,

32 A light for a revelation to the Gentiles, and a glory to your people Israel.

33 ¶ And Joseph and his mother marvelled about these things which were spoken concerning him.

34 And Simon blessed them, and he said to Mary, his mother, Behold, this one is appointed for the fall and for the rise of many in Israel, and for a sign of dispute;

35 And a sword will pierce through your own soul; so that the thoughts of the hearts of many may be revealed.

36 And Hannah the prophetess, the daughter of Phanuel, of the tribe of Asher, was of a great age; and she had lived seven years with her husband from the days of her virginity.

37 Then she became a widow for about eighty-four years, and she never left the temple, and with fasting and prayer she worshipped day and night.

38 She also stood up at that hour, and gave thanks to the Lord, and spoke concerning him to every man who was looking forward to the salvation of Jerusalem.

39 ¶ And when they had done everything according to the law of the Lord, they returned to Galilee, to their own city Nazareth.

40 The boy grew and became strong in spirit, filled with wisdom; and the grace of God was upon him.

41 ¶ And his people went every year to Jerusalem during the feast of the passover.

42 And when he was twelve years old, they went up to the feast, as they were accustomed.

43 And when the feast days were over, they returned; but the boy Jesus remained in Jerusalem; and Joseph and his mother did not know it.

44 They thought that he was with the children of their party; and when they went a day's journey, they sought for him among their own people and those who knew them.

45 But they could not find him; so they returned again to Jerusalem, looking for him.

46 After three days, they found him in the temple, sitting in the midst of the teachers, listening to them, and asking them questions.

47 And all those who heard him were amazed at his wisdom and his answers.

48 And when they saw him, they were astonished; and his mother said to him, My son, why have you done so to us? behold, I and your father have been looking for you with much anxiety.

49 He said to them, Why were you looking for me? did you not know that I would be in the house of my Father?

50 But they could not understand the word which he said to them.

51 So he went down with them and came to Nazareth; and he was subject unto them. And his mother treasured all these words in her heart.

52 And Jesus grew in his stature and in his wisdom, and in favor with God and men.

CHAPTER 3

*I*N the fifteenth year of the reign of Tiberius Caesar, during the governorship of Pontius Pilate in Judaea, when Herod was tetrarch of Galilee, and his brother Philip tetrarch of Ituraea and of the region of Trachonitis, and Lysanius tetrarch of Abilene,

2 During the high priesthood of Annas and Caiaphas, the word of God came to John, son of Zacharias, in the wilderness.

3 And he came throughout the country around Jordan, preaching the baptism of repentance for the forgiveness of sins;

4 As it is written in the book of the words of Isaiah the prophet, who said, The voice which calls in the wilderness, Prepare the way of the Lord, make the paths of our God straight in the plain.

5 Let all the valleys be filled up, and all the mountains and hills be levelled; let the crooked places be made straight, and the rough places like a plain;

6 And let every flesh see the salvation of God.

7 ¶And he said to the people, who were coming to him to be baptized, O offspring of scorpions, who has warned you to escape from the anger which is coming?

8 Therefore bring forth fruits which are worthy of repentance; and do not begin to say within yourselves, We have Abraham as our father; for I say to you that God can raise up children for Abraham from these stones.

Cf.dif. vv. 2:37-38, 42, 44, 48-49, 52; 3:4-5.

9 Behold, the axe is already placed at the root of the trees; therefore every tree which bears not good fruits will be cut down and dropped in the fire.

10 And the people asked him saying, What then shall we do?

11 He answered and said to them, He who has two shirts, let him give to him who has not; and he who has food, let him do likewise.

12 And there came also publicans to be baptized, and they said to him, Teacher, what shall we do?

13 He said to them, Do not exact anything more over what is commanded you to exact.

14 And the soldiers also asked him saying, What shall we do? And he said to them, Do not molest any man, and do not despise any man; your own wages should be enough for you.

15 ¶ While the people were placing their hope on John, and all of them were thinking in their hearts, that perhaps he is the Christ;

16 John answered and said to them, Behold, I baptize you with water; but one is coming after me, who is greater than I, the strings of whose shoes I am not worthy to untie; he will baptize you with the Holy Spirit and with fire;

17 He holds a shovel in his hand, and purifies his threshing; the wheat he gathers into his barns, and the straw he burns in the unquenchable fire.

18 Many other things also, he taught and preached to the people.

19 ¶ Now Herod the tetrarch, because he was rebuked by John concerning Herodias wife of Philip his brother, and for all the evil things that he was doing,

20 Added this also to them all, that he put John into prison.

21 ¶ It came to pass when all the people were baptized, Jesus also was baptized, and while he prayed the heaven was opened,

22 And the Holy Spirit descended on him, like a dove, and a voice from heaven, saying, You are my beloved Son, with whom I am pleased.

23 ¶ Now Jesus was about thirty years old, and he was supposed to be the son of Joseph, the son of Heli,

24 The son of Matthat, the son of Levi, the son of Melchi, the son of Jannai, the son of Joseph,

25 The son of Mattathias, the son of Amos, the son of Nahum, the son of Esli, the son of Naggai,

26 The son of Maath, the son of Mattathias, the son of Semei, the son of Joseph, the son of Juda,

27 The son of John, the son of Rhesa, the son of Zerubbabel, the son of Shealtiel, the son of Neri,

28 The son of Melchi, the son of Addi, the son of Kosam, the son of Elmodad, the son of Er,

29 The son of Jose, the son of Eliezer, the son of Jorim, the son of Mattitha, the son of Levi,

30 The son of Simon, the son of Juda, the son of Joseph, the son of Jonan, the son of Eliakim,

31 The son of Melea, the son of Mani, the son of Matta, the son of Nathan, the son of David,

32 The son of Jesse, the son of Obed, the son of Boaz, the son of Salmon, the son of Nahshon,

33 The son of Aminadab, the son of Aram, the son of Hezron, the son of Perez, the son of Juda,

34 The son of Jacob, the son of Isaac, the son of Abraham, the son of Terah, the son of Nahor,

35 The son of Serug, the son of Arau, the son of Peleg, the son of Eber, the son of Shalah,

36 The son of Cainan, the son of Arphaxad, the son of Shem, the son of Noah, the son of Lamech,

37 The son of Methuselah, the son of Enoch, the son of Jared, the son of Mahalaleel, the son of Cainan,

38 The son of Enosh, the son of Seth, the son of Adam, who was of God.

CHAPTER 4

*N*OW Jesus, full of the Holy Spirit, returned from the Jordan, and the Spirit carried him away into the wilderness,

2 Forty days, in order that he might be tempted by the adversary. And he did not eat anything in those days; and when they were over, at last he became hungry.

3 ¶ And the adversary said to him, If you are the Son of God, command this stone to become bread.

4 Jesus answered and said to him, It is written, That it is not by bread alone that man can live, but by every word of God.

5 Then Satan took him up to a high mountain, and showed him all the kingdoms of the earth in a short time.

6 And the adversary said to him, I will give you all this power and its glory, which are entrusted to me, and I give it to whom I please;

7 If therefore you worship me, it will all be yours.

8 Jesus answered and said to him, It is written, You shall worship the Lord your God, and him only you shall serve.

9 And he brought him to Jerusalem and made him to stand up on the pinnacle of the temple, and said to him, If you are the Son of God, throw yourself down from here;

10 For it is written, That he will command his angels concerning you, to watch you;

11 And they will take you up in their arms, so that even your foot may not strike a stone.

12 Jesus answered and said to him, It is said, You shall not tempt the Lord your God.

13 When the adversary was through with all his temptations, he left him for some time.

14 ¶ So Jesus returned in the power of the Spirit to Galilee; and the fame about him went out through all the country around them.

15 And he taught in their synagogues, and was praised by every man.

16 ¶ And he came to Nazareth, where he had been brought up; and he entered the synagogue on the sabbath day, as was the custom, and stood up to read.

17 And the book of the prophet Isaiah was given to him. And Jesus opened the book, and found the place where it is written,

18 The Spirit of the Lord is upon me; because of this he has anointed me, to preach good tidings to the poor; and he has sent me to heal the broken-hearted, and to proclaim release to the captives, and sight to the blind; to strengthen with forgiveness those who are bruised

19 And to preach the acceptable year of the Lord.

20 And he rolled up the scroll and gave it to the attendant, and went and sat down. And the eyes of all who were in the synagogue were fixed on him.

21 And he began to say to them, To-day this scripture is fulfilled in your ears.

22 And all testified to him, and were amazed by the words of grace which came out of his mouth. And they said, Is not this man the son of Joseph?

23 Jesus said to them, You might probably tell me this proverb, "Physician, heal yourself"; and all that we heard you did in Capernaum, do also here in your own city.

24 Then he said, Truly I say to you, No prophet is acceptable in his own city.

25 For truly I say to you, There were many widows in Israel in the days of the prophet Elijah, when the heaven was closed for three years and six months, and there was a great famine throughout the land;

26 Yet Elijah was not sent to one of them, but to Zarephath of Sidon, to a widow.

27 And there were many lepers in Israel in the days of the prophet Elisha, and yet not one of them was cleansed, except Naaman the Syrian.

28 When those who were in the synagogue heard these things, they were all filled with anger.

29 And they rose up, and took him outside the city, and brought him to the brow of the mountain, on which their city was built, that they might throw him down from a cliff.

30 But he passed through the midst of them and went away.

31 ¶ And he went down to Capernaum, a city of Galilee, and he taught them on the sabbaths.

32 And they were astonished at his teaching; because his word had power.

33 And there was in the synagogue a man who had an unclean, demonic spirit, and he cried in a loud voice,

34 And said, Leave me alone, what have we in common, O Jesus the Nazarene? have you come to destroy us? I know who you are, "Holy One of God"!

35 And Jesus rebuked him, and said, Keep quiet, and come out of him. The demon threw him in the midst, and went out of him, and did him no harm.

36 And every man was seized with amazement, and spoke among themselves, saying, What kind of word is this, that he commands unclean spirits with authority and power, and they go out!

37 And the fame about him went out through all the country around them.

38 ¶ And when Jesus left the synagogue, he entered the house of Simon. And Simon's mother-in-law was suffering with a severe fever; and they besought him for her.

39 And he stood by her, and rebuked the fever, and it left her; and she rose up immediately and ministered to them.

40 ¶ When the sun was setting, all who had sick people suffering from divers diseases brought them to him; and he laid his hand on each one of them, and healed them.

41 Demons also came out of many, who cried out saying, You are the Christ, the Son of God. And he rebuked them, and he would not allow them to speak; that they might not know that he was the Christ.

42 And in the morning, he came out and went to a desert place; and the people were looking for him, and came where he was; and they held him so that he might not leave them.

43 But Jesus said to them, I must preach the kingdom of God in other cities also; because I was sent for this.

44 And he preached in the synagogues of Galilee.

CHAPTER 5

*I*T came to pass when the people gathered around him to hear the word of God, he stood on the shore of the lake of Gennesaret.

2 And he saw two boats standing by the lake; but the fishermen had got out of them, and were washing their nets.

3 One of them belonged to Simon Peter; so Jesus went up and sat in it, and he asked to row it a little way from the shore to the water. And he sat and taught the people from the boat.

4 When he was through speaking, he said to Simon, Row out to the deep, and cast your net for a catch.

5 Simon answered and said to him, Teacher, we have toiled all night, and have caught nothing; but just because of your word, I will cast the net.

6 And when they had done this, they inclosed a great many fish; and their net was breaking.

7 So they signalled to their partners in the other boat, to come and help them. And when they came, they filled both the boats, till they were almost sinking.

8 When Simon Peter saw it, he fell at the feet of Jesus, and said to him, I beg you, my Lord, leave me alone, for I am a sinful man.

9 For he was amazed, and all who were with him, because of the catch of fish which they took.

10 So also was it with James and John, sons of Zebedee, who were partners with Simon. But Jesus said to Simon, Do not be afraid; from henceforth you will be catching men for life.

11 And they brought the boats to land, and left everything and followed him.

12 ¶ When Jesus was in one of the cities, there came a man who was covered with leprosy; and he saw Jesus and fell on his face, and besought him, and said, My Lord, if you will, you can cleanse me.

13 And Jesus stretched out his hand and touched him, and said to him, I will, be clean; and immediately his leprosy left him.

14 And he charged him not to tell any man; but go and show yourself to the priests, and make an offering for your cleansing, as Moses commanded, for a testimony to them.

15 ¶ And the fame concerning him went out the more; and many people gathered to hear him, and to be healed of their diseases.

16 But he departed into the wilderness, and prayed.

17 ¶ It came to pass on one of the days when Jesus was teaching, the Pharisees and the teachers of the law were sitting, who had come from every town of Galilee and Judaea and Jerusalem. And the power of God was present to heal them.

18 And some men brought a paralytic on a quilt-bed; and they wanted to go in and lay him before him.

19 And when they found they were not able to carry him in, because of many people, they went up on the roof, and they lowered him down on his quilt-bed from the ceiling into the midst before Jesus.

20 When Jesus saw their faith, he said to the paralytic, Man, your sins are forgiven.

21 And the scribes and the Pharisees began to reason saying, Who is this man who talks blasphemy? Who can forgive sins, except God only?

22 But Jesus knew their thoughts, and he answered and said to them, What do you reason in your heart?

23 Which is easier to say, Your sins are forgiven, or just to say, Arise and walk?

24 But that you may know that the Son of man has authority on earth to forgive sins, he said to the paralytic, I tell you, Arise, take up your quilt-bed and go to your home.

25 And immediately he rose up before their eyes, and took his quilt-bed and went to his house, praising God.

26 And every man was seized with amazement, and they praised God, and were filled with fear, saying, To-day we have seen wonders.

27 ¶ After these things, Jesus went out and saw a publican named Levi, sitting at the custom house; and he said to him, Follow me.

28 So he left everything, and rose up, and went after him.

29 And Levi gave him a great reception in his house; and there was a large gathering of publicans and others, who were guests with them.

Cf.dif. vv. 5:6, 8, 10, 18-19, 26, 29.

30 And the scribes and the Pharisees murmured and said to his disciples, Why do you eat and drink with publicans and sinners?

31 And Jesus answered and said to them, A physician is not needed for those who are well, but for those who are seriously sick.

32 I have not come to call the righteous, but the sinners to repentance.

33 ¶ They said to him, Why do the disciples of John always fast and pray, and also those of the Pharisees; but yours eat and drink?

34 He said to them, You cannot make the sons of the wedding feast fast, so long as the bridegroom is with them.

35 But the days will come, when the bridegroom is taken from them, then they will fast in those days.

36 And he told them a parable, No man cuts a piece of cloth from a new garment and puts it on a worn out garment; so that he may not cut the new, and the new piece will not blend with the old.

37 No man pours new wine into worn out skins; else the new wine will rend the skins, and the wine will run out, and the skins will be ruined.

38 But they pour new wine into new skins, and both are well preserved.

39 And no man drinks old wine, and immediately wants new wine; for he says, The old is delicious.

CHAPTER 6

*I*T came to pass on the sabbath, as Jesus walked through the wheat fields, his disciples plucked ears of wheat, and rubbed them in their hands and did eat.

2 But some of the men of the Pharisees said to them, Why are you doing what is unlawful to do on the sabbath?

3 Jesus answered and said to them, Have you not read this, what David did when he and those who were with him were hungry?

4 He entered into the house of God, and took the bread that was on the table of the Lord and did eat it, and he gave it to those who were with him; that which was unlawful to eat but only for the priests.

5 And he said to them, The Son of man is Lord of the sabbath.

6 ¶ And it came to pass on another sabbath, he entered into the synagogue and taught; and there was there a man whose right hand was withered.

7 And the scribes and the Pharisees watched him, to see if he would heal on the sabbath, so that they might find an accusation against him.

8 But he knew their thoughts, and said to the man whose hand was withered, Rise up and come to the center of the synagogue. And when he came and stood up,

9 Jesus said to them, I will ask you, What is lawful to do on the sabbath, that which is good or that which is bad? to save a life or to destroy it?

10 And he looked at all of them, and said to him, Stretch out your hand. And he stretched it out; and his hand was restored like the other.

11 But they were filled with bitterness, and discussed with each other what to do with Jesus.

12 ¶ It happened in those days, Jesus went out to a mountain to pray, and he remained all night in prayer to God.

13 And at daybreak, he called his disciples; and he chose twelve from them, whom he called apostles;

14 Simon who is called Peter, and Andrew his brother, and James and John, and Philip and Bartholomew,

15 And Matthew and Thomas, and James the son of Alphaeus and Simon who is called the Zealot,

16 And Judas the son of James, and Judas of Iscariot, who became the traitor.

17 ¶ And Jesus went down with them and stood up in the plain; and a large group of his disciples, and a large crowd of people, from all over Judaea, and from Jerusalem, and from the sea coast of Tyre and Sidon, who had come to hear his word, and to be healed of their diseases;

18 And those who were suffering from unclean spirits were healed.

19 And all the people wanted to touch him; because power proceeded from him, and he healed them all.

20 ¶ And he lifted up his eyes on his disciples and said, Blessed are you poor, for the kingdom of God is yours.

21 Blessed are you who hunger now, for you shall be filled. Blessed are you who weep now, for you shall laugh.

22 Blessed are you, when men hate you, and discriminate against you, and reproach you, and publish your names as bad, for the sake of the Son of man.

23 Be glad and rejoice in that day, for your reward is increased in heaven; for their fathers did the same to the prophets.

24 But woe to you, rich men! for you have already received your comforts.

25 Woe to you who are full! for you will hunger. Woe to you who laugh now! for you will weep and mourn.

26 Woe to you when men speak well of you! for so did their fathers to the false prophets.

27 But I say to you who hear, Love your enemies, and do good to those who hate you,

28 And bless those who curse you, and pray for those who compel you to carry burdens.

29 And he who strikes you on your cheek, offer him the other; and he who takes away your robe, do not refuse your shirt also.

30 Give to every one who asks you; and from him who takes away what is yours, do not demand it back again.

31 Just as you want men to do to you. do to them likewise.

32 For if you love those who love you, what is your favor? for even sinners love those who love them.

33 And if you do good only to those who do good to you, what is your favor? for sinners also do the same.

34 And if you lend only to him from whom you expect to be paid back, what is your favor? for sinners also lend to sinners, to be paid back likewise.

35 But love your enemies, and do good to them, and lend, and do not cut off any man's hope; so your reward will increase, and you will become sons of the Highest; for he is gracious to the wicked and the cruel.

36 Be therefore merciful, as your Father also is merciful.

37 Judge not, and you will not be judged; condemn not, and you will not be condemned; forgive, and you will be forgiven.

38 Give, and it will be given to you; good measure shaken up and running over, they will pour into your robe.* For with the measure that you measure, it will be measured to you.

39 And he told them a parable, Can a blind man take care of a blind man? will they not both fall in a pit?

40 There is no disciple who is more important than his teacher; for every man who is well developed will be like his teacher.

41 Why do you see the splinter in your brother's eye, and do not see the beam in your own eye?

42 Or how can you say to your brother, My brother, let me take out the splinter from your eye, when behold, you do not see the beam in your own eye? O hypocrites, first take out the beam from your own eye, and then you will see clearly to take out the splinter from your brother's eye.

* Lk. 6:38 - Easterners carry wheat from house to house in the folds of their robes.

Cf.dif. vv. 6: 22, 28-30, 32-35, 38-42.

43 There is no good tree that bears bad fruits, nor a bad tree that bears good fruits.

44 For every tree is known by its own fruits. For they do not gather figs from thistles, nor gather grapes from a bramble bush.

45 A good man brings out good things from the good treasure of his heart; and a bad man from the bad treasure of his heart brings out bad things; for from the abundance of the heart the lips speak.

46 Why do you call me, My Lord, my Lord, and do not do what I say?

47 Every man who comes to me and hears my words and does them, I will show you what he is like.

48 He is like a man who built a house, and dug deep, and laid its foundations upon the rock; and when the flood came, the flood beat upon that house, and could not shake it; for its foundation was laid upon a rock.

49 And he who hears and does not, is like a man who built his house on the earth without a foundation; and when the river beat against it, it fell immediately, and the fall of that house was great.

CHAPTER 7

WHEN he had finished all of these words, in the hearing of the people, Jesus entered Capernaum.

2 Now the servant of a centurion was seriously sick, one who was very dear to him; and he was near death.

3 And when he heard about Jesus, he sent to him Jewish elders, and besought him to come and heal his servant.

4 When they came to Jesus, they begged him earnestly, saying, He is worthy to have this done for him;

5 For he loves our people, and has even built us a synagogue.

6 Jesus went with them. And when he was not far from the house, the centurion sent some of his friends to him, and said, My Lord, do not trouble yourself; for I am not worthy that you should enter under my roof;

7 That is why I was not worthy to come to you; but just say a word and my boy will be healed.

8 For I am also a man in government service, and there are soldiers under my command; and I say to this one, Go, and he goes; and to another, Come, and he comes; and to my servant, Do this, and he does it.

9 When Jesus heard these things, he was amazed at him, and he turned and said to the people who followed him, I say to you, not even in Israel have I found such faith as this.

10 So those who were sent returned to the house, and found the servant who was sick, healed.

11 ¶ And it came to pass on the next day, he was going to a city called Nain; and his disciples were with him, and many people.

12 And when they came near the gate of the city, he saw a dead man being carried out, who was the only son of his mother, and his mother was a widow; and many people of the city were with her.

13 When Jesus saw her, he had compassion on her, and said to her, Weep not.

14 Then he went and touched the bier, and those who carried it stood still. And he said, Young man, I tell you, Arise.

15 And the dead man sat up, and began to speak. And he gave him to his mother.

16 And all men were seized with fear; and they praised God, saying, A great prophet is risen among us; and, God has visited his people.

17 And this word about him went out through all Judaea, and through the country around them.

Cf.dif. vv. 6:48;   7:4, 7-8, 11.

18 ¶ And John's disciples told him all these things.

19 So John called two of his disciples, and sent them to Jesus, and said, Are you the one who is to come? or are we to expect another one?

20 And they came to Jesus and said to him, John the Baptist has sent us to you, saying, Are you the one who is to come? or are we to expect another one?

21 In that very hour, he healed a great many of their diseases and plagues, and of evil spirits; and he gave sight to many blind men.

22 So Jesus answered and said to them, Go and tell John everything that you have seen and heard; that the blind see, and the lame walk, and the lepers are cleansed, and the deaf hear, and the dead rise up, and the poor are given hope.

23 And blessed is he, who does not stumble on account of me.

24 ¶ When John's disciples had gone, Jesus began to speak to the people concerning John, What did you go out to the wilderness to see? A reed which is shaken by the wind?

25 If not so, what did you go out to see? A man dressed in fine clothes? Behold, those who wear fine clothes and live delicately are in kings' houses.

26 And if not so, what did you go out to see? A prophet? Yes, I say to you, and much more than a prophet.

27 This is he of whom it is written, Behold, I send my messenger before your face, to prepare the way before you.

28 I say to you that there is no prophet among those who are born of women, who is greater than John the Baptist; and yet even the least person in the kingdom of God is greater than he.

29 And all the people who heard it, even the publicans, justified themselves before God, for they were baptized with the baptism of John.

30 But the Pharisees and the scribes suppressed the will of God in themselves, because they were not baptized by him.

31 ¶ To whom, therefore, shall I liken the men of this generation? and to what are they like?

32 They are like boys who sit in the street, and call to their friends and say, We have sung to you but you did not dance; and we have wailed to you and you did not weep.

33 For John the Baptist came, neither eating bread nor drinking wine; and you say, He is insane.

34 The Son of man came, eating and drinking; and you say, Behold, a glutton and a winebibber, and a friend of publicans and sinners!

35 And yet wisdom is justified by all its works.

36 ¶ Then one of the Pharisees came and asked him to eat with him. And he entered the house of that Pharisee and reclined as a guest.

37 Now there was in that city a woman who was a sinner; and when she knew that he was a guest in the Pharisee's house, she took an alabaster cruse of perfume,

38 And she stood behind him at his feet, weeping, and she began to wet his feet with her tears, and to wipe them with the hair of her head, and she kissed his feet, and anointed them with perfume.

39 When the Pharisee who had invited him saw it, he reasoned in himself and said, If this man were a prophet, he would have known who she was and her reputation; for the woman who has touched him is a sinner.

40 Jesus answered and said to him, Simon, I have something to tell you. He said to him, Say it, teacher. Jesus said to him,

41 There were two men who were debtors to a creditor; one of them owed him five hundred pence, and the other one fifty pence.

Cf.dif. vv. 7:22-23, 26-26, 29-30, 32, 38-39.

42 And because they had nothing to pay, he forgave them both. Which one of them will love him more?

43 Simon answered and said, I think the one to whom he forgave more. Jesus said to him, You have judged truly.

44 And he turned to the woman, and said to Simon, Do you see this woman? I entered your house, you did not give me even water for my feet; but she has wet my feet with her tears, and wiped them with her hair.

45 You did not kiss me; but she, since she entered, has not ceased to kiss my feet.

46 You did not anoint my head with oil; but she has anointed my feet with perfume.

47 For this reason, I say to you, Her many sins are forgiven, because she loved much; but he to whom little is forgiven, loves little.

48 And he said to the woman, Your sins are forgiven.

49 Then the guests began to say within themselves, Who is this man, who forgives even sins?

50 Jesus said to the woman, Your faith has saved you; go in peace.

CHAPTER 8

AND it came to pass after these things, Jesus was traveling in cities and villages, preaching and giving good news of the kingdom of God. And his twelve were with him,

2 And the women who were healed of diseases and unclean spirits, Mary who is called of Magdala, from whom seven demons went out,

3 And Joanna, the wife of Chuza the steward of Herod, and Susanna, and many others, who ministered to them of their wealth.

4 ¶ And when many people had gathered, and were coming to him from all the cities, he spoke by parables.

5 The sower went out to sow his seed. And when he sowed, some fell on the roadside; and it was trodden under foot, and the birds ate it.

6 Other fell upon the rock; and sprung up earlier, and because it had no moisture, it dried up.

7 And other fell among thistles; and the thistles sprung up with it and choked it.

8 And other fell in good and fertile ground; and sprung up and bore fruit a hundredfold. And when he said this, he cried out, He who has ears to hear, let him hear.

9 ¶ And his disciples asked him, What is this parable?

10 He said to them, To you it is granted to know the mystery of the kingdom of God; but to the rest it has to be said in figures; for while they see, they do not perceive; and while they hear, they do not understand.

11 ¶ This is the parable. The seed is the word of God.

12 Those on the roadside are those who hear the word; and the enemy comes and takes away the word from their heart, so that they may not believe and be saved.

13 Those on the rock are those who when they have heard, receive the word with joy; and yet they have no root, but their belief is for a while, and in time of trial they stumble.

14 That which fell among the thistles are those who hear the word, and then choke themselves with worries and riches and worldly covetousness, and bear no fruit.

15 But that in good soil, these are those who hear the word with pure and good heart, and keep it, and bear fruit with patience.

16 ¶ No man lights a lamp and covers it with a vessel, or puts it under the bed; but he puts it on the lamp holder, that whoever enters sees its light.

17 For there is nothing covered which will not be uncovered; and nothing hidden which will not be known, and come to light.

Cf.dif. vv. 7:44, 49;   8:2-3, 6, 8, 13-14,17.

18 Take heed how you hear; for he who has, to him shall be given; and he who has not, even that which he thinks he has shall be taken away from him.

19 ¶ And there came to him his mother and his brothers, and they were not able to speak to him because of the crowd.

20 And they said to him, Your mother and your brothers are standing outside, and they want to see you.

21 He answered and said to them, These are my mother and my brothers, those who hear the word of God and do it.

22 ¶ It came to pass on one of the days, Jesus went up and sat in a boat with his disciples; and he said to them, Let us cross to the other side of the lake.

23 And while they were rowing Jesus fell asleep; and there rose a storm of wind on the lake; and the boat was near sinking.

24 And they came up and awoke him and said to him, Our teacher, our teacher, we are perishing. He got up and rebuked the winds and the waves of water, and they quieted down, and there was a calm.

25 And he said to them, Where is your faith? But as they were frightened, they wondered, saying one to another, O who is this man, who even commands the winds, and the waves and the sea obey him?

26 And they rowed and came to the country of the Gadarenes, which is on the coast opposite Galilee.

27 And when he landed, he was met by a man from the city, who had the demon in him for a long time, and he did not wear clothes, and did not live in a house, but in the cemetery.

28 When he saw Jesus, he cried out and fell before him, and said in a loud voice, What have we in common, Jesus, Son of the Most High God? I beg you not to torment me.

29 For Jesus commanded the unclean spirit to go out of the man. For it was a long time since he was possessed, and bound with chains, and kept in fetters; but he would often break off his bonds and was driven into the desert by the demon.

30 Jesus asked him, What is your name? He said, Legion, because many demons had entered into him.

31 And they besought him not to command them to go down into the abyss.

32 Now there was there a herd of many swine feeding on the mountain; and they besought him to permit them to attack the swine. And he permitted them.

33 Then the demons went out of the man, and they attacked the swine; and that whole herd went straight to the cliff, and fell down into the lake and were drowned.

34 When the herdsmen saw what had happened, they fled and told it in the cities and in the villages.

35 And some men went out to see what had happened; and they came to Jesus, and found the man from whom the demons had gone out, dressed, and well behaved, and sitting at the feet of Jesus; and they were afraid.

36 And those who had seen it told them, how that lunatic was healed.

37 Then all the people of the Gadarenes besought him to leave them, because they were seized with a great fear; and Jesus went up into the boat and returned from thence.

38 But the man from whom the demons had gone out, besought him to remain with him; but Jesus dismissed him and said to him,

39 Return to your own house, and declare what God has done for you. And he went away, and preached throughout the city what Jesus had done for him.

40 ¶ When Jesus returned, a large multitude welcomed him, for they were all expecting him.

41 And a man named Jairus, a leader of the

synagogue, fell at the feet of Jesus, and besought him to enter into his house.

42 For he had an only daughter, about twelve years old, and she was near death. And as Jesus went with him, a large crowd pressed against him.

43 ¶ Now a woman who had the hemorrhage for twelve years, and had spent all her wealth for doctors, could not be healed by anybody.

44 She came near him from behind, and touched the edge of his cloak; and immediately her hemorrhage stopped.

45 And Jesus said, Who touched me? And when all of them denied it, Simon Peter and those who were with him said to him, Teacher, the crowds are troubling you and pressing on you, and yet you say, Who has touched me?

46 But he said, Some one has touched me, for I know that power has gone out of me.

47 When the woman saw that she could not deceive him, she came trembling, and fell down and worshipped him; and she said in the presence of all the people for what purpose she had touched him, and how she was healed immediately.

48 Jesus said to her, Have courage, my daughter; your faith has healed you; go in peace.

49 ¶ While he was still talking, there came a man from the house of the leader of the synagogue, and said to him, Your daughter has died, do not trouble the teacher.

50 Jesus heard it and said to the father of the girl, Do not be afraid, but only believe, and she will be restored to life.

51 Jesus came into the house, and he did not allow anyone to enter with him, except Simon and James and John, and the father and mother of the girl.

52 And all of them were weeping and mourning over her; but Jesus said, Do not weep, for she is not dead but asleep.

53 And they laughed at him, for they knew that she was dead.

54 Then he put everybody out, and held her by her hand, and called her, and said, Little girl, arise.

55 And her spirit returned, and she got up immediately; and he commanded to give her something to eat.

56 And her parents were amazed; but he warned them, not to tell any man what had happened.

CHAPTER 9

*T*HEN Jesus called his twelve, and gave them power and authority over all the demons, and to cure diseases.

2 And he sent them out to preach the kingdom of God, and to heal the sick.

3 And he said to them, Do not take anything for the journey, neither a staff, nor a bag, nor bread, nor money; nor have two shirts.

4 And into whatever house you enter, remain there, and depart from thence.

5 And whoever will not welcome you, when you leave that city, shake off even the sand from your feet for a testimony to them.

6 And the apostles went out, and travelled in villages and cities, preaching the gospel, and healing everywhere.

7 ¶ Now Herod the tetrarch heard of all that was done by his hand; and he was amazed, because some men said that John has risen from the dead.

8 But others, that Elijah has appeared; and others, that one of the old prophets has risen.

9 So Herod said, I have beheaded John; but who is this one concerning whom I hear these things? And he wanted to see him.

10 ¶ When the apostles returned, they told Jesus everything which they had done. And he took them all alone to a lonely place in Bethsaida.

11 When the people found it out, they went after him; and he received them, and spoke

to them concerning the kingdom of God, and he healed those who were in need of healing.

12 ¶ And when the day began to wane, his disciples came up and said to him, Dismiss the people, that they may go to the villages around us and to the farms, to lodge there, and find food for themselves; because we are in a lonely place.

13 Jesus said to them, You give them to eat. But they said, We do not have more than five loaves of bread and two fish; unless we go and buy food for all this people;

14 For there were about five thousand men. Jesus said to them, Make them sit down in groups, fifty men in each group.

15 The disciples did so, and made them all sit down.

16 And Jesus took the five loaves of bread and the two fish, and looked up to heaven, and he blessed them, and broke and gave them to his disciples, to set before the people.

17 And they all ate and were filled; and they took up fragments of what was left over, twelve baskets.

18 ¶ While he prayed by himself, and his disciples were with him, he asked them and said, What do the people say concerning me that I am?

19 They answered and said to him, John the Baptist; and others, Elijah; and others that one of the old prophets has risen.

20 He said to them, But you, what do you say that I am? Simon answered and said, The Messiah (the anointed one of God).

21 But he cautioned them, and warned them not to say this to anyone.

22 And he said to them, The Son of man must suffer a great many things, and he will be rejected by the elders and the high priests and the scribes, and they will kill him, and on the third day he will rise.

23 ¶ Then he said in the presence of everyone, He who wishes to come after me, let him deny himself, and take up his cross every day and follow me.

24 For he who wishes to save his life, shall lose it; but he who loses his life for my sake, he shall save it.

25 For how can a man be benefited, if he gain the whole world, but lose his own soul, or even weakens it?

26 For whoever is ashamed of me and of my words, the Son of man will be ashamed of him, when he comes with the glory of his Father, accompanied by his holy angels.

27 I tell you the truth, that there are men who stand here, who will not taste death, until they see the kingdom of God.

28 ¶ And it came to pass about eight days after these words, Jesus took Simon, and James and John, and went up into a mountain to pray.

29 And while he prayed, the appearance of his face was changed, and his clothes became white and dazzling.

30 And behold, two men were speaking with him, who were Moses and Elijah;

31 Who appeared in glory, and spoke concerning his departure which was to end at Jerusalem.

32 And Simon and those who were with him were heavy with sleep; and when they awoke they saw his glory, and the two men who stood with him.

33 And when they began to leave him, Simon said to Jesus, Teacher, it is better for us to remain here; and let us make three shelters, one for you, one for Moses, and one for Elijah; but he did not know what he was saying.

34 And when he had said these things, there came a cloud and overshadowed them; and they were frightened when they saw Moses and Elijah enter into the cloud.

35 And there came a voice out of the cloud, saying, This is my beloved Son; hear him.

Cf.dif. vv. 9:14, 18, 20, 22-23, 26, 31, 34.

36 And when the voice was heard, they found Jesus alone. And they kept silent, and in those days they did not tell any man what they saw.

37 ¶ And it came to pass the next day, as they came down from the mountain, they were met by many people.

38 And one of the men of that crowd cried out and said, O teacher, I beg you to have mercy on me. I have an only son,

39 And a spirit seizes him, and he suddenly cries out, and gnashes his teeth and foams; and it hardly leaves him when it has tormented him.

40 And I besought your disciples to cast it out; and they could not.

41 Jesus answered and said, O crooked and faithless generation, how long will I be with you, and preach to you? Bring your son here.

42 And as he brought him, the demon attacked him and convulsed him. And Jesus rebuked the unclean spirit, and healed the boy, and gave him to his father.

43 ¶ And they were all amazed at the greatness of God. And while every man wondered at everything which Jesus did, he said to his disciples,

44 Treasure these words in your ears; for the Son of man will be delivered into the hands of men.

45 But they did not understand this word, because it was hidden from them so that they might not know it; and they were afraid to ask him concerning this word.

46 ¶ Then a reasoning entered into their minds, as to who was the greatest among them.

47 But Jesus knew the reasoning of their heart, and he took a boy and made him stand by him.

48 And he said to them, Everyone who receives a little boy like this one in my name, receives me; and he who receives me receives him who sent me; for whoever is least among you, let him be great.

49 And John answered and said, Teacher, we saw a man casting out demons in your name; and we forbad him, because he did not come with us, as your follower.

50 Jesus said to them, Do not forbid; for he who is not against you is for you.

51 ¶ And it happened, when the days to go up on his journey were fulfilled, he set his face to go
to Jerusalem.

52 So he sent messengers ahead of him; and they went away and entered into a Samaritan village, to prepare for him.

53 But they did not receive him, because his face was set to go straight to Jerusalem.

54 When his disciples James and John saw it, they said to him, Our Lord, would you be willing that we command fire to come down from heaven and consume them, just as Elijah did?

55 He turned and rebuked them and said, You do not know of what spirit you are.

56 For the Son of man did not come to destroy lives, but to save. And they went to another village.

57 ¶ And while they were on the journey, a man said to him, My Lord, I will follow you wherever you go.

58 Jesus said to him, The foxes have holes, and the fowl of the sky a shelter; but the Son of man has no place even to lay his head.

59 He said to another, Follow me; but he said to him, My Lord, permit me first to go and bury my father.

60 Jesus said to him, Let the dead bury their own dead; but you go and preach the kingdom of God.

61 Another one said to him, I will follow you, my Lord; but permit me first to entrust my household to some one, and then come.

62 Jesus said to him, No man who puts his

Cf.dif. vv. 9:36, 39, 41-42, 44, 46, 49, 50-51, 53-54, 61.

hand on the plough handle, and looks back, is fit for the kingdom of God.

CHAPTER 10

AFTER these things, Jesus selected from his disciples seventy others, and he sent them two by two before his face, to every place and city to which he was to go.

2 And he said to them, The harvest is great, and the laborers are few; ask therefore the owner of the harvest, to bring out laborers to his harvest.

3 Go forth; behold, I send you as lambs among wolves.

4 Do not carry purses, nor bags, nor shoes; and do not salute any man on the road.

5 And to whatever house you enter, first say, Peace be to this house.

6 And if a man of peace is there, let your peace rest upon him; and if not, your peace will return to you.

7 Remain in that house, eating and drinking of what they have; for a laborer is worthy of his wages. Do not keep moving from house to house.

8 And into whatever city you enter, and they receive you, eat whatever they set before you;

9 And heal those who are sick in it, and say to them, The kingdom of God is come near to you.

10 But into whatever city you enter, and they do not receive you, go out into the street and say,

11 Even the sand of your city which cleaves to our feet, we shake it off to you; but know this that the kingdom of God has come near to you.

12 I say to you, that it will be much easier for Sodom in that day than for that city.

13 Woe to you, Chorazin! Woe to you, Bethsaida! If the mighty works which were done in you, had been done in Tyre and Sidon, perhaps they might have repented with sackcloth and ashes.

14 But, it will be easier for Tyre and Sidon at the judgment day than for you.

15 And you, Capernaum, which have exalted yourself up to heaven, you will be brought down to Sheol.

16 He who hears you hears me; and he who oppresses you oppresses me; and he who oppresses me oppresses him who sent me.

17 ¶ So the seventy whom he had sent returned with great joy, and they said to him, Our Lord, even the demons have submitted to us in your name.

18 He said to them, I saw Satan falling like lightning from heaven.

19 Behold, I give you power, to tread on snakes and scorpions, and over all the power of the enemy; and nothing shall harm you.

20 But do not rejoice in this that the demons submit to you; but rejoice because your names are written in heaven.

21 ¶ At that very hour, Jesus rejoiced in the Holy Spirit and said, I thank you, O my Father, Lord of heaven and earth, because you did hide these things from the wise and men of understanding, and did reveal them to children; yes, my Father, for so it was well pleasing in your presence.

22 And he turned to his disciples and said to them, Everything has been entrusted to me by my Father; and no man knows who is the Son, except the Father; and who is the Father except the Son, and to whomever the Son wishes to reveal him.

23 Then he turned to his disciples alone and said, Blessed are the eyes which see what you see.

24 For I say to you, that many prophets and kings desired to see what you see, and did not see it; and to hear what you hear, and did not hear it.

25 ¶ And behold, a scribe stood up to test him, and he said, Teacher, what shall I do to inherit eternal life?

Cf.dif. vv. 10:1-2, 6-7, 11-13, 15-16, 20-22, 25.

26 Jesus said to him, What is written in the law? how do you read it?

27 He answered and said to him, You must love the Lord your God with all your heart, and with all your soul, and with all your strength, and with all your mind; and your neighbor as yourself.

28 Jesus said to him, You said the truth; do this and you shall live.

29 But as he wanted to justify himself, he said to him, And who is my neighbor?

30 Jesus said to him, There was a man who went down from Jerusalem to Jericho, and the bandits attacked him, and robbed him, and beat him, and left him with little life remaining in him, and they went away.

31 And it chanced a priest was going down that road; and he saw him and passed on.

32 And likewise a Levite came and arrived at that place, and saw him and passed on.

33 But a Samaritan, as he journeyed, came where he was, and when he saw him, he had compassion on him.

34 And he came to him and bound up his wounds, and poured on them wine and oil; and he put him on his own ass, and brought him to the inn, and took care of him.

35 And in the morning, he took out two pennies and gave them to the innkeeper, and said to him, Take care of him; and whatever you spend more, when I return, I will give it to you.

36 Who therefore of these three, appears to you, became neighbor to him who fell into the hands of the bandits?

37 He said, The one who had compassion on him. Jesus said to him, You go also, and do the same.

38 ¶ And it came to pass while they were journeying, he entered into a village; and a woman named Martha received him into her house.

39 And she had a sister whose name was Mary, and she came and sat at the feet of our Lord, and listened to his words.

40 But Martha was busy with many household cares, and she came and said to him, My Lord, you do not seem to care that my sister has left me to serve alone? tell her to help me.

41 Jesus answered and said to her, Martha, Martha, you are worried and excited about many things;

42 But one thing is more necessary; and Mary has chosen the good portion for herself, which shall not be taken away from her.

CHAPTER 11

*A*ND it came to pass, while he was praying in a certain place, when he finished, one of his disciples said to him, Our Lord, teach us to pray, just as John also taught his disciples.

2 Jesus said to them, When you pray, say like this, Our Father in heaven, Hallowed be thy name. Thy kingdom come. Let thy will be done, as in heaven, so on earth.

3 Give us bread for our needs every day.

4 And forgive us our sins; for we have also forgiven all who are indebted to us. And do not let us enter into temptation; but deliver us from error.

5 And he said to them, Who is among you who has a friend, and he should go to him at midnight, and say to him, My friend, loan me three loaves,

6 For a friend has come to me from a journey, and I have nothing to set before him.

7 Would his friend from inside answer and say to him, Do not trouble me; the door is already locked, and my children are with me in bed; I cannot get up and give you.

8 I say to you, that if because of friendship he will not give him, yet because of his persistence, he will rise and give him as much as he wants.

9 I say to you also, Ask, and it shall be given to you; seek, and you shall find; knock, and it shall be opened to you.

10 For everyone who asks, receives; and he who seeks, finds; and he who knocks, it is opened to him.

11 For who is among you, a father, if his son should ask him bread, why, would he hand him a stone? and if he should ask him a fish, why, would he hand him a snake instead of a fish?

12 And if he should ask him for an egg, why, would he hand him a scorpion?

13 So if you, who err, know how to give good gifts to your children, how much more will your Father give the Holy Spirit from heaven to those who ask him?

14 ¶ And while he was casting out a demon from a dumb man, it came to pass when the demon went out, the dumb man spoke; and the people were amazed.

15 But some of the men among them said, This man casts out devils by Beelzebub, the prince of devils.

16 And others, tempting him, asked him for a sign from heaven.

17 But Jesus knew their thoughts, and said to them, Every kingdom which is divided against itself, shall be destroyed; and a house which is divided against itself shall fall.

18 And if Satan is divided against himself, how can his kingdom survive? And yet you say I am casting out devils through Beelzebub.

19 If I cast out devils through Beelzebub, by what do your sons cast them out? Therefore they will be your judges.

20 But if I cast out devils by the finger of God, then the kingdom of God is come near you.

21 When a strong man is armed and keeps watch over his courtyard, * his property is safe;

22 But if there should come one who is stronger than he, he will conquer him, and take away his armor in which he trusted, and divide his spoil.

23 He who is not with me is against me; and he who does not gather with me will scatter.

24 ¶ When an unclean spirit is gone out of a man, it goes away and travels in places where there is no water, to seek rest; and when it finds it not, it says, I will return to my own house from whence I came out.

25 And if it should come and find it warm and well furnished,

26 Then it goes away and brings seven other spirits worse than itself; and they enter and dwell there; and the end of that man will become worse than the beginning.

27 ¶ While he was saying these things, a woman out of the multitude lifted up her voice and said to him, Blessed is the womb which bore you, and the breasts which gave you suck.

28 He said to her, Blessed are they who hear the word of God and keep it.

29 ¶ And when the people were gathering, he began to say, This evil generation wants a sign; and no sign will be given to it, except the sign of the prophet Jonah.

30 For as Jonah was a sign to the Ninevites, so also will the Son of man be to this generation.

31 The queen of the south will rise up in judgment with the men of this generation, and condemn them; for she came from the far ends of the earth to hear the wisdom of Solomon; and behold, a greater than Solomon is here.

32 The men of Nineveh will rise up in judgment against this generation and condemn it; for they repented at the preaching of Jonah; and behold, a greater than Jonah is here.

33 ¶ No man lights a lamp and puts it in a hidden place, or under a basket, but on a lamp

* Lk. 11:21 - A Courtyard is often used to house cattle and sheep, the main property of an Oriental.
Cf.dif. vv. 11: 11, 13-14, 18, 21, 25, 33.

holder, so that those who enter may see its light.

34 The lamp of your body is your eye; when therefore your eye is clear, your whole body will also be lighted; but if it is diseased, your whole body will also be dark.

35 Take heed, therefore, lest the light which is in you be darkness.

36 If your whole body is lighted, and there is no part in it dark, the whole of it will give light, just as a lamp gives you light with its shining.

37 ¶ While he spoke, a Pharisee asked him to dine with him; and he entered and reclined.

38 When the Pharisee saw him, he was amazed because he did not first wash before dinner.

39 And Jesus said to him, Now you Pharisees clean the outside of the cup and the dish; but within you are full of extortion and iniquity.

40 O you shortsighted, did not he who made the outside also make the inside?

41 But give alms of what you have; and, behold, everything will be clean to you.

42 But woe to you Pharisees! who take tithes of mint and dill and every kind of vegetable, but overlook justice and the love of God. These were necessary for you to have done, and the same by no means to have left undone.

43 Woe to you Pharisees! for you love chief seats in the synagogues, and salutations in the streets.

44 Woe to you, scribes and Pharisees, hypocrites! for you are like graves that cannot be recognized, and men walk over them and know it not.

45 One of the scribes answered and said to him, Teacher, when you say these things, you reproach us also.

46 But he said, Woe also to you, scribes! for you lay heavy burdens on men, and you yourselves do not touch these burdens even with one of your fingers.

47 Woe to you! for you build the tombs of prophets, whom your fathers killed.

48 Therefore you are witnesses, and you approve the works of your fathers; for they killed them, and yet you build their tombs.

49 For this reason, the wisdom of God also said, Behold, I will send them prophets and apostles, some of them they will persecute and kill;

50 That the blood of all the prophets, which was shed since the creation of the world, may be avenged on this generation;

51 From the blood of Abel to the blood of Zacharias, who was killed between the temple and the altar; yes, I say to you, it will be avenged on this generation.

52 Woe to you, scribes! for you have taken away the keys of knowledge; you did not enter, and those who were entering you hindered.

53 When he had said these things to them, the scribes and the Pharisees were displeased, and they were enraged and criticized his words.

54 And they plotted against him in many ways, seeking to catch something from his mouth, so that they might be able to accuse him.

CHAPTER 12

WHEN a large number of people had gathered together, so as to tread on one another, Jesus began to say to his disciples, First of all, Beware you of the leaven of the Pharisees, which is hypocrisy.

2 For there is nothing that is covered, that will not be uncovered; and what is hidden that will not be known.

3 For whatever you have said in darkness will be heard in the light; and what you have whispered in the ears in the inner chambers will be preached on the housetops.

4 I say to you, my friends, Do not be afraid

of those who kill the body, and after that have nothing more they can do.

5 But I will show you of whom to be afraid; of him who after he has killed has the power to throw into hell; yes, I say to you, Fear him.

6 Are not five sparrows sold for two pennies? And yet not one of them is lost before God.

7 But so far as you are concerned, even the hairs of your head are all numbered; therefore fear not, because you are much more important than many sparrows.

8 I say to you, Whoever will acknowledge me before men, the Son of man will also acknowledge him before the angels of God.

9 But he who denies me before men, I will deny him before the angels of God.

10 And whoever says a word against the Son of man, will be forgiven; but he who blasphemes against the Holy Spirit will not be forgiven.

11 When they bring you to the synagogues before the leaders and authorities, do not worry how you will answer, or what you will say;

12 For the Holy Spirit will teach you at that very hour what you ought to say.

13 ¶ And one of the men from the crowd said to him, Teacher, speak to my brother to divide the inheritance with me.

14 Jesus said to him, Man, who appointed me a judge or a property divider over you?

15 And he said to his disciples, Beware of all covetousness, because life does not depend on abundance of wealth.

16 Then he told them a parable. The land of a rich man brought him a great many crops.

17 And he reasoned within himself and said, What shall I do, for I have no place to gather my crops?

18 So he said, I will do this; I will tear down my barns, and build them and enlarge them; and gather there all my wheat and my good things.

19 And I will say to myself, Myself, you have many good things stored up for many years; rest, eat, drink, and be happy.

20 But God said to him, O you shortsighted, this very night your life will be demanded of you; and these things which you have prepared, to whom will they he left?

21 Such is he who lays up treasures for himself, and is not rich in the things in God.

22 And he said to his disciples, Therefore I say to you, Do not worry for your life, what you will eat; nor for your body, what you will wear.

23 For the life is much more important than food, and the body than clothing.

24 Observe the ravens; for they do not sow nor reap, and they have no storerooms and barns; and yet God feeds them; how much more important are you than the fowls?

25 Who is among you, who by worrying, can add to his stature one cubit?

26 So if you are not able to do the smaller thing, why do you worry about the rest?

27 Observe the flowers, how they grow; for they do not toil nor do they spin; but I say to you, that not even Solomon with all his glory was covered like one of these.

28 And if God clothes in such fashion the grass of the field, which today is and tomorrow falls into the fireplace; how much more is he to you, O you of little faith?

29 So do not be anxious what you will eat, and what you will drink, and let not your mind be disturbed by these things.

30 For worldly people seek after all these things; and your Father knows that these things are also necessary for you.

31 But you, seek the kingdom of God; and all of these things shall be added to you.

32 Do not be afraid, O little flock; for your Father is pleased to give you the kingdom.

33 Sell your possessions and give them as alms; make for yourselves purses which do not wear out, and a treasure in heaven that

Cf.dif. vv. 12:6, 9, 14-15, 19-20, 22-26, 28-30.

does not run short, where the thief does not come near, and moth does not destroy.

34 For where your treasure is, there also will be your heart.

35 ¶ Let your girdle be fastened on your loins, and your lamps lighted.

36 And be like men who expect their master, when he will return from the wedding house; so that when he comes and knocks, they will immediately open the door for him.

37 Blessed are those servants, whom their master, when he comes, finds awake; truly I say to you, that he will gird himself and make them sit down, and come in, and serve them.

38 If he should come in the second or the third watch and find them so, blessed are those servants.

39 But know this, that if the master of the house knew at what watch the thief would come, he would have kept awake, and not allowed his house to be plundered.

40 Therefore, you also be ready; for the Son of man will come in that very hour which you do not expect.

41 ¶ Simon Peter said to him, Our Lord, do you speak this parable to us, or also to all men?

42 Jesus said to him, Who is the faithful and wise steward, whom his master will appoint over his household, to give supplies in due time?

43 Blessed is that servant, whom when his master comes will find him so doing.

44 Truly I say to you, that he will appoint him over all his wealth.

45 But if that servant should say in his heart, My master has delayed his coming; and begins to beat the servants and maidservants of his master, and then begins to eat and drink and get drunk;

46 The master of that servant will come in a day and at an hour that he does not expect or know; and he will severely punish him, and

place him with those who are not trustworthy.

47 And the servant who knows the wishes of his master, and does not make ready according to his wishes, will receive a severe beating.

48 But he who does not know, and does what is worthy of punishment will receive less beating. For to whomever more is given, of him more will be required; and to whom much is entrusted, more will be required of his hand.

49 ¶ I came to set the earth on fire; and I wish to do it, if it has not already been kindled.

50 I have a baptism to be baptized with; and I am oppressed until it is fulfilled.

51 Do you think that I have come to bring peace on earth? I say to you, No, but divisions;

52 For from henceforth there will be five in a house, who will be divided, three against two, and two against three.

53 For a father will be divided against his son, and a son against his father; a mother against her daughter, and a daughter against her mother; a mother-in-law against her daughter-in-law, and a daughter-in-law against her mother-in-law.

54 ¶ And he said to the people, When you see a cloud rise from the west, you immediately say, It will rain; and it is so.

55 And when the wind blows from the south, you say, It will be hot; and it is so.

56 O you hypocrites, you know how to discern the face of the earth and of the sky; how then is it that you do not discern this time?

57 Why do you not of yourselves judge what is right?

58 ¶ For when you go with your accuser to the district leader, while you are on the way give something and settle with him; otherwise he might take you to the judge, and the

judge will deliver you to the prison warden, and the prison warden will throw you in prison.

59 Truly I say to you, you will not come out from thence, until you pay the last penny.

CHAPTER 13

AT that time, there came some men and told him about the Galileans, whose blood Pilate had mingled with their sacrifices.

2 And Jesus answered and said to them, Do you think that those Galileans were greater sinners than all the Galileans, because this happened to them?

3 No; but I say to you, that all of you also, if you do not repent, you will perish in the same way.

4 Or those eighteen, upon whom the tower in Siloam fell, and it killed them; do you think that they were greater sinners than all the men who live in Jerusalem?

5 No, but I say to you, that unless you repent, all of you will perish like them.

6 ¶ And he spoke this parable; A man had a fig tree planted in his vineyard; and he came and sought fruit on it, and he did not find any.

7 So he said to the laborer, Behold, for three years, I have been coming and seeking fruit on this fig tree, and found none; cut it down; why should it waste the ground?

8 The laborer said to him, My lord, let it remain this year also, until I work it and fertilize it.

9 It might bear fruit; and if not, then you can cut it down.

10 ¶ While Jesus was teaching in one of the synagogues on the sabbath,

11 There was there a woman who was afflicted with rheumatism for eighteen years; and was bent down and could never straighten herself at all.

12 Jesus saw her, and called her, and said to her, Woman, you are loosened from your sickness.

13 And he laid his hand on her, and immediately she straightened up, and praised God.

14 But the leader of the synagogue answered with anger, because Jesus healed on the sabbath; and he said to the people, There are six days in which men should work; in those days you ought to come and be healed, and not on the sabbath day.

15 Jesus answered and said to him, O hypocrites, does not each one of you loosen his ox or his ass, from the manger, and go with it to give it drink?

16 This one is a daughter of Abraham, and behold, the adversary has bound her for eighteen years; was it not necessary for her to be loosened from this bond on the sabbath day?

17 And when he said these things, all who opposed him were ashamed; and all the people rejoiced over all the wonders which were done by his hand.

18 ¶ Jesus said, To what is the kingdom of God like? and to what shall I liken it?

19 It is like a grain of mustard seed, which a man took and cast into his garden, and it grew and became a large tree, and the fowls of the sky settled on its branches.

20 ¶ Again Jesus said, To what shall I liken the kingdom of God?

21 It is like the leaven which a woman took and buried in three measures of flour, until it was all leavened.

22 ¶ And he journeyed through the villages and cities, teaching, and going to Jerusalem.

23 A man asked him, Are there only a few who are to be saved? Jesus said to them,

24 Strive to enter in through the narrow door; for I say to you, that many will seek to enter in, and will not be able.

25 From the hour when the master of the house rises up and locks the door, you will

be standing outside and knocking at the door, and you will begin to say, Our Lord, our Lord, open for us; and he will answer and say, I say to you, I do not know you where you come from.

26 And you will begin to say, We have eaten and drunk in your presence, and you taught in our streets.

27 And he will say to you, I do not know you where you come from; depart from me, O you workers of iniquity.

28 There will be weeping and gnashing of teeth, when you see Abraham, and Isaac and Jacob, and all the prophets in the kingdom of God, but you thrown outside.

29 And they will come from the east and from the west, and from the south and from the north, and sit down in the kingdom of God.

30 And behold, there are some who are last, who will be first, and there are some who are first who will be last.

31 ¶ In that very day, some of the men of the Pharisees drew near and said to him, Get out and go away from here; because Herod wants to kill you.

32 Jesus said to them, Go and tell that fox, Behold, I cast out demons, and I heal today and tomorrow, and on the third day I will be through.

33 But I must do my work today and tomorrow, and I will leave the next day; because it is impossible that a prophet should perish outside of Jerusalem.

34 O Jerusalem, Jerusalem, murderess of prophets, and stoner of those who are sent to her! how many times I longed to gather your children together, as a hen which gathers her chickens under her wings, but you were not willing!

35 Behold, your house is left to you desolate; for I say to you, that you will not see me until you say, Blessed is he who comes in the name of the Lord.

CHAPTER 14

AND it came to pass when he entered the house of one of the leaders of the Pharisees to eat bread on a sabbath day, they watched him.

2 And there was a man before him, who had dropsy.

3 And Jesus answered and said to the scribes and Pharisees, Is it lawful to heal on the sabbath?

4 But they kept silent. So he took him, and healed him, and let him go.

5 And he said to them, Which one of you, if his son or his ox should fall into a pit on the sabbath day, would not immediately pull and bring him out?

6 And they could not answer him concerning this.

7 ¶ And he spoke a parable to those who were invited there, because he saw them choosing places among the front seats.

8 When you are invited of a man to a banquet house, do not go and sit in the front seat; it might be that a more honorable man than you is invited there;

9 And then he who has invited you and him will come, and say to you, Give the place to him; and you will be embarrassed when you get up and take a lower seat.

10 But when you are invited, go and sit at the lower end, so that when he who has invited you comes, he will say to you, My friend, go up and sit higher; and you will have glory before all who sit with you.

11 For whoever exalts himself will be humbled; and whoever humbles himself will be exalted.

12 He also said to him who had invited him, When you give a dinner or a supper, do not invite your friends, nor your brothers, nor your relatives, nor your rich neighbors; they might probally invite you, and you will be repaid for this.

13 But when you give a reception, invite the poor, the maimed, the lame and the blind;

14 And you will be blessed; for they have nothing to repay you; for you will be repaid at the resurrection of the righteous.

15 When one of the guests heard these things, he said to him, Blessed is he who will eat bread in the kingdom of God.

16 Jesus said to him, A man gave a great supper, and invited many.

17 And he sent his servant at supper time to tell those who were invited, Behold, everything is made ready for you, come.

18 One and all, they began to make excuse. The first said to him, I have bought a field, and I am forced to go and see it; I beg you to excuse me for being called away.

19 Another said, I have bought five yoke of oxen, and I am just going to examine them; I beg you, excuse me for being called away.

20 Another said, I have just taken a wife, and therefore I cannot come.

21 And the servant came and told his master these things. Then the master of the house was angry, and said to his servant, Go out quickly to the streets and lanes of the city, and bring in here the poor, the afflicted, the maimed and the blind.

22 And the servant said, My Lord, it has been done as you commanded, and yet there is more room.

23 Then the master said to his servant, Go out to the highways and hedges, and urge them to come in so that my house may be filled.

24 For I say to you, that not one of those men who were invited shall taste of my supper.

25 ¶ And while many people were going with him, he turned and said to them,

26 He who comes to me and does not put aside his father, and his mother, and his brothers, and his sisters, and his wife, and his children, and even his own life, he cannot be a disciple to me.

27 And he who does not take up his cross and follow me, cannot be a disciple to me.

28 For which of you, who wishes to build a tower, does not at first sit down and consider its cost, to see if he has enough to finish it?

29 Lest after he has laid the foundation, he is not able to finish it, and all who see it will mock him,

30 Saying, This man began to build, but he was not able to finish.

31 Or which king, who goes to war to fight against a king equal to him, would not at first reason, whether he is able with ten thousand to meet the one who is coming against him with twenty thousand?

32 And if not, while he is far away from him, sends envoys and seeks peace.

33 So every man of you, who would not leave all his possessions, cannot be a disciple to me.

34 Salt is good; but if the salt lose its savor, with what can it be salted?

35 It is good neither for the ground nor for fertilizing; but it is thrown out. He who has ears to hear let him hear.

CHAPTER 15

*T*HEN the publicans and sinners drew near to him to hear him.

2 And the scribes and Pharisees murmured, saying, He receives even the sinners and eats with them.

3 ¶ So Jesus told them this parable,

4 What man among you has one hundred sheep, and if one of them should get lost, would he not leave the ninety and nine in the open, and go in search of the one which is lost, until he finds it?

5 And when he finds it he rejoices, and he takes it on his shoulders.

6 And he comes to his house, and invites his friends and neighbors, and says to them, Rejoice with me, for I have found my sheep

Cf.dif. vv. 14:18, 23, 26, 31, 35.

which was lost.

7 I say to you, that such will be the joy in heaven over one sinner who repents, than over ninety and nine righteous, who need no repentance.

8 ¶ Or what woman who has ten coins, and should lose one of them, would not light a lamp and sweep the house, and search for it carefully, until she finds it?

9 And when she finds it, she calls her women friends and neighbors, and says to them, Rejoice with me, for I have found my coin which was lost.

10 I say to you, that such will be the joy before the angels of God over one sinner who repents.

11 ¶ And Jesus said to them again, A man had two sons;

12 And his younger son said to him, My father, give me the portion, which is coming to me from your house. And he divided to them his possessions.

13 And after a few days, his younger son gathered everything that was his share, and went to a far-away country, and there he scattered his wealth in extravagant living.

14 And when all he had was gone, there was a severe famine in that country; and he began to be in need.

15 So he went and got acquainted with one of the men of the city of that country; and he sent him to the field to feed the swine.

16 And he craved to fill his stomach with the husks that the swine were eating; and yet no man would give him.

17 And when he came to himself, he said, How many hired workers are now in my father's house, who have plenty of bread, and I am here perishing with hunger!

18 I will rise and go to my father, and say to him, My father, I have sinned before heaven, and before you;

19 And I am no longer worthy to be called

your son; just make me like one of your hired workers.

20 And he rose up and came to his father. And while he was yet at a distance, his father saw him, and had compassion on him, and he ran and fell on his neck and kissed him.

21 And his son said to him, My father, I have sinned before heaven and before you, and I am not worthy to be called your son.

22 But his father said to his servants, Bring the best robe and put it on him, and put a ring on his hand, and shoes on his feet;

23 And bring and kill the fat ox, and let us eat and be merry;

24 For this my son was dead, and has come to life; he was lost and is found. And they began to be merry.

25 But his elder son was in the field; and as he came near the house, he heard the voice of the singing of many.

26 And he called one of the boys, and asked him what it was all about.

27 He said to him, Your brother has come; and your father has killed the fat ox, because he received him safe and well.

28 And he became angry and would not go in; so his father came out and besought him.

29 But he said to his father, Behold, how many years I have served you, and I never disobeyed your commandment; and yet you never gave me even a kid, that I might make merry with my friends.

30 But for this son of yours, after he had wasted your wealth with harlots and come back, you have killed the fat ox.

31 His father said to him, My son, you are always with me, and everything which is mine is yours.

32 It was right for us to make merry and rejoice; for this your brother was dead and has come to life; and was lost and is found.

Cf.dif. vv. 15:8, 12-13, 15, 23, 30.

CHAPTER 16

AND he spoke a parable to his dis ciples, There was a rich man, who had a steward; and they accused him that he was wasting his wealth.

2 So his master called him and said to him, What is this that I hear concerning you? Give me an account of your stewardship; for no longer can you be a steward for me.

3 Then the steward said to himself, What will I do? for my lord will take away from me the stewardship? I cannot dig, and I am ashamed to beg.

4 Now I know what I will do, so that when I leave the stewardship, they will receive me in their houses.

5 And he called his lord's debtors, one by one, and said to the first, How much do you owe my lord?

6 He said to him, A hundred pounds of butter. He said to him, Take your note, sit down quickly, and write fifty pounds.

7 And he said to another, And you, what do you owe to my lord? He said to him, One hundred bushels of wheat. He said to him, Take your note, and sit down and write eighty bushels.

8 And the lord praised the unjust steward because he had done wisely; for the children of this world are wiser in their generation than the children of light.

9 And I also say, use this earthly wealth, however acquired, to make friends so that when it is gone, they will receive you and you will have everlasting habitation.

10 He who is faithful with little, is also faithful with much; and he who is dishonest with little, is also dishonest with much.

11 If therefore, you are not faithful with the wealth of iniquity, who will believe that there is any truth in you?

12 And if you are not found faithful with that which is not your own, who will give you that which is your own?

13 No servant can serve two masters; for either he will hate the one and like the other; or he will honor one and despise the other. You cannot serve God and mammon (wealth).

14 ¶ When the Pharisees heard all these things, because they loved money, they ridiculed him.

15 But Jesus said to them, You are the ones who make yourselves righteous before men; but God knows your hearts. For what is highly esteemed among men is disgusting in the presence of God.

16 The law and prophets were until John; from that time the kingdom of God is preached, and everyone presses to enter into it.

17 It is easier for heaven and earth to pass away than for one letter of the law to pass away.

18 He who divorces his wife and marries another commits adultery; and he who marries the one who is separated commits adultery.

19 ¶ There was a rich man, who used to wear purple and fine linen, and every day he made merry very lavishly.

20 And there was a poor man named Lazarus, who was laid down at that rich man's door, afflicted with boils;

21 He longed to fill his stomach with the crumbs that fell from the rich man's tray; the dogs also came and licked his boils.

22 Now it happened that the poor man died, and the angels carried him into Abraham's bosom; and the rich man also died and was buried.

23 And while he was tormented in Sheol, he lifted up his eyes from a distance, and saw Abraham, with Lazarus in his bosom.

24 And he called in a loud voice and said, O my father Abraham, have mercy on me, and send Lazarus to dip his finger in water and wet my tongue; for I am tormented in this flame.

Cf.dif. vv. 16:5-6, 9-11, 13-14, 16-18, 20-21.

25 Abraham said to him, My son, remember you received your pleasures when you were living, and Lazarus his hardships; and behold now he is comfortable here, and you are suffering.

26 Besides all these things, a great gulf is fixed between us and you; so that those who wish to cross over from here to you cannot, neither from there to cross over to us.

27 He said to him, If that is so, I beseech you, O my father, to send him to my father's house;

28 For I have five brothers; let him go and testify to them, so that they may not also come to this place of torment.

29 Abraham said to him, They have Moses and the prophets; * let them hear them.

30 But he said to him, No, my father Abraham; but if only a man from the dead go to them, they will repent.

31 Abraham said to him, If they will not hear Moses and the prophets, neither will they believe even if a man should rise from the dead.

CHAPTER 17

AND Jesus said to his disciples, It is impossible but that offences should come; but woe to him by whose hand they come!

2 It were better for him that an ass' millstone were hanged on his neck, and he thrown into the sea, than cause one of these little ones to stumble.

3 ¶ Beware among yourselves. If your brother should sin, rebuke him; and if he repents, forgive him.

4 And if he should offend you seven times in a day, and seven times in a day turn to you and say, I repent; forgive him.

5 ¶ And the apostles said to our Lord, Increase our faith.

6 He said to them, If you have faith, even as a grain of mustard seed, you could say to this mulberry tree, Be uprooted and planted in the sea; it would obey you.

7 ¶ Now which of you has a servant who ploughs or feeds sheep, and if he should come from the field, would say to him, Enter in and sit down?

8 But he will rather say to him, Prepare something that I may have my supper, and gird yourself and serve me until I eat and drink; and then you also can eat and drink.

9 Why, will that servant receive praise, because he did what he was commanded to do? I do not think so.

10 Even you also, when you have done all the things which are commanded you, say, We are idle servants; we have only done what was our duty to do.

11 ¶ And it came to pass, while Jesus was going to Jerusalem, he passed through Samaritan territory which is towards Galilee.

12 And when he drew near to enter a village, he was met by ten lepers, and they stood afar off;

13 And they lifted their voices saying, O Jesus, our Master, have mercy on us.

14 And when he saw them he said to them, Go, show yourselves to the priests; and while they were going, they were cleansed.

15 But one of them, when he saw that he was cleansed, turned back, and with a loud voice praised God.

16 And he fell on his face at the feet of Jesus, thanking him; and this one was a Samaritan.

17 Jesus answered and said, Were there not ten who were cleansed? where are the nine?

18 Why did they separate themselves so as not to come and give praise to God, except

---

* Lk. 6:29- That is, the books of Moses and the prophets.

this man who is of a strange people?

19 And he said to him, Arise, go, your faith has healed you.

20 ¶ When some of the Pharisees asked Jesus, when the kingdom of God would come, he answered and said to them, The kingdom of God does not come by observation.

21 Neither will they say, Behold, it is here! or, behold, it is there! for behold, the kingdom of God is within you.

22 And he said to his disciples, The days will come when you will covet to see one of the days of the Son of man, and you will not see it.

23 And if they should say to you, Behold, he is here! and behold, he is there! do not go.

24 For just as the lightning flashes from the sky, and all under the sky is lightened, such will be the day of the Son of man.

25 But first he must suffer a great many things, and be rejected by this generation.

26 Just as it happened in the days of Noah, such will it be in the days of the Son of man.

27 For they were eating and drinking, and marrying women, and giving in marriage, until the day when Noah entered the ark, and the flood came, and destroyed every man.

28 And again, just as it happened in the days of Lot; they were eating and drinking, and buying and selling, and planting and building;

29 But in the day when Lot went out of Sodom, the Lord sent down a rain of fire and sulphur from heaven, and destroyed them all.

30 Such will it be in the day when the Son of man appears.

31 In that day, he who is on the roof and his clothes in the house, will not come down to take them; and he who is in the field will not return back.

32 Just remember Lot's wife.

33 He who desires to save his life shall lose it; and he who loses his life shall save it.

34 I say to you that in that very night two will be in one bed; one will be taken away, and the other left.

35 And two women will be grinding together; one will be taken away, and the other left.

36 Two will be in the field; one will be taken, and the other left.

37 They answered and said to him, Our Lord, to what place? He said to them, Wherever the corpse is, there will the eagles gather.

CHAPTER 18

HE also spake to them a parable, that they should pray always and not get weary.

2 There was a judge in a city, who did not fear God, and had no regard for men.

3 There was a widow in that city, and she used to come to him, saying, Avenge me of my accuser.

4 And he would not for a long time; but afterwards he said within himself, Though I am not afraid of God, and have no regard for men;

5 Yet because this widow troubles me, I will avenge her, so that she may not keep coming and annoy me.

6 Then our Lord said, Hear what the unjust judge said.

7 Would not God avenge his chosen ones much more, who call upon him day and night, though he has patience with them?

8 I say to you, he will avenge them promptly. But when the Son of man comes, will he find faith on the earth?

9 ¶ And he said this parable against the men who relied upon themselves that they were righteous, and despised every man.

10 Two men went up to the temple to pray; one a Pharisee, and the other a publican.

11 And the Pharisee stood by himself, and prayed thus: O God, I thank thee, that I am not like the rest of men, extortioners, grafters, adulterers, and not like this publican.

Cf.dif. vv. 17:24, 30, 37.

12 But I fast twice a week, and I give tithes on everything I earn.

13 But the publican stood afar off, and he would not even lift up his eyes to heaven, but smote his breast, saying, O God, be merciful to me, I am a sinner.

14 I say to you, that this man went down to his house more righteous than the Pharisee. For everyone who exalts himself will be humbled; and everyone who humbles himself will be exalted.

15 ¶ They brought to him also little boys, that he might touch them; and his disciples saw them and rebuked them.

16 But Jesus called them, and said to them, Permit the children to come to me, and do not stop them; for the kingdom of heaven is for those who are like these.

17 Truly I say to you, He who will not receive the kingdom of God like a little boy will never enter into it.

18 And one of the leaders asked him and said to him, O good Teacher, what shall I do to inherit life everlasting?

19 Jesus said to him, Why do you call me good? there is no one good, except one, that is God.

20 You know the commandments: You shall not kill; You shall not commit adultery; You shall not steal; You shall not bear false witness; Honor your father and your mother.

21 He said to him, All these I have obeyed from my boyhood.

22 When Jesus heard it, he said to him, You lack one thing; go, sell everything you have, and give it to the poor, and you will have a treasure in heaven; and come and follow me.

23 But when he heard these things, he felt sad, because he was very rich.

24 And when Jesus saw that he felt sad, he said, How difficult it is for those who have wealth to enter into the kingdom of God!

25 It is easier for a rope to go through the eye of a needle, than for a rich man to enter into the kingdom of God.

26 Those who heard it said to him, Who then can be saved?

27 But Jesus said, Those things which are impossible to men are possible to God.

28 Simon Peter said to him, Behold we have left everything and followed you.

29 Jesus said to him, Truly I say to you, that there is no man who leaves houses, or parents, or brothers, or wife, or children for the sake of the kingdom of God,

30 Who will not receive many times more at this time, and in the world to come life everlasting.

31 ¶ Then Jesus took the twelve and said to them, Behold, we are going up to Jerusalem, and all things which are written by the prophets concerning the Son of man will be fulfilled.

32 For he will be delivered to the Gentiles, and they will mock him, and spit in his face.

33 And they will scourge him, and curse him, and kill him; and on the third day he will rise again.

34 But they understood not one of these things; and this saying was hidden from them, and they did not know these things which were spoken to them.

35 ¶ And when he drew near Jericho, a blind man was sitting by the roadside and begging.

36 And he heard the voice of the people passing, and asked, Who is this?

37 They said to him, Jesus the Nazarene is passing.

38 And he cried and said, O Jesus, son of David, have mercy on me.

39 And those who were going before Jesus rebuked him, to keep quiet; but he cried the more, O son of David, have mercy on me.

40 So Jesus stood still, and commanded to call him to him; and as he came near him he asked him,

41 And said to him, What do you wish me to do for you? He answered and said, My

Lord, that I may see.

42 And Jesus said to him, See; your faith has healed you.

43 And he saw immediately, and followed him, and praised God; and all the people who saw it, gave praise to God.

CHAPTER 19

AND when Jesus entered and passed through Jericho,

2 There was a man named Zacchaeus, who was rich and chief of the publicans.

3 And he wanted to see who Jesus was; but he could not because of the crowd, for Zacchaeus was small in his stature.

4 So he ran ahead of Jesus, and climbed up into a fig tree without leaves, that he might see him, because he was to pass that way.

5 When Jesus came to that place, he saw him and said to him, Make haste, come down, O Zacchaeus, for today I must remain in your house.

6 And he hastened, and came down, and welcomed him with joy.

7 Now when they all saw it, they murmured, saying, He has entered to stay in the house of a sinner.

8 But Zacchaeus rose up and said to Jesus, Behold, my Lord, half of my wealth I will give to the poor; and I will pay fourfold to every man from whom I have extorted.

9 Jesus said to him, Today life has come to this house, because he also is a son of Abraham.

10 For the Son of man came to seek and save that which was lost.

11 ¶ While they were listening to these things, he added and spoke a parable, because he was near Jerusalem, and they were expecting that the kingdom of God would appear at that very hour;

12 And he said, A great man of a noble family went to a far country to receive for him-self a kingdom, and return.

13 And he called his ten servants, and gave them ten pounds, and said to them, Do business until I come back.

14 But the people of his city hated him, and sent messengers after him, saying, We do not want him to rule over us.

15 And when he received the kingdom and returned, he commanded to call his servants, to whom he had given the money, that he might know what each one of them had gained in business.

16 The first one came and said, My lord, your pound has gained ten pounds.

17 He said to him, O good servant, because you are found faithful in a little, you will have charge over ten talents.

18 And the second came and said, My lord, your pound has gained five pounds.

19 He said to this one also, You also will have charge over five talents.

20 And another one came and said, My lord, here is your pound which was with me, which I kept laid up in a purse.

21 For I was afraid of you, because you are a harsh man; you pick up what you have not laid down, and you reap what you have not sown.

22 He said to him, I will judge you from your own mouth, O wicked servant. You knew me that I am a harsh man, and pick up what I have not laid down, and reap what I have not sown.

23 Why then did you not give my money to the exchange, so that when I came I could demand it with its interest?

24 And he said to those who stood in his presence, Take away the pound from him, and give it to him who has ten pounds.

25 They said to him, Our lord, he has already with him ten pounds.

26 He said to them, I say to you, to everyone who has shall be given; and from him who

Cf.dif. vv. 19:4, 8-9, 11, 17, 19-20, 23.

has not, even that which he has will be taken away from him.

27 But those my enemies, who were not willing that I should rule over them, bring them here, and kill them before me.

28 ¶ And when Jesus had said these things, he went forward to go to Jerusalem.

29 And when he arrived at Bethphage and Bethany, on the side of the mountain which is called the Home of Olives, he sent two of his disciples,

30 And he said to them, Go to the village which is in front of us; and when you enter it you will find a colt tied up, on which no man has ever ridden; untie it and bring it.

31 And if any man should ask you, Why do you untie it? tell him this: Our lord needs it.

32 And those who were sent went away, and found just as he had told them.

33 And as they were untying the colt, its owners said to them, Why do you untie the colt?

34 And they said to them, Our Lord needs it.

35 And they brought it to Jesus; and they put their garments on the colt, and they set Jesus on it.

36 And as he went on, they spread their garments on the road.

37 And when he came near to the descent of the Mount of the Home of Olives, the whole multitude of the disciples began to rejoice, praising God with a loud voice, for all the miracles which they had seen,

38 Saying, Blessed is the king who comes in the name of the Lord; peace in heaven and glory in the highest.

39 But some of the men of the Pharisees who were in the multitude said to him, Teacher, rebuke your disciples.

40 He said to them, I say to you, that if these should keep silent, the stones would cry out.

41 ¶ And when he drew near and saw the city, he wept over it;

42 And he said, If you had only known those who are concerned in your peace, even in this your day! but now they are hidden from your eyes.

43 But the days will come to you, when your enemies will surround you, and oppress you from every place,

44 And will overthrow you, and your children within you; and they will not leave in you a stone upon a stone; because you did not know the time when you were to be visited.

45 ¶ And when he entered the temple, he began to put out those who were buying and selling in it;

46 And he said to them, It is written, My house is the house of prayer; but you have made it a cave of bandits.

47 And he taught every day in the temple. But the high priests and the scribes and the elders of the people sought to get rid of him;

48 But they were not able to find what to do to him; for all the people hung around him to hear him.

CHAPTER 20

AND it came to pass on one of the days, while he was teaching the people and preaching in the temple, the high priests and the scribes with the elders rose up against him.

2 And they said to him, Tell us by what authority you do these things, and who gave you this authority?

3 Jesus answered and said to them, I will also ask you a word, and you tell me;

4 The baptism of John, was it from heaven or from men?

5 And they reasoned with themselves, saying, If we should say from heaven, he will say to us, Why then did you not believe him?

6 And if we should say from men, all the people will stone us; for they regard John as a prophet.

7 So they said to him, We do not know whence it is.

8 Jesus said to them, Neither will I tell you by what authority I do these things.

9 ¶ And he began to say this parable to the people, A man planted a vineyard, and leased it to laborers, and went on a journey for a long time.

10 And at the season he sent his servant to the laborers to give him of the fruit of the vineyard; but the laborers beat him and sent him back empty.

11 And again he sent another of his servants; but they beat him also, and treated him shamefully, and sent him back empty.

12 And again he sent the third one; but they wounded him also, and threw him outside.

13 Then the owner of the vineyard said, What shall I do? I will send my beloved son; perhaps they will see him and feel ashamed.

14 But when the laborers saw him, they reasoned with themselves, saying, This is the heir; come, let us kill him, and the inheritance will be ours.

15 So they cast him out of the vineyard, and killed him. What therefore will the owner of the vineyard do to them?

16 He will come and destroy those laborers, and give the vineyard to others. And when they heard it, they said, This will never happen.

17 But he looked at them and said, What is it that is written, The stone which the builders rejected, the same became the cornerstone?

18 Whoever falls on that stone will be broken; and on whomever it falls it will scatter him.

19 The high priests and the scribes sought to lay hands on him that very hour; but they were afraid of the people; for they knew that he had spoken this parable against them.

20 ¶ So they sent spies disguised as righteous men, to ensnare him by a word, and to deliver him to the judge, and then to the authority of the governor.

21 So they asked him, and said to him, Teacher, we know that you speak and teach truthfully, and you do not discriminate between men, but you teach the way of God justly.

22 Is it lawful for us to pay head-tax * to Caesar or not?

23 But he understood their craftiness and said, Why do you tempt me?

24 Show me a penny. Whose image and inscription are on it? They said, Caesar's.

25 Jesus said to them, Give therefore to Caesar that which is Caesar's and to God what is God's.

26 And they were not able to get a word from him before the people; and they were amazed at his answer, and kept silence.

27 ¶ Then came to him some of the men of the Sadducees, those who say there is no resurrection; and they asked him,

28 Teacher, Moses wrote to us, that if a man's brother should die, and has a wife without children, let his brother take his wife and raise up offspring for his brother.

29 Now there were seven brothers; the first married and died without children.

30 The second married his wife, and he died without children.

31 And the third one married her again; and likewise the seven of them; and they died leaving no children.

32 And at last the woman also died.

33 Therefore at the resurrection to which one of them will she be a wife? for seven of them married her.

34 Jesus said to them, The sons of this world marry women, and women are given to men in marriage.

Cf.dif. vv. 20:13, 16, 18, 20-21, 34.

35 But those who are worthy of the other world, and the resurrection from the dead, neither take women in marriage nor are women given in marriage to men.

36 For they cannot die again, because they are like angels; and they are sons of God, because they are sons of the resurrection.

37 Now concerning the resurrection of the dead, even Moses pointed out; for he referred to it at the Bush when he said, The Lord God of Abraham, and the God of Isaac, and the God of Jacob.

38 God is not the God of the dead but of the living; for all live to him.

39 And some of the men of the scribes answered and said to him, Teacher, you have well said.

40 And they did not dare again to question him concerning anything.

41 ¶ And he said to them, How can the scribes say concerning the Christ, that he is son of David?

42 And yet David said in the book of Psalms, The Lord said to my Lord, Sit at my right hand,

43 Until I put down your enemies under your feet.

44 If, therefore David calls him my Lord, how then can he be his son?

45 ¶ And while all the people were listening, he said to his disciples,

46 Beware of the scribes, who like to walk in long robes, and love to be greeted in the streets, and the chief seats in the synagogues, and the high places at the banquets;

47 Those who embezzle the property of widows with the pretence that they make long prayers; they will receive a greater judgment.

CHAPTER 21

JESUS then looked at the rich men who were casting their offerings into the trea sury.

2 And he also saw a poor widow, who cast in two pennies.

3 And he said, Truly I say to you, that this poor widow has cast in more than every man.

4 For all these cast into the house of the offerings of God of their abundance; but she of her poverty cast in everything she had earned.

5 ¶ While some men were talking about the temple, that it was adorned with beautiful stones and gift offerings, Jesus said to them,

6 These things which you see, the days will come when not a stone will be left upon a stone, which will not be torn down.

7 And they asked him, saying, Teacher, when will these things happen? and what is the sign when these things are about to happen?

8 He said to them, Be careful that you may not be deceived; for many will come in my name, and say, I am the Christ; and the time is near; but do not follow them.

9 And when you hear of wars and revolutions, do not be afraid; for all these things must first come to pass; but the end is not yet.

10 For nation will rise against nation, and kingdom against kingdom.

11 And there will be great earthquakes in different places, and famines and plagues; and there will be alarming sights, and great signs will appear from heaven; and the winters will be severe.

12 But before all these things, they will lay hands on you, and persecute you, and de-

* Lk. 20:21- This tax was levied on every male, and is still resented in the Orient.

liver you to the synagogues and the prisons; and they will bring you before kings and governors for the sake of my name.

13 It will be to you for a testimony.

14 Treasure it in your heart, and do not try to learn what to answer.

15 For I will give you a mouth and wisdom, which all your enemies will not be able to withstand.

16 You will be delivered up even by your parents and brothers, and your relatives and friends; and they will put some of you to death.

17 And you will be hated by every man because of my name.

18 And yet not a hair of your head will be lost.

19 By your patience you will gain your souls.

20 But when you see Jerusalem surrounded by an army, then know that its destruction is at hand.

21 Then let those who are in Judaea flee to the mountain; and let those who are within it flee; and let those who are in the fields not enter into it.

22 For these are the days of vengeance, so that everything which is written must be fulfilled.

23 But woe to those who are with child, and to those who give suck in those days! For there will be great distress in the land, and wrath to this people.

24 And they will fall by the edge of the sword, and they will be taken captive to every country; and Jerusalem will be trodden under the feet of the Gentiles, until the time of the Gentiles comes to an end.

25 ¶ And there will be signs in sun and moon and stars; and on earth distress of the nations, and confusion because of the roaring of the sea;

26 And upheaval that takes life out of men, because of fear of what is to come on earth;

and the powers of the universe will be shaken.

27 Then they will see the Son of man coming in the clouds, with a large army and great glory.

28 But when these things begin to happen, have courage, and lift up your heads; because your salvation is at hand.

29 And he said to them a parable, Look at the fig tree and all the trees;

30 When they put forth leaves, you immediately understand by them that the summer is near.

31 Even so you also, when you see these things happen, know that the kingdom of God is near.

32 Truly I say to you, This generation will not pass away until all these things happen.

33 Heaven and earth will pass away, but my words shall not pass away.

34 ¶ But take heed to yourselves, that your hearts may not become heavy by extravagance, and drunkenness, and worries of this world, and that day come suddenly upon you.

35 For like a downpour it will entrap all those who dwell on the face of all the earth.

36 Therefore keep watch all the time and pray, so that you may be worthy to escape all these things which are to happen, and that you may stand before the Son of man.

37 ¶ During the day he taught in the temple; and at night he went out, and lodged in the mountain, which is called the Home of Olives.

38 And all the people came ahead of him to the temple, to hear him.

CHAPTER 22

NOW the feast of unleavened bread, which is called the passover, was at hand.

2 And the high priests and the scribes sought how to kill him; but they were afraid of the people.

Cf.dif. vv. 21:14-15, 19, 21-22, 24-26, 28, 34-35, 37.

3 ¶ But Satan had taken possession of Judas who is called of Iscariot, who was of the number of the twelve.

4 So he went away, and spoke with the high priests and the scribes and officers of the temple, about delivering him to them.

5 And they were glad and promised to give him money.

6 And he agreed with them, and sought an opportunity to deliver him to them in the absence of the people.

7 ¶ Then the day of unleavened bread came, on which it was the custom to kill the passover lamb.

8 So Jesus sent Peter and John, and said to them, Go and prepare the passover for us to eat.

9 They said to him, Where do you wish us to prepare?

10 He said to them, Behold, when you enter the city, you will meet a man carrying a skin full of water; follow him. And wherever he enters,

11 Say to the master of the house, Our Teacher says, Where is the guest room, where I may eat the passover with my disciples?

12 And behold, he will show you an upper room, large and furnished; there make ready.

13 And they went and found just as he had said to them; and they prepared the passover.

14 ¶ And when the time came, Jesus came and sat down, and the twelve apostles with him.

15 And he said to them, I have desired with desire to eat this passover with you before I suffer;

16 For I say to you, that henceforth, I will not eat it, until it is fulfilled in the kingdom of God.

17 And he took the cup and gave thanks and said, Take this, and divide it among yourselves.

18 For I say to you, I will not drink of the fruit of the vine until the kingdom of God comes.

19 ¶ And he took bread and gave thanks and broke it, and gave it to them and said, This is my body, which is given for your sake; this do in remembrance of me.

20 And likewise also the cup, after they had eaten the supper, he said, This is the cup of the new covenant in my blood, which is shed for you.

21 But behold, the hand of him who is to betray me is on the table.

22 And the Son of man will go, just as he has been destined; but woe to the man by whose hand he will be betrayed!

23 And they began to enquire among themselves, which one of them was to do this act.

24 ¶ There was also a dispute among them, as to who is the greatest among them.

25 Jesus said to them, The kings of the Gentiles are also their owners; and those who rule over them are called benefactors.

26 But not so with you; but he who is great among you, let him be the least, and he who is a leader be like a minister.

27 For who is greater, he who sits down or he who serves? Is it not he who sits down? but I am among you as one who serves.

28 You are those who have remained with me, throughout my trials.

29 And I promise you, just as my Father has promised me, a kingdom,

30 That you may eat and drink at the table in my kingdom; and you will sit on chairs, and judge the twelve tribes of Israel.

31 ¶ And Jesus said to Simon, Simon, behold Satan wants to sift all of you as wheat;

32 But I have made supplication for you that your faith may not weaken; and even you in time will repent, and strengthen your brethren.

33 Simon said to him, My Lord, I am ready with you, even for the prison and for death.

Cf.dif. vv. 22:3, 7, 10, 21-22.25-26, 29, 31-32.

34 Jesus said to him, I say to you, Simon, the cock will not crow today, until you have denied three times that you know me.

35 And he said to them, When I sent you out without purses, and without bags, and shoes, did you lack anything? They said to him, Not a thing.

36 He said to them, From now on he who has purses, let him take them, and the bag likewise; and he who has no sword, let him sell his robe and buy for himself a sword.

37 For I say to you, that this which is written must be fulfilled in me, He will be numbered among the wicked; for all the things concerning me will be fulfilled.

38 And they said to him, Our Lord, behold here are two swords. He said to them, That is enough.

39 ¶ And he went out and went away, as it was his custom, to the Mount of the Home of Olives; and his disciples also followed him.

40 And when he arrived at a place, he said to them, Pray that you may not enter into temptation.

41 And he separated from them, about the distance of a stone's throw, and he kneeled down, and prayed,

42 Saying, O Father, if you will, let this cup pass from me; but not as I will, but your will be done.

43 And there appeared to him an angel from heaven, to strengthen him.

44 And he was in fear, and prayed earnestly; and his sweat became like drops of blood; and he fell down upon the ground.

45 Then he rose up from his prayer, and came to his disciples, and found them sleeping because of distress.

46 And he said to them, Why do you sleep? rise and pray that you may not enter into temptation.

47 ¶ While he was still speaking, behold, a multitude, and he who is called Judas, one of the twelve, coming before them; and he drew near to Jesus and kissed him. For this was the sign he had given them, He whom I kiss, it is he.

48 Jesus said to him, Judas, do you betray the Son of man with a kiss?

49 When those who were with him saw what happened, they said to him, Our Lord, shall we smite them with swords?

50 And one of them struck the servant of the high priest, and cut off his right ear.

51 But Jesus answered and said, It is enough for the present. And he touched the ear of him who was wounded, and healed it.

52 And Jesus said to the high priests and the elders and the officers of the temple, who had come against him, Have you come out against me to arrest me with swords and staves, as if you were against a bandit?

53 I was with you every day in the temple, and you did not even point your hands at me; but this is your turn, and the power of darkness.

54 ¶ And they arrested him, and brought him to the house of the high priest. And Simon followed him afar off.

55 And they kindled a fire in the midst of the courtyard, and they sat around it; and Simon also sat among them.

56 And a young woman saw him sitting by the fire, and she looked at him and said, This man also was with him.

57 But he denied, and said, Woman, I do not know him.

58 And after a little while, another saw him, and said to him, You also are one of them. But Peter said, I am not.

59 And after an hour, another one argued and said, Truly, this man also was with him; for he is also a Galilean.

60 Peter said, Man, I do not know what you are saying. And immediately while he was still speaking, the cock crew.

Cf.dif. vv. 22:37, 42, 44, 47, 49, 51-53, 59.

61 And Jesus turned and looked at Peter. And Simon remembered the word of our Lord, that he said to him, Before the cock crows you will deny me three times.

62 And Simon went outside and wept bitterly.

63 ¶ And the men who held Jesus mocked him,

64 And they covered his head, and smote him on his face, saying, Prophesy, who has struck you.

65 And many other things they blasphemed and said against him.

66 ¶ As soon as it was daybreak, the elders and the high priests and the scribes gathered together, and brought him up to their council chamber.

67 And they said to him, If you are the Christ, tell us. He said to them, If I tell you, you will not believe me.

68 And if I ask you, you will not answer me nor release me.

69 From henceforth the Son of man will sit at the right hand of the power of God.

70 And they all said, Are you then the Son of God? Jesus said to them, You say that I am.

71 And they said, Why then do we need witnesses? for we have heard it from his own mouth.

CHAPTER 23

*T*HEN the whole company of them rose up, and brought him to Pilate;

2 And began to accuse him, saying, We found this man misleading our people, and forbidding to pay the head-tax to Caesar; and he says concerning himself that he is a King, even the Christ.

3 Pilate asked him and said, Are you the king of the Jews? He said to him, You say that.

4 Then Pilate said to the high priests and the people, I cannot find any fault against this man.

5 But they shouted and said, He has stirred up our people, teaching throughout Judaea, and beginning from Galilee even to this place.

6 When Pilate heard the name Galilee, he asked if the man was a Galilean.

7 And when he knew that he was under the jurisdiction of Herod, he sent him to Herod, because he was in Jerusalem in those days.

8 When Herod saw Jesus he was exceedingly glad, for he had wanted to see him for a long time, because he had heard many things concerning him; and he hoped to see some miracle by him.

9 And he asked him many words; but Jesus gave him no answer.

10 But the high priests and the scribes stood, and accused him bitterly.

11 And Herod and his soldiers insulted him, and mocked him, and dressed him in a scarlet robe, and sent him to Pilate.

12 And that day Pilate and Herod became friends with each other; for there was a long-standing enmity between them.

13 ¶ Then Pilate called the high priests and the leaders of the people,

14 And he said to them, You brought me this man, as if he were misleading your people; and behold, I have examined him before your own eyes, and I have found no fault in this man concerning all that you accuse him.

15 Not even has Herod; for I sent him to him; and behold, he has done nothing worthy of death.

16 I will therefore chastise him, and release him.

17 For there was a custom to release to them one at the feast.

18 But all the people cried out saying, Get rid of him, and release to us Bar-Abbas;

19 Who because of sedition and murder which had happened in the city, was cast into prison.

20 Again Pilate spoke to them, desiring to release Jesus.

21 But they cried out, saying, Crucify him, crucify him.

22 And he said to them the third time, What evil has he done? I have found nothing in him, worthy of death; I will therefore chastise him, and release him.

23 But they persisted with loud voices, and asked to crucify him. And their voice and that of the high priests prevailed.

24 Then Pilate commanded to have their request granted.

25 So he released to them the one who because of sedition and murder was cast into prison, whom they asked for; and he delivered Jesus to their will.

26 ¶ And while they took him away, they laid hold of Simon, a Cyrenian, who was coming from the field, and they placed the end of the cross on him, to carry it with Jesus.

27 And many people followed him, and the women who were mourning and wailing over him.

28 But Jesus turned to them and said, O daughters of Jerusalem, do not weep over me; but weep over yourselves, and over your own children.

29 For behold, the days are coming, in which they will say, Blessed are the barren, and the wombs that never gave birth, and the breasts that never gave suck.

30 Then they will begin to say to the mountains, Fall on us; and to the hills, Cover us.

31 For if they do these things with the green wood, what will be done with dry wood?

32 ¶ And there were coming with him two others, malefactors, to be put to death.

33 And when they came to a place which is called The Skull, they crucified him there, and the malefactors, one on his right and one on his left.

34 And Jesus said, O Father, forgive them, for they know not what they are doing. And they divided his garments and cast lots over them.

35 The people stood looking on. And even the leaders of the synagogue mocked him, and said, He saved others; let him save himself, if he is the Christ, the chosen one of God.

36 And the soldiers ridiculed him, as they came near him and offered him vinegar,

37 Saying to him, If you are the king of the Jews, save yourself.

38 There was also an inscription which was written over him, in Greek and Roman, and Hebrew, THIS IS THE KING OF THE JEWS.

39 ¶ Now one of the malefactors who were crucified with him, blasphemed against him, saying, If you are the Christ, save yourself and save us also.

40 But the other rebuked him, and said to him, Do you not fear even God, for you are also in the same judgment?

41 And ours is just, for we are paid as we deserve and as we have done; but he has done nothing wrong.

42 And he said to Jesus, Remember me, my Lord, when you come in your kingdom.

43 Jesus said to him, Truly I say to you today, you will be with me in Paradise.

44 ¶ Now it was about the sixth hour, and darkness fell upon the whole earth, until the ninth hour.

45 And the sun was darkened, and the door curtains of the temple were torn in the center.

46 Then Jesus cried with a loud voice and said, O my Father, into thy hands I commit my spirit. He said this and passed away.

Cf.dif. vv. 23:26, 31-34, 38, 41, 43, 45.

47 ¶ When the centurion saw what had happened, he praised God and said, Truly this was a righteous man.

48 And all the people who were gathered together to see this sight, when they saw what had happened, returned, beating their breasts.

49 And all the acquaintances of Jesus stood afar off, and the women who had come with him from Galilee, and they were beholding these things.

50 ¶ There was a man named Joseph the counsellor of Arimathaea, a city of Judaea, a good and righteous man.

51 He did not agree with their wishes and their actions; and he waited for the kingdom of God.

52 He went to Pilate and asked for the body of Jesus.

53 And he took it down and wrapped it in fine linen, and laid it in a hewn tomb, in which no one was ever laid.

54 This was a Friday, and the sabbath was approaching.

55 ¶ The women who had come with him from Galilee were near, and they saw the tomb, and how his body was laid.

56 And they returned and prepared spices and perfumes. And on the sabbath they rested, as it is commanded.

CHAPTER 24

AND on the first day of the week, early in the morning, while it was yet dark, they came to the tomb, and brought the spices which they had prepared; and there were with them other women.

2 And they found the stone rolled away from the tomb.

3 And they entered in, but they did not find the body of Jesus.

4 And it came to pass as they were confused about this, behold, two men stood above them, and their garments were shining;

5 And they were afraid, and bowed their faces to the ground; and they said to them, Why do you seek the living among the dead?

6 He is not here, he has risen; remember that he spoke to you while he was in Galilee,

7 Saying, that the Son of man had to be delivered into the hands of sinful men,, and be crucified, and rise again on the third day.

8 And they remembered his words.

9 And they returned from the tomb, and told all these things to the eleven and to the rest.

10 They were Mary of Magdala, and Joanna, and Mary the mother of James, and the rest who were with them, who told these things to the apostles.

11 And these words appeared in their eyes as delusions; and they did not believe them.

12 But Simon rose up and ran to the tomb; and he looked in and saw the linen laid by itself, and he went away wondering in himself concerning what had happened.

13 ¶ And behold two of them were going on that day to a village called Emmaus, about six miles from Jerusalem.

14 They were talking with each other concerning all these things that had happened.

15 And while they were speaking and asking each other, Jesus came and overtook them, and walked with them.

16 But the sight of their eyes was holden, so that they could not recognize him.

17 And he said to them, What are these words that you are discussing with each other, as you walk, and are sad?

18 One of them, named Cleopas, answered and said to him, Are you a stranger alone from Jerusalem, that you do not know what has happened in it in these days?

19 He said to them, What things? They said to him, About Jesus of Nazareth, a man who was a prophet, mighty in word and deed be-

Cf.dif. vv. 23:50-51, 54;   24:11-12, 15.

fore God and before all the people.

20 And the high priests and the elders delivered him up to the judgment of death, and they crucified him.

21 But we were hoping that he was the one to save Israel; and behold, it is three days since all these things happened.

22 And some of our women also amazed us, for they went early to the tomb;

23 And when his body was not found, they came, and said to us, We saw angels there, and they said that he is alive.

24 And some of our men also went to the tomb, and they found it so, as the women had said; but they did not see him.

25 Then Jesus said to them, O dull-minded heavy-hearted, slow to believe all that the prophets have spoken.

26 Did not Christ have to suffer all these things, and to enter into his glory?

27 And he began from Moses and from all the prophets, and interpreted to them from all the scriptures concerning himself.

28 And they drew near to the village, to which they were going; and he made them think that he was going to a far place.

29 But they urged him and said, Remain with us; because the day is spent and it is near dark. So he entered to stay with them.

30 And it came to pass, as he sat at meat with them, he took bread and blessed it, and broke it, and gave it to them.

31 And immediately their eyes were opened and they recognized him; and he was taken away from them.

32 And they said one to another, Were not our hearts heavy within us, when he spoke with us on the road, and interpreted the scriptures to us?

33 ¶ And they rose up that very hour and returned to Jerusalem; and they found the eleven gathered together, and those who were with them,

34 Saying, Truly our Lord has risen, and he has appeared to Simon.

35 And they also reported those things that happened on the road, and how they knew him as he broke the bread.

36 ¶ And while they were discussing these things, Jesus stood among them, and said to them, Peace be with you; it is I; do not be afraid.

37 And they were confused and frightened, for they thought they saw a spirit.

38 Jesus said to them, Why do you tremble? and why do thoughts arise in your hearts?

39 Look at my hands and my feet, that it is I; feel me and understand; for a spirit has no flesh and bones, as you see I have.

40 When he said these things, he showed them his hands and his feet.

41 And as they still did not believe because of their joy, and they were bewildered, he said to them, Have you anything here to eat?

42 They gave him a portion of a broiled fish, and of a honeycomb.

43 And he took it, and ate before their eyes.

44 And he said to them, These are the words which I spoke to you when I was with you, that everything must be fulfilled which is written in the law of Moses, and in the prophets, and in the psalms, concerning me.

45 Then he opened their mind to understand the scriptures.

46 And he said to them, Thus it is written, and it was right that Christ should suffer, and rise from the dead on the third day;

47 And that repentance should be preached in his name for the forgiveness of sins among all nations; and the beginning will be from Jerusalem.

48 And you are witnesses of these things.

49 And I will send upon you the promise of my Father; but you remain in the city of Jerusalem, until you are clothed with power from on high.

Cf.dif. vv. 24:20-21, 23, 25, 28, 31-32, 37, 39, 41, 46-47

50 ¶ And he took them out as far as Bethany, and he lifted up his hands and blessed them.
51 And it came to pass, while he blessed them, he parted from them, and went up to heaven.

52 And they worshipped him, and returned to Jerusalem with great joy;
53 And they were always in the temple, praising and blessing God.
Amen.

Completion of the Holy Gospel of Luke the Evangelist.

ܟܘܠ ܐܘܢܓܠܝܘܢ ܩܕܝܫܐ ܕܠܘܩܐ ܡܦܫܩܢܐ ܀

THE GOSPEL ACCORDING TO
ST. JOHN

❖ ܐܘܢܓܠܝܘܢ ܩܕܝܫܐ ܕܝܘܚܢܢ ❖

CHAPTER 1

*T*HE Word was in the beginning, and that very Word was with God, and God was that Word.

2 The same was in the beginning with God.

3 Everything came to be by his hand; and without him not even one thing came to be of what was created.

4 The life was in him, and the life is the light of men.

5 And the same light shines in the darkness, and the darkness does not overcome it.

6 ¶There was a man, sent from God, whose name was John.

7 He came as a witness to testify concerning the light, so that every man might believe by means of him.

8 He was not the light, but to testify concerning the light.

9 ¶ He was the true light, which lighteth every man who came into the world.

10 He was in the world, and the world was under his hand, and yet the world knew him not.

11 He came to his own, and his own did not receive him.

12 But those who received him, to them he gave power to become sons of God, especially to those who believed in his name;

13 Those who are not of blood, nor of the will of the flesh, nor of the will of man, but born of God.

14 And the Word became flesh, and dwelt among us, and we saw his glory, a glory like that of the firstborn of the Father, full of grace and truth.

15 John witnessed concerning him and cried and said, This is the one of whom I said, He is coming after me, and yet he is ahead of me, because he was before me.

16 And of his fulness we have all received, grace for grace.

17 For the law was given by Moses; but truth and grace came into being by Jesus Christ.

18 No man has ever seen God; but the first-born of God, who is in the bosom of his Father, he has declared him.

19 ¶ This is the testimony of John, when the Jews sent to him priests and Levites from Jerusalem to ask him, Who are you?

20 And he confessed and did not deny it; but he declared, I am not the Christ.

21 Then they asked him again, What then? Are you Elijah? And he said, I am not. Are you a prophet? And he said, No.

22 Then they said to him, Who are you? so that we may give an answer to those who sent us. What do you say concerning yourself?

23 He said, I am the voice of one crying in the wilderness, Straighten the highway of the Lord, as the prophet Isaiah said.

24 Those who were sent were from the Pharisees.

25 And they asked him and said to him, Why then do you baptize, if you are not the Christ, nor Elijah, nor a prophet?

26 John answered and said to them, I baptize with water; but among you stands one whom you do not know;

27 This is the one who comes after me, and is ahead of me, the one even the strings of

Cf.dif. vv. 1:1, 3, 5, 7, 10, 13, 15, 21, 25, 27.

whose shoes I am not good enough to untie.

28 These things happened in Bethany, at the Jordan crossing, where John was baptizing.

29 ¶ The next day John saw Jesus coming to him, and he said, Behold the Lamb of God, who takes away the sin of the world!

30 This is the one of whom I said, The man who comes after me is yet ahead of me, because he was before me.

31 And I did not know him; but that he might be made known to Israel, I came to baptize with water.

32 And John testified and said, I saw the Spirit descending from heaven like a dove, and it rested upon him.

33 And yet I did not know him; but he who sent me to baptize with water, said to me, The one upon whom you see the Spirit descending and resting, he is the one who will baptize with the Holy Spirit.

34 And I saw and testified that this is the Son of God.

35 ¶ The next day John was standing, with two of his disciples;

36 And he looked at Jesus while he walked, and said, Behold, the Lamb of God!

37 And when he said it, two of his disciples heard it; and they went after Jesus.

38 And Jesus turned around and saw them following him, and he said to them, What do you want? They said to him, Rabbi (Teacher), where do you live?

39 He said to them, Come, and you will see. And they came and saw where he stayed, and they remained with him that day; and it was about the tenth hour.

40 One of them who heard John and followed Jesus, was Andrew, the brother of Simon.

41 He saw his brother Simon first, and said to him, We have found the Christ.

42 And he brought him to Jesus. And Jesus looked at him and said, You are Simon the son of Jonah; you are called Kepa (a Stone).

43 ¶ The next day Jesus wanted to leave for Galilee, and he found Philip, and said to him, Follow me.

44 Now Philip was from Bethsaida, the city of Andrew and Simon.

45 Philip found Nathanael, and said to him, We have found that Jesus, the son of Joseph, of Nazareth, is the one concerning whom Moses wrote in the law and the prophets.

46 Nathanael said to him, Can anything good come out of Nazareth? Philip said to him, Come and you will see.

47 Jesus saw Nathanael coming to him and he said of him, Behold truly an Israelite, in whom there is no guile!

48 Nathanael said to him, Whence do you know me? Jesus said to him. Even before Philip called you, while you were under the fig tree, I saw you.

49 Nathanael answered, saying to him, Rabbi, you are the Son of God, you are the King of Israel.

50 Jesus said to him, Do you believe because I told you I saw you under the fig tree? you shall see greater things than these.

51 He said to him, Truly, truly, I say to all of you, that from now on you will see the heaven opened, and the angels of God ascending and descending to the Son of man.

CHAPTER 2

ON the third day there was a marriage feast in Cana, a city of Galilee; and the mother of Jesus was there.

2 And Jesus and his disciples were also invited to the marriage feast.

3 And when the wine decreased, his mother said to Jesus, They have no wine.

4 Jesus said to her, What is it to me and to you, woman? my turn has not yet come.

5 His mother said to the helpers, Whatever he tells you, do it.

6 And there were six stone jars placed there for the purification of the Jews, which could hold several gallons each.

7 Jesus said to them, Fill the jars with water; and they filled them up to the brim.

8 Then he said to them, Draw out now, and bring it to the chief guest of the feast. And they brought it.

9 And when the chief guest tasted the water that had become wine, he did not know whence it had come; but the helpers knew, who had drawn the water. Then the chief guest called the bridegroom

10 And said to him, Every man at first brings the best wine; and when they have drunk, then that which is weak; but you have kept the best wine until now.

11 This is the first miracle which Jesus performed in Cana of Galilee, and he showed his glory; and his disciples believed in him.

12 ¶ After this he went down to Capernaum, he and his mother and his brothers, and his disciples; and they remained there a few days.

13 ¶ And the Jewish passover was nearing; so Jesus went up to Jerusalem.

14 And he found in the temple those who were buying oxen and sheep and doves, and the money changers sitting.

15 And he made a whip of cord, and drove them all out of the temple, even the sheep and the oxen and the money changers; and he threw out their exchange money, and upset their trays;

16 And to those who sold doves he said, Take these away from here; do not make my Father's house a house of trading.

17 And his disciples remembered that it is written, The zeal for your house has given me courage.

18 The Jews answered and said to him, What sign do you show us, that you are doing these things?

19 Jesus answered and said to them, Tear down this temple, and in three days I will raise it up.

20 The Jews said to him, It took forty-six years to build this temple, and will you raise it up in three days?

21 But he spoke concerning the temple of his body.

22 When he rose from the dead, his disciples remembered that he had said this; and they believed the scriptures and the word which Jesus had said.

23 ¶ Now when Jesus was in Jerusalem at the passover, during the feast, a great many believed in him, because they saw the miracles which he did.

24 But Jesus did not entrust himself to them, because he understood every man.

25 And he needed no man to testify to him concerning any man; for he knew well what was in man.

CHAPTER 3

*T*HERE was there a man of the Pharisees, named Nicodemus, a leader of the Jews;

2 He came at night to Jesus and said to him, Rabbi, we know that you are a teacher sent from God; for no man can do these miracles that you are doing, except God is with him.

3 Jesus answered and said to him, Truly, truly, I say to you, If a man is not born again,* he cannot see the kingdom of God.

4 Nicodemus said to him, How can an old man be born again? can he enter again a second time into his mother's womb, and be born?

---

* Jn. 3:3 - "Born again" in Northern Aramaic means to change one's thoughts and habits. Nicodemus spoke Southern Aramaic and hence did not understand Jesus.

Cf.dif. vv. 2:6, 8-10, 15-17, 24-25; 3:3.

5 Jesus answered and said to him, Truly, truly, I say to you, If a man is not born of water and the Spirit, he cannot enter into the kingdom of God.

6 What is born of flesh is flesh; and what is born of the Spirit is spirit.

7 Do not be surprised because I have told you that you all must be born again.

8 The wind blows where it pleases, and you hear its sound; but you do not know whence it comes and whither it goes; such is every man who is born of the Spirit.

9 Nicodemus answered and said to him, How can these things be?

10 Jesus answered and said to, You are a teacher of Israel, and yet you do not understand these things?

11 Truly, truly, I say to you, We speak only what we know, and we testify only to what we have seen; and yet you do not accept our testimony.

12 If I have told you about earthly things and you do not believe, how then will you believe me, if I tell you about heavenly things?

13 No man has ascended to heaven, except he who came down from heaven, even the Son of man who is in heaven.

14 Just as Moses lifted up the serpent in the wilderness, so the Son of man is ready to be lifted up;

15 So that every man who believes in him should not perish, but have eternal life.

16 For God so loved the world, that he even gave his only begotten Son, so that whoever believes in him should not perish, but have eternal life.

17 For God did not send his Son into the world, to condemn the world; but that the world should be saved by him.

18 He who believes in him will not be condemned; and he who does not believe has already been condemned, for not believing in the name of the only begotten Son of God.

19 And this is the judgment, that light has come into the world, and yet men have loved darkness more than light, because their works were evil.

20 For every one who does detested things hates the light, and he does not come to the light, because his works cannot be covered.

21 But he who does truthful things comes to the light, so that his works may be known, that they are done through God.

22 ¶ After these things, Jesus and his disciples came to the land of Judaea, and he remained there with them, and baptized.

23 John also was baptizing at the spring of Aenon near to Salim, because there was much water there; and they came, and were baptized.

24 For John was not yet cast into prison.

25 ¶ Now it happened that a dispute arose between one of John's disciples and a Jew about the ceremony of purifying.

26 So they came to John and told him, Teacher, he who was with you at the Jordan crossing, concerning whom you testified, behold, he also is baptizing and a great many are coming to him.

27 John answered and said to them, No man can receive anything of his own will, except it is given to him from heaven.

28 You yourselves bear me witness that I said, I am not the Christ, but only a messenger to go before him.

29 He who has a bride is the bridegroom; and the best man of the bridegroom is he who stands up and listens to him, and rejoices greatly because of the bridegroom's voice; this my joy therefore is fulfilled.

30 He must become greater and I lesser.

31 For he who has come from above is above all; and he who is of the earth is of the earth, and he speaks of earthly things; but he who has come from heaven is above all.

32 And he testifies of what he has seen and heard, and yet no man accepts his testimony.
33 He who accepts his testimony, has set his seal that God is true.
34 For he whom God has sent, speaks the words of God; for God did not give the Spirit by measure.
35 The Father loves the Son, and has placed everything under his hand.
36 He who believes in the Son has eternal life; and he who does not obey the Son, shall not see life, but the wrath of God shall remain on him.

CHAPTER 4

WHEN Jesus knew that the Pharisees had heard he made many disciples, and was baptizing more people than John,
2 Though Jesus himself did not baptize, but his disciples;
3 He left Judaea and came again to Galilee.
4 He had to go through Samaritan territory.
5 Then he came to a Samaritan city, called Sychar, near the field which Jacob had given to his son Joseph.
6 Now Jacob's well was there; and Jesus was tired by the fatigue of the journey, and sat down by the well. It was about the sixth hour.
7 And there came a woman from Samaria to draw water; and Jesus said to her, Give me water to drink.
8 His disciples had entered into the city to buy food for themselves.
9 The Samaritan woman said to him, How is it? You are a Jew, and yet you ask me for a drink, who am a Samaritan woman? For Jews have no social intercourse with Samaritans.
10 Jesus answered and said to her, If you only knew the gift of God, and who is the man who said to you, Give me a drink; you would have asked him, and he would have given you living water.

11 The woman said to him, My lord, you have no leather bucket, and no deep well; where do you get the living water?
12 Why, are you greater than our father Jacob, who gave us this well, and he himself drank from it, and his sons and his sheep?
13 Jesus answered and said to her, Everyone who drinks of this water will thirst again;
14 But whoever drinks of the water which I give him, shall never thirst; but the same water which I give him shall become in him a well of water springing up to life everlasting.
15 The woman said to him, My lord, give me of this water, so that I may not thirst again, and need not come and draw from here.
16 Jesus said to her, Go and call your husband, and come here.
17 She said to him, I have no husband; Jesus said to her, You said well, I have no husband;
18 For you have had five husbands; and the one you now have is not your husband; what you said is true.
19 Then the woman said to him, My lord, I see that you are a prophet.
20 Our forefathers worshipped on this mountain; and you say the place where men must worship is in Jerusalem.
21 Jesus said to her, Woman, believe me, the time is coming, when neither on this mountain nor in Jerusalem they will worship the Father.
22 You worship what you do not know; but we worship what we do know; for salvation is from the Jews.
23 But the time is coming, and it is here, when the true worshippers shall worship the Father in spirit and in truth; for the Father also desires worshippers such as these.
24 For God is Spirit; and those who worship him must worship him in spirit and in truth.
25 The woman said to him, I know that the

Cf.dif. vv. 4:1, 4-5, 9, 11.

Messiah (Christ) is coming; when he is come, he will teach us everything.

26 Jesus said to her, I am he, who is speaking to you.

27 ¶ While he was talking, his disciples came, and they were surprised that he was talking with a married woman; but no one said to him, What do you want? or, What are you talking with her?

28 The woman then left her water jar, and went to the city and said to the men,

29 Come and see a man who told me everything which I have done; why, is he the Christ?

30 And the men went out of the city, and came to him.

31 ¶ During the interval his disciples begged him, saying, Teacher, eat.

32 But he said to them, I have food to eat, of which you do not know.

33 The disciples said among themselves, Why, did any man bring him something to eat?

34 Jesus said to them, My food is to do the will of him who sent me, and to finish his work.

35 Do you not say that after four months comes the harvest? behold, I say to you, Lift up your eyes, and look at the fields, which have turned white and have long been ready for the harvest.

36 And he who reaps receives wages, and gathers fruits to life everlasting; so that the sower and the reaper may rejoice together.

37 For in this case the saying is true, One sows and another reaps.

38 I sent you to reap that for which you did not labor; for others labored, and you have entered into their labor.

39 ¶ A great many Samaritans of that city believed in him, because of the word of that woman, who testified, He told me everything which I have done.

40 So when the Samaritans came to him, they begged him to stay with them; and he stayed with them two days.

41 And a great many believed in him because of his word;

42 And they were saying to the woman, Henceforth it is not because of your word that we believe him; for we ourselves have heard and know, that this is indeed the Christ, the Saviour of the world.

43 ¶ Two days later, Jesus departed thence and went to Galilee.

44 For Jesus himself testified, that a prophet is not honored in his own city.

45 When he came to Galilee, the Galileans welcomed him, for they had seen all the wonders he did at Jerusalem during the feast; for they also had come to the feast.

46 Then Jesus came again to Cana of Galilee, where he had made the water wine. And there was at Capernaum a servant of a king, whose son was sick.

47 This man heard that Jesus had come from Judaea to Galilee; so he went to him and asked him to come down and heal his son; for he was near death.

48 Jesus said to him, Unless you see miracles and wonders, you will not believe.

49 The king's servant said to him, My Lord, come down before the boy is dead.

50 Jesus said to him, Go, your son is healed. And the man believed the word that Jesus said to him and went away.

51 And as he was going down, his servants met him and brought him good news, saying, Your son is healed.

52 And he asked them, At what time was he healed? They said to him, Yesterday at the seventh hour, the fever left him.

53 And his father knew that it was at that very hour when Jesus told him, Your son is healed; so he himself believed and his whole household.

54 This is again the second miracle which Jesus did, after he came from Judaea to Galilee.

CHAPTER 5

AFTER these things there was a feast of the Jews; and Jesus went up to Jerusalem.

2 Now there was at Jerusalem a baptismal pool, which is called in Hebrew Bethesda, having five entrances.

3 And at these entrances a great many sick people were lying, the blind, the lame, and the crippled; and they were waiting for the water to be stirred up;

4 For an angel of God went down at a certain time to the baptismal pool and stirred up the water; and whoever went in first after the stirring of the water was healed of any disease he had.

5 A man was there who had been sick for thirty-eight years.

6 Jesus saw this man lying down, and he knew that he had been waiting for a long time; so he said to him, Do you wish to be healed?

7 The sick man answered and said, Yes, my Lord; but I have no man, when the water is stirred up, to put me into the baptismal pool; but while I am coming, another one goes in before me.

8 Jesus said to him, Rise, take up your quilt-bed, and walk.

9 And the man was healed immediately, and he got up and took his quilt-bed and walked. And that day was the sabbath.

10 ¶ So the Jews said to him who was healed, It is the sabbath; it is not lawful for you to carry your quilt-bed.

11 He answered and said to them, He who had healed me, he told me, Take up your quilt-bed, and walk.

12 And they asked him, Who is this man who said to you, Take up your quilt-bed, and walk?

13 But he who was healed did not know who he was; for Jesus was pressed by a large crowd which was at that place.

14 After a while, Jesus found him in the temple and said to him, Behold, you are healed; do not sin again, for something worse might happen to you than the first.

15 And the man went away and told the Jews, that it was Jesus who had healed him.

16 ¶ And for this reason the Jews persecuted Jesus and wanted to kill him, because he was doing these things on the sabbath.

17 But Jesus said to them, My Father works even until now, so I also work.

18 And for this the Jews wanted the more to kill him, not only because he was weakening the sabbath, but also because he said concerning God that he is his Father, and was making himself equal with God.

19 Jesus answered and said to them, Truly, truly, I say to you, that the Son can do nothing of his own accord, except what he sees the Father doing; for the things which the Father does, the same the Son does like him also.

20 For the Father loves his Son, and he shows him everything that he does; and he will show him greater works than these, so that you may marvel.

21 For just as the Father raises the dead and gives them life, even so the Son gives life to those whom he will.

22 For the Father does not judge any man, but he has entrusted all judgment to the Son;

23 So that every man should honor the Son, just as he honors the Father. He who does not honor the Son, does not honor the Father who sent him.

24 Truly, truly, I say to you, He who hears my word, and believes him who has sent me, has everlasting life; and he does not come

Cf.dif. vv. 5:2, 6, 13, 17-18.

before the judgment, but he passes from death to life.

25 Truly, truly, I say to you, The time is coming, and it is now already here, when the dead will hear the voice of the Son of God; and those who hear it will live.

26 For as the Father has life in himself, even so he has given to the Son also to have life in himself.

27 And he has given him authority to execute judgment also, for he is the Son of man.

28 Do not wonder at this; for the time is coming, when all those who are in the graves will hear his voice,

29 And they will come out; those who have done good works to the resurrection of life; and those who have done evil works to the resurrection of judgment.

30 I can do nothing of myself; but as I hear I judge, and my judgment is just; for I do not seek my own will, but the will of him who sent me.

31 If I testify concerning myself, my testimony is not true.

32 It is another one who testifies concerning me; and I know that the testimony which he testifies concerning me is true.

33 You sent to John, and he testified concerning the truth.

34 But I do not receive any testimony from men; but I tell you these things so that you may be saved.

35 He was a lamp which burns and gives light; and you were willing to delight in his light for a while.

36 But I have a greater testimony than that of John; for the works which my Father has given me to finish, the same works which I do, testify concerning me, that the Father has sent me.

37 And the Father who sent me has testified concerning me. But you have never heard his voice, nor seen his appearance.

38 And his word does not abide in you, because you do not believe in him whom he has sent.

39 Examine the scriptures, in which you trust that you have eternal life; and even they testify concerning me.

40 Yet you will not come to me, that you might have life everlasting.

41 I do not receive any praise from men.

42 But I know you well, that the love of God is not in you.

43 I have come in the name of my Father, and you do not receive me; if another should come in his own name, you will receive him.

44 How can you believe, when you accept praise one from another, but the praise from God only, you do not want?

45 Why, do you think that I will accuse you before the Father; there is one who will accuse you, even Moses, in whom you trust.

46 For if you had believed in Moses, you would also have believed in me; because Moses wrote concerning me.

47 If you do not believe his writings, how then can you believe my words?

CHAPTER 6

AFTER these things, Jesus went to the port of the sea of Galilee, at Tiberias.

2 And a great many people followed him, because they saw the miracles which he performed on sick people.

3 So Jesus went up to the mountain, and he sat there with his disciples.

4 And the feast of the passover of the Jews was at hand.

5 ¶ And Jesus lifted up his eyes, and saw a large crowd coming to him, and he said to Philip, Where can we buy bread that all these may eat?

6 He said this merely to test him; for he knew what he would do.

7 Philip said to him, Two hundred pennies

worth of bread would not be sufficient for them, even if each one should take a little.

8 One of his disciples, Andrew the brother of Simon Peter, said to him,

9 There is a boy here, who has with him five barley loaves and two fishes; but what are these for all of them?

10 Jesus said to them, Make all the men sit down. There was much grass in that place. So the males * sat down, five thousand in number.

11 And Jesus took the bread, and blessed it, and distributed it to those who were sitting down; likewise the fish also, as much as they wanted.

12 When they were filled, he said to his disciples, Gather up the broken pieces which are left over, so that nothing is lost.

13 And they gathered them up, and filled twelve baskets with broken pieces, which were left over by those who ate from five barley loaves.

14 ¶ Then the men who saw the miracle which Jesus performed said, Truly this is the prophet who is to come into the world.

15 ¶ But Jesus knew that they were ready to come and seize him to make him a king, so he departed to the mountain alone.

16 And when evening came, his disciples went down to the sea,

17 And entered into a boat, and were going to the port of Capernaum. And now it was dark, and Jesus had not yet come to them.

18 And the sea became rough, because a strong wind was blowing.

19 And they rowed about twenty-five or thirty furlongs, and they saw Jesus walking on # the sea; and as he drew towards their boat, they became afraid.

20 But Jesus said to them, It is I, do not be afraid.

21 So they wanted to receive him into the boat; but soon the boat reached the land to which they were going.

22 ¶ The next day, the multitude which stood waiting at the seaport saw no other boat there, except the boat in which the disciples had entered, and that Jesus had not entered the boat with his disciples.

23 But other boats had come from Tiberias, near the place where they had eaten bread, when Jesus blessed it.

24 And when the people saw that Jesus was not there, nor his disciples, they entered the boats and came to Capernaum, looking for Jesus.

25 And when they found him at the seaport, they said to him, Teacher, when did you come here?

26 Jesus answered and said to them, Truly, truly, I say to you, You seek me, not because you saw the miracles, but just because you ate bread and were filled.

27 Do not work for the food which perishes, but for the food which endures unto life everlasting, which the Son of man will give you; for this one God the Father has sealed.

28 They said to him, What shall we do to work the works of God?

29 Jesus answered and said to them, This is the work of God, that you should believe in him whom he has sent.

30 They said to him, What miracle do you perform that we may see and believe in you? What have you performed?

31 Our forefathers ate manna in the wilderness; as it is written, He gave them bread from heaven to eat.

---

* Jn. 6:10 - In that culture, women and children did not eat with men, nor were they counted.

\# Jn.6:19 - The Aramaic *al* means on or by. The disciples were going from Tiberias to Capernaum, and both cities were on the same side of the Sea of Galilee. See further ver. 21.

Cf.dif. vv. 6:17, 21-22, 25.

32 Jesus said to them, Truly, truly, I say to you, It was not Moses who gave you bread from heaven; but my Father gives you the true bread from heaven.

33 For the bread of God is he who has come down from heaven, and gives life to the 34 They said to him, Our Lord, give us this bread always.

35 Jesus said to them, I am the bread of life; he who comes to me shall never hunger; and he who believes in me shall never thirst.

36 But I have said to you, that you have seen me and yet you do not believe.

37 Everyone whom my Father has given me shall come to me; and he who comes to me, I will not cast him out.

38 For I came down from heaven, not merely to do my own will, but to do the will of him who sent me.

39 This is the will of him who sent me, that I should lose nothing of all that he has given me, but should raise it up at the last day.

40 For this is the will of my Father, that whoever sees the Son and believes in him, shall have life everlasting; and I will raise him up at the last day.

41 ¶ Now the Jews murmured against him, for he said, I am the bread which came down from heaven.

42 And they said, Is this not Jesus, the son of Joseph, whose father and mother we know? how can he say, I have come down from heaven?

43 Jesus answered and said to them, Do not murmur one with another.

44 No man can come to me, except the Father who sent me draw him; and I will raise him up at the last day.

45 For it is written in the prophet, They shall all be taught by God. Everyone therefore who hears from the Father and learns from him, will come to me.

46 No man can see the Father, except he who is from God, he can see the Father.

47 Truly, truly, I say to you, He who believes in me has eternal life.

48 I am the bread of life.

49 Your forefathers ate manna in the wilderness, and yet they died.

50 This is the bread which came down from heaven, that a man may eat of it and not die.

51 I am the living bread because I came down from heaven; if any man eats of this bread, he shall live forever; and the bread which I will give, is my body, which I am giving for the sake of the life of the world.

52 ¶ The Jews argued one with another, saying, How can this man give us his body to eat?

53 Jesus said to them. Truly, truly I say to you, Unless you eat the body of the Son of man, and drink his blood, you have no life in yourselves,

54 He who eats of my body, and drinks of my blood, has eternal life; and I will raise him at the last day.

55 For my body truly is the food, and my blood truly is the drink.

56 He who eats my body and drinks my blood, will abide with me, and I with him.

57 Just as the living Father sent me, and I am living because of the Father, so whoever eats me, will also live because of me.

58 This is the bread which came down from heaven; it is not like that manna which your forefathers ate and died; he who eats of this bread shall live forever.

59 These things he said in the synagogue, while he was teaching at Capernaum.

60 ¶ Many of his disciples who heard it said, This is a hard saying; who can listen to it?

61 Jesus knew in himself that his disciples were murmuring about this; so he said to them, Does this cause you to stumble?

62 What then if you should see the Son of man ascending to the place where he was before?

Cf.dif. vv. 6:40, 51-52, 54, 56-57.

63 It is the spirit that gives life; the body is of no account; the words which I have spoken to you are spirit and life.

64 But there are some of you who do not believe. For Jesus knew for a long while who were those who did not believe, and who was to betray him.

65 And he said to them, For this reason I have told you that no man can come to me, unless it is given to him by my Father.

66 ¶ Just because of this saying, a great many of his disciples turned away, and did not walk with him.

67 So Jesus said to his twelve, Why, do you also want to go away?

68 Simon Peter answered and said, My Lord, to whom shall we go? you have the words of eternal life.

69 And we have believed and known that you are the Christ, the Son of the living God.

70 Jesus said to them, Did not I choose you, the twelve, and yet one of you is Satan? *

71 He said it concerning Judas, the son of Simon Iscariot; for he was the one of the twelve who was going to betray him.

CHAPTER 7

AFTER these things Jesus travelled in Galilee; for he did not wish to travel in Judaea, because the Jews wanted to kill him.

2 ¶ Now the Jewish feast of the tabernacles was at hand.

3 And his brothers said to Jesus, Depart from here and go to Judaea, so that your disciples may see the works that you do.

4 For there is no man, who does anything in secret and yet wants it to become known. If you are doing these things, show yourself to the people.

5 For not even his own brothers believed in Jesus.

6 Jesus said to them, My time has not yet come; but your time is always ready.

7 The world cannot hate you; but it hates me, because I testify against it, that its works are evil.

8 You go up to this feast; I am not going just now to this feast, for my time is not yet come.

9 He said these things, and remained in Galilee.

10 But when his brothers had gone up to the feast, then he also went up, not openly, but as it were in secret.

11 ¶ The Jews were looking for him at the feast and said, Where is he?

12 And there was much murmuring among the people concerning him; for some said, He is good; and others said, No, but he just deceives the people.

13 But no man spoke openly about him, because of the fear of the Jews.

14 ¶ Now about the middle period of the feast, Jesus went up to the temple and taught.

15 And the Jews marvelled, saying, How does this man know reading, when he has not been instructed?

16 Jesus answered and said, My teaching is not mine, but his who sent me.

17 He who wills to do his will, he will understand if my teaching is from God, or if I am just speaking of my own accord.

18 He who speaks of his own accord seeks glory for himself; but he who seeks the glory of him who sent him, he is true, and there is no deception in his heart.

19 Did not Moses give you the law? and yet no one of you obeys the law. Why do you want to kill me?

20 The people answered, saying, You are crazy; who wants to kill you?

---

* Jn. 6:70 - The Aramaic *satana* (Satan) is derived from *sta* , which means to slide, to slip, or to miss the mark; and applies to one who causes these results.

Cf.dif. vv. 6:63, 70;   7:4, 7, 15, 18, 20.

21 Jesus answered and said to them, I have done one work, and all of you marvel.

22 Moses gave you circumcision, not because it is from Moses, but because it is from the forefathers; and yet you circumcise a man on the sabbath.

23 So if a man is circumcised on the sabbath day, that the law of Moses may not be broken; yet you murmur at me, because I healed a whole man * on the sabbath day?

24 Do not judge by partiality, but judge a just judgment.

25 ¶ Then some of the men of Jerusalem were saying, Is not this the man whom they want to kill?

26 And yet he speaks openly, but they say nothing to him. Perhaps our elders have found out that he is the Christ?

27 Howbeit we know whence he comes; but when the Christ comes, no man will know whence he comes.

28 ¶ Jesus then lifted up his voice as he taught in the temple, and said, You know me, and you know whence I come; and yet I have not come of my own accord, but he who sent me is true, whom you do not know.

29 But I know him; because I am from him, and he sent me.

30 So they wanted to seize him; and no man laid hands on him, because his time had not yet come.

31 But a great many of the people believed in him and said, When the Christ comes, why, will he do greater wonders than this man does?

32 The Pharisees heard the people talking about him; so they and the high priests sent soldiers to arrest him.

33 And Jesus said, I am with you just a short while, and I am going to him who sent me.

34 You will seek me, but you will not find me; and where I am you cannot come.

35 Then the Jews said among themselves, Where is he going, that we cannot find him? why, is he planning to go to the countries of the Gentiles, to teach the pagans?

36 What does this word mean which he said, You will seek me and you will not find me; and where I am you cannot come?

37 ¶ Now on the greatest day, which is the last day of the feast, Jesus stood and cried out and said, If any man is thirsty, let him come to me and drink.

38 Whoever believes in me, just as the scriptures have said, the rivers of living water shall flow from within him.

39 He said this concerning the Spirit, which they who believe in him were to receive; for the Spirit was not yet given, because Jesus was not yet glorified.

40 Many of the people who heard his words were saying, This man truly is a prophet.

41 Others were saying, He is the Christ; but others said, Is it possible that Christ should come from Galilee?

42 Does not the scripture say that Christ will come from the seed of David, and from Bethlehem, the town of David?

43 So the people were divided because of him.

44 And there were some men among them, who wanted to seize him; but no man laid hands on him.

45 And the soldiers returned to the high priests and the Pharisees; and the priests said to them, Why did you not bring him?

46 The soldiers said to them, Never a man has spoken as this man speaks.

47 The Pharisees said to them, Why, have you also been deceived?

---

* Jn. 7:23 - Circumcision affected only one part of the body. Jesus here healed the whole body; and so his work on the sabbath was more important than circumcision.

48 Why, have any of the leaders or of the Pharisees believed in him,

49 Except this cursed people, who do not know the law?

50 Nicodemus, one of them, who had come to Jesus at night, said to them,

51 Does our law convict a man, unless it first hears from him, and knows what he has done?

52 They answered and said to him, Why, are you also from Galilee? * Search and see that no prophet will rise up from Galilee.

53 So everyone went to his own house.

CHAPTER 8

*T*HEN Jesus went to the mount of Olives. 2 And in the morning he came again to the temple, and all the people were coming to him; and he sat down and taught them.

3 Then the scribes and the Pharisees brought a woman who was caught in adultery; and they made her to stand in the midst.

4 They said to him, Teacher, this woman was caught openly in the act of adultery.

5 Now in the law of Moses it is commanded that women such as these should be stoned; but what do you say?

6 They said this to tempt him, that they might have a cause to accuse him. While Jesus was bent down, he was writing on the ground.

7 When they were through questioning him, he straightened himself up and said to them, He who is among you without sin, let him first throw a stone at her.

8 And again as he bent down, he wrote on the ground.

9 And when they heard it, they left one by one, beginning with the elders; and the man woman was left alone in the midst.

10 When Jesus straightened himself up, he said to the woman, Where are they? did no henceforth, do not sin again.

12 ¶ Again Jesus spoke to them and said, I am the light of the world; he who follows me shall not walk in darkness, but he shall find for himself the light of life.

13 The Pharisees said to him, You testify concerning yourself; your testimony is not true.

14 Jesus answered and said to them, Even though I testify concerning myself, my testimony is true, because I know whence I came and whither I go; but you do not know whence I came, or whither I go.

15 You judge according to the flesh; but I judge no man.

16 And if I should judge, my judgment is true; because I am not doing it alone, but I and my Father who sent me.

17 And it is written in your own law, that the testimony of two men is true.

18 I testify concerning myself, and my Father who sent me testifies concerning me.

19 They said to him, Where is your Father? Jesus answered and said to them, You know neither me, nor my Father; if you knew me, you would know my Father also.

20 These words he spoke in the treasury, while he taught in the temple; and no man arrested him, for his time had not yet come.

21 ¶ Jesus again said to them, I am going away, and you will seek me, and you will die in your sins; and where I am going you cannot come.

22 The Jews said, Why, will he kill himself? for he says, Where I am going, you cannot come.

23 And he said to them, You are from below, and I am from above; you are of this world, but I am not of this world.

---

* Jn. 7:52- Galilee was the land of the Gentiles and of mixed races, the descendants of those who were transferred to Assyria during the captivity.

Cf.dif. vv. 7:49;   8:7, 9, 10, 12.

24 I told you that you will die in your sins; for unless you believe that I am he, you will die in your sins.

25 The Jews said, Who are you? Jesus said to them, Even though I should begin to speak to you,

26 I have many things to say and to judge concerning you; but he who sent me is true; and I speak in the world only those things which I have heard from him.

27 They did not understand that he spoke to them concerning the Father.

28 Again Jesus said to them, When you have lifted up the Son of man, then you will understand that I am he, and I do nothing of my own accord; but as my Father has taught me, so I speak just like him.

29 And he who sent me is with me; and my Father has never left me alone, because I always do what pleases him.

30 ¶ While he was speaking these words, a great many believed in him.

31 Then Jesus said to the Jews who believed in him, If you abide by my word, you are truly my disciples.

32 And you will know the truth, and that very truth will make you free.

33 They said to him, We are the seed of Abraham, and we have never been enslaved to any man; how do you say, You will be free sons?

34 Jesus said to them, Truly, truly, I say to you, Whoever commits sin is a servant of sin.

35 And a servant does not remain in the house forever, but the son remains forever.

36 If therefore, the Son shall make you free, you shall truly become free.

37 I know you are the seed of Abraham; but still you want to kill me, because you have no room in you for my word.

38 I speak what I have seen with my Father; and you do what you have seen with your father.

39 They answered and said to him, Our own father is Abraham. Jesus said to them, If you were the sons of Abraham, you would be doing the works of Abraham.

40 But behold, now you want to kill me, even a man who has told you the truth, which I heard from God; this Abraham did not do.

41 But you do the works of your father. They said to him, We are not born of fornication; we have one Father, God.

42 Jesus said to them, If God were your Father, you would love me, for I proceeded and came from God; I did not come of my own accord, but he sent me.

43 Why therefore do you not understand my word? Because you cannot obey my word?

44 You are from the father of accusation, and you want to do the lusts of your father, he who is a murderer of men from the very beginning and who never stands by the truth, because there is no truth in him. When he speaks he speaks his own lie, because he is a liar, and the father of it.

45 But because I speak the truth, you do not believe me.

46 Which one of you can rebuke me because of sin? If I speak the truth, why do you not believe me?

47 He who is of God, hears God's words; for this reason you do not hear, because you are not of God.

48 The Jews answered and said to him, Did we not say well, that you are a Samaritan, and that you are crazy?

49 Jesus said to them, I am not crazy; but I honor my Father, and you curse me.

50 I do not seek my glory; there is one who seeks and judges.

51 Truly, truly, I say to you, Whoever obeys my word, shall never see death.

52 The Jews said to him, Now we are sure that you are insane. Abraham and the prophets have died; and yet you say, Whoever obeys my word, shall never taste death.

53 Why, are you greater than our father Abraham who died, and the prophets who died? Whom do you make yourself?

54 Jesus said to them, If I honor myself, my honor is nothing; but it is my Father who honors me, the one of whom you say, He is our God.

55 Yet you have not known him, but I do know him; and if I should say, I do not know him, I would be a liar like yourselves; but I do know him, and I obey his word.

56 Your father Abraham rejoiced to see my day; and he saw it and was glad.

57 The Jews said to him, You are not yet fifty years old, and yet have you seen Abraham?

58 Jesus said to them, Truly, truly, I say to you, Before Abraham was born, I was.

59 So they took up stones, to stone him; and Jesus hid himself, and went out of the temple, and he passed through the midst of them, and went away.

CHAPTER 9

A ND as Jesus passed by he saw a man who was blind from his mother's womb.

2 And his disciples asked him, saying, Teacher, who did sin, this man, or his parents, that he was born blind?

3 Jesus said to them, Neither did he sin nor his parents. But that the works of God might be seen in him,

4 I must do the works of him who sent me, while it is day; the night comes when no man can work.

5 As long as I am in the world, I am the light of the world.

6 When he said these words, he spat on the ground, and mixed clay with his saliva, and he placed it on the eyes of the blind man.

7 Then he said to him, Go and wash in the baptismal pool of Siloam. He went and washed, and he came seeing.

8 His neighbors and those who had seen him before begging, said, Is not this he who used to sit down and beg?

9 Some said, It is he; and some said, No, but he resembles him; but he said, I am he.

10 Then they said to him, How were your eyes opened?

11 He answered and said to them, A man whose name is Jesus made clay and placed it on my eyes, and he said to me, Go and wash in the water of Siloam; and I went and washed, and I see.

12 They said to him, Where is he? He said to them, I do not know.

13 ¶ So they brought to the Pharisees him who had been blind from his birth.

14 Now it was the sabbath when Jesus made the clay, and opened his eyes.

15 Again the Pharisees asked him, How did you receive your sight? He said to them, He placed clay on my eyes, and I washed, and I see.

16 Then some of the Pharisees said, This man is not from God, because he does not observe the sabbath; others said, How can a man who is a sinner do these miracles? And there was a division among them.

17 They said to the blind man again, What do you say concerning him who opened your eyes? He said to them, I say he is a prophet.

18 But the Jews did not believe concerning him, that he had been blind, and had received his sight, until they called the parents of him who had received his sight.

19 And they asked them, Is this your son, who you say was born blind? how then does he now see?

20 His parents answered and said, We know

Cf.dif. vv. 8:52; 9:3-4, 6-7, 11, 13.

that he is our son, and that he was born blind.

21 But how he sees now, or who opened his eyes, we do not know; he is of age, ask him, he will speak for himself.

22 His parents said these things because they were afraid of the Jews; for the Jews had decided already, that if any man should confess that he is the Christ, they would put him out of the synagogue.

23 For this reason his parents said, He is of age, ask him.

24 So they called a second time the man who had been blind, and said to him, Give praise to God, for we know that this man is a sinner.

25 He answered and said to them, If he is a sinner I do not know; but I do know one thing, that I was blind, and now behold, I see.

26 They said to him again, What did he do to you? How did he open your eyes?

27 He said to them, I have already told you, and you did not listen; why do you want to hear it again? why, do you also want to become his disciples?

28 Then they cursed him, and said to him, You are his disciple, but we are disciples of Moses.

29 And we know that God spoke with Moses; but as for this man, we do not know whence he is.

30 The man answered and said to them, This is surprising, that you do not know whence he is, and yet he opened my eyes.

31 We know that God does not hear the voice of sinners; but he hears the one who fears him and does his will.

32 From ages it has never been heard that a man opened the eyes of one who was born blind.

33 If this man were not from God, he could

not have done this.

34 They answered and said to him, You were wholly born in sins, and yet do you teach us? And they cast him out.

35 ¶ And Jesus heard that they had cast him out; and he found him and said to him, Do you believe in the Son of God?

36 He who was healed answered and said, Who is he, my Lord, so that I may believe in him?

37 Jesus said to him, You have seen him, and he is the one who is speaking with you.

38 He said, I do believe, my Lord; and he fell down and worshipped him.

39 Then Jesus said to him, I have come for the judgment of this world, so that those who cannot see may see, and those who see may become blind.

40 ¶ When some of the Pharisees who were with him heard these words, they said to him, Why, are we also blind?

41 Jesus said to them, If you were blind, you would have no sin; but now you say, We see; because of this your sin remains.

CHAPTER 10

*T*RULY, truly, I say to you, He who does not enter by the door into the sheepfold, but climbs up from another place, is a thief and a bandit.

2 But he who enters by the door, is the shepherd of the sheep.

3 To him the door-keeper opens the door; and the sheep hear his voice; and he calls his own sheep by their names and brings them out.

4 And when he has brought out his sheep, he goes before them; and his own sheep * follow him, because they know his voice.

5 The sheep do not follow a stranger, but they run away from him; because they do

---

* Jn. 10:4 - "His sheep" refers to the several flocks in the fold, "his own sheep" refers to his own flock.

not know the voice of a stranger.

6 Jesus spoke this parable to them; but they did not understand what he was telling them.

7 Jesus said to them again, Truly, truly, I say to you, I am the door of the sheep.

8 All who have come are thieves and bandits, if the sheep did not hear them.

9 I am the door; if any man enter by me, he shall live, and he shall come in and go out and find pasture.

10 A thief does not come, except to steal and kill and destroy; I have come that they might have life, and have it abundantly.

11 I am the good shepherd; a good shepherd risks his life for the sake of his sheep.

12 But the hired person, who is not the shepherd, and who is not the owner of the sheep, when he sees the wolf coming, leaves the sheep and runs away; and the wolf comes and seizes and scatters the sheep.

13 The hired person runs away, because he is hired, and he does not care for the sheep.

14 I am the good shepherd, and I know my own, and my own know me.

15 Just as my Father knows me, I also know my Father; and I lay down my life for the sake of the sheep.

16 I have other sheep also, which are not of this fold; them also I must bring, and they will hear my voice; and all the sheep will become one flock and one shepherd.

17 This is why my Father loves me, because I lay down my life, so that I may take it up again.

18 No man takes it away from me, but I lay it down of my own will. Therefore I have the power to lay it down, and I have the power to take it up again. This command I received from my Father.

19 ¶ There was again a division among the Jews because of these sayings.

20 And many of them said, He is insane and rambles; why do you listen to him?

21 Others said, These are not the words of a crazy man. Why, can a crazy man open the eyes of the blind?

22 ¶ Then came the feast of dedication at Jerusalem, and it was winter.

23 And Jesus was walking in the temple in Solomon's porch.

24 Then the Jews surrounded him and said to him, How long do you vex our soul with uncertainty? If you are the Christ, tell us openly.

25 Jesus answered and said to them, I have told you, but you do not believe; yet the works which I do, in the name of my Father, testify of me.

26 But you do not believe, because you are not of my sheep, just as I told you.

27 My own sheep hear my voice, and I know them, and they follow me;

28 And I give to them eternal life; and they will never perish, and no man will snatch them from my hands.

29 For my Father who gave them to me is greater than all; and no man can snatch anything from my Father's hand.

30 I and my Father are one in accord.

31 Then the Jews again took up stones to stone him.

32 Jesus said to them, I have shown you many good works from my Father; for which one of them do you stone me?

33 The Jews said to him, It is not because of the good works we stone you, but because you blaspheme; for while you are only a man, you make yourself God.

34 Jesus said to them, Is it not so written in your law, I said, you are gods?

35 If he called them gods, because the word of God was with them, and the scripture cannot be broken;

36 Yet to the one whom the Father sanctified and sent to the world, you say, You blaspheme, just because I said to you, I am the Son of God.

Cf.dif. vv. 10:8, 11, 20-21, 24, 30, 35-36.

37 If I am not doing the works of my Father, do not believe me.

38 But if I am doing them, even though you do not believe in me, believe in the works; so that you may know and believe that my Father is with me and I am with my Father.

39 ¶ And they wanted again to seize him; but he escaped from their hands.

40 And he went away to the Jordan crossing, to the place where John was, where he first baptized; and he remained there.

41 And many men came to him and said, John did not perform a single miracle; but everything which John said concerning this man is true.

42 And many believed in him.

CHAPTER 11

*N*OW there was a man who was sick, Lazarus of the town of Bethany, the brother of Mary and Martha.

2 This is the Mary who anointed the feet of Jesus with perfume and wiped them with her hair. Lazarus who was sick, was her brother.

3 His two sisters therefore sent to Jesus, saying, Our Lord, behold, the one whom you love is sick.

4 Jesus said, This is not a sickness of death, but for the sake of the glory of God, that the Son of God may be glorified on his account.

5 Now Jesus loved Martha and Mary and Lazarus.

6 When he heard he was sick, he remained two days in the place where he was.

7 After that he said to his disciples, Come, let us go again to Judaea.

8 His disciples said to him, Teacher, not long ago the Jews wanted to stone you, and yet are you going there again?

9 Jesus said to them, Are there not twelve hours in the day? If a man walks by day time, he will not stumble, because he sees the light of this world.

10 But if a man travels at night time, he will stumble, because there is no light in it.

11 Jesus said these things; and after that he said to them, Our friend Lazarus is asleep; but I am going to awake him.

12 His disciples said to him, Our Lord, if he is sleeping, he will get well.

13 But Jesus spoke of his death; and they thought that what he said was sleeping in bed.

14 Then Jesus said to them, plainly, Lazarus is dead.

15 And I am glad I was not there, for your sakes, so that you may believe; but let us walk there.

16 Then Thomas, who is called the Twin, said to his fellow disciples, Let us also go, and die with him.

17 ¶ So Jesus came to Bethany, and he found that he had been four days in the tomb.

18 Now Bethany was towards Jerusalem, a distance of about two miles.

19 And many Jews kept coming to Martha and Mary, to comfort their hearts concerning their brother.

20 When Martha heard that Jesus had come, she went out to meet him; but Mary sat in the house.

21 Then Martha said to Jesus, My Lord, if you had been here, my brother would not have died.

22 But even now I know that whatever you ask of God, he will give you.

23 Jesus said to her, Your brother will rise up.

24 Martha said to him, I know he will rise up in the resurrection at the last day.

25 Jesus said to her, I am the resurrection and the life; he who believes in me, even though he die, he shall live.

26 And whoever is alive and believes in me shall never die. Do you believe this?

27 She said to him, Yes, my Lord; I do believe that you are the Christ, the Son of God,

         Cf.dif. vv. 10:38, 40; 11:1, 4, 10, 13, 16.

who is to come to the world.

28 And when she had said these things, she went away and called her sister Mary secretly, and said to her, Our teacher has come, and he is calling you.

29 When Mary heard it, she rose up quickly and came to him.

30 Jesus had not yet come into the town, but he was still at the same place where Martha met him.

31 The Jews also who were with her in the house, comforting her, when they saw Mary rise up quickly and go out, followed her, for they thought she was going to the tomb to weep.

32 When Mary came where Jesus was, and saw him, she threw herself at his feet, and said to him, My Lord, if you had been here, my brother would not have died.

33 When Jesus saw her weeping, and the Jews weeping, who had come with her, he was moved in his spirit, and was greatly disturbed.

34 And he said, Where have you laid him? They said to him, Our Lord, come and see.

35 And Jesus was in tears.

36 The Jews then said, Look, how much he loved him!

37 Some of them said, Could not this man, who opened the eyes of that blind man, have also kept this man from dying?

38 As Jesus was disturbed in himself because of them, he came to the tomb. That tomb was a cave, and a stone was placed at the entrance.

39 Jesus said, Take away this stone. Martha, the sister of the dead man, said to him, My Lord, he is already disfigured, for he is dead four days.

40 Jesus said to her, Did not I say to you that if you believe, you will see the glory of God?

41 So they took away the stone. And Jesus lifted his eyes upwards, and said, O Father, I thank you for you have heard me,

42 And I know that you always hear me; but I say these things just because of this people who stand around, so that they may believe that you have sent me.

43 And when he had said this, he cried with a loud voice, Lazarus, come outside.

44 And the dead man came out, his hands and feet bound with burial clothes; and his face bound with a burial napkin. Jesus said to them, Loose him and let him go.

45 ¶ Many of the Jews who had come to Mary, when they saw what Jesus had done, believed in him.

46 And some of them went to the Pharisees, and told them everything Jesus had done.

47 ¶ So the high priests and the Pharisees gathered together and said, What shall we do? for this man does many miracles?

48 If we allow him to continue like this, all men will believe in him; and the Romans will come and take over both our country and our people.

49 But one of them, called Caiaphas, who was the high priest for that year, said to them, You know nothing;

50 Nor do you reason that it is much better for us that one man should die instead of the people, and not all the people perish.

51 He did not say this of himself; but because he was the high priest for that year, he prophesied that Jesus had to die for the sake of the people;

52 And not only for the sake of the people, but also to gather together the children of God who are scattered abroad.

53 And from that very day, they decided to kill him.

54 ¶ Jesus therefore did not walk openly among the Jews, but went away thence to a place which is close to the wilderness, in the province of Ephraim; and he remained there with his disciples.

Cf.dif. vv. 11:31, 35, 37-39, 48, 50, 53-54.

55 Now the Jewish passover was at hand; and many went up from the towns to Jerusalem, before the feast, to purify themselves.

56 And they were looking for Jesus, and at the temple they kept saying to one another, What do you think, will he not come to the feast?

57 But the high priests and the Pharisees had already commanded, that if any man should know where he is, to let them know, so that they might seize him.

CHAPTER 12

SIX days before the passover, Jesus came to Bethany, where Lazarus was, whom Jesus had raised from the dead.

2 And they gave him a banquet there; Martha served; but Lazarus was one of the guests who were with him.

3 Then Mary took a cruse containing pure and expensive nard, and anointed the feet of Jesus, and wiped his feet with her hair; and the house was filled with the fragrance of the perfume.

4 And Judas of Iscariot, one of his disciples, who was about to betray him, said,

5 Why was not this oil sold for three hundred pennies, and given to the poor?

6 He said this, not because he cared for the poor; but because he was a thief, and the purse was with him, and he carried whatever was put in it.

7 Jesus then said, Leave her alone; she has kept it for the day of my burial.

8 For you have the poor always with you, but me you have not always.

9 ¶ Many people of the Jews heard that Jesus was there; so they came, not only on account of Jesus, but also to see Lazarus, whom he had raised from the dead.

10 And the high priests were thinking of killing Lazarus also;

11 Because on his account a great many Jews were leaving and believing in Jesus.

12 ¶ On the next day, a large crowd which had come to the feast, when they heard that Jesus was coming to Jerusalem,

13 Took branches of palm trees, and went out to greet him, and they cried out and said, Hosanna, Blessed is the king of Israel who comes in the name of the Lord.

14 And Jesus found an ass and sat on it; as it is written,

15 Fear not, O daughter of Zion; behold, your king cometh to you, riding on the colt of an ass.

16 His disciples did not understand these things at that time; but when Jesus was glorified, then his disciples remembered that these things were written concerning him, and that they had done these things to him.

17 The people who were with him testified that he had called Lazarus from the tomb, and raised him from the dead.

18 It was on this account that large crowds went out to meet him, for they heard that he had performed this miracle.

19 The Pharisees said one to another, Do you see that you have not been able to gain anything? Behold, all the people have gone after him.

20 ¶ Now there were some Gentiles among them who had come up to worship at the feast.

21 They came and approached Philip of Bethsaida of Galilee, and asked him, saying, My lord, we would like to see Jesus.

22 Philip came and told Andrew; then Andrew and Philip told Jesus.

23 Jesus answered and said to them, The hour has come that the Son of man should be glorified.

24 Truly, truly, I say to you, that unless a grain of wheat falls and dies in the ground, it will be left alone; but if it dies, it produces much fruit.

25 He who loves his life will lose it; and he who has no concern for his life in this world will keep it unto life eternal.

26 If any man serve me, let him follow me; and where I am, there also will my servant be; he who serves me, him my Father will honor.

27 Now my soul is disturbed, and what shall I say? O my Father, deliver me from this hour; but for this cause I came to this very hour.

28 O Father, glorify your name. Then a voice was heard from heaven, I am glorified, and I shall again be glorified.

29 And the people who stood by heard it, and said, It was thunder; others said, An angel spoke to him.

30 Jesus answered and said to them, This voice was not on my account, but for your sake.

31 Now is the judgment of this world; now the leader of this world will be cast out.

32 And I, when I am lifted up from the earth, will draw every man to me.

33 He said this, to show by what kind of death he was to die.

34 The people said to him, We have heard from the law that the Christ shall remain forever; how do you say that the Son of man must be lifted up? Who is this Son of man?

35 Jesus said to them, The light is with you for a little while; walk while you have the light, so that the darkness may not overcome you; and he who walks in the darkness does not know where he goes.

36 While you have the light, believe in the light, so that you may become the sons of the light. Jesus spoke these things, and went away and hid himself from them.

37 ¶ Even though he had performed all of these miracles before them, yet they did not believe in him;

38 So that the word of the prophet Isaiah might be fulfilled, who said, My Lord, who will believe our report, and to whom has the arm of the Lord been revealed?

39 For this reason, they could not believe, because Isaiah said again,

40 Their eyes have become blind and their heart darkened, so that they cannot see with their eyes and understand with their heart; let them return and I will heal them.

41 Isaiah said these things, when he saw his glory and spoke concerning him.

42 ¶ Many of the leading men also believed in him; but because of the Pharisees they did not confess it, so that they might not be cast out of the synagogue.

43 For they loved the honor of men more than the glory of God.

44 ¶ Jesus cried out and said, He who believes in me, believes not in me but in him who sent me.

45 And he who sees me, has already seen him who sent me.

46 I have come into the world as the light, so that whoever believes in me may not remain in the darkness.

47 And he who hears my words, and does not obey them, I will not judge him; for I have not come to judge the world, but to save the world.

48 He who oppresses me and does not receive my words, there is one who will judge him; the word which I have spoken, it will judge him at the last day.

49 For I did not speak of myself; but the Father who sent me, he commanded me what to say and what to speak.

50 And I know that his commandment is life everlasting; these things therefore which I speak, just as my Father told me, so I speak.

Cf.dif. vv. 12:25, 28, 38, 40, 42, 48.

CHAPTER 13

NOW before the feast of the passover, Jesus knew the hour had come to depart from this world to his Father. And he loved his own who were in this world, and he loved them unto the end.

2 ¶ During supper, Satan put into the heart of Judas, son of Simon of Iscariot, to deliver him.

3 But Jesus, because he knew that the Father had given everything into his hands, and that he came from God, and was going to God,

4 He rose from supper and laid aside his robes; and he took an apron and tied it around his loins.

5 Then he poured water into a basin, and began to wash the feet of his disciples, and to wipe them with the apron which was tied around his loins.

6 When he came to Simon Peter, Simon said to him, You, my Lord, are you going to wash my feet?

7 Jesus answered and said to him, What I am doing, you do not know now, but later you will understand.

8 Then Simon Peter said to him, You will never wash my feet. Jesus said to him, If I do not wash you, you have no part with me.

9 Simon Peter said to him, Then, my Lord, wash not only my feet, but also my hands and my head.

10 Jesus said to him, He who has bathed does not need except to wash his feet only, for he is already all clean; so you are all clean, but not everyone of you.

11 For Jesus knew him who was to betray him; therefore he said, Not everyone of you is clean.

12 When he had washed their feet, he put on his robes and sat down; and he said to them, Do you know what I have done to you?

13 You call me, our Teacher and our Lord; and what you say is well, for I am.

14 If I then, your Lord and Teacher, have washed your feet, how much more should you wash one another's feet?

15 For I have given you this as an example, so that just as I have done to you, you should also do.

16 Truly, truly, I say to you, There is no servant who is greater than his master; and no apostle who is greater than he who sent him.

17 If you know these things, blessed are you if you do them.

18 I do not say this concerning all of you, for I know those whom I have chosen; but that the scripture might be fulfilled, He who eats bread with me has lifted up his heel against me.

19 I tell you now before it happens, that when it happens, you may believe that I am he.

20 Truly, truly, I say to you, He who receives him whom I send, receives me; and he who receives me receives him who sent me.

21 ¶ Jesus said these things, and he was disturbed in spirit, and testified and said, Truly, truly, I say to you, one of you will betray me.

22 The disciples then looked at each other, because they did not know concerning whom he spoke.

23 Now there was one of his disciples who was leaning on his bosom, the one whom Jesus loved.

24 Simon Peter winked at to him, to ask him of whom he spoke.

25 So that disciple leaned himself on the breast of Jesus, and said to him, My Lord, who is he?

26 Jesus answered and said, The one for whom I dip bread and give to him. So Jesus dipped the bread, and gave it to Judas, the son of Simon of Iscariot.

Cf.dif. vv. 13:4, 10, 22, 24-26.

27 And after the bread, Satan took possession of him. So Jesus said to him, What you are going to do, do it soon.

28 But no man of those who were sitting at the table understood what he said to him.

29 For some of them thought, because the purse was with Judas, that he ordered him to buy what was needed for the feast; or to give something to the poor.

30 Judas then received the bread and went outside immediately; it was night when he went out.

31 ¶ Jesus then said, Now the Son of man is glorified, and God is glorified by him.

32 If God is glorified by him, God will also glorify him by himself, and he will glorify him at once.

33 My sons, I am with you yet a little while, and you will want me. And just as I said to the Jews, Where I go you cannot come; so now I tell you also.

34 A new commandment I give you, that you love one another; just as I have loved you, that you also love one another.

35 By this every man shall know that you are my disciples, if you have love one for another.

36 Simon Peter said to him, Our Lord, where are you going? Jesus answered and said to him, Where I go, you cannot follow me now, but you will follow later.

37 Simon Peter said to him, My Lord, why can I not follow you now? I will even lay down my life for you.

38 Jesus said to him, Will you lay down your life for me? Truly, truly, I say to you, The cock shall not crow, until you have denied me three times.

CHAPTER 14

LET not your heart be troubled; believe in God, and believe in me also.

2 In my Father's house there are many rooms; if it were not so, I would have told you. I am going to prepare a place for you.

3 And if I go and prepare a place for you, I will come again, and take you to me, so that where I am, you may be also.

4 You know where I am going, and you know the way.

5 Thomas said to him, Our Lord, we do not know where you are going, and how can we know the way?

6 Jesus said to him, I am the way, and the truth, and the life; no man comes to my Father except by me.

7 If you had known me, you would have known my Father also; from henceforth you know him and you have seen him.

8 Philip said to him, Our Lord, show us the Father, and that is enough for us.

9 Jesus said to him, All this time I have been with you, and yet you do not know me, Philip? he who sees me, has seen the Father; and how do you say, Show us the Father?

10 Do you not believe that I am with my Father and my Father is with me? the words that I speak, I do not speak of myself; but my Father who abides with me, he does these works.

11 Believe that I am with my Father, and my Father is with me; and if not, believe because of the works.

12 Truly, truly, I say to you, He who believes in me, the works which I do he shall do also; even greater than these things he shall do, because I am going to my Father.

13 And whatever you ask in my name, I will do it for you, so that the Father may be glorified through his Son.

14 If you ask me in my own name, I will do it.

15 If you love me, then obey my commandments.

16 And I will ask of my Father, and he will give you another Comforter, to be with you for ever;

Cf. dif. vv. 13:27, 30, 32-33; 14:2, 10-11, 14.

17 Even the Spirit of the truth; whom the world cannot receive, because it has not seen him, and does not know him; but you know him because he abides with you, and is in you.

18 I will not leave you orphans, for I will come to you after a little while.

19 And the world will not see me, but you will see me; because I live, you also shall live.

20 In that day you will know that I am with my Father, and you are with me, and I am with you.

21 He who has my commandments with him and obeys them, he is the one who loves me; he who loves me will be loved by my Father, and I will love him, and reveal myself to him.

22 Judas (not of Iscariot) said to him, My Lord, why is it that you will reveal yourself to us, and not to the world?

23 Jesus answered and said to him, He who loves me, keeps my word; and my Father will love him, and we will come to him, and make a place of abode with him.

24 But he who does not love me, does not keep my word; and this word which you hear, is not mine own, but the Father's who sent me.

25 I have spoken these things to you, while I am with you.

26 But the Comforter, the Holy Spirit, whom my Father will send in my name, he will teach you everything, and remind you of everything which I tell you.

27 Peace I leave with you; my own peace I give you; not as the world gives, I give to you. Let not your heart be troubled, and do not be afraid.

28 You heard that I told you, I am going away, and I will come to you. If you loved me, you would rejoice because I am going to my Father; for my Father is greater than I.

29 And now behold, I have told you before it happens, so that when it does happen, you may believe.

30 Hereafter I will not talk much with you; for the prince of this world comes; and yet he has nothing against me.

31 But that the world may know that I love my Father, and as my Father has commanded me, so I do. Arise, let us go away from here.

CHAPTER 15

I AM the true vine, and my Father is the worker.

2 Every branch in me that does not bear fruit, he cuts out; and the one which bears fruit, he prunes so that it may bring forth more fruit.

3 You have already been pruned because of the word which I have spoken to you.

4 Remain with me and I with you. Just as a branch cannot give fruit by itself, unless it remains in the vine; even so you cannot, unless you remain with me.

5 I am the vine, you are the branches. He who remains with me and I with him, will bear abundant fruit; for without me you can do nothing.

6 Unless a man remains with me, he will be cast outside, like a branch which is withered; which they pick up and throw into the fire to be burned.

7 If you remain with me, and my words remain with you, whatever you ask shall be done for you.

8 In this the Father will be glorified, that you bear abundant fruit, and be my disciples.

9 ¶ Just as my Father has loved me, I also have loved you; remain in my love.

10 If you keep my commandments, you will remain in my love; even as I have kept my Father's commandments, and I remain in his love.

11 I have spoken these things to you, that my joy may be in you, and that your joy may be full.

12 This is my commandment, that you love one another, just as I have loved you.

13 There is no greater love than this, when a man lays down his life for the sake of his friends.

14 You are my friends, if you do everything that I command you.

15 Henceforth I will not call you servants, because a servant does not know what his master does; but I have always called you my friends, because everything that I heard from my Father I made it known to you.

16 You did not choose me, but I chose you, and I have appointed you, that you also should go and produce fruit, and that your fruit might remain; so that whatever you ask my Father in my name, he will give it to you.

17 I command these things to you, so that you love one another.

18 If the world hate you, know well that it has hated me before you.

19 If you were of the world, the world would love its own; but you are not of the world, for I have chosen you out of the world; this is why the world hates you.

20 Remember the word which I said to you, that no servant is greater than his master. If they have persecuted me, they will also persecute you; if they kept my word, they will also keep yours.

21 But they will do all these things to you for the sake of my name, because they do not know him who sent me.

22 If I had not come and spoken to them, they would be without sin; but now they have no excuse for their sins.

23 He who hates me, hates my Father also.

24 If I had not done works before their eyes, such as no other man has ever done, they would be without sin; but now they have seen and hated me and also my Father,

25 So that the word which is written in their law may be fulfilled, They hated me for no reason.

26 But when the Comforter comes, whom I will send to you from my Father, the Spirit of truth which proceeds from my Father, he will testify concerning me.

27 And you also will testify because you have been with me from the beginning.

CHAPTER 16

I HAVE spoken these things to you, so that you may not stumble.

2 For they will put you out of their synagogues; and the hour will come that whoever kills you, will think that he has offered an offering to God.

3 And these things they will do, because they have not known my Father, nor me.

4 I have spoken these things to you, that when their time does come, you may remember them, and that I told you. And these things I did not tell you before, because I was with you.

5 ¶ But now I am going to him who sent me, and yet no one of you asks me, Where are you going?

6 But because I told you these things, sorrow has come and filled your hearts.

7 But I tell you the truth, It is better for you that I should go away; for if I do not go away, the Comforter will not come to you; but if I should go, I will send him to you.

8 And when he is come, he will rebuke the world concerning sin, concerning righteousness, and concerning judgment.

9 Concerning sin, because they do not believe in me;

10 Concerning righteousness, because I go to my Father, and you will not see me again;

11 Concerning judgment, because the leader of this world has been judged.

12 Again, I have many other things to tell you, but you cannot grasp them now.

13 But when the Spirit of truth is come, he will guide you into all the truth; for he will not speak from himself, but what he hears

that he will speak; and he will make known to you things which are to come in the future.

14 He will glorify me; because he will take of my own and show to you.

15 Everything that my Father has is mine; this is the reason why I told you that he will take of my own and show to you.

16 A little while, and you will not see me; and again a little while, and you will see me, because I am going to the Father.

17 Then his disciples said to one another, What is this that he said to us, A little while, and you will not see me; and again a little while, and you will see me; and, because I am going to my Father?

18 And they said, What is this that he said, A little while? We cannot understand what he talks about.

19 Jesus knew that they desired to ask him, and he said to them, Are you inquiring among yourselves concerning this, that I told you, A little while, and you will not see me; and again a little while, and you will see me?

20 Truly, truly, I say to you, that you will weep and wail, and yet the world will rejoice; and you will be sad, but your sadness will be changed into gladness.

21 When a woman is in travail, she is depressed, because her day has arrived; but when she has given birth to a son, she no longer remembers her troubles, because of the joy that a male child * is born into the world.

22 So you also are depressed; but I will see you again, and your heart will rejoice, and your joy no man will take away from you.

23 In that day you will not ask me anything. Truly, truly, I say to you, that whatever you ask my Father in my name, he will give it to

you.

24 Hitherto you have asked nothing in my name; ask and you will receive, so that your joy may be full.

25 I have spoken these things in figures; but the time is coming, when I will not speak to you in figures, but will plainly explain to you concerning the Father.

26 In that day you will ask in my name; and I will not say to you, I will ask the Father concerning you.

27 For the Father himself loves you, because you have loved me, and have believed that I came forth from the Father.

28 I came forth from the Father, and I came into the world; again, I am leaving the world and I am going to the Father.

29 His disciples said to him, Behold, now you speak plainly, and do not utter a single figure.

30 Now we understand that you know everything; and you need no man to ask you; by this we believe that you have come forth from God.

31 Jesus said to them, Believe it.

32 For behold, the hour is coming, and it has now come, when you will be dispersed, every man to his own country, and you will leave me alone; and yet I am never alone, because the Father is with me.

33 These things I have said to you, that in me you may have peace. In the world you will have tribulation; but have courage; I have conquered the world.

CHAPTER 17

JESUS spoke these things, and then he lifted up his eyes to heaven and said, O my Father, the hour has come; glorify your Son, so that your Son may glorify you.

* Jn. 16:21 - When a girl is born in the East, the news is kept from the mother for awhile if she is in danger. If a boy is born she is at once informed to cheer her up.

Cf.dif. vv. 16:21, 31-32.

2 Since you have given him power over all flesh, so that to all whom you have given him, he may give life eternal.

3 And this is life eternal, that they might know you, that you are the only true God, even the one who sent Jesus Christ.

4 I have already glorified you on the earth; for the work which you had given to me to do, I have finished it.

5 So now, O my Father, glorify me with you, with the same glory which I had with you before the world was made.

6 I have made your name known to the men whom you gave me out of the world; they were yours and you gave them to me; and they have kept thy word.

7 Now they know that whatever you have given me is from you.

8 For the words which you gave me I gave them; and they accepted them, and have known truly that I came forth from you, and they have believed that you sent me.

9 What I request is for them; I make no request for the world, but for those whom you have given to me; because they are yours.

10 And everything which is mine, is yours; and what is yours is mine; and I am glorified by them.

11 Hereafter I am not in the world, but these are in the world; and I am coming to you. O holy Father, protect them in your name, which you have given me, that they may be one, even as we are.

12 While I was with them in the world, I protected them in your name; those you gave me I protected, and not one of them is lost, except the son of perdition, that the scripture might be fulfilled.

13 Now I am coming to you; and these things I speak while I am in the world, that my joy may be complete in them.

14 I have given them your word; and the world hated them, because they were not of the world, just as I am not of the world.

15 What I request is not that you should take them out of the world, but that you should protect them from evil.

16 For they are not of the world, just as I am not of the world.

17 O Father, sanctify them in your truth, because your word is truth.

18 Just as you sent me into the world, so I have sent them into the world.

19 And for their sakes, I am sanctifying myself, so that they also may be sanctified in the truth.

20 I am not making request for these alone, but also for the sake of those who believe in me through their word.

21 So that they all may be one; just as you, my Father, art with me, and I am with you, that they also may be one with us; so that the world may believe you sent me.

22 And the glory which you gave me, I gave to them; so that they may be one just as we are one.

23 I with them and you with me, that they may become perfected in one; so that the world may know that you sent me, and that you loved them just as you loved me.

24 O Father, I wish that those whom you have given me, may also be with me where I am; so that they may see my glory which you have given me; for you have loved me before the foundation of the world.

25 O my righteous Father, the world did not know you, but I have known you; and these have known that you have sent me.

26 And I have made your name known to them, and I am still making it known; so that the love with which you loved me may be among them, and I be with them.

Cf.dif. vv. 17:3, 5, 10, 21, 23.

CHAPTER 18

JESUS said these things and went out with his disciples across the brook Kidron, to a place where there was a garden, where he and his disciples entered.

2 Judas the traitor also knew that place; because Jesus and his disciples frequently gathered there.

3 Judas, therefore, took a company of soldiers, and also guards from the high priests and the Pharisees, and he came there with torches and lamps and weapons.

4 Jesus, knowing everything that was to happen, went out and said to them, Whom do you want?

5 They said to him, Jesus the Nazarene. Jesus said to them, I am he. Judas the traitor was also standing with them.

6 When Jesus said to them, I am he, they drew back and fell to the ground.

7 Jesus again asked them, Whom do you want? They said, Jesus the Nazarene.

8 Jesus said to them, I have told you that I am he; if then you want me, let these men go away;

9 That the word which he said might be fulfilled, Of those whom you gave me, I have lost not even one.

10 But Simon Peter had a sword, and he drew it and struck the high priest's servant, and cut off his right ear. The servant's name was Malech.

11 And Jesus said to Peter, Put the sword into its sheath; shall I not drink the cup which my Father has given me?

12 ¶ Then the soldiers and the captains, and the Jewish guards seized Jesus and bound him,

13 And they brought him first to Annas, because he was the father-in-law of Caiaphas, who was the high priest of that year.

14 Caiaphas was the one who had counselled the Jews, that it was better for one man to die instead of the people.

15 Simon Peter and one of the other disciples followed Jesus. The high priest knew that disciple, so he entered with Jesus into the courtyard.

16 But Simon stood outside near the door. Then the other disciple, whom the high priest knew, went out and told the portress, and brought in Simon.

17 The young portress then said to Simon, Why, are you also one of the disciples of this man? He said to her, No.

18 And the servants and guards were standing and making a fire, to warm themselves because it was cold; Simon also stood with them and warmed himself.

19 The high priest then questioned Jesus concerning his disciples and concerning his teaching.

20 Jesus said to him, I have spoken openly to the people, and I have always taught in the synagogue and in the temple, where all Jews assemble; and I have spoken nothing secretly.

21 Why do you ask me? ask those who heard what I have spoken to them; behold, they know everything which I said.

22 And as he said these things, one of the guards who stood by, struck Jesus on his cheek, and said to him, Is this how you answer the high priest?

23 Jesus answered and said to him, If I have spoken any evil, testify to the evil; but if it is good, why did you strike me?

24 Annas then sent Jesus bound to Caiaphas the high priest.

25 Now Simon Peter was standing and warming himself. They said to him, Why, are you also one of his disciples? He denied and said, I am not.

26 Then one of the servants of the high priest, a kinsman of him whose ear Simon had cut off, Did I not see you with him in the garden?

Cf.dif. vv. 18:3, 11-12, 14, 22.

27 Simon again denied; and at that very hour the cock crew.

28 ¶ Then they brought Jesus from Caiaphas to the praetorium; and it was morning; and they did not enter into the praetorium, so that they may not be defiled before they ate the passover.

29 Pilate then went outside where they were, and said to them, What accusation do you have against this man?

30 They answered and said to him, If he were not an evil-doer, we would not have delivered him up also to you.

31 Then said Pilate to them, Take him yourselves, and judge him according to your own law. The Jews said to him, We have no power to kill a man;

32 So that the word which Jesus had said might be fulfilled, when he signified by what kind of death he was to die.

33 Pilate then entered into the praetorium, and called Jesus and said to him. Are you the King of the Jews?

34 Jesus said to him, Do you say this of yourself, or have others told it to you concerning me?

35 Pilate said to him, Why, am I a Jew? Your own people and the high priests have delivered you to me; what have you done?

36 Jesus said to him, My kingdom is not of this world; if my kingdom were of this world, my servants would have fought so that I should not be delivered to the Jews; but now my kingdom is not from here.

37 Pilate said to him, Then are you a king? Jesus said to him, You say that I am a king.* For this I was born, and for this very thing I came to the world, that I may bear witness concerning the truth. Whoever is of the truth will hear my voice.

38 Pilate said to him, What is this truth?

And as he said this, he went out again to the Jews, and said to them, I am unable to find even one cause against him.

39 You have a custom that I should release to you one at the passover; do you wish, therefore, that I release to you this "king of the Jews"?

40 They all cried out saying, Not him, but Bar-Abbas. Now this Bar-Abbas was a bandit.

CHAPTER 19

*T*HEN Pilate had Jesus scourged.

2 And the soldiers wove a crown of thorns, and placed it on his head, and they covered him with purple robes;

3 And they said, Peace be to you, O king of the Jews! and they struck him on his cheeks.

4 Pilate again went outside and said to them, Behold, I bring him outside to you, so that you may know that I find not even one cause against him.

5 So Jesus went outside, wearing the crown of thorns and the purple robes. And Pilate said to them, Behold the man!

6 When the high priests and the guards saw him, they cried out, saying, Crucify him, crucify him! Pilate said to them, You take him and crucify him; for I find no cause in him.

7 The Jews said to him, We have a law, and according to our law he is guilty of death, because he made himself the Son of God.

8 When Pilate heard this saying, he was the more afraid;

9 So he entered again into the praetorium, and said to Jesus, Where do you come from? But Jesus gave him no answer.

10 Pilate said to him, Will you not speak even to me? Do you not know that I have the authority to release you, and I have the authority to crucify you?

---

* Jn. 18:37 - "You are making the assertion that I am a political king, but I am not."

Cf. dif. vv. 18:28, 31, 38; 19:1, 3-4.

11 Jesus said to him, You would have no authority whatever over me, if it had not been given to you from above; for this reason the sin of him who delivered me to you is greater than yours.

12 And because of this, Pilate wanted to release him; but the Jews cried out, If you release this man you are not a friend of Caesar; for whoever makes himself a king is against Caesar.

13 When Pilate heard this word, he brought Jesus outside; then he sat down on the judgment seat, at a place which is called the Stone Pavement but in Hebrew it is called, Gabbatha.

14 It was Friday of the passover, and it was about six o'clock; and he said to the Jews, Behold your king!

15 But they cried out, Take him away, take him away, crucify him, crucify him. Pilate said to them, Shall I crucify your king? The high priests said to him, We have no king except Caesar.

16 Then he delivered him to them to crucify him. So they took hold of Jesus and took him out,

17 Carrying his cross, to the place which is called The Skull, but in Hebrew it is called Golgotha;

18 Where they crucified him, and with him two others, one on either side, and Jesus between.

19 Pilate also wrote on a stone tablet, and placed it on his cross. And the writing was, THIS IS JESUS THE NAZARENE, THE KING OF THE JEWS.

20 And a great many Jews read this tablet, for the place where Jesus was crucified was near the city; and it was written in Hebrew* and in Greek and in Roman.

21 The high priests then said to Pilate, Do not write that he is the king of the Jews; but that he said, I am the king of the Jews.

22 Pilate said, What I have written, I have written.

23 ¶ Now when the soldiers had crucified Jesus, they took his clothes and divided them into four parts, a part to each of the soldiers; but his robe was without seam, woven from the top throughout.

24 So they said one to another, Let us not tear it, but cast lots for it, whose lot it shall be. And the scripture was fulfilled, which said, They divided my clothes among them, and for my robe they cast lots. These things the soldiers did.

25 ¶ Now there were standing by the cross of Jesus his mother, and his mother's sister, and Mary of Cleopas, and Mary of Magdala.

26 When Jesus saw his mother and the disciple whom he loved standing, he said to his mother, Woman, behold your son!

27 Then he said to the disciple, Behold your mother! And from that very hour the disciple took her with him.

28 After these things Jesus knew that everything was now accomplished; and that the scripture might be fulfilled, he said, I thirst.

29 Now there was a pitcher full of vinegar placed there; so they filled a sponge with vinegar and put it on the point of a reed, and placed it on his mouth.

30 ¶ When Jesus drank the vinegar, he said, It is fulfilled; and he bowed his head and gave up his spirit.

31 Now because it was Friday the Jews said, Let not these bodies remain on their crosses because the sabbath is dawning; for that sabbath was a great day. So they besought Pilate to have the legs of those who were crucified broken, and to have them lowered down.

---

* Jn. 19:20 - "Hebrew" here refers to nationality but the language of the inscription was Aramaic.

32 So the soldiers came and broke the legs of the first one, and of the other one who was crucified with him.

33 But when they came to Jesus, they saw that he was dead already, so they did not break his legs.

34 But one of the soldiers pierced his side with a spear, and immediately blood and water came out.

35 And he who saw it testified, and his testimony is true; and he knows well that what he said is true, that you also may believe.

36 For these things happened that the scripture might be fulfilled, which said, Not even a bone shall be broken in him;

37 And again another scripture which said, They shall look on him whom they pierced.

38 ¶ After these things Joseph of Arimathea, who was a disciple of Jesus, but secretly because of fear of the Jews, besought Pilate that he might take away the body of Jesus. And Pilate granted him permission. So he came and took away the body of Jesus.

39 And there came also Nicodemus, who at first had come to Jesus by night; and he brought with him a mixture of myrrh and aloes, about a hundred pints.

40 So they took away the body of Jesus, and bound it in linen cloths with the spices, according to the custom of the Jews in burial.

41 Now there was a garden in the place where Jesus was crucified; and in the garden a new tomb, in which no man was yet laid.

42 So they laid Jesus there, because the sabbath was approaching and because the tomb was near.

CHAPTER 20

ON the first day of the week, early in the morning, while it was yet dark, Mary of Magdala came to the tomb; and she saw that the stone was removed from the tomb.

2 Then she ran and came to Simon Peter and to the other disciple whom Jesus loved, and she said to them, They have taken our Lord out of that tomb, and I do not know where they have laid him.

3 So Simon and the other disciple went out, and came to the tomb.

4 And they were both running together; but that disciple outran Simon, and came first to the tomb.

5 And he looked in and saw the linen cloths lying; but he did not enter in.

6 Then Simon came after him, and entered into the tomb; and he saw the linen cloths lying,

7 And the burial napkin which was bound around his head, was not with the linen cloths, but was wrapped up and put in a place by itself.

8 Then the other disciple who had come first to the tomb also entered in, and he saw and believed.

9 For they did yet not understand from the scripture, that he had to rise from the dead.

10 So the disciples went away again to their lodging place.

11 ¶ But Mary was standing near the tomb weeping; and as she wept, she looked into the tomb;

12 And she saw two angels in white sitting, one at the head, and the other at the feet, where the body of Jesus had lain.

13 And they said to her, Woman, why do you weep? She said to them, Because they have taken away my Lord, and I do not know where they have laid him.

14 She said this and turned around, and saw Jesus standing, but she did not know that it was Jesus.

Cf.dif. vv. 19:39, 42.

15 Jesus said to her, Woman, why do you weep? and whom do you want? She thought he was the gardener, so she said to him, My lord, if you are the one who has taken him away, tell me where you have laid him, and I will go and take him away.

16 Jesus said to her, Mary. She turned around and said to him in Hebrew, Rabbuli! which means, My Teacher!

17 Jesus said to her, Do not come near me; for I have not yet ascended to my Father; but go to my brethren and say to them, I am ascending to my Father and your Father, and my God and your God.

18 Then Mary of Magdala came and brought glad tidings to the disciples, that she had seen our Lord and that he had told her these things.

19 ¶ When it was evening on that first day of the week, and the doors were shut where the disciples were staying for fear of the Jews, Jesus came, stood among them, and said to them, Peace be with you.

20 He said this, and then he showed them his hands and his side. The disciples rejoiced when they saw our Lord.

21 Then Jesus said to them again, Peace be with you; just as my Father has sent me, so I send you.

22 And when he had said these things, he gave them courage and said to them, Receive the Holy Spirit.

23 If you forgive a man his sins, they shall be forgiven to him; and if you hold a man's sins, they are held.

24 ¶ But Thomas, one of the twelve, who is called the Twin, was not there with them when Jesus came.

25 And the disciples said to him, We have seen our Lord. He said to them, Unless I see in his hands the places of the nails, and put my fingers in them, and put my hand into his side, I will not believe.

26 Eight days later, the disciples were again inside, and Thomas with them. Jesus came, when the doors were locked, and stood in the midst, and said to them, Peace be with you.

27 Then he said to Thomas, Bring your finger here, and see my hands; and bring your hand and put it into my side; and do not be an unbeliever, but a believer.

28 Thomas answered and said to him, O my Lord and my God!

29 Jesus said to him, Now you believe, because you have seen me? Blessed are those who have not seen me, and have believed.

30 ¶ Many other miracles Jesus did in the presence of his disciples, which are not written in this book;

31 Even these are written, so that you may believe that Jesus is the Christ, the Son of God; and when you believe you shall have life everlasting in his name.

CHAPTER 21

AFTER these things, Jesus showed himself again to his disciples by the sea of Tiberias; and he appeared in this way:

2 They were all together, Simon Peter, and Thomas who is called the Twin, and Nathanael of Cana of Galilee, and the sons of Zebedee, and two others of the disciples.

3 Simon Peter said to them, I am going to catch fish. They said to him, We also will come with you. So they went out and went up into the boat; and that night they caught nothing.

4 When morning came, Jesus stood by the sea side; and the disciples did not know that it was Jesus.

5 So Jesus said to them, Boys, have you got anything to eat? They said to him, No.

6 He said to them, Throw your net on the right side of the boat, and you will find. So they threw it, and they were not able to draw the net, because of the many fishes which it had caught.

       Cf.dif. vv. 20:16-18, 22-25, 27, 21:5; (next page) 21:7, 12, 15, 17-18, 23.

7 Then the disciple whom Jesus loved said to Peter, That is our Lord. When Simon heard that it was our Lord, he took his cloak and girded it around his waist, because he was naked; and he jumped into the sea to come to Jesus.

8 But the other disciples came by boat; for they were not very far from land, but about a hundred yards, and they were dragging the net of fishes.

9 When they landed, they saw burning coals set, and a fish laid on them, and bread.

10 Jesus said to them, Bring some of the fish which you have now caught.

11 So Simon Peter went up, and drew the net to land, full of large fishes, one hundred and fifty-three; and in spite of this weight, the net did not break.

12 Jesus said to them, Come, break your fast. But not one of the disciples dared to ask him who he was, for they knew he was our Lord.

13 Then Jesus drew near, and took bread and fish, and gave to them.

14 This is the third time that Jesus appeared to his disciples, since he rose up from the dead.

15 ¶ When they had broken their fast, Jesus said to Simon Peter, Simon, son of Jonah, do you love me more than these things? He said to him, Yes, my Lord; you know that I love you. Jesus said to him, Feed my male lambs.

16 He said to him again the second time, Simon, son of Jonah, do you love me? He said to him, Yes, my Lord; you know that I love you. Jesus said to him, Feed my sheep.

17 He said to him again the third time, Simon, son of Jonah, do you love me? It grieved Peter because he said to him the third time, Do you love me? So he said to him, My Lord, you understand well everything, you know that I love you. Jesus said to him, Feed my female lambs.

18 Truly, truly, I say to you, when you were young, you used to tie up your girdle yourself, and walk wherever you pleased; but when you become old, you will stretch out your hands, and another will tie up for you your girdle, and take you where you do not wish.

19 He said this, to show by what death he would glorify God. And when he had said these things, he said to him, Follow me.

20 Simon Peter turned around and saw the disciple whom Jesus loved following him, the one who leaned on the breast of Jesus at the supper, and said, My Lord, who will betray you?

21 When Peter saw him, he said to Jesus, My Lord, what about him?

22 Jesus said to him, If I wish him to remain until I come, what difference does that make to you? You follow me.

23 This word then went out among the brethren, that that disciple would not die. But what Jesus said was not that he would not die; but, If I wish that he should remain until I come back, what difference does that make to you?

24 This is the disciple who testified concerning all of these things, and who also wrote them; and we know that his testimony is true.

25 There are also a great many other things which Jesus did, which, if they were written one by one, not even this world, I believe, could contain the books that would be written.

Completion of the Holy Gospel, the announcement of John the Evangelist; which he uttered, in Greek, at Ephesus.

ܫܠܡ ܐܘܢܓܠܝܘܢ ܩܕܝܫܐ ܕܟܪܘܙܘܬܗ ܕܝܘܚܢܢ ܀
܀ ܕܡܠܠ ܝܘܢܐܝܬ ܒܐܦܣܘܣ ܀

THE
ACTS OF THE APOSTLES

✣ ܐܦܪܟܣܝܣ ܕܗܠܝܢ ܫܠܝܚܐ ܩܕܝܫܐ ✣

CHAPTER 1

THE first book have I written, O The-oph'i-lus, concerning all the things which our Lord Jesus Christ began to do and teach

2 Until the day when he ascended after he, through the Holy Spirit, had given command-ments to the apostles whom he had chosen;

3 The very ones to whom he had also shown himself alive, after he had suffered, with many wonders during the forty days, while appearing to them and talking with them concerning the kingdom of God:

4 And as he ate bread with them, he com-manded them not to depart from Jerusalem but to wait for the promise of the Father, the one of whom you have heard from me.

5 For John baptized with water; but you shall be baptized with the Holy Spirit not many days hence.

6 While they were assembled, they asked him, saying, Our LORD, will you at this time restore the kingdom to Israel?

7 He said to them, It is not for you to know the time or times, which the Father has put under his own authority.

8 But when the Holy Spirit comes upon you, you shall receive power and you shall be witnesses to me both in Jerusalem and in all Judaea also in the province of Samaria and unto the uttermost part of the earth.

9 And when he had spoken these things, he ascended while they were looking at him; a cloud * received him and he was hidden from their sight.

10 And while they looked steadfastly toward heaven as he went up, behold two men stood by them in white robes;

11 And they said to them, Men of Gal'i-lee, why do you stand gazing up into heaven? This same Jesus who has ascended from you into heaven, shall so come in like manner as you have seen him ascend into heaven.

12 ¶ Then they returned to Jerusalem from the mount which is called Ol'i-vet, home of Olives, which is near to Jerusalem, about a mile away.

13 And after they had entered into the city, they went up into an upper room, where stayed Peter and John and James and Andrew, and also Philip and Thomas, and Matthew and Bar-thol'o-mew and James the son of Al-phæ'us, and Simon the zealot, and Judas the son of James.

14 These all continued together in prayer with one accord, with the women, and Mary the Mother of Jesus, and with his brothers.

15 And in those days Simon Peter stood up in the midst of the disciples (there were there a number of men, about a hundred and twenty), and said,

16 Men and brethren, it was proper that the scripture should be fulfilled, that which the Holy Spirit foretold by the mouth of David concerning Judas, who was guide to them that seized Jesus.

17 For he was numbered with us and had a lot # in this ministry.

18 He is the one who earned for himself a field with the price of sin; and falling head-

* Ac.1:9 - Until recent days Easterners believed that clouds were living creatures.
# Ac.1:17 - "Lot" means *vote*.

Cf.dif. vv. 1:1, 3-4, 8,12, 15, 17.

149

long, he burst open in the midst and all his bowels gushed out.

19 And this very thing is known to all who dwell in Jerusalem; so that the field is called in the language of the country, Kha'kal-De'ma which is to say Ko-ri-ath'dem, the field of blood.

20 For it is written in the book of Psalms, Let his habitation be desolate, and let no one dwell in it; and let his duty be taken by another man.

21 It is necessary, therefore, that one of these men, who have been with us during all the time that our LORD Jesus went in and out among us,

22 Beginning from the baptism of John until the day he ascended from among us, become a partner with us as a witness of his resurrection.

23 So they appointed two: Joseph called Bar'sa-bas who was surnamed Justus, and Mat-thi'as.

24 And as they prayed, they said, O LORD, you know what is in the hearts of all men; show which of these two you choose,

25 That he may receive the lot to the ministry and apostleship, from which Judas has been relieved to go his own way.

26 Then they cast lots, and the lot fell upon Mat-thi'as; and he was numbered with the eleven apostles.

CHAPTER 2

AND when the day of Pen'te-cost was fulfilled, while they were assembled together,

2 Suddenly there came a sound from heaven as of a rushing mighty wind and it filled all the house where they were sitting.

3 And there appeared to them tongues which were divided like flames of fire; and they rested upon each of them.

4 And they were all filled with the Holy Spirit, and they began to speak in various languages, according to whatever the Spirit gave them to speak.

5 Now there were resident at Jerusalem, devout men and Jews from every nation under heaven.

6 And as the sound took place, all the people gathered together, and they were confused because every man heard them speak in his own language.

7 And they were all amazed and marvelled, saying one to another, Behold, are not all these who speak Gal-i-læ'ans?

8 How is it that we hear every man in our own native language?

9 Par'thi-ans and Medes and E'lam-ites and those who dwell in Mes-o-po-ta'mi-a, Jews and Cap-pa-do'ci-ans and those from Pontus and Asia Minor,

10 And those from the region of Phryg'i-a and of Pam-phyl'i-a and of Egypt, and of the regions of Lib'y-a near Cy-re'ne, and those who have come from Rome, both Jews and proselytes,

11 And those from Crete, and Arabians, behold we hear them speak in our own tongues of the wonderful works of God.

12 And they were all amazed and stunned, saying one to another, what does this mean?

13 Others mocking said, These men are full of new wine.

14 ¶ And afterwards Simon Peter stood up together with the eleven disciples, and lifted up his voice and said to them, Men of Jewish race, and all that dwell at Jerusalem, let this be known to you, and harken to my words:

15 For these men are not drunken as you suppose for behold it is but the third hour of the day. *

16 But this is that which was spoken by the prophet Joel:

* Ac.2:15 - Equivalent to nine in the morning. By custom drinking is not done until after the noonday meal.

17 It shall come to pass in the last days, said God, I will pour my spirit upon all flesh: and your sons and your daughters shall prophesy and your young men shall see visions and your old men shall dream dreams:

18 And upon my servants and upon my maidservants will I pour out my spirit in those days; and they shall prophesy:

19 And I will show wonders in heaven, and signs on the earth; blood and fire and vapor of smoke:

20 The sun shall be changed into darkness, and the moon into blood, before that great and fearful day of the Lord shall come.

21 And it shall come to pass that whoever shall call on the name of the Lord shall be saved.

22 Men of Israel, hear these words; Jesus of Nazareth, a man of God, who appeared among you by miracles and signs and wonders which God did by him among you, as you yourselves know:

23 The very one who was chosen for this purpose from the very beginning of knowledge and will of God, you have delivered into the hands of wicked men, and you have crucified and murdered him:

24 Whom God has raised up, having loosed the pains of death: because it was not possible for the grave to hold him.

25 For David said concerning him, I foresaw my Lord always, for he is on my right hand, so that I should not be shaken:

26 Therefore my heart is comforted and my glory is exalted; even my body shall rest in hope:

27 Because you will not leave my soul in the grave neither will you suffer your Holy One to see corruption.

28 You have revealed to me the way of life; you will fill me with joy with your presence.

29 Now men and brethren, permit me to speak to you openly concerning Patriarch David, who is dead and buried and whose sepulchre is with us to this day.

30 For he was a prophet, and he knew that God had sworn by an oath to him, that of the fruit of his loins, according to the flesh, he would raise up one to sit on his throne.

31 So he foresaw and spoke concerning the resurrection of Christ, that his soul was not left in the grave, neither did his body see corruption.

32 This very Jesus, God has raised up, and we are all his witnesses.

33 It is he who is exalted by the right hand of God, and has received from the Father the promise of the Holy Spirit, and has poured out gifts which you now see and hear.

34 For David did not ascend into heaven, because he himself said, The Lord said unto my Lord, Sit thou on my right hand,

35 Until I make thy foes thy footstool.

36 Therefore let all the house of Israel know assuredly that God has made this very Jesus whom you have crucified, both Lord and Christ.

37 ¶ When they heard these things, their hearts were touched and they said to Simon and the rest of the apostles, Our brethren, what shall we do?

38 Then Simon said to them, Repent and be baptized, every one of you in the name of the LORD Jesus for the remission of sins, so that you may receive the gift of the Holy Spirit.

39 For the promise was made to you and to your children, and for all of those who are far off, even as many as the very God shall call.

40 And he testified to them with many other words and besought them, saying, Save your-

selves from this sinful generation.

41 And those men among them who readily accepted his word and believed were baptized and about three thousand souls were added in that day.

42 And they continued steadfastly in the teaching, of the apostles and they took part in prayer and in the breaking of bread.

43 ¶ And fear came upon every soul: and many miracles and wonders were done by the apostles in Jerusalem.

44 And all believers were together, and had all things in common;

45 And those who had possessions sold them and divided to each man according to his need.

46 And they went to the temple every day with one accord; and at home they broke bread, and they received food with joy and with a pure heart,

47 Praising God, and finding favor with all the people. And our LORD daily increased the congregation of the church.

CHAPTER 3

*I*T came to pass as Simon Peter and John were going up together to the temple at the time of prayer, at the ninth hour, *

2 Behold a certain man, lame from his mother's womb, was carried by men who were accustomed to bring him and lay him at the gate of the temple which is called Beautiful so that he might ask alms from those who entered into the temple.

3 And when he saw Simon Peter and John entering the temple, he begged of them to give him alms.

4 And Simon Peter and John looked at him and said, Look at us.

5 And he looked at them, expecting to receive something from them.

6 Then Simon Peter said to him, Gold and silver have I none; but what I have I give to you: In the name of our LORD Jesus Christ of Naz'a-reth rise up and walk.

7 And he took him by the right hand and lifted him up; and in that very hour his legs and his feet received strength.

8 And he, leaping up, stood and walked, and entered with them into the temple, walking and leaping and praising God.

9 And all the people saw him walking and praising God;

10 And they recognized that he was the beggar who had sat daily and asked alms at the gate which is called Beautiful; and they were filled with amazement and wonder at what had happened.

11 ¶ And as he was assisted by Simon and John, all the people ran in astonishment towards them to the porch that is called Solomon's.

12 And when Simon Peter saw it, he said to them, Men of Israel, why are you wondering at this man or why are you looking at us as though by our own power or authority we had made this man to walk?

13 The God of Abraham and of Isaac and of Jacob, the God of our Fathers has glorified his Son Jesus whom you delivered up and denied him in the presence of Pilate when he was determined to let him go.

14 But you denied the Holy One and the Righteous and asked a murderer to be given to you;

15 And killed the Prince of Life, whom God has raised from the dead; all of us are his witnesses.

16 Faith in his name has healed this man whom you see and know and made him strong; it is the faith in him which has granted this healing before you all.

* Ac. 3:1- Three in the afternoon.

Cf.dif. vv. 2:41-43, 45, 47;   3:2, 8, 12, 15-16.

17 But now, my brethren, I know that you did this through ignorance just as your leaders did it.

18 But those things, which God before had preached by the mouth of all the prophets, that his Christ should suffer, he has so fulfilled.

19 Repent, therefore, and be converted, that your sins may be blotted out when the times of tranquility shall come to you from before the presence of the LORD;

20 And he shall send to you One who has been prepared for you, even Jesus Christ;

21 Whom the heaven must receive until all the things which God has spoken by the mouth of his holy prophets, since the world began should be fulfilled.

22 For Moses said, The LORD shall raise up a prophet like me for you from among your brethren; listen to him in all that he shall say to you.

23 And it shall come to pass that every soul which will not listen to that prophet, shall be lost from her people.

24 Yea, and all the prophets from Samuel and those that follow after, as many as have spoken, and preached have likewise foretold of these days.

25 You are the children of the prophets, and of the covenant which God made with our fathers, saying to Abraham, By your seed shall all the kindred of the earth be blessed.

26 Now it was for you first, God appointed and sent his Son to bless you if you turn and repent from your evils.

CHAPTER 4

AND while they were speaking these words to the people, the priests and the Sad'du-cees and the leaders of the temple rose up against them,

2 Being infuriated that they taught the people and preached through Jesus the resurrection from the dead.

3 And they laid hands on them and detained them until the next day, for it was now eventide.

4 Howbeit many of them who heard the word believed; and the number of the men was about five thousand.

5 ¶ And the next day, the leaders and the elders and the scribes gathered together;

6 And also Annas the high priest, and Ca'iaphas and John and Alexander and those who were of the family of the high priest.

7 And when they had made them to stand in the midst, they asked, By what power or by what name have you done this?

8 Then Simon Peter, filled with the Holy Spirit, said to them, Leaders of the people and elders of the house of Israel, listen.

9 If we are convicted today by you, concerning the good which has been done to a sick man, on the ground of by what means he was healed;

10 Then let it be known to you, and to all the people of Israel, By the name of Jesus Christ of Nazareth, whom you crucified, and whom God raised from the dead, behold this man stands before you, healed.

11 This is the stone which you builders have rejected, which is become the head of the corner.

12 There is no salvation by any other man; for there is no other name under heaven given among men, whereby we must be saved.

13 Now when they had heard the speech of Simon Peter and John, which they had spoken boldly, and perceived that they were unlearned and ignorant men, they marvelled; and they recognized them that they had been with Jesus.

14 And because they saw the lame man who was healed standing with them they could say nothing against them.

15 But when they had commanded them to be taken aside out of the council, they conferred among themselves,

Cf.dif. vv. 3:17, 19-22, 24, 26; 4:1, 3, 8-9, 13.

16 Saying, What shall we do to these men? for behold a miracle has openly been performed by them and it is known to all that dwell in Jerusalem; and we cannot deny it.

17 But, so that this news should not spread further among the people, let us threaten them, that they speak henceforth to no man in this name.

18 And they called them, and commanded them not to speak at all nor teach in the name of Jesus.

19 But Simon Peter and John answered and said to them, Whether it be right before God to listen to you more than to God, you judge.

20 For we cannot stop speaking about the things which we have seen and heard.

21 So when they had further threatened them, they let them go; for they found no cause to punish them because of the people: for all men praised God for that which was done.

22 For the man on whom this miracle of healing had been wrought, was more than forty years old.

23 ¶ After they were released, they went to their brethren and told them all that the high priests and elders had said.

24 And when they heard this, they all together lifted up their voice to God and said, O LORD, you are the God who has made heaven and earth and the seas and all that in them is:

25 You are the One who spoke through the Holy Spirit by the mouth of your servant David when he said, Why did the people rage and the nations devise worthless things?

26 The kings and the rulers of the earth have revolted and have taken counsel together against the LORD and against his Anointed.

27 For truly, they assembled in this very city, together with both Herod and Pilate and with the Gentiles and with the people of Israel, against your holy Son Jesus,

28 To execute whatever your hand and your will had previously decreed to take place.

29 And even now, O LORD, look and see their threatenings; and grant to your servants that they may freely preach your word,

30 Just as your hand is freely stretched out for healings, and wonders and the miracles which are done in the name of your holy Son Jesus.

31 And when they had petitioned and made their supplications, the place in which they were assembled together was shaken, and they were all filled with the Holy Spirit and they spoke the word of God boldly.

32 ¶ Now the congregation of the believers were of one soul and of one mind; not one of them spoke of the property he possessed as his own; but everything they had was in common.

33 And the apostles testified with great power concerning the resurrection of Jesus Christ; and they were all greatly favored.

34 There was not a man among them who was destitute; for those who possessed fields and houses sold them and brought the money for the things that were sold,

35 And placed them at the disposal of the disciples; and the proceeds were then given to every man according to his needs.

36 Now Joseph whom the apostles surnamed Bar'na-bas (which is, interpreted, the son of consolation), a Levite of the country of Cy'prus,

37 Had a field and he sold it and brought the price and placed it at the disposal of the apostles.

CHAPTER 5

BUT a certain man called An-a-ni'as, together with his wife named Shapphi'ra, sold his field.

2 And he took some of the price and hid it, and his wife also knew of it, and he brought

some of the money and placed it at the disposal of the apostles.

3 And Simon Peter said to him, An-a-ni'as, why has Satan so filled your heart that you should lie to the Holy Spirit and hide part of the money of the price of the field?

4 Was it not your own before you sold it? And after it was sold, had you not the sole authority over its price? What made you think to do this thing? You have not only lied to men but to God.

5 And when An-a-ni'as heard these words, he fell down and died; and great fear came upon all of those who heard these things.

6 The younger men among them arose, and moved his body aside. Then they took him out and buried him.

7 Three hours later his wife also came in, not knowing what had happened.

8 Simon Peter said to her, Tell me if you sold the field for this price? She said, Yea, for this price.

9 Then Simon Peter said to her, Because you have been partners to tempt the Spirit of the LORD, behold the feet of the men who have buried your husband are at the door, and they shall carry you out also.

10 And in that very hour she fell down at their feet and died, and the young men came in and found her dead, and they picked her up and carried her away and buried her by the side of her husband.

11 And great fear came upon all the congregation and upon all who heard what had happened.

12 Many miracles and signs were wrought among the people by the apostles, and they were all gathered together in the portico * of Solomon.

13 And of the unbelievers, no one dared to interfere with them, but the people held them in respect.

14 And the number of those who believed in the LORD was greatly increased by multitudes, both of men and women.

15 They even brought out the sick into the streets and laid them on bed quilts so that when Simon Peter should happen to pass by, his shadow might fall upon them.

16 Many came to them from other cities around Jerusalem, bringing the sick and mentally afflicted, and they were all healed.

17 ¶ Then the high priest was filled with jealousy and all of those who were with him, for they were adherents to the teachings of the Sad'du-cees,

18 So they laid hold on the apostles and arrested them and bound them in prison.

19 But during the night, the angel of the LORD opened the door of the prison and brought them forth and said to them,

20 Go, stand in the temple and speak to the people all these words of life.

21 Accordingly they went out early in morning and entered into the temple and taught the people. But the high priest and those who were with him called their associates and the elders of Israel, and sent to the prison to bring the apostles.

22 And when those who were sent by them, went, and did not find them in the prison, they returned,

23 Saying, We found the prison carefully locked and also the guards standing at the doors; and we opened them but found no man there.

24 When the high priest and the leaders of the temple heard these words, they were astonished at them and they were reasoning how it could happen,

25 When a man came and informed them, Behold! The men whom you put in prison are standing in the temple and teaching the people.

* Ac.5:12- Portico or Arcade - Strangers and the poor often stayed at these places.
Cf.dif. vv. 5:6-7, 9-10, 12-18, 21, 23-24.

26 Then the leaders went with the soldiers to bring them, not by force, for they were afraid that the people might stone them.

27 And when they had brought them, they made them stand before the whole council, and the high priest proceeded,

28 Saying, Did we not strictly command you not to teach any man in this name? And behold, you have filled Jerusalem with your doctrine; and intend to bring the blood of this man upon us.

29 Then Simon Peter with the rest of the apostles answered and said to them, We must obey God rather than men.

30 The God of our fathers has raised up Jesus whom you murdered when you crucified him on the cross.

31 This very one God has appointed a Prince and a Saviour, and has lifted him up by his right hand so that he may grant repentance and forgiveness of sins to Israel.

32 And we are the witnesses of these words; so is also the Holy Spirit whom God has given to those who believe in him.

33 When they heard these words, they were enraged and thought to murder the apostles.

34 Then one of the Phar'i-sees whose name was Ga-ma'li-el, a teacher of the law and honored by all the people, rose up and ordered them to take the apostles outside for a little while;

35 Then he said to them, Men of Israel, take heed to yourselves, and find out what is the best for you to do about these men.

36 For before these days, rose up Theu'das, boasting himself to be a great man; and about four hundred men followed him: he was slain; and those who followed him were scattered and nothing came of them.

37 After him rose up Judas, the Gal-i-le'an, in the days when people were registering for the head tax, and he misled many people into following him. He died; and all of those who followed him were dispersed.

38 So now I tell you, Keep away from these men and let them alone; for if this thought and this work is of men, it will fail and pass away.

39 But if it be of God, you cannot suppress it, lest perchance you find yourself standing in opposition to God.

40 And they listened to him, and they called the apostles, and scourged them, and commanded them not to speak in the name of Jesus, and let them go.

41 The apostles went out from the presence of the council rejoicing that they had been worthy to suffer abuse for the sake of his name.

42 And they did not cease to teach daily in the temple and at home and to preach concerning our LORD Jesus Christ.

CHAPTER 6

AND in those days, when the number of disciples had increased, the Hel'len-ist converts murmured against the Hebrew converts because their widows were discriminated against in the daily distribution.

2 So the twelve apostles called the whole multitude of the converts and said to them, It is not good that we should leave the word of God and serve food. *

3 Wherefore, brethren, examine and select from among you seven men of good repute who are full of the Spirit of the LORD and of wisdom, so that we may appoint them to this task.

4 And we will give ourselves continually to prayer and to the ministry of the word.

5 This suggestion pleased the whole people

---

* Ac. 6:2- In the East, food is distributed on a cloth, in wooden or copper trays and set before the people.

     Cf.dif. vv. 5:26-27, 30-32, 34-35, 37, 39, 41-42; 6:1-3.

so they chose Stephen, a man full of faith and the Holy Spirit, and Philip and Proch'o-rus and Ni-ca'nor and Ti'mon and Par'me-nas and Nic'o-las, a proselyte of An'ti-och.

6 These men stood before the apostles: who, as they prayed, laid their hands on them.

7 And the word of God spread; and the number of the converts in Jerusalem increased greatly; and many people of Jewish faith became converts.

8 ¶ Now Stephen was full of grace and power and did great wonders and miracles among the people.

9 Then there arose certain men of the synagogue, which is called the synagogue of the Lib'er-tines, and Cy-re'ni-ans and Al-ex-an'dri-ans and Ci-li'ci-ans and persons from Asia Minor, and they debated with Stephen.

10 But they were unable to stand up against the wisdom and the spirit by which he spoke.

11 Then they sent men and instructed them to say, We have heard him speak blasphemous words against Moses and against God.

12 And they stirred up the people and the elders and the scribes, and they rose up against him and seized him and brought him into the midst of the council.

13 And they appointed false witnesses who said, This man does not cease to speak against the law and against this holy land:

14 For we have heard him say that Jesus of Nazareth shall destroy this country and shall change the customs which Moses entrusted to you.

15 Then all who were seated at the council looked at him and saw that his face was like the face of an angel.

CHAPTER 7

𝒯HEN the high priest asked Stephen, Are these things so?

2 He said, Men, brethren and our fathers, harken: The God of glory appeared to our father Abraham when he was still in Mes-o-po-ta'mi-a before he came to dwell in Ha'ran.

3 And he said to him, Get out of your land and from your relatives and come into the land which I shall show you.

4 Then Abraham left the land of the Chal-de'ans and he came and settled in Ha'ran and from thence, after his father's death, God removed him into this land in which you now live.

5 And he gave him no inheritance in it, no, not so much as to set his foot on: yet he promised that he would give it as an inheritance to him and to his posterity, when as yet he had no son.

6 God spoke to him and said, Your descendants will be settlers in a foreign land where they will be enslaved and mistreated for a period of four hundred years.

7 But the people to whom they will be enslaved I will condemn, said God, and after that, they shall go out and serve me in this land.

8 God gave Ab'raham the covenant of circumcision; and then Abraham begat Isaac, and circumcised him on the eighth day; and Isaac begat Jacob; and Jacob begat our twelve patriarchs.

9 And our forefathers were jealous of Joseph; so they sold him into Egypt; but God was with him.

10 And he saved him from all his oppressors and gave him favor and wisdom before Pharaoh, king of Egypt; and Pharaoh appointed Joseph an overlord over Egypt and over all his house.

11 Now there came a famine which brought great distress throughout Egypt and in the land of Ca'naan so that our forefathers found no sustenance.

12 But when Jacob heard that there was wheat in Egypt, he sent out our forefathers on their first venture.

Cf.dif. vv. 6:6-7, 9-11; 7:2, 4, 6, 8-9, 12.

13 When they went the second time, Joseph made himself known to his brothers; and Joseph's family was made known to Pharaoh.
14 Then Joseph sent and brought his father Jacob and all his family, seventy-five souls in number.
15 So Jacob went down to Egypt where he and our forefathers died.
16 And he was removed to Sy'chem and buried in the sepulchre which Abraham had bought for a sum of money from the sons of Ha'mor.
17 But when the time of the promise was at hand, which God had sworn to Abraham, the people had already increased and become strong in Egypt,
18 Till another king reigned over Egypt who knew not Joseph.
19 He dealt deceitfully with our kindred, ill treated our forefathers, and commanded that they cast out their male children to the end that they might not live.
20 During that very period Moses was born, and he was favored before God, so that for three months he was nourished in his father's house.
21 And when he was cast away by his mother, Pharaoh's daughter found him and reared him as a son for herself.
22 So Moses was trained in all the wisdom of the E-gyp'tians and he was well versed in his words and also in his deeds.
23 And when he was forty years old, it came into his heart to visit his brethren, the children of Israel.
24 When he saw one of his own kindred mistreated, he avenged him and did justice to him, and killed the E-gyp'tian who had mistreated him.
25 For he thought his brethren, the Is'ra-el-ites, would understand that God would grant them deliverance by his hand, but they understood not.

26 And the next day he found them quarreling one with another and he pleaded with them that they might be reconciled, saying, Men, you are brothers; why are you wronging one another?
27 But the one who was wronging his fellow thrust him aside and said to him, Who appointed you leader and judge over us?
28 Perhaps you want to kill me as you killed the Egyptian yesterday.
29 And because of this saying, Moses fled and took refuge in the land of Ma'di-an where two sons were born to him.
30 And when he had completed forty years, there appeared to him in the wilderness of Mount Si'nai, an angel of the LORD in a flame of fire in a bush.
31 When Moses saw it, he wondered at the sight: and as he drew near to look at it, the LORD spoke to him in a loud voice,
32 Saying, I am the God of your fathers, the God of Abraham and of Isaac and of Jacob. And Moses trembled and dared not look at the sight.
33 Then the LORD said to him, Take off your shoes from your feet, for the ground on which you stand is holy.
34 Already I have seen the affliction of my people in Egypt, I have heard their groans, and I have come down to deliver them. And now come, I will send you into Egypt.
35 This Moses whom they had denied, saying, Who appointed you leader and judge over us?, this very one God sent to be a leader and deliverer to them by the hand of the angel which had appeared to him in the bush.
36 It was he who brought them out after he had performed miracles, wonders, and signs in the land of Egypt and in the Red sea and in the wilderness for forty years.
37 This is the Moses who said to the children of Israel, The LORD your God will raise up for you a prophet, like me, from among

your brethren; give heed to him.

38 It was he who was in the congregation in the wilderness with the angel who spoke to him and to our fathers in Mount Sinai: He is the one who received the living words to give to us.

39 Yet our fathers would not listen to him, but they left him, and in their hearts turned towards Egypt.

40 They said to Aar'on, Make us gods to go before us, for this very Moses who brought us out of the land of Egypt, we do not know what has become of him.

41 And they made a calf for themselves in those days and offered sacrifices to idols and were pleased with the work of their hands.

42 Then God turned and gave them up that they might worship the host of heaven as it is written in the book of the prophets, O Is'ra-el-ites, why have you offered me slain animals or sacrifices during the period of forty years in the wilderness?

43 Indeed you have borne the tabernacle of Mo'loch and the star of the god Rem'phan; and you have made images to worship them; therefore I will remove you beyond Bab'ylon.

44 Behold the tabernacle of the testimony of our fathers was in the wilderness just as he who spoke to Moses had commanded him to make it after the pattern which he had shown him.

45 And this very tabernacle, our fathers, together with Joshua, brought into the land which God took away from the peoples whom he drove out before them and gave it to them for an inheritance, and it was handed down until the days of David:

46 Who found favor before God and asked that he might find a dwelling place for the God of Jacob.

47 But Solomon built God a house.

48 Yet the Most High did not dwell in temples made with hands for, as the prophet had said,

49 Heaven is my throne, and earth is the footstool under my feet. What kind of house will you build me? says the LORD, or Where is the place of my rest?

50 Behold, has not my hand made all these things?

51 O you stubborn and insincere in heart and hearing, you always resist the Holy Spirit: as your fathers did, so do you.

52 Which of the prophets have not your fathers persecuted and murdered? Especially have they slain those who foretold the coming of the Righteous One whom you betrayed and murdered.

53 You received the law by the disposition of angels, and have not kept it.

54 ¶ When they heard these things, they were enraged, and gnashed their teeth at him.

55 But he, full of faith and Holy Spirit, looked up to heaven and saw the glory of God and Jesus standing at the right hand of God.

56 And he said, Behold I see the heavens opened and the Son of Man standing at the right hand of God.

57 Then they cried out with a loud voice, and stopped their ears and with one accord, shouted threats against Stephen.

58 And they seized him and took him outside the city and began to stone him. Those who testified against him placed their clothes under the care of a young man called Saul.

59 And they stoned Stephen as he prayed, saying, Our LORD Jesus, accept my spirit.

60 And as he knelt down, he cried with a loud voice and said, Our LORD, do not hold this sin against them. When he had said this, he passed away.

Cf.dif. vv. 7:39, 43-45, 47, 49, 51-52, 57-58, 60.

CHAPTER 8

SAUL was pleased to have had a part in the murder of Stephen. At that very time there was severe persecution against the church at Jerusalem; and they were all, with the exception of the apostles, dispersed throughout the towns of Judæ'a and Sama'ria.

2 And devout men picked up Stephen and buried him, and they mourned over him in great sorrow.

3 As for Saul, he continued to persecute the church of God, entering into houses and dragging out men and women and delivering them to prison,

4 ¶ So that they that were scattered abroad went everywhere preaching the word of God.

5 Then Philip went down to a Samaritan city and preached to them about Christ.

6 And when the people of that place heard his word, they gave heed and listened attentively to everything Philip said, because they saw the miracles which he did.

7 Many who were mentally afflicted, cried with loud voices and were restored; and others who were paralytic and lame, were healed.

8 And there was great joy in that city.

9 Now there was there a man called Semon, who had lived in that city a long time, and who had deceived the Samaritan people by his magic, boasting of himself and saying, I am the greatest one.

10 And both the noblest and the least followed him, saying, He is the greatest power of God.

11 All of them listened to him, because for a long time he had bewitched them with his sorceries.

12 But when they believed Philip, preaching the things concerning the kingdom of God in the name of our LORD Jesus Christ, they were baptized, both men and women.

13 Semon himself also believed and was baptized and attached himself to Philip, and as he saw the miracles and great signs performed by his hand, he marvelled greatly.

14 Now when the apostles at Jerusalem heard that the Samaritan people had accepted the word of God, they sent to them Simon Peter and John,

15 Who, when they went down, prayed over them that they might receive the Holy Spirit.

16 For as yet it had not come upon them although they had been baptized in the name of our Lord Jesus.

17 Then they laid their hands on them and they received the Holy Spirit.

18 And when Semon saw that the Holy Spirit was given by the laying on of the apostles' hands, he offered them money,

19 Saying, Give me also this authority so that on whomsoever I lay hands, he may receive the Holy Spirit.

20 Simon Peter said to him, Let your money perish with you because you have thought that the gift of God may be purchased with wealth.

21 You have no part nor lot in this faith because your heart is not right in the sight of God.

22 Repent, therefore, of this evil of yours, and beseech God that he may perhaps forgive you for the guile which is in your heart.

23 For I see your heart is as bitter as gall and you are in the bonds of iniquity.

24 Then Semon answered and said, Pray God for me so that none of these things which you have spoken may come upon me.

25 Now when Simon Peter and John had testified and taught them the word of God, they returned to Jerusalem after they had preached in many Samaritan villages.

26 ¶ And the angel of the LORD spoke to Philip, saying, Arise, and go south by way of the desert that leads down from Jerusalem to Gaza,

Cf.dif. vv. 8:1, 3-4, 6-7, 9, 12-16, 21-23, 25-26.

27 So he arose and went: and he was met by a eunuch, who had come from E-thi-o'pi-a; an official of Can'da-ce, queen of the E-thi-o'pi-ans, who had the charge of all her treasure, and had come to worship at Jerusalem.
28 While he was returning, sitting in his chariot, he read the book of the prophet I-sa'iah.
29 And the Spirit said to Philip, Go near and keep close to the chariot.
30 And as Philip drew near and heard him reading from the book of the prophet I-sa'iah, he said to him, Do you understand what you are reading?
31 And the E-thi-o'pi-an said, How can I understand unless some one teach me? and he invited Philip to come up and sit with him.
32 The portion of the scripture which he was reading was this: He was led like a lamb to the slaughter, and like a ewe sheep before the shearer, so he opened not his mouth:
33 In his humiliation, he suffered imprisonment and judgment: none can tell his struggle, for even his life is taken away from the earth.
34 And the eunuch said to Philip. I pray you, of whom does this prophet speak? of himself or of some other man?
35 Then Philip opened his mouth and began at that same scripture and preached to him concerning our LORD Jesus.
36 And as they went on their way, they came to a place where there was water; and the eunuch said, Behold here is water; what prevents me from being baptized?
37 * And Philip said, If you believe with all your heart, you may. And he answered and said, I believe that Jesus Christ is the Son of God.
38 And he commanded the chariot be stopped: and both went down into the water, and Philip baptized the eunuch.

39 And when they came up from the water, the Spirit of the LORD caught Philip away and the eunuch saw him no more: and he went on his way rejoicing.
40 Philip was found at Az-o'tus: and from there he traveled around and preached in all the cities till he came to Cæs-a-re'a.

CHAPTER 9

NOW Saul was still filled with anger and with threats of murder against the disciples of our LORD,
2 And he asked the high priests to give him letters to the synagogues at Damascus, that if he should find anyone, men or women, following this faith, he might bring them bound to Jerusalem.
3 And as he journeyed, he came near Damascus: and suddenly a light from the sky shone round about him;
4 And he fell to the ground, and heard a voice saying to him, Saul, Saul, why do you persecute me? You make it hard for yourself by kicking against the pricks.
5 Saul answered and said, Who are you my LORD? and our LORD said, I am Jesus of Nazareth whom you persecute:
6 * And he, trembling and astonished, said, LORD, what will you have me to do? And the LORD said to him, Arise and go into the city, and there you will be told what you must do.
7 And the men who journeyed with him stood speechless, hearing only a voice, but seeing no man.
8 And Saul arose from the ground, but he could not see even though his eyes were open; and they led him by the hand and brought him into Damascus.
9 And he was unable to see for three days during which he neither ate nor drank.

* Ac.8:37; Ac. 9:6 - Carried from the King James Version.
Cf.dif. vv. 8:27, 29-34, 36;   9:2-6, 8.

10 ¶ Now there was in Damascus a disciple named An-a-ni'as, and the LORD said to him in a vision, An-a-ni'as. And he said, Behold, I am here, my LORD.

11 And our LORD said to him, Arise, and go into the street which is called Straight and enquire at the house of Judas for Saul of the city of Tarsus: for behold, he is praying,

12 And he has seen in a vision a man named An-a-ni'as coming in and laying his hand on him to restore his sight.

13 Then An-a-ni'as said, My LORD, I have heard from many concerning this man, how much misery he has brought to your saints in Jerusalem.

14 And behold here also he has authority from the high priests to bind all who call on your name.

15 But the LORD said to him, Arise and go: he is the agent whom I have chosen for myself to carry my name to the Gentiles and kings, and the children of Israel:

16 For I will show him how great things he must suffer for my name's sake.

17 Then An-a-ni'as went to him at the house, and laying his hands on him, said, Saul, my brother, our LORD Jesus, who appeared to you on the way when you were coming, has sent me that you may receive your sight and be filled with the Holy Spirit.

18 And in that hour, there fell from his eyes something like scales; and his eyesight was restored; and he arose and was baptized.

19 And when he had received food, he was strengthened, and he remained several days with the disciples in Damascus.

20 From that time on, he preached in the Jewish synagogues concerning Jesus, that he is the Son of God.

21 But all those who heard him were amazed and said: Is this not he who persecuted those who called on this name in Jerusalem and behold, he was sent here for that very pur-pose that he might bring them bound to the high priests?

22 But Saul became more powerful and he made the Jews who dwelt in Damascus tremble when he proved that Jesus is the Christ.

23 After he had been there many days, the Jews plotted against him to kill him.

24 But their conspiracy was made known to Saul, how they watched the gates of the city day and night to kill him.

25 Then the disciples placed him in a basket and let him down over the wall during the night.

26 Then Saul went to Jerusalem, and wanted to join the disciples, but they were all afraid of him, and could not believe that he was a convert.

27 But Bar'na-bas took him and brought him to the apostles, and told them how he had seen the LORD on the way, and how he had spoken to him, and how in Damascus he had spoken openly in the name of Jesus.

28 So he went in and out with them at Jerusalem.

29 And he spoke openly in the name of Jesus, and debated with the Jews who understood Greek: but they wanted to kill him.

30 And when the brethren knew it, they brought him by night to Cæs-a-re'a, and from thence they sent him to Tarsus.

31 ¶ Then the church throughout Judæa and Galilee and Samaria was at peace, and strengthened itself and developed obedience and reverence to God, and by the consolation of the Holy Spirit, it increased in numbers.

32 ¶ And it came to pass, while Simon Peter traveled to various cities, he came down also to the saints who dwelt at the city oú Lyd'da.

33 And there he found a man named Æ 'ne-as, who had been paralyzed and had lain in bed eight years.

34 And Simon Peter said to him, Æ 'ne-as, Jesus Christ heals you: Arise, and make your bed. And he arose immediately.

35 And all who dwelt at Lyd'da and Sharon saw him and turned to God.

36 ¶ Now there was in the city of Joppa a woman disciple called Tab'i-tha, which means gazelle and interpreted Dorcas; she was rich in good works and in charitable acts.

37 And it came to pass in those days, that she was sick, and died: they bathed her, and laid her in an upper room.

38 And the disciples heard that Simon Peter was in the city of Lyd'da, which is beside Joppa; they sent to him two men, desiring him to come to them without delay.

39 Then Simon Peter arose and went with them. And when he had arrived, they took him to the upper room where all the widows were gathered around her weeping and they showed him shirts and cloaks which Tab'i-tha had given them when she was alive.

40 But Simon Peter put all the people out and knelt down and prayed; then he turned to the body and said, Tab'i-tha, arise. And she opened her eyes, and when she saw Simon Peter, she sat up.

41 And he gave her his hand, and lifted her up; then he called the saints and widows and presented her to them alive.

42 And this was known throughout the city and many believed in our LORD.

43 Peter remained in Joppa many days, staying at the house of Simon Bur-sa'ya, the tanner.

CHAPTER 10

*T*HERE was in Cæs-a-re'a a man called Cornelius, a centurion of the regiment which is called the Italian,

2 A righteous and God-fearing man as were all his household; which gave much alms to the people, and always sought after God.

3 Very openly in a vision about three o'clock in the afternoon he saw an angel of God who came in to him, and said to him, Cornelius.

4 And he looked at the angel and was afraid, and he said, What is it, my LORD? And the angel said to him, Your prayers and your alms have come up for a memorial before God.

5 And now send men to the city of Joppa, and bring here Simon who is called Peter:

6 Behold he is staying with Simon Bur-sa-ya, the tanner, whose house is by the seaside.

7 And when the angel who spoke to him had departed, Cornelius called two of his household, and a soldier who believed in God and was obedient to him;

8 And he related to them everything that he had seen, and sent them to Joppa.

9 ¶ The next day, while they were on their journey, drawing near to the city, Simon Peter went up upon the housetop to pray about noontime.

10 And he became hungry, and wanted to eat: but while they were preparing food for him, he was seized with a sudden faintness.

11 And he saw the sky open and something fastened at the four corners, resembling a large linen cloth, was let down from heaven to the earth:

12 And there were in it all kind of fourfooted beasts, and creeping things of the earth, and fowls of the air.

13 And there came a voice to him, saying, Simon Peter, rise; kill and eat.

14 But Simon Peter said, Far be it, my LORD; for I have never eaten anything which was unclean and defiled.

15 And again the voice came to him a second time, What God has cleansed, you should not call unclean.

16 This happened the third time: then the cloth was lifted up to the heaven.

17 Now while Simon Peter was bewildered, wondering in himself what the vision he had seen should mean, the men who were sent by

Cf.dif. vv. 9:36, 39; 10:5, 7, 10-11, 13-14, 16-17.

163

Cornelius arrived, and enquired for the house in which Simon Peter had been staying, and they came and stood at the door of the court-yard.

18 And from there they called and asked if Simon who is called Peter stayed there.

19 While Simon Peter meditated about the vision, the Spirit said to him, Behold three men seek you.

20 Arise, go down, and go with them, with-out doubt in your mind: for I have sent them.

21 Then Simon Peter went down to the men and said, I am the man you seek. What is the purpose of your mission?

22 They said to him, A man called Cornelius, a righteous and God-fearing centurion of whom all the Jewish people speak well, was told in a vision by a holy angel to send and bring you to his house and to hear words from you.

23 So Simon Peter brought them into the place where he was staying and welcomed them. The next day he arose and went with them, and a few men from amongst the breth-ren of Joppa accompanied him.

24 ¶ And the next day they entered Cæs-a-re'a. And Cornelius was waiting for them, and all his relatives and also his dear friends were assembled with him.

25 And just as Simon Peter was entering, Cornelius met him and threw himself at his feet and worshipped him.

26 But Simon Peter raised him, saying, Stand up; I am but a man also.

27 And after he had talked with him, he went in and found a great many people had come there.

28 So he said to them, You know well that it is unlawful for a Jew to associate with a stranger who is not of his tribe; but God has showed me that I should not call any man common or unclean.

29 This is why I came at once when you sent for me: but now let me ask you, for what reason have you sent for me?

30 Then Cornelius said to him, Four days I have been fasting; and at three o'clock in the afternoon while I was praying in my house, a man dressed in white garments stood be-fore me.

31 And said to me, Cornelius, your prayer has been heard, and your alms are a memo-rial before God.

32 But send to the city of Joppa and bring Simon, who is called Peter; behold he is stay-ing in the house of Simon Bur-sa'ya, the tan-ner, by the seaside: and he will come and talk with you.

33 At that very time I sent for you, and you have done well to come. Behold we are all here present before you, and we wish to hear everything commanded thee from God.

34 ¶ Then Simon Peter opened his mouth and said, Of a truth I perceive that God is no respecter of persons:

35 But among all people, he who fears him and works righteousness is accepted with him.

36 For God sent the word to the children of Israel, preaching peace and tranquility by Jesus Christ: he is the LORD of all.

37 And you also are familiar with the news which was published throughout Judæa, which sprang from Galilee, after the baptism preached by John;

38 Concerning Jesus of Nazareth, whom God anointed with the Holy Spirit and with power, and who, because God was with him, went about doing good and healing all who were oppressed of the devil.

39 And we are witnesses of all things which he did throughout the land of Judæa and in Jerusalem. This very one the Jews crucified on a cross and killed him:

40 Him God raised on the third day, and showed him openly;

41 Not to all the people, but to us who have been chosen by God to be his witnesses, for we did eat and drink with him after his resurrection from the dead.

42 And he commanded us to preach to the people and to testify, that it is he who was ordained by God to be the judge of the living and of the dead.

43 To him, all the prophets testified that whosoever believes in his name shall receive remission of sins.

44 ¶ While Simon Peter spoke these words, the Holy Spirit descended on all who heard the word.

45 And the Jewish converts who had come with him were seized with amazement because the gift of the Holy Spirit was poured out on the Gentiles also;

46 For they heard them speak with divers tongues, and magnify God.

47 Then Simon Peter said to them, Can any man forbid water, that these people who have received the Holy Spirit, just as we have, should not be baptized?

48 And he commanded them to be baptized in the name of our LORD Jesus Christ. And they urged him to remain with them a few days.

CHAPTER 11

A ND the apostles and the brethren who were in Judæa heard that the Gentiles also had received the word of God.

2 And when Simon Peter had come up to Jerusalem, those who upheld the circumcision contended with him,

3 Saying he had entered into the houses of uncircumcised men and had eaten with them.

4 Then Simon began to recite the facts one after another, saying,

5 As I was praying in Joppa, I saw in a vision something like a linen cloth descending from the sky, and it was tied at its four corners; and it came even to me.

6 And as I looked at it, I saw that there were in it fourfooted beasts, and creeping things of the earth, and fowls of the air.

7 Then I heard a voice saying to me, Simon, arise, kill and eat.

8 And I said, Far be it, my Lord: for never has anything defiled and unclean entered my mouth.

9 But again the voice from heaven said to me, What God has cleansed, do not call unclean.

10 This happened three times: then everything was lifted up into heaven.

11 And in that very hour, three men who were sent to me by Cornelius from Cæs-a-re'a came and stood at the gate of the courtyard where I was staying.

12 And the spirit said to me, Go with them, doubting nothing. And these six brethren accompanied me, and we entered the man's house.

13 And he related to us how he had seen an angel in his house, who stood and said to him, Send to the city of Joppa, and bring Simon who is called Peter;

14 And he shall speak to you words by which you and all of your household shall be saved.

15 And as I began to speak, the Holy Spirit came on them, as on us at the beginning.

16 Then I remembered that word of our LORD, when he said, John indeed baptized with water; but you shall be baptized with the Holy Spirit.

17 Now, therefore, if God has equally given the gifts to the Gentiles who believe in our LORD Jesus Christ, just as he gave to us, who am I that I should dispute God?

18 When they heard these words, they held their peace and glorified God, saying, Perhaps God has also granted to the Gentiles repentance unto life.

Cf.dif. vv. 10:41, 47-48; 11:1, 3, 5, 7, 11, 17-18.

19 ¶ Now those who had been dispersed by the persecution which occurred on account of Stephen, traveled as far as Phoe-ni'ci-a and even to the land of Cyprus, and to An'ti-och, preaching the word to none but to the Jews only.

20 But there were some men among them from Cyprus and from Cyrene; these men entered into An'ti-och and spoke to the Greeks and preached concerning our LORD Jesus.

21 And the hand of the LORD was with them: and a great number believed, and turned to the LORD.

22 ¶ Then tidings of these things came to the attention of the members of the congregation at Jerusalem: and they sent Bar'na-bas to An'ti-och.

23 When he came there and saw the grace of God, he was glad, and he pleaded with them that they should follow our LORD with all their hearts.

24 For he was a good man, and full of the Holy Spirit and of faith: and many people were added to our LORD.

25 Then Bar'na-bas departed to Tar'sus, to seek for Saul.

26 And when he had found him, he brought him to An'ti-och. And for the whole year they assembled together in the church, and taught a great many people. The disciples were called Christians first at An'ti-och and from that time on.

27 And in those days came prophets from Jerusalem to An'ti-och.

28 ¶ And one of them, named Ag'a-bus, stood up and foretold by the spirit, that a great famine was to come throughout the land: the famine which occurred in the days of Clau'di-us Cæ'sar.

29 Then the disciples, each one according to his ability, determined to set aside for relief to the brethren who dwelt in Ju-dæ'a.

30 This they did, and sent it there to the elders by the hands of Bar'na-bas and Saul.

CHAPTER 12

*N*OW at that very time Herod the king surnamed A-grip'pa seized some of the people of the church to oppress them.

2 And he killed James the brother of John with the sword.

3 And when he saw that this pleased the Jews, he proceeded to arrest Simon Peter also. This happened during the days of unleavened bread.

4 So he seized him and put him in prison and delivered him to the care of sixteen soldiers to keep him, so that he might deliver him to the Jewish people after the passover.

5 And while Simon Peter was kept in the prison, continual prayer was offered for him to God by the church.

6 And on the very night before the morning that he was to be delivered up, while Simon Peter was sleeping between two soldiers, bound with two chains, and others were guarding the doors of the prison,

7 The angel of the LORD stood over him, and a light shone in all the prison: and the angel touched him on the side and awoke him, and said to him, Rise up quickly. And the chains fell off from his hands.

8 And the angel said to him, Bind on your girdle and put on your sandals. And so he did. And again he said to him, Put on your robe and follow me.

9 And he went out, and followed the angel, not knowing that what was done by the angel was true, but thought he saw a vision.

10 When they had passed the first and the second guard, they came to the iron gate and it opened to them of its own accord; and when they had gone out, and had passed one street, the angel departed from him.

11 And when Simon Peter came to himself

he said, Now I surely know, that the LORD has sent his angel and has delivered me out of the hand of Herod, the king, and from all that the Jews were conspiring against me.

12 And when he understood, he went to the house of Mary the mother of John, whose surname was Mark; because many brethren were gathered there praying.

13 When he knocked at the door of the courtyard, a little girl named Rhoda came out to answer.

14 And when she recognized Simon's voice, because of her joy she did not open the door to him, but ran back and told, Behold Simon Peter stands at the gate of the courtyard.

15 They said to her, You are confused. But she argued that it was so. Then said they, Perhaps it is his angel.

16 But Simon Peter continued knocking at the door; and they went out, and saw him, and were astonished.

17 But he motioned to them with his hand to keep quiet; then he entered and related to them how the LORD had brought him out of the prison. And he said, Tell these things to James, and to our brethren. And he went out, and departed for another place.

18 Now when it was morning, there was great tumult among the soldiers as to what had become of Simon Peter.

19 When Herod had sought him and could not find him, he sentenced the guards and commanded that they should be put to death. And Simon Peter left Ju-dæ'a and stayed at Cæs-a-re'a.

20 ¶ Herod was angry with the people of Tyre and Sidon, but they assembled together and came to him, and they appealed to Blas'tus, the king's chamberlain, and asked him that they might have peace, because their country was dependent upon the kingdom of Herod for food supplies.

21 Upon the set day Herod, arrayed in royal apparel, sat upon the throne and addressed the assembly.

22 And all the people shouted, saying, This sounds like the voice of God speaking and not that of a man.

23 And because he did not give the glory to God, in that very hour an angel of the LORD smote him, and he was eaten by disease and died.

24 But the gospel of God continued to be preached and to reach many.

25 Bar'na-bas and Saul, after they had fulfilled their ministry, returned from Jerusalem to An'ti-och, and took with them John whose surname was Mark.

CHAPTER 13

*N*OW there were in the church at An'ti-och prophets and teachers; Bar'na-bas, and Simeon who was called Ni'ger, and Lu'cius from the city of Cy-re-ne, and Man'a-el, * who was the son of the man who brought up Herod the tetrarch, and Saul.

2 As they fasted and prayed to God, the Holy Spirit said to them, Appoint for me Saul and Bar'na-bas for the work to which I have called them.

3 So, after they had fasted and prayed, and laid their hands on them, they sent them away.

4 ¶ Thus these two were sent forth by the Holy Spirit, and went down to Se-leu'ci-a; and from there they sailed to Cy'prus.

5 And when they had entered the city of Sal'a-mis, they preached the word of our LORD in the synagogues of the Jews: and John ministered unto them.

6 And when they had traveled the whole island as far as the city of Pa'phos, they found a Jewish sorcerer, who was a false prophet

* Ac.13:1 - or, Manaen.

Cf.dif. vv. 12: 11-12, 15, 17, 20, 22-24;   13:1-2, 5-6.

and whose name was Bar-Shu'ma:

7 Who was very close friend to a wise man, the proconsul whose name was Ser'gi-us Pau'lus, who called for Saul and Bar'na-bas, and desired to hear from them the word of God.

8 But Bar-Shu'ma the sorcerer (whose name is interpreted Elymas) withstood them, seeking to turn away the proconsul from the faith.

9 Then Saul, who is called Paul, filled with the Holy Spirit, looked at him,

10 And said, O man full of every kind of subtlety and of all evil things, you son of the devil and enemy of all righteousness, will you not cease to pervert the right ways of the LORD?

11 And now the hand of the LORD is against you, and you shall be blind, and shall not see the sun for a time. And in that very hour there fell on him a mist and darkness; and he went about seeking some one to lead him by the hand.

12 And when the proconsul saw what had happened, he was amazed, and believed the teaching of the LORD.

13 Then Paul and Bar'na-bas sailed from the city of Pa'phos, and came to Per'ga, a city in Pam-phyl'i-a: and John separated from them and went to Jerusalem.

14 But they left Per'ga and came to An'ti-och, a city in Pi-sid'i-a, and on the Sabbath day they went into the synagogue and sat down.

15 And after the reading of the law and the prophets, the elders of the synagogue sent to them, saying, O men and brethren, if you have a word of encouragement for the people, speak.

16 So Paul stood up, and lifting his hands said, O men of Israel, and those of you who fear God, hear my words:

17 The God of this people of Is'ra-el chose our forefathers, and exalted and multiplied them when they dwelt as strangers in the land of Egypt, and with a strong arm he brought them out of it.

18 And he fed them in the wilderness for forty years.

19 And he destroyed seven nations in the land of Ca'naan, and he gave them their land for an inheritance.

20 And for a period of four hundred and fifty years he gave them judges until the time of the prophet Samuel.

21 Then they asked for a king, and God gave them Saul the son of Kish, a man of the tribe of Benjamin, for a period of forty years.

22 And when in time God took Saul away he raised up to them David to be their king; concerning whom he testified and said, I have found David, the son of Jesse, a man after my own heart, to do my will.

23 Of this man's seed God has, according to his promise, raised to Israel a Saviour, Jesus:

24 Before whose coming, he had sent John to preach the baptism of repentance to all the people of Israel.

25 And as John fulfilled his ministry, he said, Whom do you think I am? I am not he. But behold there comes one after me the strings of whose shoes I am not worthy to untie.

26 O men and brethren, descendants of the family of Abraham, and whosoever among you fears God, to you is the word of salvation sent.

27 For in as much as the inhabitants of Jerusalem and their leaders did not understand him nor the books of the prophets which are read every Sabbath day, they condemned him; but all the things which were written have been fulfilled.

28 And though they found no cause for his death, they asked Pilate that they might kill him.

29 And when they had fulfilled all that was

Cf.dif. vv. 13:7, 10-11, 13, 18-19, 22, 24-28.

written of him, they lowered him from the cross and laid him in a sepulchre.

30 But God raised him from the dead;

31 And for many days he was seen by them who had come up with him from Galilee to Jerusalem, and they are now his witnesses to the people.

32 And behold we also preach to you that that very promise which was made to our fathers,

33 Behold God has fulfilled it unto us their children, for he has raised up Jesus, just as it is written in the second psalm, You are my son, this day I have begotten you.

34 And God raised him from the dead, no more to return to corruption, as he said, I will give you the sure mercies of David.

35 And again he said in another place, You shall not suffer your Holy One to see corruption.

36 ¶ For David, after he had served his own generation with the will of God, passed away; though he was a greater man than his fathers, yet he saw corruption.

37 But he whom God raised did not see corruption.

38 Be it known to you, therefore, brethren, that through this very one is preached to you the forgiveness of sins:

39 And by him all that believe are justified from all things, from which you could not be justified by the law of Moses.

40 Beware, therefore, lest that which is written in the prophets may come upon you.

41 Be careful, O you despisers, for you shall wonder and perish: for I will do a great work in your day which you will not believe even if a man tell it to you.

42 ¶ And as Paul and Bar'na-bas were leaving them, the people besought them to speak these things to them the next sabbath.

43 Now when the congregation was dismissed, a great many Jews, and also pros-elytes who feared God, followed Paul and Bar'na-bas: who, speaking to them, persuaded them to continue in the grace of God.

44 And the next sabbath day the whole city gathered to hear the word of God.

45 But when the Jews saw the great crowd, they were filled with envy, and they bitterly opposed the words of Paul, and they blasphemed.

46 Then Paul and Bar'na-bas said to them boldly, It was necessary that the word of God should first be spoken to you: but because you reject it, you have decided against yourselves and you are unworthy of everlasting life, so behold, we turn to the Gentiles.

47 For so has our Lord commanded us, as it is written, I have set you to be a light to the Gentiles, that you should be for salvation unto the ends of the earth.

48 ¶ And when the Gentiles heard this, they were glad and glorified God; and as many as were ordained to eternal life believed.

49 And the word of the Lord was published throughout all that region.

50 But the Jews stirred up the chief men of the city and the rich women who worshipped God with them, so that they stirred up a persecution against Paul and Bar'na-bas, and expelled them beyond their borders.

51 And as they went out, they shook off the dust of their feet upon them, and they came to the city of I-co'ni-um.

52 And the disciples were filled with joy, and with the Holy Spirit.

CHAPTER 14

AND Paul and Bar'na-bas entered into the Jewish synagogue and addressed the people in such manner that a great many of the Jews and of the Greeks believed.

2 But the Jews who would not listen stirred up the Gentiles to oppress the brethren.

3 So they remained there for a long time,

and spoke boldly concerning the LORD, and he gave them testimony to the word of his grace, by means of signs and wonders which he performed by their hands.

4 But the people of the city were divided: part held with the Jews, and part followed the apostles.

5 And they were menaced by both the Gentiles and the Jews with their leaders with disgrace and by threats to stone them with stones.

6 And when they became aware of it, they departed and took refuge in Ly'stra and Derbe, cities of Lyc-ao'ni-a, and the villages near by.

7 And there they preached the gospel.

8 ¶ And there dwelt in the city of Ly'stra a cripple who had been lame from his mother's womb, who never had walked.

9 He heard Paul speak; and when Paul saw him and perceived that there was faith in him to be healed,

10 He said to him with a loud voice, I say to you, in the name of our LORD Jesus Christ, stand upright on your feet. And he leaped and walked.

11 And when the people saw what Paul had done, they lifted their voices and said in the language of the country, The gods have come down to us in the likeness of men.

12 So they called Bar'na-bas, the chief of the gods; and Paul, they called Hermes, because he was the chief speaker.

13 Then the priest of the chief of gods whose shrine was outside the city, brought oxen and garlands to the gate of the courtyard where they stayed, and he wanted to offer sacrifices to them.

14 When Bar'na-bas and Paul heard of this, they rent their clothes, and leaped to their feet and went out to the crowd, crying out

15 And saying, Men, what are you doing? We also are ordinary human beings like you, who preach to you that you should turn from these useless things to the living God who made heaven and earth and the sea and all things that are therein,

16 Who in generations past suffered all nations to walk in their own ways.

17 Nevertheless he left himself without testimony, in that he bestowed good on them from heaven, and gave them rain, and caused the fruits to grow in their seasons, and satisfied their hearts with food and gladness.

18 And even though they said these things they had difficulty in restraining the people from offering sacrifice to them.

19 ¶ But there came there Jews from I-co'ni-um and An'ti-och and stirred up the people against them, and they stoned Paul and dragged him out of the city, supposing him to be dead.

20 Howbeit, as the disciples gathered around him, he rose up and entered again into the city: and the next day he departed from there with Bar'na-bas, and they came to the city of Der'be.

21 ¶ And when they had preached the gospel to the people of that city, and had converted many, then they returned to the city of Lys'tra, and to I-co'ni-um, and An'ti-och,

22 Strengthening the souls of the converts, and exhorting them to continue in the faith, and telling them that only through much tribulation can we enter into the kingdom of God.

23 And when they had ordained them elders in every church, and had prayed with them with fasting, they commended them to our LORD, on whom they believed.

24 And after they had traveled through the country of Pi-sid'i-a, they came to Pamphyl'i-a.

25 And when they had preached the word of the LORD in the city of Per'ga, they went down to At-ta'li-a:

26 And thence they sailed and came to An'ti-och, because from there they had been recommended to the grace of the LORD, for the work which they fulfilled.

27 And as the whole congregation was gathered together, they related everything that God had done to them, and how he had opened the door of faith to the Gentiles.

28 And there they remained a long time with the disciples.

CHAPTER 15

AND certain men who had come down from Judæ'a taught the brethren, Unless you be circumcised in accordance with the custom of the law you cannot be saved.

2 And there was great dissension and controversy between them and Paul and Bar'na-bas, and it reached such a point that it was necessary for Paul and Bar'na-bas and others with them to go up to Jerusalem to the apostles and elders concerning this question.

3 They were given an escort and sent on their way by the church, and they traveled through all Phoe-ni'ci-a and the territory of the Sa-mar'i-tans, declaring the conversion of the Gentiles; and they caused great joy to all the brethren.

4 On their arrival at Jerusalem, they were received by the church, and by the apostles and elders; and they reported everything that God had done with them.

5 But some of the men who had been converted from the sect of the Phar'i-sees rose up and said, You must circumcise them and command them to keep the law of Moses.

6 ¶ Then the apostles and elders assembled to consider this matter.

7 And after much controversy, Simon Peter rose up and said to them, Men and brethren, you know that from the early days God chose that from my mouth the Gentiles should hear the word of the Gospel and believe.

8 And God, who knows what is in the heart, has testified concerning them, and has given them the Holy Spirit just as he did to us.

9 And he did not discriminate between us and them, because he purified their hearts by faith.

10 Now therefore why do you tempt God by putting a yoke upon the necks of the disciples, which neither our fathers nor we were able to bear?

11 But we believe that through the grace of the LORD Jesus Christ, we shall be saved even as they.

12 Then the whole congregation was silent, and listened to Paul and Barnabas, who were declaring the miracles and signs among the Gentiles and everything which God had wrought by their hands.

13 And when they had ceased speaking, James rose up and said, Men and brethren, hear me:

14 Simon Peter has told you how God from the beginning chose a people from the Gentiles for his name.

15 And with this the words of the prophets agree, as it is written,

16 After this I will return, and I will set up again the tabernacle of David which has fallen down; and I will repair what has fallen from it, and I will set it up:

17 So that the men who remain may seek after the LORD, and also all the Gentiles upon whom my name is called; so said the LORD who does all these things.

18 ¶ The works of God are known from the very beginning.

19 Because of this I say, Do not trouble those who turn to God from among the Gentiles:

20 But let us send word to them that they abstain from defilement by sacrifices to idols, and from fornication, and from animals strangled, and from blood.

21 For Moses, from the very early centuries, had preachers in the synagogues in every city to read his books on every sabbath day.

22 ¶ Then the apostles and elders, with the whole church, chose men from among themselves and sent them to An'ti-och with Paul and Bar'na-bas; namely, Judas who is called Bar'sa-bas and Silas, men who were leaders among the brethren:

23 And they wrote a letter and sent it by them after this manner; The apostles and elders and brethren to the brethren of the Gentiles in An'ti-och and Sy'ria and Ci-li'ci-a, greetings.

24 We have heard that certain men have gone out and disturbed you with words, thus upsetting your souls, saying, You must be circumcised, and keep the law: on these things we have never commanded them.

25 Therefore, we have considered the matter while we are assembled, and we have chosen and sent men to you with our beloved Paul and Bar'na-bas,

26 Men who have dedicated their lives for the name of our LORD Jesus Christ.

27 And we have sent with them Judas and Silas, so that they may tell you the same things by word of mouth.

28 For it is the will of the Holy Spirit and of us, to lay upon you no additional burden than these necessary things;

29 That you abstain from sacrifices offered to idols, and from blood, and from animals strangled, and from fornication: when you keep yourselves from these things, you will do well. Remain steadfast in our LORD.

30 ¶ Now when those who were sent came to An'ti-och and when the whole people were gathered together, they delivered the epistle:

31 And when they had read it, the people rejoiced and were comforted.

32 And Judas and Silas, being prophets themselves also, confirmed the brethren with gracious words.

33 And after they had been there some time, the brethren let them go in peace to the apostles.

34 * Notwithstanding it pleased Silas to abide there still.

35 Paul also and Bar'na-bas remained in An'ti-och, teaching and preaching the word of God, with many others also.

36 ¶ And some days after, Paul said to Bar'na-bas, Let us return and visit the brethren in every city where we have preached the word of God and see how they do.

37 Now Bar'na-bas wanted to take John who was also called Mark.

38 But Paul was unwilling to take him with them, because he had left them when they were in Pam-phyl'i-a, and had not gone with them.

39 And because of this dispute, Paul and Bar'na-bas separated from each other: and Bar'na-bas took Mark, and they sailed to Cy'prus,

40 But Paul chose Silas and departed, being commended by the brethren to the grace of God.

41 And he traveled through Syr'i-a and Ci-li'cia, establishing churches.

CHAPTER 16

*T*HEN he arrived at the city of Der'be and Lys'tra: there was there a disciple whose name was Timo'the-us, the son of a Jewess convert, but whose father was a Syr'i-an.

2 And all the disciples of Lys'tra and I-co'ni-um gave good testimony concerning him.

3 Paul wanted to take this man with him, so he took him and circumcised him because of the Jews who were in that region; for they all knew that his father was a Syr'i-an.

* Ac.15:34 - not found in Eastern text.
Cf.dif. vv. 15:21, 23, 25, 28-30, 32, 36;   16:1, 3.

4 And as they went through the cities, they preached and taught the people to obey the decrees which the apostles and elders had written at Jerusalem.

5 And so the churches were established in the faith, and increased in number daily.

6 ¶ Then they traveled through the countries of Phryg'i-a and Ga-la'tia, and the Holy Spirit forbade them to speak the word of God in Asia Minor.

7 And when they came to the country of Mys'ia, they wanted to go from thence to Bi-thyn'i-a: but the spirit of Jesus permitted them not.

8 And when they had left Mys'ia, they came to the country of Tro'as.

9 And, in a vision of the night, there appeared to Paul a man resembling a Mac-e-do'ni-an, standing and begging him, saying, Come over to Mac-e-do'ni-a and help me.

10 And after Paul had seen this vision, we were desirous to leave for Mac-e-do'ni-a at once, because we understood that our LORD had called us to preach the gospel to them.*

11 When we sailed from Tro'as, we came in a direct course to Sam-o-thra'cia, and from thence on the following day, we came to the city Ne-ap'o-lis;

12 And from thence to Phi-lip'pi, which is the capital of Mac-e-do'ni-a, and is a colony: and we were in that city on some holidays.

13 And on the sabbath day we went outside the city gate to the river side because a house of prayer was seen there, and when we were seated, we spoke to the women who had gathered there.

14 And a certain woman, named Lyd'i-a, a seller of purple of the city of Thy-a-ti'ra, feared God; her heart was so touched by our LORD that she listened to what Paul said.

15 And she was baptized together with her household, and she begged us, saying, If you are sincerely convinced that I believe in our LORD, come and stay in my house; and she urged us strongly.

16 ¶ And it came to pass, as we went to the house of prayer, we were met by a young girl who was possessed of a spirit, and who did for her masters a great business by fortune telling.

17 And she followed Paul and us, crying and saying, These men are the servants of the most high God, and they preach to you the way of salvation.

18 And she did this for many days. So Paul was indignant and said to the spirit, I command you in the name of Jesus Christ to come out of her. And it left her the same hour.

19 And when her masters saw that the hope for their business was lost with her power, they seized Paul and Silas and beat them and brought them to the market place.

20 And they brought them before the soldiers and the city magistrates and said, These men are Jews, and they create disturbances in our city,

21 And they preach customs to us which are not lawful for us to accept and practice, because we are Romans.

22 And a large crowd gathered against them. Then the soldiers stripped them of their clothes and gave command to scourge them.

23 And when they had flogged them severely, they cast them into prison, charging the jailer to watch them carefully.

24 He, having received the charge, brought them in and put them into the inner chamber of the prison, and fastened their feet in the stocks.

25 ¶ Now at midnight Paul and Silas prayed and glorified God; and the prisoners heard them.

* Ac.16:10 - The author, Luke, used "they" and "them" in referring to Paul, Timothy and Silas when he was not with them. He used "we" and "us" when he was with them.
Cf.dif. vv. 16:4, 6-7, 9-10, 12-13, 16-17, 19-20, 22, 25.

26 And suddenly there was a great earthquake, so that the foundations of the prison were shaken, and immediately all the doors were opened, and the bands of all were loosed.

27 When the keeper of the prison awoke, and saw that the prison doors were open, he took a sword and would have killed himself, for he thought the prisoners had escaped.

28 But Paul cried with a loud voice and said to him, Do not harm yourself, for we are all here.

29 Then he lighted a lamp, and sprang in, trembling, and threw himself at the feet of Paul and Silas.

30 And he brought them out, and said, Sirs, what must I do to be saved?

31 And they said to him, Believe in our LORD Jesus Christ, and both you and your household will be saved.

32 And they spoke to him the word of the LORD, and to all who were of his household.

33 And he took them at that hour of the night and washed their wounds; and then was baptized in that very hour, he and all his household.

34 And when he had brought them up into his house, he set food before them; and he and all the members of his household rejoiced, believing in God.

35 In the morning, the soldiers sent the lictors to tell the prison warden to release those men.

36 And when the keeper of the prison heard this, he went in and told Paul, saying, The soldiers have sent orders to release you: now therefore depart, and go in peace.

37 But Paul said to him, Not having committed any offense, they flogged us, Roman citizens, in the presence of the people, and they cast us into prison; and now do they let us out secretly? No verily; let them come themselves and fetch us out.

38 And the lictors went and told the soldiers these words which were told to them: and when they heard that Paul and Silas were Roman citizens, they were afraid.

39 And they came to them and urged them to get out and depart from the city.

40 And they went out of the prison and entered into the house of Lydia where they saw the brethren and comforted them, and departed.

CHAPTER 17

*T*hey passed by the cities of Am-phip'o-lis and Ap-ol-lo'ni-a, and came to Thes-sa-lo-ni'ca, where there was a synagogue of the Jews.

2 And Paul, as was his custom, went in to join them, and for three sabbaths, he spoke to them from the scriptures,

3 Interpreting and proving that Christ had to suffer, and rise again from the dead; and that he is the same Jesus Christ whom I preach to you.

4 And some of them believed and joined Paul and Silas; and many of them were Greeks who feared God, and many of them were well known women, a goodly number.

5 But the Jews, being jealous, secured a band of bad men from the streets of the city and formed a great mob, who caused disturbances in the city, and who came and assaulted the house of Jason, and sought to bring them out from it and deliver them to the mob.

6 And when they failed to find them there, they dragged forth Jason and the brethren who were there and brought them before the authorities of the city, crying, These are the men who have created disturbances throughout the world, and behold, they have come here also,

7 And Jason has welcomed them: and all of them are against the decrees of Cæ'sar, say-

ing that there is another king, Jesus.

8 The authorities of the city and all the people were alarmed when they heard these things.

9 So they took bail from Jason and some of the brethren and then let them go.

10 Then the brethren immediately sent away Paul and Silas by night to the city of Be-re'a: and when they arrived there, they entered into the synagogue of the Jews.

11 For the Jews there were more liberal than the Jews who were in Thes-sa-lo-ni'ca, in that they gladly heard the word daily, and searched the scriptures to find out if these things were so.

12 And many of them believed; and of the Greeks were many men and notable women.

13 But when the Jews of Thes-sa-lo-ni'ca found out that the word of God was preached by Paul in the city of Be-re'a, they came there also; and ceased not to stir up and alarm the people.

14 Then the brethren sent Paul away to go to the sea; but Silas and Ti-mo'the-us remained in that city.

15 And those who escorted Paul went with him as far as the city of Athens: and when they were leaving him, they received from him an epistle to Silas and Ti-mo'the-us requesting them to come to him in haste.

16 ¶ Now while Paul waited for them at Athens, he saw the whole city full of idols, and he murmured thereat in his spirit.

17 And he spoke in the synagogue to the Jews and to those who feared God, and in the market place daily with them who were there.

18 Philosophers, also, who were of the teaching of Ep'i-cu-rus, and others, who were called Sto'ics, argued with him. And some of them said, What does this babbler want? And others said, He preaches foreign gods:

because he preached to them Jesus and his resurrection.

19 So they arrested him and brought him to the court house which is called Ar-e-op'a-gus, and said to him, May we know what is this new doctrine which you preach?

20 For you proclaim strange words to our ears and we want to know what these things mean.

21 (For all the Athenians and the strangers who were there, were uninterested in anything except something new to tell or to hear.)

22 When Paul stood in the court at Ar-e-op'a-gus, he said, Men of Athens, I see that above all things you are extravagant in the worship of idols.

23 For as I walked about, and viewed the house of your idols, I found an altar with this inscription, THIS IS THE ALTAR OF THE UNKNOWN GOD, whom therefore, while you know him not but yet worship, is the very one I am preaching to you.

24 For the God, who made the world and all things therein, and who is the LORD of heaven and earth, does not dwell in temples made with hands;

25 Neither is he ministered to by human hands, nor is he in need of anything, for it is he who gave life and breath to all men.

26 And he has made of one blood all nations of men to dwell on all the face of the earth, and he has appointed seasons by his command, and has set limits to the age of men;

27 So that they should seek and search after God, and find him by means of his creations, because he is not far from any one of us:

28 For in him we live, and move, and have our being; as some of your own wise men have said, For we are his kindred.

29 ¶ Now therefore, man, being of the family of God, is not bounden to worship resemblances made of gold or silver or stone

Cf.dif. vv. 17:11-12, 14-16, 18-19, 22-23, 26-27, 29.

shapen by the skill and knowledge of man into resemblances of the Deity.

30 For the times of ignorance God has made to pass, and at this time he has commanded all men, everywhere, to repent.

31 For he has appointed a day in which he will judge all the earth with righteousness by the man whom he has chosen; he who has turned every man towards his faith; for that, he has raised him from the dead.

32 ¶ And when they heard of the resurrection of the dead, some mocked: and others said, We will hear you again on this matter.

33 So Paul left them.

34 Some of them, however, followed him and were converted; one of them was Di-o-nys'ius, one of the judges of Ar-e-op'a-gus, and a woman named Dam'a-ris, and others with them.

CHAPTER 18

THEN Paul departed from Athens, and came to Corinth;

2 And there he found a Jew named A'qui-la, from the region of Pontus, who had just arrived from Italy with his wife Pris-cil'la, because Clau'di-us Cæs'ar had commanded all Jews to leave Rome: and Paul went to them.

3 And because he was of the same trade, he stayed with them and worked with them: for they were saddle makers by trade.

4 And he spoke in the synagogue every sabbath, and persuaded the Jews and the pagans.

5 And when Silas and Ti-mo'the-us came from Mac-e-do'ni-a, Paul felt he was not free to speak, because the Jews opposed him and blasphemed as he testified that Jesus is the Christ.

6 So he shook his garments and said to them, From henceforth I am not to be blamed for what I am about to do; I am going to the Gentiles.

7 And he departed thence, and entered into the house of a certain man named Titus, a devout man whose household had joined the synagogue.

8 And Crispus, the chief of the synagogue, believed in our LORD, together with all his household; and many of the Corinthians hearing him believed in God and were baptized.

9 Then the LORD spoke to Paul in a vision, Be not afraid, but speak and be not silent.

10 For I am with you, and no man can harm you: and I have many people in this city.

11 For he had already been in Corinth a year and six months and had taught the word of God among them.

12 ¶ And when Gal'li-o was proconsul of A-cha'ia, the Jews made insurrection with one accord against Paul; and they brought him to the judgment seat,

13 Saying, This fellow persuades men to worship God contrary to the law.

14 And as Paul was desirous to open his mouth and speak, Gal'li-o said to the Jews, If your accusations were based on something criminal, fraudulent, or vicious, I would welcome you properly, O Jews:

15 But if they are a mere question of words and names and concerning your law, you can settle it better among yourselves; for I do not wish to be a judge of such matters.

16 And he drove them from his judgment seat.

17 Then the pagans seized Sos'the-nes, the priest of the synagogue, and beat him before the judgment seat. And Gal'li-o disregarded these things.

18 And after Paul had remained there many days, he bade the brethen farewell and sailed for Syria, and with him Pris-cil'la and A'qui-la; having shorn his head in Cen'chre-a: because he had vowed a vow.

19 And they came to Eph'e-sus, and Paul entered into the synagogue and spoke to the Jews.

20 When they wanted him to tarry a longer time with them, he consented not;

21 Saying, I must by all means celebrate the coming feast as is my custom at Jerusalem; but I will return to you again, God willing.

22 And he left A'qui-la and Pris-cil'la at Eph'e-sus and sailed and when he landed at Cæs-a-re'a, he went up and saluted the members of the church, and went on to An'ti-och.

23 ¶ And after he had spent some special days there he departed and traveled all through the country of Phryg'i-a and Ga-la'tia, increasing disciples in all of them.

24 And a certain Jew named A-pol'los, a native of Al-ex-an'dri-a, an eloquent man and well versed in the scriptures, came to Eph'e-sus.

25 He had been converted to the way of the LORD, and was fervent in the spirit; he spoke and taught very fully concerning Jesus, but he knew only the baptism of John.

26 And he began to speak boldly in the synagogue: and when A'qui-la and Pris-cil'la heard him, they took him to their home, and fully showed him the way of the LORD.

27 And when he was disposed to go to A-cha'ia, the brethren gave him a warm reception and wrote to the disciples to welcome him, and when he had come, he greatly helped all believers by means of grace.

28 For he forcefully and publicly argued against the Jews, proving by the scriptures that Jesus is the Christ.

CHAPTER 19

AND it came to pass, that while A-pol'los was at Cor'inth, Paul traveled through the northern countries and came to Eph'e-sus, and inquired of the disciples whom he found there,

2 Have you received the Holy Spirit since you were converted? They answered and said to him, We have not even heard that there is a Holy Spirit.

3 Then he said to them, By what baptism then were you baptized? They said, By the baptism of John.

4 Then said Paul, John verily baptized the people with the baptism of repentance, saying unto them that they should believe on him who should come after him, that is, Jesus Christ.

5 When they heard these things, they were baptized in the name of our LORD Jesus Christ.

6 And when Paul laid his hands on them, the Holy Spirit came on them; and they spoke in divers tongues, and prophesied.

7 And there were in all twelve persons.

8 Then Paul entered into the synagogue, and spoke openly for a period of three months, persuading the people concerning the kingdom of God.

9 But some of them were stubborn, and they disputed and cursed the way of God in the presence of the assembly. Then Paul withdrew, and separated the disciples from them, and he spoke to them daily in the school of a man named Ty-ran'us.

10 And this continued for two years until all who dwelt in Asia Minor, both Jews and Arameans (Syrians), heard the word of God.

11 And God wrought great miracles by the hands of Paul:

12 So that even when, of the clothes on his body, pieces of garments were brought and laid upon the sick, diseases were cured, and even the insane were restored.

13 ¶ Now certain Jews, who went about exorcising evil spirits, invoked the name of our LORD Jesus over those who were possessed, saying, We adjure you in the name of Jesus whom Paul preaches.

14 And there were seven sons of one Sce'va, a Jew, and chief of the priests, who did this.

15 And the insane man answered and said to them, Jesus I recognize and Paul I know; but who are you?

16 Then the insane man leaped on them, and overpowered them, and prevailed against them, so they fled out of that house naked and wounded.

17 And this became known to all the Jews and Arameans (Syrians) who dwelt at Eph'e-sus; and fear fell on them all, and the name of our LORD Jesus Christ was magnified.

18 And many of them that believed came, and told their faults, and confessed what they had done.

19 Many magicians also gathered together their books and brought them and burned them before the presence of the people; and they counted the price of them, and it amounted to fifty thousand pieces of silver.

20 So mightily grew the faith of God and greatly increased in numbers.

21 ¶ When these things had been accomplished, Paul made up his mind to travel through all of Mac-e-do'ni-a and A-cha'ia, and then to go to Jerusalem, saying, After I have been there, I must also see Rome.

22 So he sent to Mac-e-do'ni-a two men of those who had ministered to him, Ti-mo'the-us and E-ras'tus; but he himself stayed in Asia Minor for some time.

23 And at that time there was a great uprising against those who followed in the way of God.

24 There was here a silversmith named De-me'tri-us, who made silver shrines for Ar'te-mis, thus greatly enriching the craftsmen of his trade.

25 He called together all the craftsmen of his trade, with the workmen of like occupation, and said to them: Men, you know that all of our earnings are derived from this craft.

26 You also hear and see that not only the E-phe'si-ans, but almost throughout all Asia Minor, this Paul has persuaded, and turned away many people simply by saying that gods made by the hands of men are not gods,

27 So that not only is this craft doomed, but also the temple of the great goddess Ar'te-mis will be disregarded, and the goddess of all Asia Minor, even she whom all peoples worship, will be despised.

28 And when they heard these things they were filled with wrath, and cried out, saying, Great is Ar'te-mis of the E-phe'si-ans.

29 And the whole city was in tumult: and they rushed together to the theatre, and there seized and carried along with them Ga'ius and Ar-is-tar'chus, Mac-e-do'ni-ans, members of Paul's escort.

30 And Paul wanted to go into the theatre, but the disciples stopped him.

31 And likewise some of the chiefs of Asia Minor, because they were his friends, sent to him, begging him not to risk his life by entering the theatre.

32 Now the multitude in the theatre was greatly confused; some cried one thing, and some another; and many of them did not know why they had assembled together.

33 And the Jews who were there appointed a Jew named Al-ex-an'der. And when he rose up, he gestured with his hand and would have addressed the people.

34 But when they knew he was a Jew, all of them cried out with one voice for about two hours, Great is Ar'te-mis of the E-phe'si-ans.

35 The mayor of the city finally quieted them, saying, Men of Eph'e-sus, who among men does not know that the city of the E-phe'si-ans is the seat of great Ar'te-mis and her image that fell from heaven.

36 Since, therefore, no man can contradict this, you should keep quiet, and do nothing hastily.

37 For you have brought these men here who have neither robbed temples nor have they reviled our goddess.

38 But if De-me'tri-us and the men of his trade have a case against any man, behold there is a proconsul in the city; let the craftsmen come forward and settle with one another in the court.

39 But if you want something else, it must be determined in a lawful assembly.

40 For even now we are in danger of being charged with sedition, for we cannot give an answer concerning this day's meeting, because we have assembled for no reason, and have been tumultuous without a cause.

41 And when he had said these things, he dismissed the assembly.

CHAPTER 20

AND after the tumult had ceased, Paul called to him the disciples and comforted them and kissed them and then departed and went to Mac-e-do'ni-a.

2 And when he had traveled through those countries and had comforted them with many words, he came to Greece.

3 There he remained three months. But the Jews laid a plot against him, just as he was about to sail for Syria, so he decided to return to Mac-e-do'ni-a .

4 And there accompanied him, as far as Asia Minor, Sop'a-ter of the city of Be-re'a and Ar-is-tar'chus and Se-cun'dus of Thes-sa-lo-ni'ca and Ga'ius of the city of Der'be and Ti-mo'the-us of Ly'stra, and from Asia Minor Tych'i-cus and Troph'i-mus.

5 These men went before us, and waited for us at Tro'as.

6 But we departed from the Mac-e-do'ni-an city of Phi-lip'pi, after the days of unleavened bread, and sailed and arrived at Tro'as in five days, where we staved seven days;

7 ¶ And on the first day of the week, while the disciples were assembled to break bread,

Paul preached to them, and because he was ready to leave the next day, he prolonged his speech until midnight.

8 Now there was a great glow of light from the torches in the upper chamber, where we were gathered together.

9 And a young man named Eu'ty-chus was sitting at the floor opening above and listening, and as Paul prolonged his speech, the youth fell into a deep sleep, and while asleep he fell down from the third loft, and was taken up as dead.

10 And Paul went down and bent over him and embraced him and said, Do not be excited for he still lives.

11 And when he was come up again, and had broken bread and eaten, he continued to speak till daybreak; then he departed to journey by land.

12 And they carried away the young man alive, and rejoiced over him exceedingly.

13 But we went on board the ship, and sailed to the port of As'sos, where we were to take in Paul: as he had commanded us when he left to travel by land.

14 When we had welcomed him at As'sos, we took him on board and came to Mit-y-le'ne.

15 And we sailed thence the next day towards the island of Chi'os; and the following day we arrived at Sa'mos, and tarried at Tro-gyl'li-um; and the next day we came to Mi-le'tus.

16 For Paul had determined not to stop at Eph'e-sus, fearing he might be delayed there; because he was hastening, if it were possible for him, to celebrate the day of Pentecost at Jerusalem.

17 ¶ And from Mi-le'tus he sent and called the elders of the church of Eph'e-sus.

18 And when they had come to him, he said to them, You know from the very first day that I entered Asia Minor, how I have been with you always,

Cf.dif. vv. 19:38, 40; 20:1, 4, 7-9, 16.

19 Serving God with great humility and with tears and amid the trials which were brought upon me by conspiracies of the Jews.

20 And yet I did not neglect to preach to you about those things which were good for your souls, and I taught in the streets and from house to house.

21 Thus testifying both to the Jews and to the Syr'i-ans, about repentance toward God and faith in our LORD Jesus Christ.

22 And now I am on my way to Jerusalem, bound in the spirit, not knowing what will happen to me there:

23 Save that in every city the Holy Spirit testifies to me, saying that bonds and afflictions await me.

24 But to me my life is nothing; I am not afraid. I desire only that I may finish my course with joy and finish the ministry, which I have received from our LORD Jesus, to testify the gospel of the grace of God.

25 And now I know that you, among whom I have traveled and preached the kingdom of God, shall see my face no more.

26 Therefore, I testify to you this very day that I am innocent of the blood of all.

27 For I have never shunned to declare to you, all the will of God.

28 Take heed therefore to yourselves and to all the flock, over which the Holy Spirit has appointed you overseers, to feed the church of Christ which he has purchased with his blood.

29 For I know this, that after I have departed, fierce wolves will attack you, which will not spare the flock.

30 Also from among yourselves, men shall arise, speaking perverse things to draw away disciples after them.

31 Therefore watch, and remember, that for three years, night and day, I did not cease to teach every one of you with tears.

32 And now I commend you to God, and to the word of his grace, which is able to build you up, and to give you an inheritance among all the saints.

33 I have never coveted silver, or gold, or apparel.

34 Indeed you yourselves know, that my own hands have provided for my needs and for those who have been with me.

35 I have showed you all things, how that one must work hard, and be mindful of the weak, and remember the words of our LORD Jesus, how he said, It is more blessed to give than to receive.

36 And when he had thus spoken, he knelt down and prayed with them all.

37 And they all wept bitterly, and they embraced him and kissed him;

38 But they were most distressed because of the words he spoke, that they would not see his face again. And they accompanied him to the ship.

CHAPTER 21

AND it came to pass, after we separated from them, we sailed a straight course to the Island of Co'os, and the following day we arrived at Rhodes, and from thence to Pat'a-ra:

2 And we found there a ship sailing to Phe-ni'cia, and we went on board, and set forth.

3 Then we reached the Island of Cyprus, and passed it on the left hand, and sailed to Syria, and from thence we landed at Tyre, for there the ship was to unload her cargo.

4 And because we found disciples there, we stayed with them seven days: and every day they said to Paul through the Spirit, that he should not go up to Jerusalem.

5 After these days, we departed on our journey, and they all escorted us on our way with their wives and children, till we were out of the city: then they knelt down by the seaside and prayed;

6 And when we had kissed one another good-bye, we took ship; and they returned to their homes.

7 We sailed from Tyre and arrived at the city of Ak-ka (Ptol-e-ma'is), and we saluted the brethren who were there, and tarried with them a day.

8 On the next day we departed and came to Cæs-a-re'a: and we went in and stayed at the house of Philip the evangelist, who was one of the seven.

9 He had four daughters, virgins, who prophesied.

10 And as we were there many days, there came down from Judæa a prophet named Ag'a-bus.

11 And when he was come unto us, he took Paul's girdle, and bound his own feet and hands, and said, Thus says the Holy Spirit, So shall the Jews at Jerusalem bind the man that owns this girdle, and shall deliver him into the hands of the Gentiles.

12 And when we had heard these words, both we and the natives of the place, besought him not to go up to Jerusalem.

13 Then Paul answered and said, Why do you weep and break my heart? For I am ready not only to be bound, but also to die at Jerusalem, for the sake of the name of our LORD Jesus Christ.

14 And when he would not listen to us, we ceased, saying, Let the will of our LORD be done.

15 After those days, we made our preparations and went up to Jerusalem.

16 And there came with us some of the disciples from Cæs-a-re'a, bringing with them a brother who was among the first converts, named Mna'son, a native of Cyprus, who had before received us at his house.

17 When we arrived at Jerusalem, the brethren welcomed us gladly.

18 And the next day when all the elders were present we went in with Paul unto James.

19 And when we had saluted them, Paul told them in successive order everything that God had done among the Gentiles by his ministry.

20 And when they heard it, they glorified God, and said to Paul, Our brother, see how many thousands there are in Judæa who are believers; and they are all zealous of the law;

21 But they have been informed about you, that you teach all the Jews who are among the Gentiles to forsake the law of Moses, stating that they ought not to circumcise their children, neither to follow after the customs of the law.

22 Now, therefore, they have heard that you have come here.

23 Do, therefore, what we tell you: We have four men who have vowed to purify themselves;

24 Take them and go purify yourself with them, and pay their expenses so that they may shave their heads: then every one will know that what has been said against you is false, and that you yourself have fulfilled the law and obey it.

25 As for the believers amongst the Gentiles, we have written that they should abstain from the things sacrificed to idols, and from fornication, and from what is strangled, and from blood.

26 Then Paul took the men and on the next day he was purified with them and then he entered into the temple, informing them how to complete the days of purification, until the gift of every one of them was offered.

27 ¶ And when the seventh day approached, and the Jews from Asia Minor saw him in the temple, they stirred up all the people against him and laid hands on him,

28 And cried out, saying, Men of Israel, help: This is the man who teaches everywhere against our people, against the law, and

Cf.dif. vv. 21:7, 15-16, 19, 21-23, 26-28.

against this place; and further, he has brought Syr-i-ans into the temple, and has defiled this holy place.

29 For they had previously seen Troph'i-mus, the E-phe'sian, with him in the city, and they thought he had entered into the temple with Paul.

30 So the whole city was in a tumult, and all the people ran together; they seized Paul and dragged him out of the temple; and the doors were immediately shut.

31 And as the mob sought to kill him, the news reached the captain of the company, that all the city was in an uproar.

32 He immediately took a centurion and many soldiers, and ran down to them: and when they saw the chief captain and the soldiers, they ceased beating Paul.

33 Then the chief captain came near him and took him, and commanded him to be bound with two chains. Then he inquired, Who is he and what has he done?

34 And some of the mob cried against him one thing, some another: and because of their confusion he was unable to know what was true, so he commanded him to be taken to headquarters.

35 And when Paul reached the stairs, the soldiers bore him because of the violence of the people.

36 For a great many people followed after, crying, and saying, Away with him.

37 And as Paul was about to be led into headquarters, he said to the chief captain, May I speak to you? The captain said, Can you speak Greek?

38 Are you not that Egyptian who some time ago created disturbances and led out into the desert four thousand malefactors?

39 But Paul said, I am a Jew of Tarsus in Ci-li'cia, a citizen of a well-known city: I beg you, permit me to speak to the people.

40 ¶ And when he had given him permis-sion, Paul stood on the stairs and beckoned with his hand to them. And when they were quiet, he spoke to them in the Hebrew (Ara-maic) tongue and said to them.

CHAPTER 22

BRETHREN and fathers, hear my defense which I now make to you.

2 And when they heard him speak to them in the Hebrew tongue (Aramaic), they were the more quiet: And he said,

3 I am a Jew, born in Tarsus of Ci-li'cia, yet I was brought up in this city under the care and guidance of Ga-ma'li-el, and trained perfectly according to the law of our fathers, and was zealous toward God, just as you are also.

4 And I persecuted this religion to the death, binding and delivering into prisons both men and women.

5 The high priest and all the elders can so testify about me, for it was from them that I received letters to go to the brethren at Dam-ascus, to bring those who were there bound to Jerusalem to be punished.

6 And it came to pass as I drew near to Dam-ascus, at about noon, suddenly a great light from heaven shone round about me.

7 And I fell to the ground, and heard a voice saying to me, Saul, Saul, why do you perse-cute me?

8 And I answered and said, Who are you, my LORD? And he said to me, I am Jesus of Naz'a-reth, whom you persecute.

9 And the men who were with me saw the light, but they did not hear the voice that spoke to me.

10 And I said, What shall I do, my LORD? And our LORD said to me, Arise, and go into Da-mas'cus; and there it shall be told to you all things which are appointed for you to do.

11 And when I could not see for the glory of

that light, being led by the hand of them that were with me, I came into Da-mas'cus.

12 And a certain man, An-a-ni'as, a righteous man according to the law, as testified by all the Jews concerning him,

13 Came to me and said, My brother Saul, receive your sight. And instantly my eyes were opened and I looked upon him.

14 And he said to me, The God of our fathers has appointed you to know his will, and to see the Righteous One, and to hear the voice of his mouth.

15 And you shall be a witness for him before all men, of all that you have seen and heard.

16 And now why do you delay? Arise, and be baptized and wash away your sins calling on the name of the LORD.

17 And it came to pass that when I returned here to Jerusalem and while praying in the temple,

18 I saw a vision, saying to me, Make haste, and get quickly out of Jerusalem: for they will not receive your testimony concerning me.

19 And I said, My LORD, they know that I imprisoned and beat, in every synagogue, those who believed in you:

20 And when the blood of your martyr Stephen was shed, I also was standing by, and was in accord with his slayers, and was in charge of the garments of them who stoned him.

21 Then he said to me, Depart: for I will send you afar to preach to the Gentiles.

22 ¶ They had given Paul audience up to this word, and then they lifted up their voices, and cried out, Away with such a fellow from the earth: for it is not fit that he should live.

23 And as they cried out and cast off their robes, and threw dust into the air,

24 The chief captain commanded him to be brought into the castle, and ordered that he should be examined by scourging; that he might know for what cause they cried so against him.

25 And when they had bound him with thongs, Paul said to the centurion who stood over him, Is it lawful for you to scourge a Roman citizen who is uncondemned?

26 When the centurion heard that, he went to the chief captain and said, Be careful what you do: for this man is a Roman citizen.

27 Then the captain came and said to him, Tell me, are you a Roman? Paul said, Yes.

28 And the captain answered and said, I obtained Roman citizenship with a great sum of money. Paul answered, But I was free born to it.

29 Immediately those who were ready to scourge him left him alone, and the captain was afraid when he found out that he was a Roman citizen, because he had bound him.

30 ¶ The next day, because he desired to know the truthfulness of the charges which the Jews had brought against Paul, he unbound him and commanded the high priests and all their council to appear before him, and he took Paul and brought him down, and set him before them.

CHAPTER 23

*A*ND as Paul beheld their assembly, he said, Men, my brethren, I have lived in all good conscience before God until this day.

2 ¶ And the high priest An-a-ni'as commanded those who stood by his side to strike Paul on the mouth.

3 Then Paul said to him, God shall smite you, O you hypocrite: for you sit to judge me according to the law, yet you yourself transgress the law, when you command that I be smitten.

4 And those who stood by said to him, Do you even revile the high priest of God?

5 Then Paul said to them, Brothers, I did not know that he was a high priest: for it is written, You shall not revile the ruler of your people.

6 Now when Paul perceived that part of the people were Sad'du-cees, and the others were Phar'i-sees, he cried out in the assembly, Men, my brethren, I am a Phar'i-see, the son of a Phar'i-see: and it is because of the hope of the resurrection of the dead that I am here to be judged.

7 And when he had said this, there arose a dissension between the Phar'i-sees and the Sad'du-cees: and the people were divided.

8 For the Sad'du-cees say there is no resurrection, neither angels nor soul: but the Phar'i-sees believe in them.

9 Then there arose a great cry: and the scribes that were of the party of the Phar'i-sees rose up, and argued, saying, We find no fault with this man: and if a spirit or an angel has spoken to him, there is nothing wrong in that.

10 ¶ And because there was a great disturbance among them, the chief captain, fearing that they might tear Paul to pieces, sent Roman soldiers to go and seize him from among them and bring him into the castle.

11 During the night, our LORD appeared to Paul and said, Be strong, for as you have testified concerning me at Jerusalem, so also you are to testify at Rome.

12 And when it was morning, certain of the Jews banded together and bound themselves under oath, that they would neither eat nor drink till they had killed Paul.

13 And those who had sworn to this conspiracy were more than forty persons.

14 And they went to the priests and elders, and said, We have bound ourselves under an oath, not to taste anything till we have killed Paul.

15 Now you and the leaders of the council ask the captain to bring him to you, as though you were desirous to have a thorough investigation of his acts, and we are ready to kill him before he shall arrive here.

16 When Paul's nephew heard this plot, he went into the castle and told Paul.

17 Then Paul sent for and called one of the centurions, and said, Take this young man to the captain, for he has something to tell him.

18 So the centurion took the young man, and brought him to the chief captain and said, Paul, the prisoner, called me and begged me to bring this young man to you, for he has something to tell you.

19 Then the captain took the young man by his hand, and drew him aside, and asked him, What have you to tell me?

20 And the young man said to him, The Jews have decided to ask you to bring Paul down tomorrow to their council, as though they were desirous to learn something more from him.

21 You must not listen to them: for behold more than forty of them, who have bound themselves with an oath neither to eat nor to drink till they have killed him, are lying in wait for him: and behold they are ready and awaiting your reply.

22 Then the captain dismissed the young man and charged him, Let no man know that you have informed me of these things.

23 ¶ And he called to him two centurions, and said, Go and make ready two hundred Roman soldiers to go to Cæs-a-re'a and seventy horsemen and two hundred spearmen, to leave at nine o'clock tonight.

24 And provide also an animal that they may set Paul on, and carry him safe to Felix the governor.

25 And he wrote a letter after this manner and gave it to them:

26 Clau'di-us Lys'ias to the most excellent governor Fe'lix, greetings.

27 This man was seized by the Jews who intended to kill him: but I intervened with Roman soldiers and rescued him, when I understood he was a Roman citizen.

28 And because I wanted to know the cause for which they accused him, I took him down to their council.

29 And I found that only concerning questions of their law was he accused, and that he had done nothing worthy of bonds or of death.

30 And when I was informed that the Jews had plotted secretly against him, I immediately sent him to you, and I have ordered his accusers to go and contend with him before you. Farewell.

31 ¶ Then the Roman soldiers as it was commanded them, took Paul and brought him by night to the city of An-tip'a-tris.

32 And the next day the horsemen dismissed the footmen so that they might return to the castle:

33 And they brought him to Cæs-a-re'a, and delivered the letter to the governor, and also presented Paul before him.

34 And when the governor had read the letter, he asked Paul of what province he was. And when he learned that he was of Ci-li'cia;

35 He said to him, I will give you an audience when your accusers arrive. And he commanded him to be kept in the Præ-to'ri-um of Herod.

CHAPTER 24

AND after five days An-a-ni'as the high priest went down with the elders, together with Ter-tul'lus, the orator, and they informed the governor against Paul.

2 And when he was called forth, Ter-tul'lus began to accuse him, saying, It is through you that we enjoy great tranquility, and owing to your care many excellent things have been done for this people.

3 And we all, everywhere, receive your favors, O most excellent Fe'lix.

4 But while I desire not to weary you with lengthy discussions, nevertheless, I beg you to hear in brief our humble complaint.

5 We have found this man to be a pestilent fellow and a worker of sedition among the Jews throughout the world, for he is the ringleader of the sect of the Naz'a-renes.

6 He sought to defile our temple: therefore when we seized him, we would have judged him according to our law.

7 But the chief captain Lys'ias came, and by force took him away out of our hands and sent him to you,

8 Then he commanded his accusers to come to you. Now when you question him, you can learn for yourself concerning all these things of which we accuse him.

9 The Jews also witnessed against him, declaring that these things were true.

10 Then the governor beckoned to Paul to speak. Paul answered and said, For in as much as I know that you have been a judge for many years to this people, therefore I do the more cheerfully answer in my own defense:

11 So that you may understand, that it is not more than twelve days since I went up to Jerusalem to worship.

12 And they neither found me in the temple disputing with any man, nor have I had an assembly either in their synagogues or in the city:

13 Nor can they prove before you the things of which they accuse me.

14 But this I confess, that in that very teaching which they mention, I worship the God of my fathers, believing all things which are written in the law and in the prophets:

15 And I have the same hope in God which they themselves hold, that there shall be a

Cf.dif. vv. 23:27, 29, 31-33;   24:1-4, 7, 9-10, 12-14.

resurrection of the dead, both of the just and unjust.

16 For this reason, I labor to have always a clear conscience before God and before men.

17 Now after many years, I came to my own people to distribute alms and to present an offering.

18 So these men found me purifying myself in the temple, not in a crowd, nor in a riot, except the riot which was caused by the Jews who had come from Asia Minor,

19 Who ought to have been here with me before you, to make whatever accusations they have against me.

20 Or else let these same people here say, what fault they found in me when I stood before their council.

21 Except it be for this one saying which I cried standing before them, It is for the resurrection of the dead that I am tried before you this day.

22 But because Fe'lix was thoroughly familiar with this teaching, he deferred them, saying, When the chief captain comes down, I will give you a hearing.

23 And he commanded a centurion to keep Paul in comfort, and that none of his acquaintances should be prevented from ministering to him.

24 ¶ And after a few days, Fe'lix with his wife Dru-sil'la, who was a Jewess, sent for Paul, and heard him concerning the faith of Christ.

25 And as he spoke with them concerning righteousness, holiness, and the judgment to come, Fe'lix was filled with fear, and said, You may go, and when I have opportunity I will send for you.

26 Since he was expecting a bribe from Paul, he often sent for him to be brought and conversed with him.

27 And when he had completed two years, another governor succeeded him whose name was Por'ci-us Fes'tus: and Fe'lix, to do the Jews a favor, left Paul a prisoner.

CHAPTER 25

*N*OW when Fes'tus arrived at Cæs-a-re'a, after three days he went up to Jerusalem.

2 Then the high priests and Jewish leaders informed him against Paul.

3 They besought him as a favor to send for him and bring him to Jerusalem, for they were plotting to kill him on the way.

4 But Fes'tus answered that Paul should be kept at Cæs-a-re'a, and that he himself was shortly going there.

5 Therefore, said he, let those who are able among you come down with us and accuse the man about any offense which can be found against him.

6 And when he had tarried there eight or ten days, he went down to Cæs-a-re'a, and the next day he sat on the judgment seat and commanded Paul to be brought.

7 And when he was come, the Jews who had come from Jerusalem surrounded him, and brought against him many serious charges which they could not prove.

8 Then Paul answered, I have committed no offense against the Jewish law, or against the temple, or against Cæsar.

9 But Festus, because he was willing to do the Jews a favor, said to Paul, Would you be willing to go to Jerusalem and there be tried of these things before me?

10 Paul answered and said, I stand before Cæsar's judgment seat, where I ought to be tried: I have done no wrong to the Jews, as you very well know.

11 If I had committed any crime or had done anything worthy of death, I should not refuse to die: but if there is no truth in the charges made against me, then no man may deliver me to them just to please them. I appeal to

Cæsar.

12 Festus, when he had conferred with his counsellors, decreed, You have appealed to Cæsar. You will go to Cæsar.

13 ¶ Some days later, King A-grip'pa and Ber-ni'ce came down to Cæs-a-re'a to greet Festus.

14 And when they had been with him several days, Festus related Paul's case to the king, saying, There is a certain prisoner left by Felix:

15 And when I was in Jerusalem, the high priests and the elders of the Jews informed me about him, and asked to have judgment against him.

16 I told them, It is not the Roman custom to give up a man to be slain, until his accusers come and accuse him face to face, and give him a chance to defend himself against the charges.

17 So when I arrived here, the following day, without any delay, I sat on the judgment seat and commanded the man to be brought before me.

18 When his accusers stood up with him, they were unable to prove, as I had expected, any serious charges against him.

19 But they had certain grievances against him relative to their own worship and to one named Jesus, now dead, whom Paul affirmed to be alive.

20 And because I was not well acquainted with their controversy, I said to Paul. Would you be willing to go to Jerusalem, and there be tried of these matters?

21 But he appealed to be kept as a prisoner for a trial before Cæ'sar. I accordingly commanded him to be kept in custody till I might send him to Cæ'sar.

22 Then A-grip'pa said to Festus, I would like to hear this man myself; and Festus replied, Tomorrow, you shall hear him.

23 ¶ The next day A-grip'pa and Ber-ni'ce came with great pomp, and entered into the court house, accompanied by the chief captains and principal men of the city. Festus commanded and Paul was brought in.

24 Then Festus said, King A-grip'pa and all men who are here present with us, against this man whom you see, all the Jewish people have complained to me both at Jerusalem and also here, crying that he ought not to live any longer.

25 But when I found he had done nothing worthy of death, and because he himself had appealed to be kept in custody for a trial before Cæsar, I commanded to send him.

26 But I do not know what to write Caesar concerning him, therefore I was pleased to bring him before you, and especially before you, O King A-grip'pa, so that when he is questioned, I may find somewhat to write.

27 For it is not proper to send a prisoner, without writing down the charges against him.

CHAPTER 26

*T*HEN A-grip'pa said to Paul, You have permission to speak in your own behalf. Then Paul stretched forth his hand, and answered, saying,

2 In view of all the things whereof I am accused by the Jews, I consider myself blessed, O King A-grip'pa, to defend myself today before you.

3 Especially because I know you are familiar with all the customs and questions and laws of the Jews: wherefore, I beg you to hear me patiently.

4 Even the Jews themselves, if they would be willing to testify, know well my manner of life from my childhood which started first among mine own people at Jerusalem.

5 For they have been acquainted with me a long time, and know that I was brought up with the excellent doctrine of the Phar'i-sees.

Cf.dif. vv. 25:15-21, 25;   26:2-3, 5.

6 And now I stand and am on trial for the hope of the promise made of God to our fathers.

7 It is to the fulfillment of this hope that our twelve tribes expect to come, by means of earnest prayers day and night. And for this very hope's sake, I am accused by the Jews, O King A-grip'pa.

8 How can you judge? Is it improper to believe that God can raise the dead?

9 For I at the very beginning was determined that I ought to do many things contrary to the name of Jesus of Nazareth.

10 Which I also did at Jerusalem: I cast many of the saints into prison, having received authority from the chief priests; and when some were put to death, I took part with those who condemned them.

11 And I tortured them in every synagogue, thus compelling them to blaspheme the name of Jesus; and being exceedingly mad against them, I also went to other cities to persecute them.

12 I was on the way to Damascus for this purpose, with authority and commission from the chief priests, when,

13 At mid-day on the road, O king, I saw a light from heaven more powerful than that of the sun, shining round about me and upon those who journeyed with me.

14 When we all fell to the ground, then I heard a voice speaking unto me, in the Hebrew tongue (Ar-a-ma'ic), Saul, Saul, why do you persecute me? It is hard for you to kick against the pricks.

15 And I said, My LORD, who are you? And our LORD said to me, I am Jesus of Nazareth whom you persecute.

16 Then he said to me, Rise and stand upon your feet: for I have appeared to you for this purpose, to appoint you a minister and a witness both of these things in which you have seen me, and of those things in which you will also see me again.

17 And I will deliver you from the Jewish people, and from the other people to whom I send you;

18 To open their eyes, that they may turn from darkness to light, and from the power of Satan unto God, and receive forgiveness of sins, and a portion with the saints who are of the faith in me.

19 Whereupon, O King A-grip'pa, I did not disobey the heavenly vision:

20 But I preached first to them of Damascus and at Jerusalem, and throughout all the villages of Judæa, and then to the Gentiles, that they might repent and turn to God and do works worthy of repentance.

21 For these causes the Jews seized me in the temple, and wanted to kill me.

22 But God has helped me to this very day, and behold I stand and testify to the humble and to the great, saying nothing contrary to Moses and the prophets, but the very things which they said were to take place;

23 That Christ should suffer, and that he should be the first to rise from the dead, and that he should preach light to the people and to the Gentiles.

24 ¶ And while Paul was pleading in this manner, Festus cried with a loud voice: Paul, you are overwrought. Much study has made you mad.

25 But Paul said to him, I am not mad, O most excellent Festus; but I speak the words of truth and soberness.

26 And King A-grip'pa is also familiar with these things, and this is why I am speaking openly before him: because I think not one of these words has been hidden from him; for they were not done in secret.

27 King A-grip'pa, do you believe the prophets? I know that you believe.

28 Then King A-grip'pa said to him, With little effort you almost persuade me to become a Christian. *

29 And Paul said, I pray God that not only you, but also all of those who hear me today, were as I am, except for these bonds.

30 ¶ Then the king arose, and the governor, and Ber-ni'ce and they that sat with them:

31 And when they had departed, they talked between themselves, saying, This man has done nothing worthy of death or of imprisonment.

32 Then Agrip'pa said to Festus, This man could have been released had he not appealed to Cæsar.

CHAPTER 27

*T*HEN Festus commanded him to be sent to Cæsar in Italy, and he delivered Paul together with other prisoners to a centurion of the company of Se-bas'ti-an named Julius.

2 When we were ready to sail, we embarked in a ship of the city of Ad-ra-myt'ti-um, bound for Asia Minor, and there boarded the ship with us, Ar-is-tar'chus a Mac-e-do'ni-an of the city of Thes-sa-lo-ni'ca.

3 And the next day, we arrived at Sidon. And the centurion treated Paul with kindness, permitting him to visit his friends and to rest.

4 Then we sailed from thence, and because the winds were contrary, we had to sail towards Cyprus.

5 And when we had sailed over the sea of Ci-li'cia and Pam-phyl'i-a, we arrived at Myra, a city of Lycia.

6 And there the centurion found a ship from Al-ex-an'dri-a bound for Italy; and he put us on board of it.

7 And because for a number of days she sailed slowly, we arrived with difficulty towards the Island of Cni'dus; and because the wind would not allow us to sail in a straight course, we had to sail around Crete towards the city of Sal-mo'ne;

8 And as we hardly passed around it, we arrived at a place which is called The Fair Havens; and nearby was the city of La-se'a.

9 There we remained for a long time, till also the day of the Jewish fast was over and, since it had now become dangerous for any one to sail, Paul gave them advice,

10 Saying, Men, I see that this voyage will be beset with hardship and with great loss, not only to the cargo of our ship but also of our lives.

11 Nevertheless, the centurion listened to the master and owner of the ship more than to the words of Paul.

12 ¶ And as the harbor was not commodious for wintering in, many of us were desirous to sail from thence, and if possible to reach and winter in a harbor at Crete, which is called Phe-ni'ce, which lies towards the south.

13 And when the south wind blew softly, they thought they could reach their destination as they had desired, and we sailed around Crete.

14 A short while after, there arose against us a hurricane called Ty-phon'ic Eu-roc'ly-don.

15 And when the ship was caught, and could not bear against the wind, we let her drive.

16 And as we passed under the lee of an island which is called Clau'da, we could hardly man the ship's boat.

---

* Ac.26:28 - The possibility that King Agrippa actually *was* converted here is proposed by David Anderson, *The Two Ways of the First Century Church* (pp.189-194, 1989), and may be further suggested by the translation of J.W. Etheridge (*Apostolic Acts and Epistles, from the Peschito...* 1859) who translates this, "(Within) a little thou persuadest me to become a Christian". -D.J.M.

Cf.dif. vv. 26:28;   27:1-2, 4, 7-9, 12-13.

17 And when we had launched it, we began undergirding and repairing the ship; and because we were afraid of grounding, we lowered the sail, and so we drifted.

18 And as the violent storm raged against us, the next day we threw our belongings into the sea.

19 And on the third day we threw overboard with our own hands the tackling of the ship.

20 And as the winter was so severe that for many days, neither sun nor stars could be seen, all hope of surviving was given up.

21 And as no man among them had eaten anything, Paul stood up in the midst of them, and said, Men, if you had listened to me, we would not have sailed from Crete, and we would have been spared this loss and suffering.

22 Now let me counsel you not to be depressed: for not a single life among you will be lost, but only the ship.

23 For there has appeared to me this night the angel of God to whom I belong and whom I serve,

24 And he said to me, Fear not, Paul; you must stand before Cæsar: and behold, God has given to you all of them who sail with you.

25 Therefore, men, be of good cheer: for I have confidence in God, that it shall be just as it was told me.

26 However, we will be cast upon an island.

27 And after fourteen days of being lost and weary in the sea of A'dri-a, about midnight the sailors thought they were drawing near to land.

28 So they cast the sounding lead, and found twenty fathoms; and again, they sailed a little farther, and took soundings and found fifteen fathoms.

29 Then, fearing lest we find ourselves caught between the rocks, they cast four anchors from the stern of the ship, and prayed

for the dawning of day.

30 The sailors sought to desert the ship; so they lowered the ship's boat into the sea, under pretense that they were going in it to make fast the ship to the land.

31 And when Paul found it out, he said to the centurion and to the soldiers, Unless these men remain on board the ship, you cannot be saved.

32 Then the soldiers cut off the ropes of the ship's boat from the ship and let her drift.

33 But Paul till the early morning kept begging them all to eat, saying to them, Today is the fourteenth day since you have tasted anything because of fear.

34 Wherefore, I pray you to take some food for the sustenance of your life; for not a hair shall be lost from the head of any of you.

35 And when he had thus spoken, he took bread, and gave thanks to God in the presence of them all; and when he had broken it, they began to eat.

36 Then they were all cheerful, and received nourishment.

37 We were in all, on board, two hundred and seventy-six persons.

38 And when they had eaten enough, they lightened the ship by taking the wheat and throwing it into the sea.

39 When it was day, the sailors did not know what land it was; but they saw an inlet close to the shore, and thought if it were possible they would thrust the ship there.

40 So they cut off the anchors from the ship, and threw them into the sea, and loosed the rudder ropes, then they hoisted the topsail to the wind, and sailed toward shore.

41 But the ship struck on a shoal between two deep places in the sea, and went aground; and the forward part rested upon the bottom and could not be moved, but the stern broke by the violence of the waves.

42 And the soldiers sought to kill the pris-

oners, lest some of them should swim away and so escape.

43 But the centurion stopped them from doing this, because he was willing to save Paul; so he commanded those who could swim to cast themselves first into the sea and get to land.

44 The others he made cross over on boards and on broken pieces of the ship. In this manner, all of them escaped and reached shore safely.

CHAPTER 28

AFTERWARDS they learned that the island was called Mel'i-ta.

2 And the barbarians who inhabited it showed us much kindness: for they kindled a fire and called us all to warm ourselves, because of heavy rain and the cold.

3 And Paul picked up a bundle of sticks, and laid them on the fire and a scorpion driven by the heat, came out and bit his hand.

4 And when the barbarians saw it hanging from his hand, they said, It may be that this man is a murderer, whom though he has been rescued from the sea, yet justice does not permit him to live.

5 But Paul shook his hand and threw the viper into the fire, and felt no harm.

6 However, the barbarians expected he would immediately swell up and fall to the ground dead: but after they had waited for a long while, and saw he had not been harmed, they changed their talk, and said that he was a god.

7 There were villages in that region, belonging to a man whose name was Pub'li-us, the chief man of the island; and he gladly received us at his house for three days.

8 But the father of Pub'li-us was sick with fever and dysentery: so Paul went in to where he was lying and prayed, then he laid his hand on him and healed him.

9 So when this was done, others also sick in the island, came, and were healed.

10 The inhabitants honored us with great honors: and when we departed from thence, they ladened us with provisions.

11 ¶ After three months we departed, sailing in an Al-ex-an'dri-an ship, which had wintered in the island, and which bore the sign of Castor and Pollux.

12 Landing at Syracuse, we remained there for three days.

13 From there we circled around, and arrived at Rhe'gi-um city. After a day the south wind blew in our favor, and in two days, we came to Pu-te'o-li, an Italian city,

14 Where we found brethren who invited us; and we stayed with them seven days: then we departed for Rome.

15 When the brethren there heard of us, they came out to meet us as far as the street which is called Ap'pi-i-fo'rum and The Three Taverns. When Paul saw them, he thanked God, and was greatly encouraged.

16 ¶ Then we entered Rome, and the centurion gave permission to Paul to live wherever he pleased with a soldier to guard him.

17 And after three days, Paul sent and called the Jewish leaders; and when they were come together, he said to them, Men and my brethren, though I have done nothing against the people and the law of my fathers, yet I was delivered from Jerusalem in bonds into the hands of the Romans,

18 Who, when they had examined me, would have released me, because they found in me no cause worthy of death.

19 But as the Jews stood against me I was obliged to appeal to Cæsar; not that I had anything of which to accuse my own people.

20 This is the reason I begged you to come, for I wish to see you and to relate these things to you; because it is for the hope of Israel I am bound with this chain.

21 And they said to him, We have neither received a letter concerning you from Judæ'a, nor have any of the brethren who have come from Jerusalem made any evil report about you.

22 Nevertheless, we desire to hear what you have to say, but if it is concerning this teaching, we know well that it is not acceptable to any one, and we do not want to hear about it.

23 So they appointed a day for him and many gathered together and came to him where he was staying; and he explained to them about the Kingdom of God, thus testifying and persuading them concerning Jesus, both out of the law of Moses, and out of the prophets, from morning till evening.

24 And some of them harkened to his words, but others paid no attention.

25 And as they were dismissed, disagreeing among themselves, Paul said to them this saying, Well spoke the Holy Spirit by the mouth of the prophet I-sa'iah against your fathers,

26 Saying, Go to this people and say, Hearing you shall hear, and shall not understand; and seeing you shall see and shall not perceive:

27 For the heart of this people is hardened and their ears are dull of hearing, and their eyes have they closed; lest they should see with their eyes, and hear with their ears, and understand with their heart, and repent before me, and I should forgive them.

28 ¶ Let this be known to you therefore: that this salvation of God is sent to the Gentiles, for they will listen to it.

29 * And when he had said these words, the Jews departed arguing much among themselves.

30 ¶ And Paul hired a house for himself at his own expense and lived in it for two years; there he received all who came to him,

31 Preaching the kingdom of God, and teaching openly about our LORD Jesus Christ, without hindrance.

Here endeth the Acts of the Twelve Apostles.

❖ ܟܬܒܐ ܕܟܠܗܘܢ ܫܠܝܚܐ ܕܫܠܡ ܫܠܡ ❖

---

* Ac.28:29 - "This verse is not found in any Syriac MS." (p.205, *Syriac New Testament and Psalms*, United Bible Society). "The later editions place it in the margin." (Murdock, p.276, *The New Testament, A Literal Translation*). -D.J.M.

Cf.dif. vv. 28:21-22, 24-25, 27, 30.

THE GENERAL EPISTLE OF

JAMES

❖ ܟܬܒܐ ܕܝܥܩܘܒ ܫܠܝܚܐ ❖

CHAPTER 1

JAMES, a servant of God and of our LORD Jesus Christ, to the twelve tribes which are scattered among the Gentiles, greeting.

2 ¶ MY brethren, take it as a joy to you when you enter into many and divers temptations;

3 For you know that the trial of faith will increase your patience.

4 And let patience be a perfect work, that you may be perfect and entire, lacking nothing.

5 If any of you lack wisdom, let him ask of God, who gives to all men liberally and with grace; and it shall be given him.

6 But let him ask in faith, not doubting. For he who doubts is like the waves of the sea driven by the wind and tossed.

7 Thus let not that man expect that he will receive anything of the LORD.

8 A double-minded man is unstable in all his ways.

9 Let the brother of low estate rejoice because he is exalted.

10 Let the rich man rejoice in his humbleness: because as the flower of the grass, so shall he pass away.

11 For as the sun rises with its burning heat and causes the grass to wither, and the flower to fall and its beauty to perish: so also shall the rich man fade away in his ways.

12 Blessed is the man who endures temptations: for when he is tested, he shall receive the crown of life, which God has promised to those who love him.

13 Let no man say when he is tempted, I am tempted of God: for God cannot be tempted with evil, neither does he tempt any man:

14 But every man is tempted by his own lust; and he covets and is enticed.

15 Then when lust has conceived, it brings forth sin: and sin when it has matured, brings forth death.

16 Do not err, my beloved brethren.

17 Every good and perfect gift is from above, and comes down from the Father of lights, with whom there is no variableness nor shadow of change.

18 It is he, who begot us of his own will with the word of truth, that we should be the firstfruits of his creatures.

19 ¶ Therefore, my beloved brethren, let every man be swift to hear, and slow to speak, and slow to anger:

20 For the wrath of man does not bring about the righteousness of God.

21 Wherefore cast away all filthiness, and all the multitude of evil things, and receive with meekness the engrafted word, which is able to save your souls.

22 ¶ But you be doers of the word, and not hearers only, deceiving your own selves.

23 For if any be a hearer of the word, and not a doer, he is like a man who sees his face in a mirror;

24 For he sees himself and goes his way, and forgets how he looked.

25 But whoever looks into the perfect law of liberty, and abides in it, is not merely a hearer of the word which can be forgotten but a doer of the work, and this man shall be blessed in his work.

Cf.dif. vv. 1:1, 5, 8-9, 11, 17, 21, 25.

26 If any man thinks that he ministers to God, and does not control his tongue, he deceives his own heart, and this man's ministry is in vain.

27 For a pure and holy ministry before God, the Father, is this, To visit the fatherless and the widows in their affliction, and to keep himself unspotted from the world.

CHAPTER 2

*M*Y brethren, do not, with hypocrisy, uphold the glorious faith of our LORD Jesus Christ.

2 For if there should enter into your synagogue a man with gold rings and costly garments, and there should also enter a poor man in soiled clothing;

3 And you should attend to the one who wears the beautiful clothing, and say to him, Sit here in a good place; and say to the poor man, Stand up there, or sit here before our footstool;

4 Are you not then showing partiality, and thereby give preference to evil thoughts?

5 Hear this, my beloved brethren, Has not God chosen the poor of the world who are rich in faith, to be heirs of the kingdom which God has promised to those who love him?

6 But you have despised the poor. Do not rich men exalt themselves over you and drag you before the judgment seat?

7 Do not they blaspheme against that good name by which you are called?

8 If you fulfil the law of God by this, as it is written, Thou shalt love thy neighbor as thyself, you do well:

9 But if you discriminate among men, you commit sin and you will be condemned by the law as transgressors of the law.

10 For whoever shall keep the whole law, except that he fail in but one statute, he is guilty as to the whole law.

11 For he who said, Thou shalt not commit adultery, said also, Thou shalt not kill. Now if you do not commit adultery, but you kill, you have become a transgressor of the law.

12 So speak and so act, as men who are to be judged by the law of liberty.

13 For a judgment without mercy will be on him, who does not show mercy; for you exalt yourselves by having mercy over judgment.

14 ¶ Though a man say he has faith, what profit is it, my brethren, if he does not have works? Can faith save him?

15 If a brother or sister be naked, and lacking of daily food,

16 And one of you say to them, Depart in peace, be warmed, and be filled; yet you do not give to them those things which are needed for the body, what does it profit?

17 Even so faith, without works, is dead, by itself.

18 For a man may say, You have faith, and I have works: show me your faith without your works, and I will show you my faith by my works.

19 You believe that there is one God; you do well. The devils also believe, and they tremble.

20 Would you know, O weak man, that faith without works is dead?

21 Was not our father Abraham justified by works, when he raised Isaac his son upon the altar?

22 You can see, how his faith helped his works, and how by works his faith was made perfect.

23 And the scripture was fulfilled which said, Abraham believed God, and it was accounted to him for righteousness: and he was called the Friend of God.

24 You see then, how a man by works becomes righteous, and not by faith only.

25 Likewise also was not Rahab the harlot, justified by works, when she welcomed the

spies, and sent them out another way?

26 For as the body without the spirit is dead, so also faith without works is dead.

CHAPTER 3

*M*Y brethren, do not allow doubtful teachers among you; but know, that we are under a great judgment.

2 For in many things we all stumble. Anyone who does not offend in word, this one is a perfect man, and able also to subdue his whole body.

3 Behold, we put bits into the mouths of horses, that they may obey us; and we turn about their whole body.

4 Behold also the ships, great as they are, when driven by severe winds, they are turned about with a very small rudder, wherever the pilot wishes.

5 Even so the tongue is a little member, and boasts great things. Likewise, a small fire sets ablaze the large forests.

6 The tongue is a fire, and the sinful world like a forest: that very tongue, while it is among our members, can defile our whole body, and set on fire the records of our race which have rolled down from the beginning: and in the end it is consumed by fire.

7 For every kind of beasts, and of birds, and of creatures of the sea and of the land are under the subjugation of the will of man.

8 But the tongue no man can tame; it is an unruly evil, full of deadly poison.

9 By it we bless the LORD and the Father; and by it we curse men, who are made in the image of God:

10 Out of the same mouth proceed curses and blessings. My brethren, these things ought not so to be.

11 Can there spring forth from the same fountain, both sweet water and bitter water?

12 Can the fig tree, my brethren, bear olives? Or the vine, figs? likewise also salt water cannot be made sweet.

13 Who is wise among you and has training? let him prove his words by his good deeds, in the humbleness of wisdom.

14 But if you have bitter envying among you, or strife in your hearts, do not boast and do not lie against the truth.

15 This wisdom does not come from above, but it is earthly, sensual, devilish.

16 For wherever envy and strife are, there is confusion and every sort of evil.

17 But the wisdom that is from above is first pure then full of peace, and gentle, obedient, full of mercy and good fruits, without partiality, and without hypocrisy.

18 And the fruit of righteousness is sown in peace by the peacemakers.

CHAPTER 4

*F*ROM whence come conflicts and quarrels among you? Is it not from the lusts that war in your members?

2 You covet, and do not obtain; you kill and envy, but you cannot possess; you strive and fight, yet you have nothing, because you do not ask.

3 You ask and you do not receive because you do not ask sincerely, you ask that you may satisfy your lusts.

4 O you adulterers! Do you not know that the love for worldly things is enmity with God? Whosoever, therefore, esteems worldly things is the enemy of God.

5 Or do you think that the scripture said in vain, The pride that dwells in us is provoked by jealousy?

6 But our LORD has given us abundant grace. Therefore he said, God humbles the proud, but gives grace to the humble.

7 Submit yourselves therefore to God. Resist Satan, and he will flee from you.

8 Draw near to God, and he will draw near to you. Cleanse your hands, O you sinners!

Cf.dif. vv. 3:1, 5-7, 12-13; 4:5-6.

And purify your hearts, O you of doubtful mind!

9 Humble yourselves, and mourn; let your laughter be turned to weeping, and your joy to sorrow.

10 Humble yourselves before the LORD and he shall lift you up.

11 Do not speak against one another, my brethren, for he who speaks against his brother, and judges his brother, speaks against the law, and judges the law; but if you judge the law, you are not a doer of the law, but a judge of it.

12 For there is one lawgiver and judge, who is able to save and to destroy: who are you to judge your neighbor?

13 ¶ What then shall we say of those who say, Today or tomorrow we will go to a certain city, and will work there a year, and will trade and prosper?

14 They do not know what will happen tomorrow! For what is our life? It is but a vapour, which appears for a little while, and then vanishes away.

15 Instead of that they should say, If the LORD will, we shall live, and do this, or that.

16 But now they are proud in their boasting: all such pride is evil.

17 Therefore he who knows to do good, and does not do it, to him it is sin.

CHAPTER 5

O YOU rich men, weep and howl for the miseries which shall come upon you!

2 Your riches are destroyed and rotted, and your garments are moth-eaten.

3 Your gold and silver are tarnished, and the rust of them will be a testimony against you, and shall eat your flesh. The treasures which you have heaped together will be as fire to you for the last days.

4 Behold, the wage of the labourers, who have reaped down your fields, that which you have fraudulently kept back, cries: and the cry of the reapers has already entered into the ears of the LORD of sabaoth.

5 For you have had your luxuries on earth and have been greedy; you have fed your bodies as for the day of slaughter.

6 You have condemned and murdered the righteous; and yet he does not resist you.

7 ¶ But you, my brethren, be patient, until the coming of the LORD, just as the husbandman waits for the precious crops of his field, and has long patience for it, until he receives the early and the latter rain.

8 You be patient also: strengthen your hearts: for the coming of our LORD is at hand.

9 Complain not one against another, my brethren, lest you be condemned: for behold judgment is at hand.

10 My brethren, take the prophets who have spoken in the name of the LORD, for an example of patience in your suffering.

11 Behold, we count them happy who endure. You have heard of the patience of Job, and you have seen what the LORD did for him at the end; for the LORD is very merciful and compassionate.

12 ¶ But above all things, my brethren, do not swear, neither by heaven, neither by the earth, neither by any other oath: but let your words be yes, yes, and no, no; lest you fall under condemnation.

13 ¶ If any among you be afflicted, let him pray. If any be merry, let him sing psalms.

14 ¶ And if any be sick, let him call for the elders of the church; and let them pray over him, anointing him with oil in the name of our LORD:

15 And the prayer of faith shall heal the sick, and our LORD shall raise him up; and if he has committed sins, they shall be forgiven him.

16 ¶ Confess your faults one to another, and

pray one for another, that you may be healed. The effectual fervent prayer of a righteous man is powerful.

17 Even Elijah, who was a weak man like ourselves, prayed earnestly that it might not rain upon the land, and it did not rain for three years and six months.

18 And he prayed again, and the heaven gave rain, and the earth brought forth her fruits.

19 My brethren, if any of you do err from the way of the truth, and some one converts him from his error,

20 Let him know that he who converts a sinner from the error of his way, shall save his soul from death, and shall wipe out a multitude of sins.

Here ends the epistle of James the apostle.

❖ ܟܠܡ ܝܥܩܘܒ ܕܐܓܪܬܐ ܫܠܡܬ ❖

THE FIRST EPISTLE GENERAL OF

PETER

❖ ܟܬܒܐ ܕܦܛܪܘܣ ܫܠܝܚܐ ❖

CHAPTER 1

*P*ETER, an apostle of Jesus Christ, to the chosen ones and pilgrims, scattered throughout Pontus, Ga-la'tia, Cap-pa-do'cia, Asia Minor and Bi-thyn'i-a,

2 Who have been chosen by the foreknowledge of God the Father, through sanctification of the Spirit, to be obedient and to sprinkle the blood of our LORD Jesus Christ: Grace to you and peace, be multiplied.

3 ¶ Blessed be God, the Father of our LORD Jesus Christ, who by his abundant mercy has again renewed us spiritually to a lively hope by the resurrection of Jesus Christ from the dead,

4 To an inheritance incorruptible and undefiled, that does not fade away, and is prepared in heaven for you,

5 While you are kept by the power of God through faith, for the life eternal which is ready to be revealed at the last time.

6 Wherein you will rejoice for ever, though at present you are sorrowful for a while, through diverse trials which have come upon you:

7 So that the proof of your faith, being much more precious than refined gold which has been purified by fire, may be made manifest for the glory and honour and praise at the appearing of Jesus Christ,

8 Whom you have not seen, but whom you yet love, and in whose faith you rejoice with exceeding joy that cannot be described;

9 And you will receive the reward for your faith, even the salvation of your souls.

10 For which very salvation the prophets searched diligently when they prophesied concerning the grace which was to be given to you.

11 They searched to find out at what time it would be revealed, and the Spirit of Christ which dwelt in them testified beforehand the sufferings of Christ, and the glory that should follow.

12 And everything they were searching for was revealed to them because they did not seek for their own benefit, but they prophesied the things which concerned us, the things which now have been revealed to you by those who have preached the gospel to you through the Holy Spirit sent from heaven; which things the angels also desire to look into.

13 ¶ Wherefore gird up the loins of your mind, be wide awake, and hope for the joy that is coming to you at the revelation of our LORD Jesus Christ;

14 Like obedient children, not partakers again in those sinful desires for which you once lusted in your ignorance:

15 But be you holy in all your conduct, as he who has called you is holy;

16 Because it is written, Be you holy, even as I am holy.

17 And if you call on the Father, who is impartial and who judges every man according to his works, conduct yourselves reverently during the time of your sojourning here:

18 Knowing that you have not been redeemed from your empty works which you have received from your fathers by corruptible silver and gold;

Cf.dif. vv. 1:1, 6-9, 12-13, 17-18.

19 But with the precious blood of the Lamb without blemish and without spot which is Christ:

20 Who verily was foreordained for this very purpose, before the foundation of the world, and was manifest in these last times, for your sakes,

21 Who by him do believe in God, who raised him up from the dead, and gave him glory; that your faith and hope might rest on God.

22 Let your souls be sanctified by obedience to the truth, and be filled with sincere love, so that you may love one another with pure and perfect hearts:

23 Being born again, not of corruptible seed, but of incorruptible, by the word of God, which lives and abides for ever.

24 For all flesh is as grass, and all its glory is as the flower of the field. The grass withers and the flower fades away:

25 But the word of our God endures for ever. And this is the very word which has been preached to you.

CHAPTER 2

THEREFORE lay aside all malice and all guile, and hypocrisies, and envies, and evil accusations,

2 And become like newborn babes, and long for the word, as for pure and spiritual milk, that you may grow to salvation by it:

3 If so be you have tasted and found out that the LORD is good.

4 The one to whom you are coming is the living stone, whom men have rejected, and yet he is chosen and precious with God;

5 You also, as living stones, build up yourselves and become spiritual temples and holy priests to offer up spiritual sacrifices, acceptable to God by Jesus Christ.

6 For as it is said in the scriptures, Behold, I lay in Sion, a chief corner stone, approved, precious: and he who believes on him shall not be ashamed.

7 It is to you who believe, therefore, that this honour is given; but to those who are disobedient, he is a stumbling stone and a stone of trouble.

8 And they stumble over it because they are disobedient to the word for which they were appointed.

9 But you are a chosen people; ministers to the kingdom, a holy people, a congregation redeemed to proclaim the glories of him who has called you out of darkness to his marvelous light:

10 You, who in the past were not considered a people, but who are now the people of God: who had not obtained mercy, but who now have mercy poured out upon you.

11 ¶ Dearly beloved, I beseech you as strangers and pilgrims, abstain from carnal desires, which war against the soul;

12 And let your conduct be good before all men, so that those who speak evil words against you, may see your good works and glorify God at the day of trial.

13 Submit yourselves to all human authority for God's sake: whether it be to kings, because of their power,

14 Or to judges because from them officers are sent for the punishment of offenders, and to bestow honour on those who do good.

15 For such is the will of God, that by your good works you may silence the mouth of foolish men, who know not God.

16 Act as free men, and not as men who use their liberty as a cloak for their maliciousness; but as the servants of God.

17 Honour all men. Love your brethren. Fear God. Honour the king.

18 ¶ And the servants among you, let them be submissive to their masters with due respect, not only to those who are good and gentle, but also to those who are severe and difficult.

Cf.dif. vv. 1:22;   2:2, 4-5, 7-9, 13-15, 18.

19 For such men have favor before God; because of a good conscience they endure sorrows which come upon them unjustly.

20 What praise have they who endure suffering because of their faults? But when you do good, and are made to suffer, and you take it patiently, then your glory is greater with God.

21 For to this purpose you were called: because Christ also died for us, leaving us an example, that we should follow in his footsteps.

22 Who did no sin, neither was guile found in his mouth:

23 Who, wen he was reviled, he did not revile again: when he suffered he did not threaten, but committed his cause to him who judges righteously:

24 And he bore all our sins, and lifted them with his body on the cross, that we being dead to sin, should live through his righteousness: and by his wounds you were healed.

25 For you had gone astray like sheep, but you have now returned to the Shepherd and the Guardian of your souls.

CHAPTER 3

*L*IKEWISE, you wives, be submissive to your own husbands, so that those who obey not the word may be won without difficulty through your good example.

2 When they see that you conduct yourselves with respect and modesty.

3 And do not adorn yourselves with outward adornments such as plaiting your hair, or the wearing of ornaments of gold, or costly apparel:

4 But adorn yourselves by the spiritual man within you, with meek pride which is incorruptible and an ornament which is rich in the sight of God.

5 For so also in the past did the holy women, who trusted in God, adorn their lives and were submissive to their own husbands:

6 Even as Sara was submissive to Abraham and called him my LORD: whose daughters you are by reason of good works, and so long as you are not confused by any kind of false value.

7 Likewise, you husbands, live with your wives with understanding, and hold them with tenderness like delicate vessels, because they also will inherit with you the gift of everlasting life; do this that you may not be hindered in your prayers.

8 ¶ Finally, live in harmony, share the suffering of those who suffer, be affectionate one to another, and be kind and gentle:

9 Not rendering evil for evil, nor railing for railing, but instead of these, render blessing; for to this end you have been called, that you may inherit a blessing.

10 Now, therefore, he who desires eternal life and wants to see good days, let him refrain his tongue from evil, and his lips that they speak no guile:

11 Let him refrain from evil and do good; let him seek peace and pursue it.

12 For the eyes of the LORD are on the righteous, and his ears are open to their prayers, but the countenance of the LORD is against the wicked.

13 And who is he that can harm you if you are zealous followers of that which is good?

14 But, and if you suffer for righteousness' sake, you are blessed: and be not afraid of those who terrify you, neither be troubled.

15 ¶ But sanctify the LORD Christ in your hearts: and be ready to give an answer in meekness and reverence to everyone who seeks from you a word concerning the hope of your faith:

16 Having a good conscience; so that they who speak evil of you, as of evil doers, may be ashamed as men who belittle your good works in Christ.

Cf.dif. vv. 2:20-21, 24; 3:1-2, 4, 6-8, 10, 15-16.

17 For it is better, if it is the will of God, that you suffer for good deeds, rather than for evil doing.

18 For Christ also once suffered for our sins, a just man for sinners, that he might bring you to God, wherefore while he died in the flesh, he lives in the Spirit.

19 And he preached to the souls imprisoned in Sheol;

20 Those who in the past were disobedient; and in the days of Noah, when the Spirit of God had patience, he commanded an ark to be made in the hope of their repentance, but only eight souls entered into it, and were saved by it floating upon the water.

21 You also are saved in that very manner by baptism, not merely by washing the filth from the body, but by confessing God with a clean conscience, and by the resurrection of Jesus Christ,

22 Who is taken up to heaven, and is at the right hand of God; angels and authorities and powers being made subject to him.

CHAPTER 4

FORASMUCH then as Christ has suffered for you in the flesh, arm yourselves also with this very thought; he who subdues his body ceases from all sin;

2 That he should no longer live the rest of his time in the flesh to the lusts of men, but to the will of God.

3 For the time past sufficed to have wrought the will of the pagans when you lived in lasciviousness, drunkenness, revellings, indecent singing, and worship of idols.

4 And behold, they think it strange that you do not indulge with them in the past excesses, and they blaspheme against you.

5 And they shall answer to God who is to judge the quick and the dead.

6 For, for this cause the gospel was preached also to those who are dead: that they might be judged according to men in the flesh, and live according to God in spirit.

7 ¶ But the end of all things is at hand: be devout therefore, and be mindful of prayer.

8 And above all things have fervent charity towards one another: because charity covers a multitude of sins.

9 Be hospitable to strangers without grudging.

10 So let everyone of you according to the gift he has received from God, minister the same to your fellowmen, like good stewards of the manifold grace of God.

11 If any man preach, let him preach the word of God; and if any man minister, let him do it according to the ability which God has given him: so that in everything you do, God may be glorified through Jesus Christ, to whom belongs glory and honour for ever and ever. Amen.

12 ¶ My beloved, do not think it strange at the trials that come upon you, as though some strange thing happened to you: because these things are to prove you.

13 But rejoice, for you are partakers of Christ's sufferings; and when his glory shall be revealed you may be glad also with exceeding joy.

14 If you are reproached for the name of Christ, blessed are you: for the glorious Spirit of God rests upon you.

15 But let none of you suffer the fate of a murderer, or a thief, or a malefactor.

16 If any man suffers as a Christian, let him not be ashamed: but let him glorify God through that very name.

17 For the time is come that judgment must begin with the house of God: and if it first begins with us, what shall be the end of those who do not obey the gospel of God?

18 And if the righteous scarcely be saved, how shall the wicked and the sinner stand judgment?

19 Therefore let those who suffer according to the will of God commit their souls to him in well doing, as to a faithful Creator.

CHAPTER 5

I EXHORT the ministers who are among you, for I also am a minister and a witness of the sufferings of Christ, and a partaker of the glory that shall be revealed.

2 Feed the flock of God which is entrusted to your care and shepherd them spiritually, not by constraint, but willingly; not for filthy lucre, but with all your heart.

3 Live not as overlords over the flock, but as good examples to them.

4 And when the chief Shepherd shall appear, you shall receive a crown of glory that will not fade away.

5 And you too, young people, submit yourselves to your elders; and clothe yourselves with humility toward one another, for God resists the proud, and gives grace to the humble.

6 Humble yourselves therefore under the mighty hand of God, that he may exalt you in due time: 7 Casting all your cares upon God; for he cares for you.

8 ¶ Be vigilant, and be cautious; because your adversary, the devil, as a roaring lion, walks about, seeking whom he may devour:

9 Rise up, therefore, against him, as you are steadfast in the faith, knowing that your brethren who are in the world also suffered these same afflictions.

10 But the God of all grace, who has called us to his eternal glory by Christ Jesus, whom God has given to us; will strengthen us to endure these little afflictions that we may be made steadfast and remain in him for ever.

11 To him be glory and dominion and honour for ever and ever. Amen.

12 ¶ By Sil-va'nus, a faithful brother, I have written you these things briefly according to my opinion, exhorting and testifying that this is the true grace of God wherein you stand.

13 The chosen church which is at Bab'y-lon, and Mark, my son, salutes you.

14 Greet one another with a holy kiss. Peace be with you all who are in Christ.

Amen.

Here ends the epistle of Peter the Apostle.

❖ ܟܠܗ ܥܩܝܒܐ ܐܓܪܬܐ ܫܠܡܬ ❖

THE SECOND EPISTLE GENERAL OF
PETER

❖ ܐܓܪܬܐ ܕܬܪܬܝܢ ܕܦܛܪܘܣ ܫܠܝܚܐ ❖

CHAPTER 1

SIMON Peter, a servant and apostle of Jesus Christ, to those who through the righteousness of our LORD and Saviour Jesus Christ have been made equal with us in the precious faith;

2 Grace and peace be multiplied to you through the knowledge of our LORD Jesus Christ,

3 Who has given us all things that pertain to the power of God, for life and worship of God, through the knowledge of him who has called us by his glory and excellence;

4 Whereby are given unto us exceeding great and precious promises: that by these you might be partakers of the divine nature, having escaped the corruption that is in the world through lust.

5 And beside this, giving all diligence, add to your faith, virtue; and to virtue, knowledge;

6 And to knowledge, self-control; and to self-control, patience; and to patience; godliness;

7 And to godliness, brotherly kindness; and to brotherly kindness, love.

8 For when these things are found among you and abound, you are not empty nor unfruitful in the knowledge of our LORD Jesus Christ.

9 But he who lacks these things is blind, and cannot see afar off, and has forgotten that he was cleansed from his former sins.

10 For this very reason, my brethren, be diligent; for through your good deeds, you make your calling and your election sure: and when you do these things, you shall never fall:

11 For by so doing, an entrance shall be given freely to you into the everlasting kingdom of our LORD and Saviour Jesus Christ.

12 ¶ Wherefore I will not be negligent to put you always in remembrance of these things, though you know them well; and you rely on this very truth.

13 Therefore I think it is right, as long as I am in this body, to stir you up by putting you in remembrance;

14 Knowing that shortly I must depart this life, even as our LORD Jesus Christ has shown me.

15 Be diligent always, that you may be able to keep these things in remembrance; even after my departure.

16 For we have not followed cunningly devised fables, when we made known to you the power and coming of our LORD Jesus Christ, for we were eye-witnesses of his majesty.

17 For he received from God the Father honor and glory, when there came such a voice to him from the excellent and majestic glory, This is my beloved Son, in whom I am well pleased.

18 And this very voice which came from heaven we also heard when we were with him on the holy mount.

19 We have also a true word of prophecy; you do well when you look to it for guidance, as you look to the lamp that shines in a dark place until the dawn of day, when the sun will shine in your hearts:

20 Knowing this first, that not every prophetic writing is made clear in its own book.

21 For the prophecy did not come by the will of man, but holy men of God spoke when they were inspired by the Holy Spirit.

CHAPTER 2

*B*UT there were false prophets also among the people, even as there will be false teachers among you, who shall bring in damnable heresies, even denying the LORD who has redeemed them, and thus bringing upon themselves swift destruction.

2 Many will follow their pernicious ways, by reason of whom the way of truth shall be evil spoken of.

3 And through covetousness, they will exploit you with feigned words: whose judgment from the very beginning has not ceased and their damnation is always active.

4 God did not spare the angels, who sinned, but cast them down to hell and delivered them into chains of darkness, to be reserved for tormenting judgment;

5 And did not spare the old world, but saved Noah the preacher of righteousness, with his family, eight in all, when he brought the flood upon the wicked people;

6 And set afire the cities of Sodom and Gomorrah, and condemned them with an upheaval, making them an example to those who hereafter should live ungodly;

7 And delivered righteous Lot, mortified by the filthy conduct of the lawless:

8 For while that pious man dwelt among them, in seeing and hearing their unlawful deeds, his righteous soul was vexed from day to day.

9 The LORD knows how to deliver from distress those who revere him, and he will reserve the wicked to be punished at the judgment day.

10 And especially will he punish those who follow after filthy lusts of the flesh, and have no respect for authority. Arrogant and self-willed are they who do not tremble when they blaspheme against the glory;

11 Whereas angels who are greater in power and might do not bring upon themselves the condemnation of blasphemy.

12 But these men, as natural brute beasts, made for slaughter and destruction, speak evil of the things which they do not understand; and shall utterly perish in their own corruption;

13 And shall receive the reward of iniquity as they consider it a delightful thing to revel in the daytime. Spots and blemishes have they who sport themselves with their own deceivings as they feast in idleness;

14 And have eyes full of adultery, and of sin that does not cease: beguiling, unstable souls are they whose hearts are well versed in covetousness: accursed sons are they.

15 Who have forsaken the right way and are gone astray, following the way of Ba'laam, the son of Be-or, who loved the wages of unrighteousness;

16 But who was rebuked for his iniquity: a dumb ass, speaking with man's voice, halted the folly of the prophet.

17 These men are springs without water, as clouds that are carried with a tempest; the mist of darkness is reserved to them forever.

18 For when they speak great swelling words of vanity, they allure through the sensual lusts of the flesh; but there are those who flee at a word of warning from those who live in error.

19 They, while they promise liberty, themselves are the slaves of corruption: for a man is overcome by whatever it is that enslaves him.

20 For if after they have escaped the pollutions of the world through knowledge of our LORD and Saviour Jesus Christ, they are again entangled by these very things, and overcome, the latter end is worse with them

than the beginning.

21 Verily it would have been better for them not to have known the way of righteousness, than, after they have known it, to turn from the holy commandment that was delivered to them.

22 It will come to pass with them according to the true proverb, The dog returns to his own vomit, and the sow that was washed to her wallowing in the mire.

CHAPTER 3

*I*T has been a long time since I have written you, my beloved, but now I write you this second epistle; in both of them I have endeavored to stir up your pure minds by way of remembrance:

2 That you may be mindful of the words which were spoken before by the holy prophets, and of the commandment, given through us, the Apostles of our LORD and Saviour:

3 Knowing this first, that there shall come in the last days mockers who scoff, following after their own lusts,

4 And saying, Where is the promise of his coming? for since our fathers passed away, all things continue as they were from the beginning of the creation.

5 Of this they are willingly ignorant: that by the word of God the heavens were of old, and the earth standing out of water, and in the water;

6 And those men, because of whose deeds the world of that time was overflowed with water, perished:

7 But the present heavens and earth are sustained by his word, and are reserved for fire on the day of judgment which is the day of destruction of ungodly men.

8 But, my beloved, do not forget this one thing, that one day is with the LORD as a thousand years, and a thousand years as one day.

9 The LORD is not negligent concerning his promises, as some men count negligence; but is longsuffering toward you, not wishing that any should perish, but that all should come to repentance.

10 But the day of the LORD will come as a thief in the night, when the heavens shall suddenly pass away, and the universe shall separate as it burns, and the earth also and the works that are in it, shall pass away.

11 Now since all these things are to be dissolved, what manner of persons ought you to be in your holy conduct and godliness,

12 Looking for and longing for the coming of the day of God, wherein the heavens being tested with fire shall be dissolved, and the elements shall melt with fervent heat?

13 Nevertheless we, according to his promise, look for new heavens and a new earth, in which dwells righteousness.

14 ¶ Therefore, my beloved, while you look for these things, be diligent that you may be found by him in peace, without spot, and blameless.

15 And consider that the long suffering of the LORD is salvation; even as our beloved brother Paul also, according to the wisdom given to him, has written to you;

16 As also in all his epistles, he spoke concerning these things, in which there are certain things so hard to be understood that those who are ignorant and unstable pervert their meaning, as they do also the other scriptures, to their own destruction.

17 You therefore, my beloved, seeing that you know these things beforehand, beware, lest you follow the error of the lawless, and fall from your own steadfastness.

18 But grow in grace and in the knowledge of our LORD and Saviour Jesus Christ, and of God the Father. To him be glory both now and forever, and through all eternity. Amen.

Here ends the second epistle of Peter the Apostle.

❖ ܪܘܠܐ ܘܐܝܠܗܝ ܦܝܬܐ ܪܐܝܪ ܐܝܠܐ ❖

The Second Epistle of Peter is not found in the text which is called the Peshitta, but is included in other ancient texts.

THE FIRST EPISTLE GENERAL OF

JOHN

❖ ܟܬܒܐ ܕܝܘܚܢܢ ܫܠܝܚܐ ❖

CHAPTER 1

HE who was from the beginning, the one whom we have heard and seen with our eyes, looked upon and handled with our hands, we declare to you that he is the word of life.

2 For the life was manifested, and we have seen it, and bear witness to it, and preach to you eternal life, which was with the Father, and was revealed to us;

3 It is that which we have seen and heard that we declare to you, so that you also may have fellowship with us: and truly our fellowship is with the Father and with his Son Jesus Christ.

4 And these things we write to you, that our joy in you may be complete.

5 ¶ This then is the good news which we have heard from him, and declare to you, that God is light, and in him is no darkness at all.

6 If we say that we have fellowship with him and yet live in darkness, we lie, and do not follow the truth:

7 But if we live in the light, as he is in the light, we have fellowship with one another, and the blood of Jesus his Son cleanses us from all sin.

8 If we say that we have no sin, we deceive ourselves, and the truth is not in us.

9 If we confess our sins, he is faithful and just to forgive us our sins, and to cleanse us from all unrighteousness.

10 If we say that we have not sinned, we make him a liar and his word is not in us.

CHAPTER 2

MY little children, these things I write to you, that you do not sin. And if any man sin, we have an advocate with the Father, Jesus Christ the righteous:

2 And he is the propitiation for our sins: and not for ours only, but also for the sins of the whole world.

3 ¶ And hereby we do know that we know him, if we keep his commandments.

4 He who says, I know him, and does not keep his commandments, is a liar, and the truth is not in him.

5 But whoso keeps his word, in him verily is the love of God perfected: hereby we know that we are in him.

6 He who says, he abides in him ought himself also so to walk, even as he walked.

7 ¶ My beloved, I do not write a new commandment to you, but an old commandment which you had from the beginning. The old commandment is the word which you have already heard.

8 Again, a new commandment I do write to you, which thing is true in Him and in you: because the darkness is past, and the true light now shines.

9 He who says he is in the light but hates his brother, is therefore in darkness even until now.

10 He who loves his brother abides in the light, and there is no cause for displeasure in him.

11 But he who hates his brother is in dark-

Cf.dif. vv. 1:1, 4, 6; 2:3, 6-8.

ness, and walks in darkness, and does not know where he is going, because that darkness has blinded his eyes.

12 I write to you, little children, because your sins are forgiven you for his name's sake.

13 I write to you, fathers, because you have known him who is from the beginning. I write to you, young men, because you have overcome the evil one. I write to you, little children, because you have known the Father.

14 I have written to you, fathers, because you have known him that is from the beginning. I have written to you, young men, because you are strong, and the word of God abides in you, and you have overcome the evil one.

15 Love not the world, neither the things that are in the world. If any love the world, the love of the Father is not in him.

16 For all that is in the world, the lust of the body, and the covetousness of the eyes, and the pride of material things; does not come from the Father, but is of the world.

17 And the world passes away, and the lust thereof: but he who does the will of God abides forever.

18 ¶ My children, it is the last time: and as you have heard that a false Christ shall come, even now there are many false Christs, and from this we know that it is the last time.

19 They went out from among us, but they were not of us; for if they had been of us, they would have continued with us; but they left us, that it might be known they did not belong to us.

20 But you have been anointed by the Holy One, and you are enabled to distinguish between men.

21 I have written to you not because you do not know the truth, but because you know it, and that no lie comes out of the truth.

22 Who is a liar but he who denies that Jesus is the Christ? He is a false christ, and whoever denies the Father, denies the Son also.

23 Whoever denies the Son, the same does not believe in the Father; but whoever acknowledges the Son, acknowledges the Father also.

24 Let that, therefore, abide in you which you have heard from the very beginning. For if that which you have heard from the beginning shall remain in you, you also shall continue in the Father and in the Son.

25 And this is the promise that he has promised us, even eternal life.

26 These things I have written to you concerning those who seduce you.

27 And you also, if the anointing which you have received from him abides among you, need no one to teach you: that same anointing which is of God, will teach you all things; it is a truth, and there is no lie in it; and even as I have taught you, abide in it.

28 And now, my children, abide in him; that, when he shall appear, we may not be ashamed before him, but have pride at his coming.

29 If you know that he is righteous, you know also that every one who does righteousness is of him.

CHAPTER 3

SEE how abundant the love of the Father is toward us, for he has called us sons and made us: therefore the world does not know us because it did not know him.

2 My beloved, now we are the sons of God, and as yet it has not been revealed what we shall be: but we know that when he shall appear, we shall be in his likeness; for we shall see him as he is.

3 ¶ Let every man who has this hope in him purify himself, even as he is pure.

4 Whoever commits sin commits evil: for

      Cf.dif. vv. 2:18, 20, 22-23, 27-29;   3:1, 4.

---

all sin is evil.

5 And you know that he was manifested to take away our sins; and in him is no sin.

6 Whoever abides in him does not sin: and whoever sins has not seen him, neither known him.

7 My children, let no man deceive you; he who does righteousness is righteous, just as Christ is righteous.

8 He who commits sin is of the devil; because the devil has been a sinner from the beginning. For this purpose the Son of God appeared, that he might destroy the works of the devil.

9 Whoever is born of God does not commit sin because God's seed is in him; and he cannot sin because he is born of God.

10 In this the children of God can be distinguished from the children of the devil: whoever does not practice righteousness and does not love his brother, does not belong to God.

11 ¶ For this is the commandment that you have heard from the beginning, that you must love one another,

12 Not as Cain, who belonged to the wicked one and slew his brother. And why did he kill him? Because his own works were evil, and those of his brother were righteous.

13 So be not surprised, my brethren, if the world hates you.

14 We know that we have passed from death to life, because we love our brethren. He who does not love his brother abides in death.

15 Whosoever hates his brother is a murderer: and you know that no murderer has eternal life abiding in him.

16 By this we know his love for us, because he laid down his life for us: and we ought to lay down our lives for our brethren.

17 Whoever has worldly goods, and sees his brother in need, and shuts his mercy from him, how can the love of God dwell in him?

18 My children, let us not love one another in word and in tongue, but in deed and in truth.

19 ¶ And by this we shall know that we are of the truth, and shall assure our hearts before he comes.

20 For if our hearts condemns us, how much more, then, will God who is greater than our hearts and knows all things.

21 My beloved, if our hearts do not condemn us, then we have confidence before God.

22 And whatever we ask, we receive from him, because we keep his commandments, and do those things that are pleasing to him.

23 And this is his commandment, That we should believe on the name of his Son Jesus Christ, and love one another, as he has commanded us.

24 Whosoever keeps his commandments will be guarded by him, and he will dwell in him. And by this we know that he abides in us, by the Spirit which he has given us.

CHAPTER 4

MY beloved, do not believe every prophecy, but examine the prophecies to find out if they are of God: because many false prophets have appeared in the world.

2 The Spirit of God is known by this: Every prophecy which declares that Jesus Christ is come in the flesh is from God.

3 And every prophecy which does not declare that Jesus Christ has come in the flesh is not from God: but it is the prophecy of the false Christ, of whose coming you have heard, and who is even now already in the world.

4 But you are of God, my children, and have overcome them: because he who is among you is greater than he who is in the world.

5 They are of the world; therefore they speak of the world, and the world hears them.

1 John 5

God is love.

6 But we are of God: he who knows God hears us; he who is not of God does not hear us. By this we know the spirit of truth and the spirit of error.

7 ¶ My beloved, let us love one another: for love is from God; and every one who loves is born of God, and knows God.

8 He who does not love, does not know God; for God is love.

9 By this was the love of God toward us made known, for God sent his only begotten Son into the world, that we might live through him.

10 Herein is love, not that we loved God, but that God loved us, and sent his Son to be the propitiation for our sins.

11 My beloved, if God so loved us, we ought also to love one another.

12 No man has seen God at any time. If we love one another, God abides in us, and his love is perfected in us;

13 Hereby we know that we abide in him, and he in us, because he has given us of his Spirit.

14 ¶ And we have seen and do testify that the Father sent his Son to be the Saviour of the world.

15 Whosoever shall confess that Jesus is the Son of God, God abides in him, and he in God.

16 And we have believed and have known the love that God has for us. God is love; and he who dwells in love, abides in God.

17 Herein is his love made perfect in us, so that we may have boldness in the day of judgment: because as he is, so are we in this world.

18 There is no fear in love; but perfect love casts out fear: because fear is tormenting. He who fears is not made perfect in love.

19 We love God because he first loved us.

20 ¶ If a man say, I love God, and yet hates his brother, he is a liar: for he who does not love his brother whom he has seen, how can he love God whom he has not seen?

21 And this commandment we have from him, That he who loves God loves his brother also.

CHAPTER 5

*W*HOSOEVER believes that Jesus is the Christ is born of God: and everyone who loves him who begat him, loves him also who is begotten of him.

2 And by this we know that we love the children of God, when we love God, and keep his commandments.

3 For this is the love of God, that we keep his commandments: And his commandments are not difficult.

4 For whoever is born of God triumphs over the world: and this is the victory which conquers the world, even our faith.

5 Who is he who triumphs over the world but he who believes that Jesus is the Son of God?

6 ¶ This is he who came by water and blood, even Jesus Christ; not by water only, but by water and blood. And the Spirit testifies that that very Spirit is the truth.

7 For there are three that bear record in heaven, the Father, the Word, and the Holy Ghost: and these three are one.

8 And there are three to bear witness, the Spirit, and the water, and the blood: and these three are one.

9 If we accept the testimony of men, how much greater is the testimony of God: for this is the testimony of God, which he has testified of his Son.

10 He who believes on the Son of God has this testimony in himself: he who does not believe God, has made him a liar; because he does not believe the record that God gave of his Son.

11 And this is the testimony, that God has

Cf.dif. vv. 4:18; 5:1, 8.

given to us eternal life, and this life is in his Son.

12 He who believes on the Son has life; he who does not believe on the Son of God does not have life.

13 ¶ These things I have written to you who believe on the name of the Son of God; that you may know that you have eternal life.

14 And this is the confidence that we have in him, that if we ask anything according to his will, he hears us:

15 For if we beseech him to hear us concerning the things that we ask of him, we are assured that we have already received from him those things that we desire.

16 ¶ If any man see his brother commit a sin which is not worthy of death, let him ask and life will be granted him, if he has not committed a sin worthy of death. There is a sin worthy of death: I do not say that he shall pray for it.

17 All unrighteousness is sin: but there is a sin which is not worthy of death.

18 ¶ We know that everyone who is born of God does not sin: for he who is born of God watches himself, and the evil one does not come near him.

19 And we know that we are of God, and the whole world lies in wickedness.

20 And we know that the Son of God has come, and has given us an understanding, that we may know Him who is true, and we are in him who is true, even in his Son Jesus Christ. This is the true God, and eternal life.

21 My children, keep yourselves from idols.

Here ends the epistle of John the Apostle.

✥ ܟܠܗ ܝܘܚܢܢ ܕܐܓܪܬܐ ܫܠܡܬ ✥

THE SECOND EPISTLE OF
JOHN

❖ ܐܓܪܬܐ ܕܬܪܬܝܢ ܕܝܘܚܢܢ ܫܠܝܚܐ ❖

*T*HE minister, to the mother church, and her children, those whom I love in the truth, and not I only, but also all those who have known the truth,

2 For the sake of the truth which dwells in us and is with us for ever,

3 Grace be with us, mercy, and peace, from God the Father, and from the LORD Jesus Christ, the Son of the Father, in truth and love.

4 ¶ I rejoiced greatly that I found some of your children living in the truth, as we have received a commandment from the Father.

5 And now I beseech you, O mother church, not as though I wrote a new commandment to you, but that which we had from the beginning, that we love one another.

6 And this is love, that we walk according to his commandments. This is the commandment, that as you have heard from the beginning, you should follow it.

7 For many deceivers have appeared in the world, who do not acknowledge that Jesus Christ has come in the flesh. Such a person is a deceiver and an antichrist.

8 Look to yourselves, that you lose not those things which you have accomplished, but that you receive a full reward.

9 Whosoever transgresses, and does not abide in the teaching of Christ, does not have God. He who abides in His doctrine, has both the Father and the Son.

10 If anyone comes to you, and does not bring this doctrine, do not welcome him to your house, neither bid him to eat:

11 For he who bids him to eat is partaker of his evil works.

12 ¶ I have many things to say to you, which I do not want to write with paper and ink: but I trust to come to you, and speak face to face, that our joy may be full.

13 The children of your elect sister Church greet you. Grace be with you. Amen.

Here ends the second epistle of John the Apostle.

❖ ܫܠܡܬ ܐܓܪܬܐ ܕܬܪܬܝܢ ܕܝܘܚܢܢ ܫܠܝܚܐ ❖

Cf.dif. vv. 1, 3, 7-8, 10-11, 13.

THE THIRD EPISTLE OF

JOHN

❖ ܪܘܚܢ ܕܝܠܗ ܕܝܘܚܢܢ ܐܓܪܬܐ ❖

*T*HE elder, to the well beloved Gaius, whom I love in the truth.

2 Our beloved, I pray above all things, that you may prosper and be in good health, even as your soul prospers.

3 For I rejoiced greatly, when the brethren came and testified concerning the truth that is in you, even as you live a true life.

4 I have no greater joy than to hear that my children follow the truth.

5 Our beloved, you do faithfully that which you do to the brethren, especially to those who are strangers;

6 Who have borne witness concerning your love before the whole church: for the good things which you have done for them by supplying their needs, as is pleasing to God,

7 Because they have gone forth for his name's sake, taking nothing from the Gentiles.

8 We, therefore, ought to welcome such, so that we may be fellow helpers to the truth.

9 ¶ I wrote to the church, that Di-ot're-phes, who loves to have the preeminence among them, would not receive us.

10 Therefore, if I come, I will mention the things which he did, gossiping against us with malicious words: and not content with this, he not only did not receive the brethren, but also forbade those who would like to receive them, and cast them out of the church.

11 Our beloved, do not follow that which is evil, but that which is good. He who does good is of God: but he who does evil has not seen God.

12 De-me'tri-us has good report of all men, and of the church, and of the truth itself: yea, we also testify for him; and we know that our testimony is true.

13 ¶ I had many things to write, but I do not want to write them to you with ink and pen:

14 But I trust I shall shortly see you, and we shall speak face to face.

15 Peace be to you. Our friends salute you. Salute the friends every one by his name.

Here ends the third epistle of John the Apostle.

❖ ܫܠܡ ܐܓܪܬܐ ܕܝܘܚܢܢ ܪܘܚܢ ܕܝܠܗ ❖

The Second and Third Epistles of John are not included in the text which is called Peshitta, but are included in other old texts.

Cf.dif. vv. 6, 9, 10, 13.

THE GENERAL EPISTLE OF

JUDE

❖ ܟܘܠܐ ܟܙܩܡܘܐ ܟܐܝܪܟ ❖

JUDE, the servant of Jesus Christ, and brother of James, to the Gentiles who have been called, and are beloved by God the Father, and are protected by Jesus Christ,

2 Mercy, and peace, with love, be multiplied unto you.

3 ¶ My beloved, I write to you with all diligence concerning our common salvation, and it is needful that I write and exhort you also to earnestly contend for the faith which was once delivered to the saints.

4 For certain men have falsely entered among you, and these were foreordained from the very beginning to this condemnation; they are ungodly men, turning the grace of God into lasciviousness, and denying the only LORD God, and our LORD Jesus Christ.

5 I will, therefore, remind you, though you once knew this, that God, having redeemed and saved the people out of the land of Egypt, afterward destroyed those who did not believe.

6 And the angels that did not keep their first estate but left their own habitation, he has reserved in everlasting chains under darkness unto the judgment of the great day.

7 Even as Sodom and Gomorrah and the neighbouring cities which in like manner gave themselves over to fornication, and followed after other carnal lusts, are condemned to judgment and placed under everlasting fire;

8 Likewise also, these filthy dreamers defile the flesh, despise authority, and blaspheme against the glory.

9 Yet Michael, the archangel, when contending with the devil about the body of Moses, did not dare to bring railing accusation against him, but said, The LORD rebuke thee.

10 But these men blaspheme against those things about which they do not know: and what they know naturally as dumb beasts, in those things they corrupt themselves.

11 Woe unto them! for they have gone in the way of Cain, and ran greedily after the error of Balaam for reward, and have perished in the rebellion of Korah.

12 These people are those who lead a wasteful, feasting life and are blemished; they do not shepherd themselves in reverence; they are clouds without rain, driven by winds; trees whose blossoms have withered, without fruit; having died a second time, pulled up by the roots;

13 Raging waves of the sea, foaming out their own shame; wandering stars, to whom is reserved the blackness of darkness for ever.

14 And Enoch also, the seventh from Adam, prophesied of these, saying, Behold, the LORD cometh with ten thousands of his saints,

15 To execute judgment upon all, and to punish all who are ungodly for all their un-

godly deeds which they have ungodly committed, and for all the harsh words which the ungodly sinners have spoken. *

16 These are the ones who murmur and complain, following after their own lusts, and their mouths speak idle flattering words, praising people for the sake of gain.

17 But you, my beloved, remember the words which were spoken before by the apostles of our LORD Jesus Christ;

18 How they told you there will be mockers until the end of time, and they will always follow their own ungodly lusts.

19 These are those who prefer to associate with selfish people because they do not have the Spirit in them.

20 But you, my beloved, build up yourselves anew in the holy faith through the Holy Spirit, by means of prayer.

21 Keep ourselves in the love of God, looking for the mercy of our LORD Jesus Christ and for the life which is ours forever.

22 And on some of them whoever they may be, heap coals of fire:

23 And when they repent, have mercy on them with compassion; despise even a garment which is spotted with the things of the flesh.

24 ¶ Now unto him who is able to keep you from falling, and to present you faultless before the presence of his glory with exceeding joy,

25 To the only God our Saviour, through Jesus Christ our LORD, be glory and majesty, dominion and power, both now and for ever, Amen.

Here ends the epistle of Jude the Apostle.

❖ ܪܘܠܐ ܟܪܝܘܥܘܪܕ ܪܕܝܠܪ ܫܘܠܐ ❖

The Epistle of Jude is not found in the text which is called Peshitta, but is written in the other ancient texts.

* Jude 14-15 - citation from the *Book of Enoch* (ch.2): "Behold, he comes with ten thousands of his saints, to execute judgment upon them, and destroy the wicked, and reprove all the carnel for everything which the sinful and ungodly have done, and committed against him." - translated by Richard Lawrence, *The Book of Enoch the Prophet*, Kegan Paul, Trench & Co., 1883 . For a more recent translation and commentary on Enoch, see vol.1 of *The Old Testament Pseudepigrapha: Apocalyptic Literature and Testaments*, Edited by J. Charlesworth, Doubleday, 1983.

Cf.dif. vv. 16, 19-23.

THE REVELATION

OF ST. JOHN THE DIVINE

✧ ܓܠܝܢܐ ܕܝܘܚܢܢ ✧

CHAPTER 1

*T*HE Revelation of Jesus Christ, which God gave to him, to show unto his servants those things which must soon come to pass, he sent and signified it by his angel to his servant John:

2 Who bore record of the word of God and of the testimony of Jesus Christ and of all things that he saw.

3 Blessed is he who reads and they who listen to the words of this prophecy, and keep those things which are written in it: for the time is at hand.

4 ¶ John to the seven churches which are in Asia: Grace be to you, and peace, from him who is, and who was, and who is to come; and from the seven spirits which are before his throne;

5 And from Jesus Christ, who is the faithful witness, and the first to arise from the dead, and the prince of the kings of the earth unto him who loved us and washed us from our sins in his own blood,

6 And has made us a spiritual Kingdom unto God and his Father; to him be glory and dominion for ever and ever. Amen.

7 ¶ Behold he comes with the clouds; and every eye shall see him, even the men who pierced him: and all the kindreds of the earth shall wail over him. Even so, Amen.

8 I am Alpha and Omega, * the beginning and the ending says the LORD God, who is, and who was, and who is to come, the Almighty.

9 ¶ I, John, your brother, and companion in suffering, and in the hope of Jesus Christ, was in the island which is called Patmos, because of the word of God, and because of the testimony of Jesus Christ.

10 The Spirit of prophecy came upon me on the LORD'S day, and I heard behind me a great voice, as of a trumpet, saying, I am Alpha and Omega, the first and the last: and,

11 What you see, write in a book, and send it to the seven churches; to Eph'e-sus, and to Smyrna, and to Per'ga-mos, and to Thy-a-ti'ra, and to Sardis, and to Philadelphia, and to La-od-i-ce'a.

12 And I turned to see the voice that spoke to me. And as I turned, I saw seven golden candlesticks;

13 And in the midst of the seven candlesticks one resembling the Son of man, wearing a long vestment and girded round his breast with a golden girdle.

14 His head and his hair were white like wool, as white as snow; and his eyes were as a flame of fire;

15 And his feet were like the fine brass of Lebanon, as though they burned in a furnace; and his voice was as the sound of many waters.

16 And he had in his right hand seven stars: and out of his mouth came a sharp two-edged sword: and his countenance was as the sun shining in its strength.

17 And when I saw him, I fell at his feet as dead. And he laid his right hand upon me, saying, Fear not; I am the first and the last:

18 I am he who lives, and was dead; and, behold, I am alive for evermore. Amen; and have the keys of death and of hell.

* Rev. 1:8- Eastern version says *Aleph and Tau.*

Cf.dif. vv. 1:6-8, 16.

19 Write, therefore, the things which you have seen, and the things which are, and the things which shall be hereafter;

20 The mystery of the seven stars which you saw in my right hand, and the seven golden candlesticks. The seven stars are the angels of the seven churches: and the seven candlesticks are the seven churches.

CHAPTER 2

TO the angel * of the church of Eph'e-sus write: These things says the Omnipotent; who holds the seven stars in his right hand, who walks in the midst of the seven golden candlesticks;

2 I know your works, and your labour, and your patience, and how you cannot endure those who are ungodly: you have tried those who say they are apostles, and are not, and you have found them liars:

3 And you have patience, and you have borne burdens for my name's sake, and have not wearied.

4 Nevertheless I have something against you, because you have left your first love.

5 Remember therefore from whence you have fallen and repent and do the first works; or else I will come to you very soon, and I will remove your candlestick from its place except you repent.

6 But this you have in your favour, you hate the works of the Nic-o-la'i-tanes, which I also hate.

7 He who has ears, let him hear what the Spirit says unto the churches: To him who overcomes, I will give to eat of the tree of life, which is in the midst of the paradise of my God.

8 ¶ And to the angel of the church in Smyrna write, These things says the first and the last, which was dead and is alive:

9 I know your works and your suffering and poverty, but you are rich, and I know the blasphemy of those who say they are Jews, and are not, but are of the synagogue of Satan.

10 Fear none of those things which you shall suffer: behold, the devil will cast some of you into prison, that you be tried; and you will be oppressed for ten days: be faithful even to death, and I will give you a crown of life.

11 He who has ears, let him hear what the Spirit says to the churches; He who overcomes shall not be hurt by the second death.

12 ¶ And to the angel of the church in Per'ga-mos write: These things says he who has the sharp two-edged sword;

13 I know your works and where you dwell even where Satan's seat is: And you uphold my name, and you did not deny my faith, even in those days when that witness of mine appeared, that faithful one of mine who was slain among you, where Satan dwells.

14 But I have a few things against you, because you have there those who hold the teaching of Balaam, who taught Balac to cast a stumblingblock before the children of Israel, to eat things sacrificed to idols, and to commit adultery.

15 And also you have those among you who hold to the teaching of the Nic-o-la'i-tanes.

16 Repent; or else I will come to you very soon, and will fight against them with the sword of my mouth.

17 He who has ears, let him hear what the Spirit says to the churches; To him who overcomes, I will give to eat of the hidden manna, and I will give him a white stone, and on the stone a new name written, which no man knows except he who receives it.

18 ¶ And unto the angel of the church in Thy-a-ti'ra write: These things says the Son of God, who has eyes like unto a flame of fire, and whose feet are like fine brass from Leba-non;

* Rev.2:1 - Angel in this case means the appointed head of the church.
Cf.dif. vv. 2:5, 11, 13, 15-18.

19 I know your works, and love and faith, and service, and also your patience; and your last works are to be more abundant than the first.

20 Notwithstanding I have a few things against you, because you allowed that woman of yours Jezebel, who calls herself a prophetess, to teach and to seduce my servants to commit fornication and to eat things sacrificed to idols.

21 And I gave her time to repent, but she did not repent from her fornication.

22 Behold I will cast her into a sick bed and those who commit adultery with her into great tribulation, unless they repent of their deeds.

23 And I will kill her children with death; and all the churches shall know that I am he who searches the reins and hearts: and I will give unto everyone of you according to your works.

24 But I say unto you, the rest of you in Thy-a-ti'ra, those of you who do not have this doctrine, and those who have not known, as they say, the depths of Satan, that I will not put upon you another burden.

25 But hold fast to that which you already have till I come.

26 And he who overcomes, and keeps my works unto the end, to him I will give authority over the nations:

27 And he shall shepherd them with a rod of iron; like the vessels of the potter, they shall be shattered: even as I was disciplined by my Father.

28 And I will give him the morning star.

29 He who has ears, let him hear what the Spirit says unto the churches.

CHAPTER 3

AND unto the angel of the church in Sardis write; These things says he who has the seven Spirits of God, and the seven stars; I know your works; you have a name that you are alive and yet you are dead.

2 Awake, and hold fast to the things which remain but are ready to die; for I have not found your works perfect before my God.

3 Remember, therefore, just as you have received and heard, so hold fast and repent. And if, therefore, you do not awake, I will come against you as a thief, and you shall not know at what hour I will come upon you.

4 But you have a few members at Sardis who have not defiled their names; and they shall walk with me in white for they are worthy.

5 He who overcomes, the same shall be clothed in white robes; and I will not blot his name out of the book of life, but I will confess his name before my Father, and before his angels.

6 He who has ears, let him hear what the Spirit says unto the churches.

7 ¶ And to the angel of the church in Philadelphia write; These things says he who is the holy one, he who is true, he who has the key of David, he who opens and no man shuts; and shuts, and no man opens;

8 I know your works: and behold, I have set before you an open door, which no man can lock, for you have but little strength and yet you have obeyed my word, and have not denied my name.

9 Behold I turn over those of the synagogue of Satan, who say that they are Jews, and are not, but do lie; behold, I will make them to come and worship before your feet, and to know that I have loved you.

10 Because you have kept the word of my patience, I also will keep you from the hour of temptation, which shall come upon all the world, to try those who dwell upon earth.

11 Behold I come quickly. Hold that fast which you have, so that no man take your crown.

12 He who overcomes I will make a pillar in the temple of my God, and he shall not go out again: and I will write upon him the name of my God and the name of the new Jerusalem which comes down out of heaven from my God: and I will write upon him my new name.

13 He who has ears, let him hear what the Spirit says to the churches.

14 ¶ And unto the angel of the church in La-od-i-ce'a write; These things says the Amen, the faithful, and true witness, the beginning of the creation of God;

15 I know your works, that you are neither cold nor hot; it is better to be either cold or hot.

16 So then because you are lukewarm, and neither cold nor hot, I will spue you out of my mouth.

17 Because you say, I am rich and my wealth has increased, and I need nothing; and you do not know that you are miserable, and a wanderer, and poor, and blind, and naked:

18 I advise you to buy of me gold refined in the fire, that you may become rich; and white raiment, that you may be clothed, so that the shame of your nakedness does not appear; and anoint your eyes with salve that you may see.

19 I rebuke and chastise all those whom I love: be zealous, therefore, and repent.

20 Behold, I stand at the door, and knock: if any man hear my voice and open the door, I will come in to him and will sup with him, and he with me.

21 To him who overcomes I will grant to sit with me on my throne, even as I also overcame, and have sat down with my Father on his throne.

22 He who has ears, let him hear what the Spirit says to the churches.

CHAPTER 4

AFTER these things I looked and behold a door was open in heaven: and the first voice which I heard was like a trumpet talking with me; which said, Come up here, and I will show you things which must come to pass.

2 And immediately I was in the spirit: and behold, a throne was set in heaven, and one sat on the throne.

3 And he who sat resembled a stone of jasper and sardonyx and round about the throne was a rainbow resembling emeralds.

4 Round about the throne were four and twenty seats; and upon the seats I saw four and twenty elders sitting, clothed in white robes; and they had on their heads crowns of gold.

5 And out of the throne proceeded lightnings and thunderings and noises: and there were seven lamps of fire burning before the throne, which are the seven Spirits of God.

6 And before the throne was a sea of glass resembling crystal: and in the midst of the throne, and round about it, and in front of the throne, were four beasts, full of eyes before and behind.

7 And the first beast was like a lion, and the second beast was like a calf, and the third beast had a face of a man, and the fourth beast was like a flying eagle.

8 And the four beasts had each of them six wings about it; and they were full of eyes within; and they had no rest day and night saying, Holy, holy, holy, the LORD God Almighty, who was and is, and is to come.

9 And when those wild beasts give glory and honor and thanks to him who sat on the throne, who lives for ever and ever,

10 The four and twenty elders fall down before him who sat on the throne, and worship him who lives for ever and ever, and cast their crowns before the throne, saying,

11 You are worthy, O our Holy LORD and God, to receive glory and honor and power, for you have created all things, and by you, they are, and by your will, they are and were created.

CHAPTER 5

AND I saw on the right hand of him who sat on the throne a book, written within and on the back and sealed with seven seals.

2 Then I saw a mighty angel proclaiming with a loud voice, Who is worthy to open the book, and to loose the seals thereof?

3 And no man in heaven above, nor in earth, neither under the earth, was able to open the book, neither to look on it.

4 And I wept exceedingly, because no man was found worthy to open the book, neither to look on it.

5 And one of the elders said unto me, Weep not; behold the Lion of the tribe of Juda, the Scion of David, has prevailed and he will open the book, and the seven seals thereof.

6 And I beheld, and lo, in the midst of the elders, stood a Lamb as it had been slain, having seven horns and seven eyes, which are the seven Spirits of God sent forth into all the earth.

7 And he came and took the book from the right hand of him who sat upon the throne.

8 And as he took the book, the four wild beasts and the four and twenty elders fell down before the Lamb, and everyone of them had a harp and a cup of gold full of incense, and these were the prayers of the saints.

9 And they sang new praise saying. You are worthy to take the book, and to open the seals thereof; for you were slain, and have redeemed us to God by your blood, out of every tribe, and tongue, and people, and nation;

10 And have made them to our God kings and priests: and they shall reign on the earth.

11 And I saw, and I heard as it were the voice of many angels round about the throne, and the beasts, and the elders: and their number was ten thousand times ten thousand, and thousands of thousands;

12 Saying with a loud voice, Worthy is the Lamb that was slain to receive power, and riches, and wisdom, and might, and honor, and glory, and blessing.

13 And every creature which is in heaven, and on the earth, and under the earth, and all that are in the sea, and all that are in them, I heard saying, To him who sits on the throne and to the Lamb be blessing, and honor, and glory, and dominion for ever and ever.

14 And the four beasts said, Amen. And the four and twenty elders fell down and worshipped him who lives for ever and ever.

CHAPTER 6

I SAW when the Lamb opened one of the seven seals, and I heard one of the four beasts saying in a voice as of thunder, Come and see.

2 And I saw, and beheld a white horse, and he who sat on him had a bow, and a crown was given to him: and he went forth conquering, and to conquer.

3 ¶ And when he opened the second seal, I heard the second beast say, Come and see.

4 And there went out another horse, and it was red, and to him who sat on it was given power to take away peace from the earth, that people should kill one another: and there was given to him a great sword.

5 ¶ And when he had opened the third seal, I heard the third beast say, Come and see. And behold, I saw a black horse; and he who sat on him had a pair of balances in his hand.

6 And I heard a voice in the midst of the four beasts say, A measure of wheat for a penny, and three measures of barley for a

Cf.dif. vv. 4:11;   5:6, 9-11; 6:1-2, 4, 6.

penny; and see that you do not damage the oil and the wine.

7 ¶ And when he had opened the fourth seal, I heard the fourth beast saying, Come and see.

8 And I looked, and beheld a pale horse; and the name of him who sat on him was Death, and Hell followed after him. And power was given him over the fourth part of the earth, to kill with sword, and with famine, and with death, and with the wild beasts of the earth.

9 ¶ And when he had opened the fifth seal, I saw under the altar the souls of those who had been slain for the sake of the word of God and for the testimony of the Lamb which they had:

10 And they cried with a loud voice saying, How long, O LORD, holy and true, do you not judge and avenge our blood on those who dwell on the earth?

11 And a white robe was given to every one of them; and it was said to them, that they should rest yet for a little while, until the time should be fulfilled when their fellowservants and their brethren should be killed also as they had been.

12 ¶ And I beheld when he had opened the sixth seal, and behold, there was a great earthquake; and the sun became black as sackcloth of hair, and the moon became as blood;

13 And the stars of heaven fell to the earth, even as a fig tree casts her green figs when she is shaken by a mighty wind.

14 And the heavens separated, as a scroll when it is rolled separately; and every mountain and island shifted from its resting place.

15 And the kings of the earth, and the great men, and the captains of thousands, and the rich, and the mighty men, and every bondman, and every freeman, hid themselves in caves, and in clefts of the mountain;

16 And said to the mountains and rocks: Fall on us, and hide us from the face of him who sits on the throne, and from the wrath of the Lamb:

17 For the great day of his wrath is come, and who shall be able to stand?

CHAPTER 7

AND after these things, I saw four angels standing on the four corners of the earth, holding the four winds of the earth, that the wind should not blow on the earth, nor on the sea, nor on any tree.

2 And I saw another angel, and he ascended from the direction of the rising sun, having the seal of the Living God: and he cried with a loud voice to the four angels to whom it was given to hurt the earth and the sea, saying,

3 Do not hurt the earth, neither the sea, nor the trees, till we have sealed the servants of our God upon their brows.

4 And I heard the number of those who were sealed: and it was a hundred and forty and four thousand, of all the tribes of the children of Israel.

5 Of the tribe of Juda were sealed twelve thousand; of the tribe of Reuben, twelve thousand; of the tribe of Gad, twelve thousand;

6 Of the tribe of A'ser, twelve thousand; of the tribe of Nep'tha-lim, twelve thousand; of the tribe of Ma-nas'ses, twelve thousand;

7 Of the tribe of Simeon, twelve thousand; of the tribe of Levi, twelve thousand; of the tribe of Is'sa-char, twelve thousand;

8 Of the tribe of Zab'u-lon, twelve thousand; of the tribe of Joseph, twelve thousand; of the tribe of Benjamin, twelve thousand.

9 ¶ After these things, I beheld, and lo, a great multitude, which no man could number, of every nation and people, and kindred and tongue, stood before the throne, and in the presence of the Lamb, clothed with white

robes and with palms in their hands;

10 And cried with a loud voice, saying, Salvation to our God, who sits upon the throne, and to the Lamb.

11 And all the angels stood round about the throne, and about the elders and the four beasts, and fell before his throne on their faces, and worshipped God.

12 Saying, Amen: Blessing, and glory, and wisdom, and thanksgiving, and honor, and power and might to our God for ever and ever. Amen.

13 And one of the elders answered and said to me, Who are these who are arrayed in white robes? And from whence did they come?

14 And I said to him, My LORD, you know. And he said to me, These are those who came out of great tribulation, and have washed their robes, and made them white in the blood of the Lamb.

15 Therefore they are before the throne of God, and serve him day and night in his temple; and he who sits on the throne shall shelter them.

16 They shall hunger no more; neither thirst anymore; neither shall they be stricken by the sun, nor by the heat.

17 For the Lamb who is in the midst of the throne shall shepherd them, and shall lead them to fountains of living water. And God shall wipe away all tears from their eyes.

CHAPTER 8

AND when he opened the seventh seal, there was silence in heaven for about the space of half an hour.

2 ¶ Then I saw the seven angels, who stood before God; and seven trumpets were given to them.

3 And another angel came and stood at the altar, and he had a golden censer; and abundant incense was given to him, that he might offer it with the prayers of all saints upon the golden altar which was before the throne.

4 And the smoke of the incense which came with the prayers of the saints, ascended up before God out of the angel's hand.

5 And the angel took the censer, and filled it with fire of the altar, and cast it upon the earth: and there were voices and thunderings and lightnings, and an earthquake.

6 And the seven angels, who had the seven trumpets prepared themselves to sound.

7 ¶ The first angel sounded, and there followed hail and fire mingled with water, and they were poured upon the earth: and a third part of the earth was burnt up and a third part of the trees was burnt up, and all green grass was burnt up.

8 ¶ Then the second angel sounded, and as it were a great mountain aflame with fire was cast into the sea: and the third part of the sea became blood;

9 And the third part of the creatures which were in the sea, and had life, died; and the third part of the ships were destroyed.

10 ¶ And the third angel sounded, and there fell a star from heaven, burning as though it were a lamp, and it fell upon the third part of the rivers, and upon the fountains of waters;

11 And the name of the star is called Wormwood: and the third part of the waters became wormwood; and many men died of the waters, because they were made bitter.

12 ¶ And the fourth angel sounded, and the third part of the sun was eclipsed, and the third part of the moon, and the third part of the stars; so that the third part of them was darkened, and the day was darkened for a third part of it, and the night likewise.

13 And I beheld, and heard an eagle having a tail red as it were blood, flying through the midst of heaven, saying with a loud voice, Woe, woe, woe to those who dwell on the earth, by reason of the other sounds of the

trumpets of the three angels which are yet to sound!

CHAPTER 9

AND the fifth angel sounded, and I saw a star fall from heaven upon the earth: and to him was given the key of the bottomless pit.

2 And he opened the bottomless pit; and there arose a smoke out of the pit, as smoke belching from a great furnace; and the sun and the air were darkened by reason of the smoke of the pit.

3 And there came out of the smoke locusts upon the earth: and to them was given power, as the scorpions of the earth have power.

4 And it was commanded them that they should not hurt the grass of the earth, neither any green thing, neither any tree: but only those men who do not have the seal of God on their brows.

5 And they were commanded that they should not kill them, but that they should be tormented five months: and their torment was as the torment of a scorpion when it strikes a man.

6 So in those days men shall seek death, and shall not find it; and shall desire to die, and death shall flee from them.

7 And the shapes of the locusts were like unto horses prepared for battle; and on their heads were, as it were, crowns like gold, and their faces were as faces of men.

8 And they had hair as the hair of women, and their teeth were as the teeth of lions.

9 And they had breastplates, as though they were breastplates of iron; and the sound of their wings was as the sound of chariots of many horses running to battle.

10 And they had tails like unto scorpions, and there were stings in their tails: and they had power to hurt men five months.

11 And they had a king over them, who was the angel of the bottomless pit, whose name in Hebrew is, A-bad'don, but in Greek his name is A-poll'yon.

12 The first woe is passed; and behold, two more woes follow after.

13 ¶ And the sixth angel sounded, and I heard a voice from the horns of the golden altar which is before God,

14 Saying to the sixth angel which had the trumpet, Loose the four angels which are bound by the great river Euphrates.

15 And the four angels were loosed, those which were prepared for that hour, and for that day, and for that month, and for that year, so that they might slay the third part of men.

16 And the number of the army of the horsemen was two hundred thousand thousand: and I heard the number of them.

17 And thus I saw the horses in the vision, and those who sat on them, and they had breastplates of fire, and of jacinth, and of brimstone: and the heads of the horses were as the heads of lions, and out of their mouths issued fire and smoke and brimstone.

18 And by these three plagues, was the third part of men slain, by the fire, and by the smoke, and by the brimstone, which issued out of their mouths.

19 For the power of the horses was in their mouths, and in their tails: for their tails were like unto serpents and had heads, and with them they do harm.

20 And the rest of the men who were not killed by these plagues, neither repented of the works of their hands, that is to say, the worship of devils and idols of gold and silver and brass and stone and of wood, which can neither see nor hear;

21 Nor repented of their murders, nor of their witchcraft, nor of their fornication, nor of their thefts.

Cf.dif. vv. 9:1, 15-16, 19.

CHAPTER 10

*A*ND I saw another mighty angel coming down from heaven, clothed with a cloud: and the rainbow of the cloud was upon his head, and his face was as though it were the sun, and his legs as pillars of fire:

2 And he had in his hand a little book open: and he set his right foot upon the sea, and his left foot on the land,

3 And cried with a loud voice as when a lion roars, and when he had cried, seven thunders sounded their voices.

4 And when the seven thunders had spoken, I was about to write: but I heard a voice from heaven saying, Seal up those things which the seven thunders uttered, and do not write them.

5 And the angel which I saw standing upon the sea and on the land raised his right hand to heaven, and

6 Swore by him who lives for ever and ever, who created heaven and the things which are therein, and the earth and the things which are therein, and the sea and the things which are therein, that there should be no more reckoning of time:

7 But in the days of the voice of the seventh angel, when he shall begin to sound, the mystery of God will be fulfilled, as he has proclaimed to his servants, the prophets.

8 ¶ And the same voice which I had heard from heaven, spoke to me again, saying, Go and take the little book which is open in the hand of the angel which stands on the sea and on the land.

9 And I went to the angel, and as I was about to say to him, Give me the little book, he said to me, Take it and eat it; and it shall make your belly bitter, but it shall be sweet as honey in your mouth.

10 So I took the little book out of the hand of the angel, and ate it; and it was sweet as honey in my mouth: but as soon as I had eaten it, my belly was bitter.

11 Then he said unto me, You must prophesy again about many peoples and nations and the heads of nations and kings.

CHAPTER 11

*A*ND there was given to me a reed like unto a rod: and the angel stood, saying, Arise and anoint the temple of God, and the altar, and those who worship therein.

2 But leave out the outer court of the temple, and do not anoint it; for it has been given to the Gentiles; and they shall tread the holy city under foot for forty and two months.

3 Then I will give power to my two witnesses, and they shall prophesy a thousand and two hundred and three score days, clothed in sackcloth.

4 These are the two olive trees, and the two candlesticks, standing before the LORD of the earth.

5 And if any man desires to harm them, fire will come out of their mouths and will consume their enemies: and if any man desires to harm them, he must in this manner be killed.

6 These have power to control the sky, so that it will not rain in those days: and have power over waters to turn them into blood, and to smite the earth with all plagues, as often as they will.

7 And when they have finished their testimony, the wild beast which ascends out of the bottomless pit, shall make war against them and shall overcome them.

8 And their dead bodies shall be upon the street of the great city, which spiritually is called Sodom and Egypt, where also their LORD was crucified.

9 And their dead bodies will be seen by the peoples and kindred and nations and tongues for three days and a half, and it will not be permitted to bury their dead bodies in graves.

Cf.dif. vv. 10:1-3, 5-6, 11;   11:3, 6, 8-9.

10 And those who dwell upon the earth shall rejoice over them, and make merry, and shall send gifts one to another; because these two prophets tormented those who dwelt on the earth.

11 And after three days and a half, the spirit of life from God entered into them, and they stood upon their feet; and great fear fell on those who saw them.

12 And they heard a great voice from heaven saying to them, Come up here. And they went up to heaven in a cloud; and their enemies saw them.

13 And at the same hour there was a great earthquake, and the tenth part of the city fell, and the number of men killed in the earthquake was seven thousand: and the survivors were frightened, and they gave glory to God.

14 The second woe is passed; and behold, the third woe comes quickly.

15 And the seventh angel sounded, and there were great sounds of thunders, saying, The kingdoms of this world have become the kingdom of our LORD, and of his Christ; and he shall reign for ever and ever.

16 And the four and twenty elders, who sat before the throne of God on their seats, fell upon their faces, and worshipped God.

17 Saying, We give thanks to you, O LORD God Almighty, who is, and was, because you have taken to yourself your great power and have reigned.

18 And the nations were angry, and your wrath has come, and the time of the dead, that they should be judged, and to reward your servants, the prophets, and the saints, and those who fear your name, small and great; and to destroy those who corrupt the earth.

19 ¶ And the temple of God was opened in heaven, and there was seen in his temple the ark of his covenant; and there were lightnings, and thunderings, and voices, and an earthquake, and a great hailstorm.

CHAPTER 12

AND a great sign was seen in heaven; a woman clothed with the sun, with the moon under her feet, and upon her head a crown of twelve stars:

2 And she being with child cried, travailing in birth, and pained to be delivered.

3 ¶ And there appeared another sign in heaven; and behold, there was a great dragon of fire, having seven heads and ten horns, and seven crowns upon his heads.

4 And his tail cut off a third of the stars of heaven and cast them to the earth; and the dragon stood before the woman who was ready to be delivered, so as to devour her child as soon as it was born.

5 And she brought forth a male child, who was to shepherd all the nations with a rod of iron: and her child was caught up to God, and to his throne.

6 And the woman fled into the wilderness, where she had a place prepared by God, that they should feed her there a thousand and two hundred and three score days.

7 And there was war in heaven: Michael and his angels fought against the dragon; and the dragon and his angels fought,

8 But did not prevail; neither was their place found any longer in heaven.

9 Thus the great dragon was cast out, that old serpent called the Devil and Satan, who deceives the whole world: he was cast out on the earth, and his angels were cast out with him.

10 And I heard a loud voice in heaven saying, Now the deliverance and the power and the kingdom of our God, and the power of his Christ, has been accomplished: for the accuser of our brethren, who accused them before God day and night, is cast down.

11 And they have conquered him by the blood of the Lamb, and by the word of their testimony; and they did not spare themselves even unto death.

Cf.dif. vv. 12:2, 5-8, 10-11.

12 Therefore rejoice, O ye heavens and you who dwell in them. Woe to the inhabitants of the earth, and of the sea! for the Devil has come down to you; and his wrath is great, because he knows that his time is short.

13 ¶ And when the dragon saw that he was cast down to the earth, he pursued the woman who had given birth to a son.

14 And to the woman were given two wings of a great eagle, that she might fly from the presence of the serpent to the wilderness, into her place, where she would be nourished for years, and months, and days.

15 Then the serpent sent a flood of water out of his mouth after the woman, so that he might cause her to be swept away by the flood.

16 But the earth helped the woman, and the earth opened its mouth, and swallowed up the water which the dragon had gushed out of his mouth.

17 And the dragon was enraged at the woman, and he went to make war with the remnant of her seed, who keep the commandments of God, and have the testimony of Jesus.

CHAPTER 13

AND as I stood on the sand of the sea, I saw a wild beast rise up out of the sea, having ten horns and seven heads, and upon his horns ten crowns, and upon his heads blasphemous words.

2 And the wild beast which I saw was like to a leopard, and his feet were as the feet of a bear, and his mouth as the mouth of a lion: and the dragon gave him his power, and his throne, and great authority.

3 And one of his heads was as though mortally wounded; but his deadly wound was healed: and all the world wondered about the wild beast.

4 And they worshipped the dragon because he had given power to the beast : who can prevail against him to fight him?

5 And there was given to him a mouth that he might utter great things and blasphemies; and power was given to him to make war for forty and two months.

6 And he opened his mouth in blasphemy against God, to blaspheme his name and his dwelling place, and those who dwell in heaven.

7 And power was given to him over every tribe and kindred and tongue, and nation, and it was given to him to make war with the saints, and to overcome them.

8 And all who dwell upon the earth shall worship him, even those whose names are not written in the book of life of the Lamb slain from the foundation of the world.

9 If any man has ears, let him hear.

10 He who leads into captivity, shall go into captivity; he who kills with the sword, must be killed with the sword. Here is the patience and the faith of the saints.

11 ¶ And I beheld another wild beast coming up out of the earth; and he had two horns like a lamb, and he spoke as a dragon.

12 And all the power of the first wild beast before him was exercised by him, and he caused the earth and those who dwell therein to worship the first beast, whose deadly wound was healed.

13 And he wrought great wonders, to such an extent that he could even make fire come down from heaven on the earth in the sight of men,

14 Beguiling those who dwell on the earth to make an image to the wild beast who was wounded by the sword and yet lived.

15 And he had power to give life to the image of the wild beast, and to cause all those who would not worship the image of the wild beast to be killed.

Cf.dif. vv. 12:13-14;   13:1, 5-7, 9-11, 14-15.

16 And he compelled all, both small and great, rich and poor, freemen and slaves to receive a mark on their right hands or on their brows:

17 So that no man might buy or sell, except he who had the mark of the name of the beast, or the code number of his name.

18 Here is wisdom. Let him who has understanding decipher the code number of the beast: for it is the code number of the name of a man; and his number is six hundred sixty-six (Nero Caesar).

CHAPTER 14

AND I looked, and, lo, the Lamb stood on mount Sion, and with him a hundred forty and four thousand in number, having the name of his Father written on their brows.

2 Then I heard a voice from heaven, as the sound of many waters, and as the sound of a great thunder: and the voice I heard was as the music of many harpists playing on their harps:

3 And they sang a new song before the throne, and before the four beasts and the elders: and no man was able to learn that song, except the hundred forty and four thousand who were redeemed from the earth.

4 These are those who were not defiled with women for they are virgins. These are those who follow the Lamb wheresoever he goes. These were redeemed by Jesus, from among men, to be the first fruits to God and to the Lamb.

5 And in their mouth was found no deceit: for they are without fault.

6 ¶ And I saw another angel fly in the midst of heaven, having the everlasting gospel, to preach to those who dwell on the earth, and to every nation, and kindred, and tongue, and people,

7 Saying, with a loud voice, Serve God and give glory to him; for the hour of his judgment has come: and worship him who made heaven and earth, and the sea, and the fountains of waters.

8 And another angel, a second followed him, saying, Babylon has fallen, that great city, which made all nations drink of the wine of the passion of her whoredom.

9 Then another angel, a third, followed them, saying with a loud voice, If any man worship the beast and his image, and receive his mark on his brow, or on his hand,

10 He also shall drink of the wine of the wrath of God, which is mixed with bitterness in the cup of his anger; and he shall be tormented with fire and brimstone in the presence of the holy angels and before the throne:

11 And the smoke of their torment will rise for ever and ever: and those who worship the beast and his image will have no rest day or night.

12 Here is the patience of the saints: here are they who keep the commandments of God and the faith of Jesus.

13 And I heard a voice from heaven saying, Write, Blessed are the dead who die in the LORD from henceforth: Yes, says the Spirit, that they may rest from their labours, for their works will follow them.

14 And I looked, and lo, I saw a white cloud, and upon the cloud sat one resembling the Son of man, having on his head a crown of gold, and in his hand a sharp sickle.

15 ¶ And another angel came out of the temple, and after he cried with a loud voice to him who sat on the cloud,

16 He thrust his sickle upon the earth; and the earth was harvested.

17 ¶ And another angel came out of the temple which is in heaven; and he also had a sharp sickle.

Cf.dif. vv. 14:2-10, 13, 16.

18 Then out from the altar came another angel, who had power over fire; and cried with a loud voice to him who had the sharp sickle, saying, Thrust in your sharp sickle and gather the clusters of the vineyards of the earth, for her grapes are fully ripe.

19 And the angel thrust his sickle into the earth, and gathered the vineyards of the earth, and cast the grapes into the winepress of the wrath of the great God.

20 And the winepress was trodden until the juice which came out reached even to the horse bridles, and the circumference of the winepress was a thousand and six hundred furlongs.

CHAPTER 15

*A*ND I saw another sign in heaven, great and marvelous, seven angels having the seven last plagues; for in them is fulfilled the wrath of God.

2 And I saw as it were a sea of glass mingled with fire: and those who were victorious over the beast, and over his image, and over the number of his name, were standing on the sea of glass, and had the harps of God.

3 And they were singing the song of Moses the servant of God, and the song of the Lamb, saying, Great and marvelous are your works, LORD God Almighty; just and true are your ways, O King of ages.

4 Who shall not fear you, O LORD, and glorify your name? For you only are holy: All nations shall come and worship before you; for your righteousness has been revealed.

5 And after these things, I looked, and behold the temple of the tabernacle of the testimony in heaven was opened:

6 And the seven angels, having the seven plagues, came out of the temple, clothed in pure and fine linen, and having their breast girded with golden girdles.

7 And one of the four beasts gave to the seven angels seven golden vials, full of the wrath of God who lives for ever and ever.

8 And the temple was filled with smoke from the glory of God and from his power; and no man was able to enter into the temple, until the seven plagues of the seven angels were fulfilled.

CHAPTER 16

*A*ND I heard a great voice saying the seven angels, Go your ways, and pour out the seven vials of the wrath of God upon the earth.

2 And the first went and poured out his vial upon the earth; and there came a severe and malignant sore upon the men who had the mark of the beast, and upon those who worshipped his image.

3 ¶ Then the second angel poured out his vial upon the sea; and it became as the blood of a dead man, and every living soul died in the sea.

4 ¶ And the third angel poured out his vial upon the rivers and fountains of waters; and they became blood.

5 Then I heard the angel who has charge over waters say, You are righteous, O Holy One, who is and was, because you have condemned them.

6 For they have shed the blood of saints and prophets, and you have given them blood to drink; for they are worthy.

7 And I heard another out of the altar say, Yes, O LORD God Almighty, true and righteous are your judgments.

8 ¶ And the fourth angel poured out his vial upon the sun; and power was given to him to scorch men with fire.

9 And men were scorched by intense heat, and they blasphemed the name of God, who has power over these plagues: and they did not repent to give him glory.

10 And the fifth angel poured out his vial on the throne of the wild beast; and his kingdom was darkened; and they gnawed their tongues from pain,

11 And blasphemed the God of heaven because of their wounds and sores; and did not repent of their deeds.

12 ¶ Then the sixth angel poured out his vial upon the great river Eu-phra'tes; and its waters dried up, that the way of the king of the East might be prepared.

13 And I saw three unclean spirits like frogs coming out of the mouth of the dragon, and out of the mouth of the wild beast, and out of the mouth of the false prophet.

14 For they are the spirits of devils, who work miracles which go forth to the kings of the whole world, to gather them to the battle of that great day of God Almighty.

15 And behold, I come as a thief. Blessed is he who watches and keeps his garments, lest he must walk naked, and they see his shame.

16 And he gathered them together in a place which in the Hebrew tongue is called Ar-ma-ged'don.

17 ¶ Then the seventh angel poured out his vial into the air; and there came a great voice out of the temple from the throne, saying, It is done.

18 And there were voices, and thunders, and lightnings; and there was a great earthquake, the like of which had never happened since man was upon the earth, so mighty an earthquake, and so great.

19 And the great city was divided into three parts, and the cities of the nations fell: and great Bab-y'lon came in remembrance before God, to give to her the cup of the wine of the fierceness of his wrath.

20 And every island fled away, and the mountains could not be found.

21 And great hail, about the size of a talent, fell out of heaven upon men: and men blasphemed God because of the plague of the hail; for the destructive force of the hail was exceedingly great.

CHAPTER 17

*T*HEN came one of the seven angels which had the seven vials and talked with me, saying, Come, I will show you the condemnation of the great harlot who sits upon many waters:

2 With whom the kings of the earth have committed adultery, and the inhabitants of the earth have been made drunk with the wine of her adultery.

3 So he carried me away in the spirit into the wilderness: and I saw a woman sitting on a scarlet wild beast inscribed with many words of blasphemy and having seven heads and ten horns.

4 And the woman was arrayed in purple and scarlet, and adorned with gold and precious stones and pearls; and she had a golden cup in her hand full of abominations and filthiness of her adultery on earth.

5 And upon her forehead was a name written, that not all could understand, BABYLON THE GREAT, THE MOTHER OF HARLOTS AND ABOMINATIONS OF THE EARTH.

6 And I saw that the woman was drunk with the blood of the saints, and with the blood of the martyrs of Jesus: and when I saw her, I wondered with great amazement.

7 And the angel said to me, Why do you wonder? I will tell you the mystery of the woman, and of the wild beast that carries her, which has the seven heads and the ten horns.

8 The wild beast that you saw was, and is not, and is ready to come up from the bottomless pit and go to be destroyed: and those who dwell on earth whose names were not

Cf.dif. vv. 16:10-11, 14-15, 21;   17:4-6, 8.

written in the book of life from the foundation of the world, shall wonder when they behold the beast that was, and is not, and now whose end has come.

9 Here is understanding for him who has wisdom. The seven heads are seven mountains, on which the woman sits.

10 And there are seven kings of whom five have fallen, and one is, and the other has not yet come; and when he comes he shall continue only for a short time.

11 And the wild beast that was, and no longer is, even he is the eighth, and is one of the seven destined to be destroyed.

12 And the ten horns which you saw are ten kings who have received no kingdom as yet; but receive authority as kings for one hour with the beast.

13 These are in one accord, and they shall give their strength and authority to the beast.

14 They will make war with the Lamb, and the Lamb shall conquer them: for he is LORD of lords, and King of kings; and those who are with him are called, and chosen, and faithful.

15 Then he said to me, The waters which you saw, where the harlot sits, are peoples, and multitudes, and nations, and tongues.

16 And the ten horns, and the wild beast which you saw shall hate the harlot, and shall make her desolate and naked, and shall eat her flesh, and burn her with fire.

17 For God has put into their hearts to do his will, and to be of one accord, and to give their Kingdom to the wild beast, until the words of God shall be fulfilled.

18 And the woman whom you saw is that great city, which has dominion over the kings of the earth.

CHAPTER 18

AFTER these things, I saw another angel come down from heaven, having great power; and the earth was lightened by his glory.

2 And he cried with a mighty voice, saying, Babylon the great is fallen, and has become a habitation of those possessed with devils, and the shelter of every foul spirit and the shelter of every unclean and detestable bird and the shelter of every unclean and loathsome wild beast.

3 Because all nations have drunk of the wine of her wrath, and the kings of the earth have committed adultery with her, and the merchants of the earth have become rich through the power of her trade.

4 ¶ And I heard another voice from heaven, saying, Come out of her, O my people, so that you may not become partakers of her sins, and are not smitten by her plagues.

5 For her sins have reached up to heaven, and God has remembered her iniquities.

6 Reward her even as she has rewarded you, and return unto her a double portion according to her works: in the cup which she has mixed, mix for her double.

7 For as much as she has glorified herself and lived deliciously, give her so much torment and sorrow: for she says in her heart, I sit a queen, and am no widow and shall see no sorrow.

8 Therefore, her plagues shall come in one day, death, and mourning, and famine; and she shall be burned with fire: for mighty is the LORD God who judges her.

9 And the kings of the earth who committed adultery and lived deliciously with her, shall weep and mourn and wail over her, when they see the smoke of her burning,

10 Standing afar off for the fear of her torment, saying, Woe, woe, that great city Babylon, that mighty city! for in one hour you have been condemned.

Cf.dif. vv. 17:9-11, 13-14, 16-17;   18:2, 4, 6, 8.

11 And the merchants of the earth shall weep and mourn over her; for no man buys their merchandise any more:

12 Never again will there be cargoes of gold, and silver, and precious stones, and pearls, and fine linen and purple, and silk, and scarlet, and every kind of aromatic wood, and all manner of vessels of ivory, and all manner of vessels of most precious wood, and of brass, and iron, and marble,

13 And cinnamon, and perfumes and spices and myrrh, and frankincense, and wine, and oil, and fine flour, and wheat, and cattle, and sheep, and horses, and chariots, and hides, and slaves.

14 And the fruits which your soul lusted after are departed from you, and all things which were luxurious and goodly are lost to you, and you shall never find them any more at all.

15 The merchants of these things, who were made rich by her, shall stand afar off for the fear of her torment, and they shall weep and wail,

16 Saying, Woe, woe, that great city, which was clothed with fine linen and purple, and scarlet, inlaid with gold, and precious stones and pearls! for in one hour these great riches are destroyed.

17 And every shipmaster, and all the travelers in ships, and sailors, and all those who labor at sea stood afar off,

18 And cried when they saw the smoke of her burning, saying, What city is like to this great city!

19 And they threw dust on their heads, and cried, weeping and wailing, saying, Woe, woe, that great city, where all who had ships on the sea were made rich by reason of her preciousness! for in one hour she is destroyed.

20 Rejoice over her, O heaven, and angels, apostles, and prophets, for God has avenged you on her.

21 And a mighty angel took up a stone like a great millstone, and cast it into the sea, saying, So shall that great city Babylon be overthrown with violence, and shall be found no more at all.

22 And the sound of harpers, and musicians, and singers and trumpeters, shall not be heard in you again; and no craftsman, of whatever craft he be shall be found any more in you;

23 And the light of a lamp shall shine no more at all in you; and the voice of the bridegroom and of the bride shall be heard no more at all in you: for your merchants were the great men of the earth; for by your sorceries were all peoples deceived.

24 And in her was found the blood of prophets, and of saints, and of all who were slain upon the earth.

CHAPTER 19

AND after these things, I heard a great voice of a great multitude in heaven, saying, Alleluia; Salvation, and power, and glory, and honor to our God:

2 For his judgments are true and righteous: for he has condemned the great harlot, who has corrupted the earth with her adultery, and has avenged the blood of his servants at her hand.

3 And a second time, they said, Alleluia. And her smoke rose up for ever and ever.

4 And the four and twenty elders and the four beasts fell down and worshipped God who sat on the throne, saying, Amen, Alleluia.

5 And a voice came out from the throne, saying, Praise our God, all you his servants, and you who fear him, both small and great.

6 And I heard as it were the voice of a great multitude, and as the voice of many waters, and as the sound of mighty thunderings, saying, Alleluia: for our LORD God, omnipotent, reigns.

Cf.dif. vv. 18:12-14, 16, 21;   19:1.

7 Let us be glad and rejoice, and give glory to him: for the time of the marriage feast of the Lamb has come, and his bride has made herself ready.

8 And it was given to her that she should be arrayed in fine pure linen, clean and white: for fine linen is the righteousness of saints.

9 And he said to me, Write, Blessed are those who are invited to the wedding feast of the Lamb. Then he said to me, These words of mine are the true sayings of God.

10 And I fell at his feet to worship him. And he said to me, Do not do that: I am your fellow servant, and of your brethren who have the testimony of Jesus: worship God: for the testimony of Jesus is the spirit of prophecy.

11 ¶ And I saw heaven opened, and behold, I saw a white horse; and he who sat upon him was called Faithful and True, and in righteousness he judges and makes war.

12 His eyes were as a flame of fire, and on his head were many crowns; and he had names written, and one of the names written, no man knew but he himself.

13 And he was clothed with a vesture dipped in blood: and he called his name, The Word of God.

14 And the armies which were in heaven followed him on white horses clothed in fine linen, pure and white.

15 And out of his mouth came a sharp two-edged sword, that with it he should smite the nations: and he shall rule them with a rod of iron: and he shall tread the winepress of the fierceness and wrath of Almighty God.

16 And he had a name written on his vesture and on his thigh, KING OF KINGS, AND LORD OF LORDS.

17 And I saw an angel standing in the sun; and he cried with a loud voice, saying to all the fowls that fly in the midst of heaven, Come and gather yourselves together for the great supper of God;

18 That you may eat the flesh of kings, and the flesh of captains, and the flesh of mighty men, and the flesh of horses, and of those who sit on them, and the flesh of all men, both free and bond, both small and great.

19 Then I saw the wild beast and the kings of the earth, and their armies gathered together to fight against him who sat on the horse, and against his armies.

20 And the wild beast was taken and with him the false prophet who wrought miracles before him with which he deceived those who had received the mark of the wild beast, and those who worshipped his image. These both were cast alive into a lake of fire burning with brimstone.

21 And the others were slain by the sword that came out from the mouth of him who sat upon the horse: and all the fowls were filled with their flesh.

CHAPTER 20

AND I saw an angel come down from heaven, having the key of the bottomless pit, and a great chain in his hand.

2 And he seized the dragon, that old serpent, which is the Tempter and Satan, who deceived the whole world, and bound him a thousand years,

3 And cast him into the bottomless pit, and shut him up and set a seal over him, that he should no more deceive the nations until the thousand years should be fulfilled: after that he will be loosed for a short time.

4 ¶ And I saw thrones, and they sat upon them, and judgment was given to them: and the souls of those who were beheaded for the witness of Jesus, and for the word of God, and who had not worshipped the wild beast, neither his image, nor had received his mark upon their foreheads or on their hand, lived and reigned with their Christ these thousand years. * But the rest of the dead lived not

* Rev.20:8 - "But the rest..." retained from the King James Version.

again until the thousand years were finished.

5 This is the first resurrection.

6 Blessed and holy is he who has part in the first resurrection: over them the second death has no power, but they shall be the priests of God and of his Christ, and they shall reign with him a thousand years.

7 And when the thousand years come to an end. Satan shall be loosed out of his prison,

8 And shall go out to deceive the nations which are in the four corners of the earth, even to China and Mongolia, to gather them together for war: the number of them is as the sand of the sea.

9 And they went up on a broad plain, and surrounded the camp of the saints and the beloved city: and fire came down from God out of heaven and consumed them.

10 And the devil who deceived them was cast into the lake of fire and brimstone, where also are the beast and the false prophet; and shall be tormented day and night for ever and ever.

11 ¶ And I saw a great white throne and him who sat on it, from whose presence the earth and the heavens fled away; and there was no place found for them.

12 Then I saw the dead, small and great, stand before the throne; and the books were opened: and another book was opened, which is the book of life: and the dead were judged by those things which were written in the books, according to their works.

13 And the sea gave up the dead which were in it; and death and hell gave up the dead which were in them: and they were judged every man according to his works.

14 And death and Sheol were cast into the lake of fire. This is the second death, which is the burning fire.

15 And whosoever was not found written in the book of life was cast into the lake of fire.

CHAPTER 21

AND I saw a new heaven and a new earth: for the first heaven and the first earth had passed away; and the sea was no more.

2 And I saw the holy city, new Jerusalem, coming down from God, prepared as a bride adorned for her husband.

3 And I heard a great voice from heaven saying, Behold, the tabernacle of God is with men, and he will dwell with them, and they shall be his people, and the very God shall be with them, and be their God;

4 And he shall wipe away all tears from their eyes; and there shall be no more death, neither sorrow nor wailing, neither shall there be any more pain: for the former things have passed away.

5 And he who sat upon the throne said, Behold, I make all things new. Then he said to me, Write: for these are the trustworthy and true words of God.

6 And he said to me, I am Aleph and Tau, Alpha and Omega, the beginning and the end. I will freely give of the fountain of living water to him who is thirsty.

7 He who overcomes shall inherit these things; and I will be his God, and he shall be my son.

8 But as for the fearful, and the unbelieving, and the sinful, and the abominable, and murderers, and those who commit adultery, and the magicians, and the idolators, and all liars, their portion shall be in the lake that burns with fire and brimstone: which is the second death.

9 ¶ And there came to me one of the seven angels who had the seven vials full of the seven last plagues, and he talked with me, saying, Come, I will show you the bride, the wife of the Lamb.

10 And he carried me away in the spirit onto a great and high mountain, and showed me

Cf. dif. vv. 20:8-9, 12-14; 21:5-8.

that great city, the holy Jerusalem, descending out of heaven from God,

11 Having the glory of God, radiant as a brilliant light, resembling a very precious gem; like a jasper stone, clear as crystal:

12 It had a wall great and high, and it had twelve gates, with names inscribed thereon, which are the names of the twelve tribes of the children of Israel:

13 On the east were three gates; on the north three gates; on the south three gates; and on the west three gates.

14 And the wall of the city had twelve foundations, and on them the twelve names of the twelve apostles of the Lamb.

15 And he who talked with me had a measuring rod of golden reed to measure the city, and its gates, and its wall.

16 And the city was laid four-square, and the length was the same as the breadth: and he measured the city with the reed, about twelve furlongs, twelve thousand paces. And the length and breadth and the height were equal.

17 And he measured the wall thereof, a hundred and forty and four cubits, according to the measure of a man, that is, of the angel.

18 And the wall was constructed of jasper: and the city itself was pure gold, resembling clear glass.

19 And the foundations of the wall of the city were adorned with all kinds of precious stones. The first foundation was jasper; the second sapphire; the third chalcedony; the fourth, emerald;

20 The fifth, sardonyx; the sixth, sardius; the seventh, chrysolyte; the eighth, beryl; the ninth, topaz; the tenth, chrysoprasus; the eleventh, jacinth; the twelfth, amethyst.

21 And the twelve gates were adorned with twelve pearls; one for each of the gates, and each gate was made of a single pearl; and the great street of the city was of pure gold. as it were transparent glass.

22 But I saw no temple therein: for the LORD Almighty and the Lamb are the temple of it.

23 The city has no need of the sun, neither of the moon, to shine in it: for the glory of God lightens it, and the Lamb is the lamp of it.

24 And the people who have been saved shall walk by that very light: and the kings of the earth shall bring their own glory and the honor of the people into it.

25 And the gates of it shall not be barred by day: for there is no night there.

26 And they shall bring the glory and the honor of the people into it.

27 And there shall not enter into it anything which defiles, nor he who works abominations and lies; only those shall enter whose names are written in the Lamb's book of life.

CHAPTER 22

AND he shewed me a pure river of water of life, clear as crystal, gushing out of the throne of God and of the Lamb.

2 In the midst of the great street of the city, and on either side of the river, was the tree of life, which bore twelve kind of fruits, and each month it yielded one of its fruits; and the leaves of the trees were for the healing of the people.

3 And that which drops shall be no more: but the throne of God and of the Lamb shall be in it; and his servants shall serve him:

4 And they shall see his face; and his name shall be on their foreheads.

5 And there shall be no night there; and they shall neither need a candle, nor the light of the sun; for the LORD God shines on them: and they shall reign for ever and ever.

6 ¶ And he said unto me, These sayings are faithful and true: and the LORD God who is the spirit of the prophets sent his angel to show to his servants the things which shortly must come to pass.

7 Behold, I am coming soon: blessed is he who keeps the sayings of the prophecy of this book.

8 And I, John, who heard and saw these things, when I had heard and seen them, I fell down to worship before the feet of the angel who showed me these things.

9 And he said to me, Do not do that: I am your fellow servant, and of your brethren the prophets, and of those who keep the words of this book: worship God.

10 Then he said to me, Do not seal the words of the prophecy of this book: for the time is at hand.

11 He who is unjust will continue to be unjust: and he who is filthy will continue to be filthy: and he who is righteous will continue to do righteousness: and he who is holy will continue to be holy.

12 Behold, I am coming soon, and my reward is with me, to give every man according as his work shall be.

13 I am Aleph and Tau, Alpha and Omega, the beginning and the end, the first and the last.

14 Blessed are those who do his commandments, that they may have the right to the tree of life, and may enter in through the gates into the city.

15 For without are the vicious, and magicians, and the immoral, and murderers, and idolaters, and whoever loves to tell lies.

16 ¶ I, Jesus, have sent my angel to testify to you these things in the churches. I am the root and the offspring of David, and the bright and morning star.

17 And the Spirit and the bride say Come. And let him who hears, say Come. And he who is thirsty, let him come. And whosoever will, let him take of the living water freely.

18 ¶ I testify to every man who hears the words of the prophecy of this book, If any man shall add to these things, God shall add to him the plagues that are written in this book:

19 And if any man shall take away from the words of the book of this prophecy, God shall take away his portion from the tree of life, and from the holy city, and from the things which are written in this book.

20 He who testifies these things says, Surely I am coming soon. Amen. Come, LORD Jesus.

21 ¶ The grace of our LORD Jesus Christ be with you all, all you holy ones. Amen.

Here ends the Revelation given to the holy John the Apostle and Evangelist.

❖ ܪܐ ܟܠܗ ܐܡܝܢ ❖

THE EPISTLE OF PAUL THE APOSTLE TO THE
ROMANS

❖ ܪ̈ܗܘܡܝܐ ܕܠܘܬ ܐܓܪܬܐ ܫܠܝܚܐ ܦܘܠܘܣ ❖

CHAPTER 1

*P*AUL, a servant of Jesus Christ, called to be an apostle, and chosen to proclaim the gospel of God

2 Which was promised from early days by his prophets in the holy scriptures,

3 Concerning his son who was born in the flesh of the seed of the house of David,

4 And who came to be known as the Son of God with power and with the Holy Spirit, because he arose from the dead, and he is Jesus Christ our LORD,

5 And by him we have received grace and apostleship among all the Gentiles, so that they may hear the faith which is under his name,

6 And in which you also are of them, and are called by Jesus Christ;

7 To all who are in Rome, beloved of God, called and sanctified: Grace and peace be unto you from God our Father, and from our LORD Jesus Christ.

8 ¶ First, I thank my God through Jesus Christ for you all, that your faith has been heard of throughout the world.

9 For God, whom I serve in spirit in the gospel of his Son, is my witness that unceasingly I make mention of you in my prayers;

10 Beseeching that, if the way is open to me by the will of God, I may come to you.

11 For I long to see you, and to impart to you the gift of the Spirit, in order that you may be strengthened by it,

12 And that we may be comforted together by our mutual faith.

13 Now I want you to know, my brethren, that often I have wanted to come to you, but I have been prevented thus far, that I might have some fruit among you also, even as among other Gentiles,

14 Greeks and Barbarians, the wise and the unwise; for it is my duty to preach to everybody.

15 So I am eager to preach the gospel to you who are in Rome also.

16 ¶ For I am not ashamed of the gospel of Christ: for it is the power of God unto salvation to every one who believes; whether they are Jews first, or Arameans (Syrians). *

17 For therein is the righteousness of God revealed from faith to faith: as it is written, The righteous shall live by faith.

18 ¶ For the wrath of God is revealed from heaven against all the iniquity and wickedness of men who unjustly suppress the truth;

19 Because that which may be known of God is manifested to them for God has revealed it unto them.

20 For, from the very creation of the world, the invisible things of God have been clearly seen and understood by his creations, even his eternal power and Godhead; so that they are without excuse.

21 For they knew God and did not glorify him and give thanks to him as God, but became vain in their imaginations, and their

---

* Ro.1:16 - "...some of the first converts to Chrsitianity were Arameans. Jesus had preached in Tyre and Sidon. The seventy disciples were sent out into Syria...Galilee was only a short distance from Tyre and Sidon." - Lamsa, p.179, *New Testament Commentary*, AJ Holman Co., 1945.

Cf.dif. vv. 1:1, 3-5, 14, 16, 21.

hearts were darkened so that they could not understand.

22 And while they thought within themselves that they were wise, they became fools,

23 And they have changed the glory of the uncorruptible God for an image made in the likeness of corruptible man, and in the likeness of birds, and of four-footed beasts, and of creeping things on the earth.

24 That is why God also gave them up to uncleanness through the lusts of their hearts, to dishonor their own bodies between themselves:

25 And they have changed the truth of God for lies, and worshipped and served the created things more than their Creator to whom belong glory and blessings for ever. Amen.

26 Therefore God has given them up to vile passions: for even their women have changed the natural use of their sex into that which is unnatural:

27 And likewise also their men have left the natural use of the women and have run wild with lust toward one another, male with male committing shameful acts, and receiving in themselves the due recompense of their error.

28 And as they did not consent in themselves to know God, God has given them over to a weak mind, to do the things which should not be done; as,

29 Being filled with all manner of iniquity, fornication, bitterness, malice, extortion, envy, murder, strife, deceit, evil thoughts,

30 Slanderers, backbiters, haters of God, revilers, proud boasters, inventors of evil things, the weak-minded, disobedient to their parents;

31 These have no respect for a covenant. They know neither love nor peace, nor is there mercy in them;

32 Knowing the judgment of God, that those who commit such things, he condemns to death, they not only do them, but also associate with those who practice them.

CHAPTER 2

*T*HEREFORE you are inexcusable, O man, to judge your neighbor: for in judging your neighbor, you condemn yourself; for even you who judge practice the same things yourself.

2 But we know that the judgment of God is rightly against those who commit such things.

3 What do you think, O man? Do you think that you who judge those who practice such things, while you commit them yourself, will escape the judgment of God?

4 Do you stand against the riches of his goodness and forbearance, and the opportunity which he has given you, not knowing that the goodness of God leads you to repentance?

5 Because of the hardness and impenitence of your heart you are laying up for yourself a treasure of wrath for the day of wrath and the revelation of the righteous judgment of God;

6 Who will render to every man according to his deeds:

7 To those who continue patiently in good works seeking glory and honor and immortality, he will give eternal life.

8 But to those who are stubborn and do not obey the truth, but obey iniquity, to them he will render indignation and wrath,

9 Suffering and affliction, for every man who does evil, for the Jews first, and also for the Syrians.

10 But glory, honor and peace for every one who does good, to the Jews first, and also to the Syrians.

11 For there is no respect of persons with God.

Cf.dif. vv. 1:24, 28, 32; 2:1-3, 5, 9, 11.

12 For those who have sinned without law, shall also perish without law: and those who have sinned in the law, shall be judged by the law,

13 For it is not the hearers of the law who are righteous before God, but it is the doers of the law who shall be justified.

14 For if the Gentiles, who do not have the law, do by nature the things contained in the law, these having not the law, are a law unto themselves.

15 And they show the work of the law written on their hearts; and their conscience also bears them witness, when their thoughts either rebuke or defend one another,

16 In the day when God shall judge the secrets of men according to my gospel by Jesus Christ.

17 ¶ Now if you who are called a Jew, trust on the law and are proud of God,

18 And because you know his will, and know the things which must be observed, which you have learned from the law,

19 And you have confidence in yourself that you are a guide of the blind and a light to them who are in darkness,

20 An instructor of the foolish, a teacher of children, you are the semblance of knowledge and of truth as embodied in the law.

21 Now, therefore, you teach others but fail to teach yourself. You preach that men should not steal, yet you steal.

22 You say, Men must not commit adultery, yet you commit adultery. You despise idols, yet you rob the sanctuary.

23 You are proud of the law but you dishonor God by breaking the law.

24 For the name of God is blasphemed among the Gentiles through you, as it is written.

25 ¶ For circumcision is profitable only if you keep the law: but if you break the law, then circumcision becomes uncircumcision.

26 Therefore, if the uncircumcision keep the statutes of the law, behold would not the uncircumcision be counted for circumcision?

27 And the uncircumcision which fulfills the law naturally, will condemn you, who, while in possession of the scripture and circumcision, transgress the law.

28 For it is not the one who is outwardly a Jew, who is the real Jew; neither is circumcision that which is seen in the flesh.

29 But a real Jew is one who is inwardly so, and circumcision is of the heart, spiritually and not literally; whose praise is not from men but from God.

CHAPTER 3

WHAT then is the superiority of the Jew? or what is the importance of circumcision?

2 Much in every way: because the Jews were the first to believe in the words of God.

3 For what if some had not believed, could their unbelief nullify the faith of God?

4 Far be it: only God is true and no man is wholly perfect; as it is written, That you may be justified by your words, and triumph when you are judged.

5 Now if our iniquity serves to establish the righteousness of God, what then shall we say? Is God unjust when he inflicts his anger? I speak as a man.

6 Far be it: for then how could God judge the world?

7 For if the truth of God is made abundant through my falsehood to his glory, why then am I to be judged as a sinner?

8 As for those who blaspheme against us, saying that we say, Let us do evil that good may come, their condemnation is reserved for eternal justice.

9 ¶ What then do we uphold that is superior? We have already decided concerning both Jews and Syrians, for they are all under sin.

Cf.dif. vv. 2:15, 18, 20-23, 27-29;　3:2-4, 7-9.

10 As it is written, There is none righteous, no, not one:

11 There are none who understand, there are none who seek after God.

12 They are all gone astray and they have been rejected: there are none who do good, no, not one.

13 Their throats are like open sepulchres; their tongues are deceitful; the venom of asps is under their lips.

14 Their mouths are full of cursing and bitterness.

15 They are over-quick to shed blood.

16 Destruction and misery are in their ways.

17 They have not known the way of peace.

18 There is no fear of God before their eyes.

19 Now we know that whatever the law says, it is said to those who are under the law: so that every mouth may be shut, and all the world may become guilty before God.

20 For by the deeds of the law, no flesh shall be justified before his presence: for by means of the law, sin is known.

21 ¶ But now the righteousness of God without the law is manifested, and the very law and prophets testify to it;

22 But the righteousness of God is by the faith of Jesus Christ to every one, also to every man who believes in him, for there is no discrimination:

23 For all have sinned and are short of the glory of God:

24 For they are freely bestowed righteousness by the grace of God through the salvation which is in Jesus Christ, *

25 Whom God has foreordained to be a propitiation through faith in his blood for the remission of our sins that are past;

26 By the opportunity which God has given

us through his forbearance, for the manifestation of his righteousness at the present time, that he might be declared righteous; and for the justification of righteousness to him who is in the faith of our LORD Jesus Christ.

27 Where is boasting then? It is worthless. By what law? of works? No: but by the law of faith.

28 Therefore we conclude that it is by faith a man is justified and not by the works of the law.

29 Why? Is he the God of the Jews only? Is he not also God of the Gentiles? Yes, he is God of the Gentiles also;

30 Because it is one God, who justifies the circumcision by faith, and uncircumcision by the same faith.

31 Why, then? Do we nullify the law through faith? Far be it: on the contrary, we uphold the law.

CHAPTER 4

WHAT then shall we say concerning Abraham, the chief of our forefathers, who lived according to the flesh before God called him?

2 For if Abraham were justified by works, he had reason to be proud; but not before God.

3 For what said the scripture? Abraham believed in God, and it was counted to him for righteousness.

4 But to him who works, wages are not considered as a favor but as that which is due to him.

5 And to him who works not, but only believes in him who justifies sinners, his faith is counted for righteousness.

6 Just as David also said about the blessed-

---

* Ro.3:24 - The Aramaic word *Porkana* means "salvation" and not "redemption" as translated by the King James Version. *Porkdana* is derived from the Aramaic word *prak*, "to save". *Mekhar* and *zban* mean "to purchase", "redeem" or "acquire". Neither of these words occur here (Lamsa, *ibid*, p.183).

ness of the man, whom God declared righteous without works,

7 Saying, Blessed are they whose iniquities are forgiven, and whose sins are wiped away.

8 Blessed is the man whose sins God will not hold against him.

9 Now, therefore, is this blessedness on account of circumcision, or on account of uncircumcision? for we say that Abraham's faith was accounted to him for righteousness.

10 How then was it given to him? by means of circumcision, or in uncircumcision? It was not given in circumcision, but in uncircumcision.

11 For he received circumcision as a sign and a seal of the righteousness of his faith while he was uncircumcised: that he might become the father of all them who believe, though they be not circumcised, that righteousness might be given to them also;

12 So that the father of circumcision is not only to those who are of circumcision, but also to those who walk in the steps of the faith of our father Abraham while he was yet uncircumcised.

13 For the promise to Abraham and his seed that he should inherit the world was not made through the law, but through the righteousness of his faith.

14 For if they had become heirs by means of the law, then faith would have been empty and the promise made of no effect.

15 For the law causes provocation; for where there is no law, there is no transgression.

16 Therefore it is by faith that we will be justified by grace; so that the promise might be sure to all his seed; not only to him who is of the law, but also to him who is of the faith of Abraham who is the father of us all,

17 As it is written, I have made you a father of many peoples, in the presence of the God in whom you have believed, who quickens the dead, and who invites those who are not

yet in being, as though they were present.

18 For he who was hopeless trusted in hope, that he might become the father of many peoples, as it is written, So shall your seed be.

19 His faith never weakened even when he examined his old body when he was a hundred years old, and the deadness of Sarah's womb.

20 He did not doubt the promise of God as one who lacks faith; but his faith gave him strength, and he gave glory to God.

21 He felt assured that what God had promised him, God was able to fulfill.

22 Therefore it was given to him for righteousness.

23 ¶ That his faith was given for righteousness, was not written for his sake alone,

24 But for us also, for he will number us also, who believe in him who raised our LORD Jesus Christ from the dead;

25 Who was delivered up for our offences and arose that he might justify us.

CHAPTER 5

*T*HEREFORE, being justified by faith, let us have peace with God through our LORD Jesus Christ;

2 Through him we have been brought by faith into this grace wherein we stand, and are proud in the hope of the glory of God.

3 And not only so, but we also glory in our tribulations: knowing that tribulation perfects patience in us;

4 And patience, experience; and experience, hope:

5 And hope causes no one to be ashamed; because the love of God is poured in our hearts by the Holy Spirit which is given to us.

6 But Christ at this time, because of our weaknesses, died for the sake of the wicked.

7 Hardly would any man die for the sake of

Cf.dif. vv. 4:7-10, 12-17, 19-21, 23-24; 5:2-3, 7.

the wicked: * but for the sake of the good, one might be willing to die.

8 God has here manifested his love toward us, in that, while we were yet sinners, Christ died for us.

9 Much more then, being justified by his blood, we shall be delivered from wrath through him.

10 For if when we were enemies, we were reconciled to God by the death of his Son, much more, being reconciled, we shall be saved by his life.

11 And not only so, but we also glory in God through our LORD Jesus Christ, by whom we have now received the reconciliation.

12 ¶ Just as sin entered into the world by one man, and death by means of sin, so death was imposed upon all men, inasmuch as they all have sinned:

13 For until the law was given, though sin was in the world, it was not considered sin, because there was no law.

14 Nevertheless, death reigned from Adam to Moses, even over them who had not sinned in the manner of the transgression of the law by Adam, who is the likeness of him that was to come.

15 But the measure of the gift of God was not the measure of the fall. If therefore, because of the fall of one, many died, how much more will the grace and gift of God, because of one man, Jesus Christ, be increased ?

16 And the effect of the gift of God was greater than the effect of the offence of Adam: for while the judgment from one man's offence resulted in condemnation of many, the gift of God in forgiveness of sins resulted in righteousness to many more.

17 For if by one man's offence, death reigned, how much more those who receive abundance of grace and of the gift of righteousness shall reign in life by one, Jesus Christ.

18 In like manner as by one man's offence, condemnation came upon all men, even so by the righteousness of one man, will the victory unto life be to all men.

19 For as by one man's disobedience many were made sinners, so by the obedience of one man, shall many be made righteous.

20 The introduction of the law caused sin to increase, and when sin had increased, grace became abundant.

21 Just as sin had reigned through death, so grace shall reign through righteousness unto eternal life by our LORD Jesus Christ.

CHAPTER 6

WHAT shall we then say? Shall we continue in sin, that grace may abound?

2 Far be it. How shall we who are dead to sin, continue to live in it?

3 Do you not know, that those of us who have been baptized into Jesus Christ have been baptized into his death?

4 Therefore, we are buried with him by baptism into death: so that as Jesus Christ arose from the dead by the glory of his Father, even so we also shall walk in a new life.

5 For if we have been planted together with him in the likeness of his death, so shall we be also in the likeness of his resurrection:

6 For we know, that our old selves are crucified with him, so that the sinful body might be destroyed, that henceforth we should not serve sin.

7 For he that is dead is freed from sin.

8 Now if we are dead with Christ, let us believe that we shall also live with Christ:

9 We know that Christ rose from the dead,

---

* Ro.5:7 - The Aramaic word *rashiaa*, which means "wicked," has been confused with the Aramaic word *zadika*, "righteous" [as construed in the Greek texts]". -Lamsa, *ibid.*, p.192.

and dies no more; and that death has no more dominion over him.

10 For in dying he died once to sin: and in living he lives to God.

11 Likewise, you also must consider yourself as being dead to sin, but alive to God through Jesus Christ our LORD.

12 Let not sin therefore reign in your mortal body, that you should obey it in the lusts thereof.

13 Neither should you yield your members as instruments of iniquity to sin: but yield yourselves to God, just as if you were men who had risen from among the dead, and let your members be instruments of righteousness to God.

14 Sin shall not have dominion over you: for you are no longer under the law, but under grace.

15 ¶ What then? Shall we sin because we are not under the law, but under grace? Far be it.

16 Do you not know, that to whom you yield yourselves servants to obey, his servants you are, for you obey him, whether it be to sin or whether it be of obedience to righteousness?

17 But thank God that you, who were once the servants of sin, now obey from the heart that form of doctrine which has been delivered to you.

18 Now, being made free from sin, you become the servants of righteousness.

19 I speak after the manner of men because of the weakness of your flesh: for as you have yielded your members to the servitude of uncleanness and iniquity, so now yield your members to the servitude of righteousness and holiness.

20 For when you were the servants of sin, you were free from righteousness.

21 What kind of fruit did you have then, in the things of which you are now ashamed? for the end thereof is death.

22 But now being made free from sin, and become servants to God, your fruits are holy, and the end thereof is life everlasting.

23 For the wages of sin is death; but the gift of God is eternal life through our LORD Jesus Christ.

CHAPTER 7

*D*O you not know, my brethren, I speak to them who know the law, that the law has authority over a person as long as he lives?

2 Just as a woman is bound by the law to her husband as long as he lives; but if her husband should die, she is freed from the law of her husband.

3 Thus if, while her husband is alive, she should be attached to another man, she becomes an adulteress: but if her husband is dead, she is free from the law; so that she is not an adulteress though she becomes another man's wife.

4 Wherefore, my brethren, you also are become dead to the law by the body of Christ; that you might become another's, even to him who arose from the dead, so that you may bring forth fruit to God.

5 For when we were in the flesh, the wounds of sin, which were by the law, worked in our members to bring forth fruits to death.

6 But now we are freed from the law, being dead to that which had hold upon us; and we should henceforth serve in newness of spirit and not in the oldness of the letter.

7 ¶ What shall we say then? Is the law sin? Far be it. I would not have known the meaning of sin, except by means of the law: for I would never have known the meaning of lust, except the law said, Thou shalt not covet.

8 So by means of this commandment, sin found an occasion and provoked in me every kind of lust. For without the law sin was dead.

9 Formerly I lived without the law: but when

the commandment came, sin came to life and I died.

10 And the commandment which was ordained to life I found to be for death.

11 For sin, finding occasion by the commandment, misled me and by it killed me.

12 Wherefore the law is holy and the commandment holy, and just, and good.

13 ¶ Has then that which is good, become death to me? Far be it. But sin that is exposed as sin and works death in me for that which is good, will be the more condemned by means of the law.

14 For we know that the law is spiritual: but I am of the flesh enslaved to sin.

15 For I do not know what I do: and I do not do the thing which I want, but I do the thing which I hate. That is exactly what I do.

16 So then if I do that which I do not wish to do, I can testify concerning the law that it is good.

17 Now then it is not I who do it, but sin which dominates me.

18 Yet I know that it does not fully dominate me, (that is in my flesh) but as far as good is concerned, the choice is easy for me to make, but to do it, that is difficult.

19 For it is not the good that I wish to do, that I do: but it is the evil that I do not wish to do, that I do.

20 Now if I do that which I do not wish, then it is not I who do it, but the sin which dominates me.

21 I find therefore, that the law agrees with my conscience when I wish to do good, but evil is always near, distracting me.

22 For I delight in the law of God after the inward man:

23 But I see another law in my members, warring against the law of my mind, and it makes me a captive to the law of sin which is in my members.

24 O wretched man that I am! Who shall deliver me from this mortal body?

25 I thank God through our LORD Jesus Christ. Now therefore with my mind I am a servant of the law of God; but with my flesh I am a servant of the law of sin.

CHAPTER 8

*T*HERE is therefore no condemnation to them who walk in the flesh after the Spirit of Jesus Christ.

2 For the law of the Spirit of life which is in Jesus Christ has made you free from the law of sin and death.

3 For the law was weak through the weakness of the flesh, so God sent his own Son in the likeness of sinful flesh, on account of sin, in order to condemn sin by means of his flesh:

4 That the righteousness of the law might be fulfilled in us, for we do not walk after the things of the flesh, but after the Spirit.

5 For they who are after the flesh, do mind the things of the flesh; but they who are after the Spirit, do mind the things of the Spirit.

6 To be carnally minded is death; but to be spiritually minded is life and peace;

7 Because the carnal mind is enmity against God: for it is not subject to the law of God, because it cannot be.

8 So then, they who are in the flesh cannot please God.

9 But you are not in the flesh, but in the spirit if the Spirit of God truly dwells within you. Now if any man does not have the Spirit of Christ, he does not belong to him.

10 And if Christ is within you, the body is dead because of sin: but the Spirit is life because of righteousness.

11 And if the Spirit of Him who raised our LORD Jesus Christ from the dead dwells within you, so he who raised Jesus Christ from the dead will also quicken your mortal bodies by his Spirit that dwells within you.

12 ¶ Therefore, my brethren, we are not indebted to the flesh to live after the flesh.

13 For if you live after the flesh, you will die: but if you, through the Spirit, subdue the deeds of the body, you shall live.

14 Those who are led by the Spirit of God, are the sons of God.

15 For you have not received the spirit of bondage, to be in fear again; but you have received the Spirit of adoption, whereby we cry, Abba, Avon, Father, our Father.

16 And this Spirit bears witness to our spirit, that we are the children of God:

17 And if children, then heirs; heirs of God, and joint heirs with Jesus Christ; so that if we suffer with him, we shall also be glorified with him.

18 ¶ For I reckon that the sufferings of the present time are not worthy to be compared with the glory which shall be revealed in us.

19 For the earnest expectation of all mankind waits for the manifestation of the sons of God.

20 For man was made subject to vanity, not willingly, but by reason of him who gave him free will in the hope he would choose rightly.

21 Because man himself shall be delivered from the bondage of corruption into the glorious liberty of the children of God.

22 For we know that the whole creation groans and labors in pain to this day.

23 ¶ And not only they, but ourselves also, who have the first fruits of the Spirit, even we groan within ourselves, waiting for the adoption, that is, the redemption of our bodies.

24 For we live in hope: but hope that is seen is not hope: for if we see it, why should we yet hope?

25 But if we hope for that which we do not see, then do we wait for it in patience.

26 Likewise the Spirit also helps our weaknesses: for we do not know what is right and proper for us to pray for: but the Spirit prays for us with that earnestness which cannot be described.

27 And he who searches the hearts knows what is the mind of the Spirit, for the Spirit prays for the saints according to the will of God.

28 ¶ And we know that all things work together for good to them that love God, to them who are the called according to his purpose.

29 He knew them in advance and he marked them with the likeness of the image of his Son that he might be the first-born among many brethren.

30 Moreover, those he did mark in advance, he has called, and those he has called, he has declared righteous, and those he has declared righteous, he has glorified.

31 What then shall we say concerning these things? If God be for us, who can be against us?

32 If he did not spare his own Son, but delivered him up for us all, why will he not freely give us all things with him?

33 Who is to complain against the chosen ones of God? It is God who justifies.

34 Who is he who condemns? It is Christ who died and rose again, and he is at the right hand of God making intercession for us.

35 What shall separate me from the love of Christ? tribulation, or imprisonment, or persecution, or famine, or nakedness, or peril, or sword?

36 As it is written, For your sake we die every day, and we are accounted as lambs for the slaughter.

37 But in all these things we are more than conquerors through him who loved us.

38 For I am persuaded, that neither death, nor life, nor angels, nor empires, nor armies, nor things present, nor things to come,

39 Nor height, nor depth, nor any other crea-

Cf.dif. vv. 8:13, 15, 19-22, 24, 26-27, 29-30, 32, 34, 36, 38.

ture shall be able to separate me from the love of God, which is in Jesus Christ our LORD.

CHAPTER 9

I TELL the truth through Christ, and I do not lie, my conscience also bears me witness through the Holy Spirit,

2 That I am exceedingly sorrowful, and the pain which is in my heart never ceases.

3 For I have prayed that I myself might be accursed because of Christ for the sake of my brethren and my kinsmen according to the flesh,

4 Who are Israelites; to whom belongs the adoption, and the glory, and the covenants and the law, and the rituals therein, and the promises;

5 Whose are the fathers, from among whom Christ appeared in the flesh, who is God over all, to whom are due praises and thanksgiving, for ever and ever. Amen.

6 It is not as though the word of God had actually failed. For all those who belong to Israel are not Israelites:

7 Neither, because they are of the seed of Abraham are they all his children: for it was said, In Isaac shall your seed be called.

8 That is, it is not the children of the flesh who are the children of God; but the children of the promise who are reckoned as descendants.

9 For this is the word of promise, I will come at this season, and Sarah shall have a son.

10 And not only this; but Rebecca also, even though she had relations with one only, our father Isaac;

11 Before her children were born, or had done good or evil, the choice of God was made known in advance; that it might stand, not by means of works, but through him who made the choice.

12 For it was said, The elder shall be the servant of the younger.

13 As it is written, Jacob have I loved but Esau have I hated.

14 ¶ What shall we say then? Is there injustice with God? Far be it.

15 For he said to Moses also, I will have mercy on him whom I love, and I will have compassion on him whom I favor.

16 Therefore, it is not within reach of him who wishes, nor within the reach of him who runs, but it is within the reach of the merciful God.

17 For in the scripture, he said to Pharaoh, It was for this purpose that I have appointed you, that I might shew my power in you, so that my name might be preached throughout all the earth.

18 Thus he has mercy on whom he pleases, and he hardens whom he pleases.

19 Perhaps you will say, Why then does he yet find fault? For who can resist his will?

20 However, O man, who are you to question God? Shall the thing formed say to him who formed it, Why have you made me like this?

21 Does not the potter have power over his clay, to make out of the same lump vessels, one to be formed and the other for service?

22 Now then, if God wanted to shew his anger, and make his power known, would he not then, after the abundance of his patience, bring wrath upon the vessels of wrath which were ready for destruction?

23 But he poured his mercy upon the favored vessels, which were prepared for the glory of God.

24 Namely, ourselves, the called ones, not of the Jews only, but also of the Gentiles.

25 As he said also in Hosea, I will call them my people, who were not my own people; and her beloved, who was not beloved.

26 And it shall come to pass, that in the place where it was said you are not my people;

there shall they be called the children of the living God.

27 Isaiah also preached concerning the children of Israel: Though the number of children of Israel should be as the sand of the sea, only a remnant shall be saved.

28 For whatever the LORD has determined and decreed, he shall bring to pass upon the earth.

29 Just as Isaiah had said before, If the LORD of Hosts had not increased the remnant, we should have been like Sod'om, and should have resembled Go-mor'rah.

30 ¶ What shall we say then? That the Gentiles who followed not after righteousness have attained to righteousness; that is, the righteousness which is the result of faith.

31 But Israel, who followed after the law of righteousness, has not attained to the law of righteousness.

32 Why? Because it was not sought by faith, but by the works of the law. So they stumbled at that stumbling-stone.

33 As it is written, Behold, the prophet I give to Zion becomes a stumblingstone, and rock of offence: but whoever believes on him shall not be ashamed.

CHAPTER 10

MY brethren, my heart's desire and prayer to God for Is'ra-el is that they might be saved.

2 For I can testify for them that there is in them a zeal for God, but not according to the true knowledge.

3 For they know not the righteousness of God, but seek to establish their own righteousness, and because of this, they have not submitted themselves to the righteousness of God.

4 For Christ is the end of the law for righteousness to every one who believes.

5 ¶ For Moses writes of the righteousness of the law thus: Whoever shall do these things shall live by them.

6 But the righteousness which is of faith, says thus: Do not say in your heart, Who has ascended to heaven, and brought Christ down to earth?

7 And who has descended into the abyss of Sheol and brought up Christ from the dead?

8 But what does it say? The answer is near to you, even in your mouth, and in your heart: that is, the word of faith, which we preach;

9 So if you will confess with your mouth our LORD Jesus, and will believe in your heart that God raised him from the dead, you shall be saved.

10 For the heart which believes in him, shall be declared righteous, and the mouth that confesses him shall live.

11 For the scripture says, Whosoever believes on him shall not be ashamed.

12 And in this, it does not discriminate between the Jews and the Syrians: for the same LORD over all is rich unto all who call upon him.

13 For whoever shall call on the name of the LORD shall be saved.

14 ¶ How then can they call on him on whom they have not believed? Or how can they believe on him whom they have never heard? Or how can they hear without a preacher?

15 Or how can they preach, if they are not sent forth? As it is written, How becoming are the feet of those who preach peace, and of those who bring good tidings.

16 For all have not heard the preaching of the gospel. For Isaiah said, My LORD, who has believed the echoes of our voice?

17 So then faith comes by hearing, and hearing by the word of God.

18 But I say, Have they not heard? And behold the echoes of their voices have gone out over all the earth, and their words unto the ends of the world.

19 But I say, Did not Israel know? First Moses spoke thus, I will provoke you to jealousy by a people that are not my people, and I will make you angry by a reckless people.

20 Then Isaiah dared, and said, I appeared to those who did not seek me, and was found by those who did not ask for me.

21 But to Israel he said, All the day long I have stretched out my hands to a quarrelsome and disobedient people.

CHAPTER 11

I SAY, then, has God rejected his people? Far be it. For I also am an Israelite, a descendant of Abraham, of the tribe of Benjamin.

2 God has not rejected his people which he foreknew. Do you not know what the scripture says of Elijah? How he complained to God against Israel, saying,

3 My LORD, they have killed your prophets and have demolished your altars; and I am left alone; and they seek my life.

4 And it was said to him in a vision: Behold I have reserved for myself seven thousand men, who have not knelt on their knees to worship Baal.

5 Even so at the present time a remnant is preserved, elected by the grace.

6 And if by grace, then it is not by works: otherwise grace is no more grace. But if by works, then it is not by grace: otherwise work is no more work.

7 What then? Israel has not obtained that which he sought; but the elected ones have obtained it, and the rest were blinded in their hearts.

8 As it is written, God has given them a stubborn spirit, eyes that cannot see, and ears that cannot hear, to this very day.

9 And David said, Let their table become a snare, and a trap and a stumblingblock, and a recompense unto them.

10 Let their eyes be darkened, that they may not see, and let their backs be bowed down always.

11 ¶ I say then, Have they stumbled that they should fall? Far be it. But rather by their stumbling salvation has come to the Gentiles, in order to make them zealous.

12 Now if their stumbling has resulted in riches to the world, and their condemnation in riches to the Gentiles; how much more is their restoration?

13 It is to you Gentiles that I speak, inasmuch as I am the apostle to the Gentiles, and perhaps magnify my ministry:

14 But if I am able to make those who are my flesh zealous, I may thus save some of them.

15 And if their rejection has resulted in reconciliation of the world, how much more will their restoration be? Indeed it will be life from the dead.

16 For if the first fruit is holy, the rest of the lump is also holy; and if the root is holy, so are the branches.

17 And if some of the branches were cut off, and you who are a branch of a wild olive tree have been grafted in their place, and you have become a partaker of the root and fatness of the olive tree;

18 Do not boast over the branches. For if you boast, it is not you who sustains the root, but the root sustains you.

19 Perhaps you may say, The branches were cut off that I might be grafted in their place.

20 Well; they were cut off because of their unbelief, but you exist by faith. Be not highminded, but fear God.

21 For if God did not spare the natural branches, it may well be he will not spare you.

22 Consider therefore the goodness and severity of God: on those who fell, severity; but on you, goodness, if you continue in his

goodness: otherwise you also will be cut off.

23 And even they, if they do not abide in their unbelief, will be grafted in: for God is able to graft them in again.

24 For if you who have been cut from the wild olive tree, which is natural to you, and grafted contrary to your nature to become a good olive tree: how much more fruitful would they be, if they were grafted into their natural olive tree?

25 I am desirous, my brethren, that you should know this mystery, so that you may not be wise in your own conceits; for blindness of heart has to some degree befallen Israel, until the fulness of the Gentiles shall come in.

26 And then all Israel shall be saved: as it is written, A deliverer shall come out of Zion, and he shall remove ungodliness from Jacob:

27 And then they shall have the same covenant from me, when I have forgiven their sins.

28 ¶ Now according to the gospel, they are enemies for your sake. But according to election, they are beloved for the fathers' sakes.

29 For God does not withdraw his gift and his call.

30 Just as you were formerly disobedient to God and have now obtained mercy because of their disobedience,

31 Likewise, they are also disobedient now to the mercy which is upon you, that there may be mercy upon them also.

32 For God has included all men in disobedience, that he might have mercy on every man.

33 ¶ O the depth of the riches, the wisdom, and the knowledge of God! for no man has searched his judgment, and his ways are inscrutable.

34 For who has known the mind of the LORD? or who has been his counsellor?

35 Or who has first given to him and then received from him?

36 For of him, and through him, and to him, are all things: to him be glory and blessing, for ever and ever. Amen.

CHAPTER 12

I BESEECH you therefore, brethren, by the mercies of God, that you present your bodies a living sacrifice, holy and acceptable to God, by means of reasonable service.

2 Do not imitate the way of this world, but be transformed by the renewing of your minds, that you may discern what is that good and acceptable, and perfect will of God.

3 For I say, through the grace which is given to me, to all of you, not to think of yourselves beyond what you ought to think; but to think soberly, every man according to the measure of faith which God has distributed to him.

4 For as we have many members in one body, and all members have not the same function,

5 So we, being many, are one body in Christ, and every one members one of another.

6 Having then gifts differing according to the grace that is given to us; some have the gift of prophecy, according to the measure of faith,

7 Some have the gift of ministration, in his ministry; and some of teaching, in his teaching.

8 Some of consolation, in consoling: he that gives, let him do it with sincerity; he that rules, with diligence; he that shows mercy, with cheerfulness.

9 Let not your love be deceitful. Abhor that which is evil; cleave to that which is good.

10 Be kindly affectioned one to another with brotherly love; in honor preferring one another;

11 Not slothful in business; fervent in spirit, serving the LORD;

12 Rejoicing in hope; patient in tribulation; continuing instant in prayer.

13 Distributing to the necessity of saints; given to hospitality.

14 Bless them which persecute you; bless, and curse not.

15 Rejoice with them that rejoice, and weep with them that weep.

16 Be of the same mind one toward another. Mind not vain glory, but associate with those who are humble. Be not wise in your own conceits.

17 Recompense to no man evil for evil. But be careful to do good things before the presence of all men.

18 If it be possible, as much as lies in you, live peaceably with all men.

19 Dearly beloved, avenge not yourselves, but rather give place unto wrath; for it is written, Vengeance is mine: I will execute justice for you, said the LORD. *

20 Therefore if your enemy hunger, feed him; if he thirst, give him drink; for in so doing, you shall heap coals of fire on his head.

21 Be not overcome of evil, but overcome evil with good.

CHAPTER 13

*L*ET every soul be subject to the sovereign authorities. For there is no power which is not from God: and those who are in authority are ordained by God.

2 Whoever therefore resists the civil authority, resists the command of God: and they that resist, shall receive judgment to themselves.

3 For judges are not a menace to good works, but to evil. Now if you do not wish to be afraid of the authority, then do good, and you will be praised for it.

4 For he is the minister of God to you for good. But if you do that which is wrong, be afraid; for he is not girded with the sword in vain; for he is the minister of God, and an avenger of wrath upon those who commit crime.

5 Wherefore, we must be obedient, not only in fear of wrath, but also for our conscience sake.

6 For, for this reason you pay head tax also: for they are ministers of God who are in charge of these things.

7 Render therefore, to every one as is due to him: head tax to him who is in charge of head tax, duty to him who is in charge of custom; reverence to whom reverence is due, and honor to whom honor is due.

8 Owe no man anything, but love one another: for he who loves his neighbor has fulfilled the law,

9 Which says, Thou shalt not kill, Thou shalt not commit adultery, Thou shalt not steal, Thou shalt not covet; and if there is any other commandment, it is fulfilled in this saying, namely, Thou shalt love thy neighbor as thyself.

10 Love does not work evil to his neighbor because love is the fulfillment of the law.

11 Know this also, that now is the time and the hour that we should awake from our sleep, for now our salvation is nearer than when we believed.

12 The night is far spent, the day is at hand; let us therefore cast off the works of darkness, and let us put on the armor of light.

13 Let us walk decently, as in the daylight; not in clamor and drunkenness, not in the

---

* Ro. 12:19b - In the Syriac text, this verse is more literally translated by Murdock: "...For it is written: If thou dost not execute judgment for thyself, I will execute judgment for thee, saith God." (p.296. *The New Testament, A Literal Translation from the Syriac*)- D.J.M.

practice of immorality, not in envy and strife. 14 But clothe yourselves with our LORD Jesus Christ, and take no heed for the lusts of the flesh.

CHAPTER 14

He who is weak in the faith, assist him. And be consistent in your reasoning.
2 For one believes that he may eat all things: another who is weak, eats vegetables.
3 Let not him who eats despise him who eats not; and let not him who eats not judge him who eats: for God has received him also.
4 Who are you to judge another man's servant? for if he is a success, he is a success to his master; and if he is a failure, he is a failure to his master. As for his success, he will succeed for it is in the power of his master to make him succeed.
5 One person values one day above another: another values all days alike. Let every man be sure in his own mind.
6 He who is mindful concerning a day's duty is considerate of his master; and every one who is not mindful concerning a day's duty, is inconsiderate of his master. And he who is wasteful, is detrimental to his master even though he confesses it to God; and he who is not wasteful, is not wasteful to his master, yet he likewise tells it to God.
7 For none of us lives to himself, and none of us dies to himself.
8 For whether we live, we live unto our LORD; and whether we die, we die unto our LORD: whether we live therefore, or die, we belong to our LORD.
9 For to this end even Christ both died and came back to life, and rose to be LORD both of the dead and living.
10 Why, then, do you judge your brother? or why do you despise your brother? for we must all stand before the judgment seat of Christ.

11 For it is written, As I live, said the LORD, every knee shall bow to me, and every tongue shall confess me.
12 So then every one of us shall answer for himself to God.
13 Let us not therefore judge one another any more: but rather be mindful of this, that you should never place a stumblingblock in the way of your brother.
14 For I know, and I have confidence in the LORD Jesus, that nothing unclean comes from him: but to him who believes a thing to be unclean, to him only is it unclean.
15 But now if you have caused your brother to grieve on account of meat, then you are not living in harmony. Do not make food a cause to destroy a man for whose sake Christ died.
16 Let not our blessings be a reproach to any one:
17 For the kingdom of God is not meat and drink, but righteousness and peace and joy in the Holy Spirit.
18 For he who serves Christ in these things is acceptable to God and is approved by men.
19 Now let us strive after peace, and help one another.
20 And let us not, because of food, destroy the work of God. All things indeed are pure; but it is wrong for the man who eats with offence.
21 It is better that we neither eat meat nor drink wine nor do any other thing whereby we cause our brother to stumble.
22 You who have a certain belief, keep it to yourself, before God. Blessed is he who does not condemn himself by doing those things which he believes to be wrong.
23 For he who is doubtful and eats, violates his beliefs: for whatever is not of faith, is sin.

Cf.dif. vv. 14:1-2, 4-6, 11, 14-16, 19-20, 22-23.

CHAPTER 15

WE then who are strong ought to bear the weaknesses of the weak, and not seek to please ourselves.

2 Let every one of us please his neighbor in good and constructive ways.

3 For even Christ pleased not himself: but as it is written, The reproaches of those who reproached you have fallen on me.

4 For whatever things were written of old were written for our learning, that we through patience and comfort of the scriptures might have hope.

5 Now the God of patience and consolation grant you to regard one another to be equally worthy through the example of Jesus Christ;

6 That you may with one mind and one mouth glorify God, even the Father of our LORD Jesus Christ.

7 Therefore be close and bear one another's burdens, just as Christ also brought you close to the glory of God.

8 ¶ Now I say that Jesus Christ was a minister of the circumcision, for the truth of God, to confirm the promises made to the fathers:

9 And that the Gentiles might glorify God for his mercies which were poured upon them; as it is written, Therefore I will praise you among the Gentiles, and sing unto your name.

10 And again he says, Rejoice, ye Gentiles, with his people.

11 And again, he says, Praise the LORD, all ye Gentiles; and praise him, all ye nations.

12 And again Isaiah said, There shall be a root of Jesse, and he that shall rise will be a prince to the Gentiles; and in him shall the Gentiles trust.

13 Now may the God of hope fill you with all joy and peace so that by faith you may abound in hope, through the power of the Holy Spirit.

14 ¶ And I myself am persuaded concerning you, my brethren, that you also are filled with the same goodness, and made perfect with all knowledge, able also to admonish others.

15 Nevertheless, my brethren, I have written rather boldly to you, in order to remind you of the grace which is given to me by God,

16 That I may become a minister of Jesus Christ among the Gentiles, ministering the gospel of God, that the offering up of the Gentiles might be acceptable and sanctified by the Holy Spirit.

17 I am proud therefore to glory in Jesus Christ before God.

18 For I can scarcely speak of anything which Christ has not wrought by me for the obedience of the Gentiles, by word and deed,

19 Through mighty miracles and wonders, and by the power of the Spirit of God; so that from Jerusalem I went round about as far as Il-lyr'i-cum, and I have fully preached the gospel of Christ.

20 And I have strived to preach the gospel, not at any place where Christ's name had already been preached, because I did not want to build on another's foundation:

21 But as it is written, Those to whom he was never mentioned, they shall see him: and those who have not heard of him, they shall be made obedient.

22 This is the reason why I have been many times prevented from coming to you.

23 But now since I have no place in these countries, and as I have been desirous for many years past to come to you,

24 When I leave for Spain, I hope to come to see you: and I hope that you will escort me thence after I have more or less fully enjoyed my visit.

25 But now I am going to Jerusalem to minister unto the saints.

26 For the brethren in Mac-e-do'ni-a and A-

cha'ia have been pleased to take part in helping the poor saints which are at Jerusalem.

27 They have been eager to do it, because they are indebted to them, for if the Gentiles have been made partakers with them, of their spiritual things, they are indebted to minister to them in material things.

28 When, therefore, I have accomplished this and have finished distributing to them this kind of help, I will cross over toward you on my way to Spain.

29 I know that, when I come to you, I shall come in the fulness of the blessing of the gospel of Christ.

30 Now, I beseech you, my brethren, by our LORD Jesus Christ, and by the love of the Spirit, that you should strive together with me in your prayer to God for me;

31 That I may be delivered from those who are disobedient in Judæa; and that the assistance which I carry to the saints in Jerusalem may be well accepted.

32 So that I may come to you with joy by the will of God, and may with you be refreshed.

33 Now may the God of peace be with you all. Amen.

CHAPTER 16

I ENTRUST to your care Phe'be, our sister, who is a deaconess of the church which is at Cen'chre-a:

2 That you may receive her in our LORD, with the respect which is due saints, and that you may assist her in whatever she may need of you: for she has been a help to many, and to me also.

3 Salute Pris-cil'la and A'qui-la, fellow-workers with me in Jesus Christ,

4 Who have risked their necks for my sake: I am not the only one grateful to them, but also all the churches of the Gentiles.

5 Likewise salute the congregation that is in their house. Salute my well beloved E-pæn'e-tus, who is the first-fruits of A-cha'ia unto Christ.

6 Greet Mary, who has labored hard among you.

7 Salute An-dro-ni'cus and Junia, my kinsmen, who were prisoners with me, and well-known among the apostles, and who were believers in Christ before me.

8 Greet Am'pli-as, my beloved in our LORD.

9 Salute Ur'bane, our fellow-worker in Christ, and Sta'chys, my beloved.

10 Salute A-pel'les, chosen in our LORD. Salute the members of the household of Ar-is-to-bu'lus.

11 Salute He-ro'di-on my kinsman. Greet the members of the household of Nar-cis'sus, who are in our LORD.

12 Salute Try-phe'na and Try-pho'sa, who labor in the LORD. Salute the beloved Per'sis, who labored hard in our LORD.

13 Salute Rufus chosen in our LORD, and his mother, who is also a mother to me.

14 Salute A-syn'cri-tus, Phle'gon, Hermas, Patrobas, Hermes, and the brethren who are with them.

15 Salute Phi-lol'o-gus, and Julia, Ne're-us and his sister, and O-lym'pas, and all the saints who are with them.

16 Salute one another with a holy kiss. The churches of Christ salute you.

17 ¶ Now I beseech you, my brethren, beware of those who cause divisions and offences contrary to the doctrine which you have been taught; keep away from them.

18 For those who are such do not serve our LORD Jesus Christ, but their own belly; and by smooth words and fair speeches deceive the hearts of the simple people.

19 But your obedience is known to every one. I rejoice therefore on your behalf: and I want you to be wise in regard to good things,

and pure concerning evil things.

20 The God of peace will soon crush Satan under your feet. The Grace of our LORD Jesus Christ be with you.

21 ¶ Ti-mo'the-us, my fellow-worker, and Lucius, and Jason, and So-sip'a-ter, my kins-men, salute you.

22 I Ter'tius, who wrote this epistle, salute you in the LORD.

23 Ga'ius, my host and of the whole church, salutes you. E-ras'tus, the chamberlain of the city, salutes you; and Quar'tus, a brother.

24 Now I entrust you to God who will con-firm you in my gospel which is preached con-cerning Jesus Christ, in the revelation of the mystery, which was hidden since the world began,

25 But now is made manifest by the scrip-tures of the prophets; and by the command of the eternal God, and is made known to all the peoples for the obedience of faith:

26 For God is the only wise one, and to him be glory through Jesus Christ for ever and ever: Amen.

27 The grace of our LORD Jesus Christ be with you all. Amen.

Here endeth the epistle to the Romans; which was written from Corinthus and sent by Phebe, deaconess of the church of Cenchrea.

❖ ܘܫܠܝܚܐ ܡܢ ܐܬܟܬܒܬ ܪܗܘܡܝܐ ܕܠܘܬ ܐܓܪܬܐ ܫܠܡܬ ❖

THE FIRST EPISTLE OF PAUL THE APOSTLE TO THE
CORINTHIANS

❖ ܐܓܪܬܐ ܕܠܘܬ ܩܘܪܝܢܬܝܐ ܩܕܡܝܬܐ ❖

CHAPTER 1

*P*AUL, called to be an apostle of Jesus Christ through the will of God, and brother Sos'the-nes,

2 Unto the church of God which is at Corinth, the invited and holy ones who are sanctified by Jesus Christ, and to all of them in every place who invoke the name of our LORD Jesus Christ, both theirs and ours:

3 Grace be unto you, and peace, from God our Father and from our LORD Jesus Christ.

4 ¶ I thank my God always on your behalf, for the grace of God that has been given to you by Jesus Christ;

5 For in everything you are enriched by him, in all utterance, and in all knowledge;

6 Because the testimony of Christ has been confirmed in you:

7 And you do not lack any of his gifts but wait for the manifestation of our LORD Jesus Christ:

8 Who will also strengthen you to the end so that you may be blameless in the day of our LORD Jesus Christ.

9 God, by whom you have been called to the fellowship of his Son Jesus Christ our LORD, is trustworthy.

10 ¶ Now I beseech you, my brethren, in the name of our LORD Jesus Christ, to be of one accord, and let there be no divisions among you but be perfectly united in one mind and in one thought.

11 For I have been informed about you, my brethren, by the household of Chlo'e that there are disputes among you.

12 Now this I say, because there are some among you who say, I am a follower of Paul; and some who say, I am a follower of A-pol'los; and some who say, I am a follower of Ce'phas; and some who say, I am a follower of Christ.

13 Why? Is Christ divided? or was Paul crucified for you? or were you baptized in the name of Paul?

14 ¶ I confess to my God that I have baptized none of you, except Cris'pus and Ga'ius;

15 So no man can say that I have baptized in my own name.

16 And I baptized also the household of Steph'a-nas. I do not know whether I have baptized any one else.

17 ¶ For Christ did not send me to baptize but to preach the gospel: and not to rely on the wisdom of words, lest the cross of Christ should be in vain.

18 For the preaching of the cross * to those who have gone astray is foolishness; but to us who are saved it is the power of God.

19 For it is written, I will destroy the wisdom of the wise, and I will do away with the understanding of the prudent.

20 Where is the wise? where is the scribe? where is the learned of this world? Has not God made foolish the wisdom of this world?

21 Because all the wisdom which God had

---

* 1 Co.1:18 - "...in the eyes of Jews and pagans, death on the cross represented a political and moral defeat. The crucified persons were accursed ones (Deut.21:23; Gal.3:13). -Lamsa, *NT Commentary*, p.231.

Cf.dif. vv. 1:2, 6-7, 9-10, 12, 14, 16-17, 20-21.

given was not sufficient for the world to know God, it pleased God to save those who believe by the simple gospel.

22 For the Jews demand signs, and the Syrians seek after wisdom:

23 But we preach Christ crucified, which is a stumbling block to the Jews and foolishness to the Syrians. *

24 But for those who are called, both Jews and Syrians, Christ is the power of God and the wisdom of God.

25 Because the foolishness of God is wiser than men; and the weakness of God is stronger than men.

26 For consider also your own calling, my brethren, not many among you are wise in terms of worldly things, and not many among you are mighty, and not many among you belong to the nobility.

27 But God has chosen the foolish ones of the world to put the wise to shame; and God has chosen the weak ones of the world to embarrass the mighty;

28 And he has chosen those of humble families in the world, and the lowly, and those who are insignificant, in order to belittle those who consider themselves important,

29 So that no man should boast in his presence.

30 But you also belong to God through Jesus Christ who, from God, is wisdom and righteousness and sanctification, and salvation to all of us.

31 As it is written, He who glories, let him glory in the LORD.

CHAPTER 2

AND I, my brethren, when I came to you, did not come with excellency of speech, nor did I preach to you with learning the mystery of God.

2 For I did not pretend to know anything among you, except Jesus Christ, and even him crucified.

3 And I was with you with much reverence for God and in trembling.

4 And my speech and my preaching was not with enticing words of wisdom, but in demonstration of the Spirit and of power,

5 So that your faith might not rest in the wisdom of men, but in the power of God.

6 Howbeit we do discuss wisdom with those who have comprehension, yet not the wisdom of this world, nor of the rulers of this world who pass away:

7 But we discuss the wisdom of God shown in a mysterious way, and it is hidden, but which God ordained before the world for our glory:

8 Which none of the rulers of the world knew: for had they known it, they would not have crucified the LORD of glory.

9 But as it is written, The eye has not seen, and the ear has not heard, and the heart of man has not conceived the things which God has prepared for those who love him.

10 But God has revealed them to us by his Spirit: for the Spirit searches everything, even the depths of God.

11 For what man knows the mind of man, save the spirit of man which is in him? even so, no man knows the mind of God, except the Spirit of God.

12 Now we have received not the spirit of the world, but the spirit that is from God, that we may understand the gifts that are given to us by God.

13 For the things which we discuss are not dependent on the knowledge of words and man's wisdom, but on the teaching of the

---

* 1 Co.1:22-23 - "The Jews at this time were still expecting a Messiah to perform great wonders and to establish the Davidic kingdom forever. Thus the preaching of the restoration and salvation through a crucified man...was a stumbling block...To [the Syrians] death was the end. When a prophet or leader died, his mission died with him". - Lamsa, *NT Commentary*, pp.233-234.

      Cf.dif. vv. 1:22, 26-28, 30;   2:1-2, 6-7, 11-13.

Spirit; thus explaining spiritual things to the spiritually minded.

14 For the material man rejects spiritual things, for they are foolishness to him: neither can he know them, because they are spiritually discerned.

15 But the spiritual man discerns every thing, and yet no man can discern him.

16 For who knows the mind of the LORD, that he may teach it? But we have the perception of Christ.

CHAPTER 3

SO I, my brethren, could not converse with you as with spiritual men, but as with worldly men and even as with little children in Christ.

2 I have fed you with milk, and not with meat: for hitherto you were unable to eat it, and even now you are not ready for it;

3 Because you are still worldly: for as long as there is among you envying and strife and divisions, are you not worldly and still following after the material things?

4 For while one says, I am a follower of Paul; and another, I am a follower of Apollos; are you not worldly?

5 ¶ Who then is Paul, and who is Apollos, but ministers through whom you were converted; each one is gifted according as the LORD gave to him.

6 I have planted, Apollos watered; but God gave the increase.

7 So then neither he who plants, nor he who waters deserves the credit; but God who gives the increase.

8 Thus the planter and the waterer are equal: and each one shall receive his own wages according to his own labor.

9 For we work together with God: you are God's work and God's building.

10 According to the grace of God which is given to me, as a wise masterbuilder, I have laid the foundation, and another builds upon it. But let every man be careful how he builds thereon.

11 For other foundation can no man lay than that which is already laid, which is Jesus Christ.

12 Now if any man build on this foundation gold, silver, or precious stones, or wood, or hay, or stubble;

13 Every man's work shall be plainly seen: for the light of day shall expose it, because it shall be revealed by fire; and the fire shall test every man's work and show of what sort it is.

14 And the builder whose work survives shall receive his reward.

15 And the one whose work shall be burned, he shall suffer loss: but he himself shall be rescued, even as one who has been saved from the fire.

16 Do you not know that you are the temple of God, and that the Spirit of God dwells in you?

17 And whoever defiles the temple of God, God will destroy; for the temple of God is holy, and that temple is you.

18 ¶ Let no man deceive himself. Whoever among you thinks he is wise in this world, let him consider himself a fool so that he may become wise.

19 For the wisdom of this world is foolishness before God. For it is written, He catches the wise in their own craftiness.

20 And again, The LORD knows that the thoughts of the wise are vain.

21 Therefore, let no man boast about men. For all things are yours;

22 Whether Paul, or Apollos, or Cephas, or the world, or life, or death, or things present, or things to come; all things are yours;

23 And you are of Christ, and Christ is of God.

Cf.dif. vv. 2:14-16;   3:3, 5, 13-14, 17-18, 21, 23.

CHAPTER 4

THIS is the way you should consider us: as the servants of Christ, and stewards of the mysteries of God.

2 Henceforth it is required of stewards, that every one of them must be faithful.

3 But as for me, it is of little importance that I am judged by you or by any one else: because I do not judge myself.

4 For I know nothing of which I am guilty; yet I may not be right in this, for my judge is the LORD.

5 Therefore do not judge before the time, until the LORD comes, and brings to light the hidden things of darkness, and reveals the thoughts of the hearts; then shall every man have praise from God.

6 ¶ These things, my brethren, concerning myself and Apollos I have pictured for your sakes; that in our example you may learn not to think beyond that which is written, and let no one exalt himself over his fellow man, on account of any man.

7 For who has inquired into you? And what do you have which was not given to you? and if you did receive it, then why do you boast, as if you had not received it?

8 ¶ For a long time you have been full and enriched, and you have waxed strong without our counsel. And I would to God you were as kings, so that we also might share with you.

9 For I think God has placed us, the apostles, last as if we were condemned to death: for we have become a spectacle to the world, and to angels, and to men.

10 We are fools for Christ's sake, but you are wise in Christ; we are weak, but you are strong; you are praised, but we are despised.

11 Even to this very hour we both hunger and thirst, and are naked and mistreated and have no permanent home;

12 And labor, working with our own hands: being cursed we bless, being persecuted, we endure it;

13 Being reviled, we intreat;: we are looked upon as the refuse of the world, and we are the revilement of every man to this day.

14 I do not write these things to make you feel ashamed, but to advise you as beloved children.

15 For though you have ten thousand instructors in Christ, yet you will have not many fathers: for in Jesus Christ I have begotten you through the gospel.

16 I beseech you therefore, to follow me.

17 This is why I have sent Ti-mo'the-us to you, who is my beloved son and faithful in the LORD, who shall remind you of my manner of life in Christ, just as I teach in all the churches.

18 There are some among you who are puffed up, thinking I am unwilling to come to you.

19 But I will come to you very soon, if the LORD wills, and then I shall find out not the words of these men who exalt themselves, but their power.

20 For the kingdom of God is not in the word, but in power.

21 Now what do you desire? Shall I come to you with a rod, or with love and in the spirit of meekness?

CHAPTER 5

IT is reported that immorality is common among you, and such immorality as is not known among pagans, that even a

---

* 1 Co.5:1 - "Where polygamy is still practiced, it is not unusual for a son to fall in love and marry one of his father's wives [cf. Reuben, Gen.35:22; Absalom, 2 Sam.16:21f.; Adonijah, I Kings 2:17]...But such practices among the Jews were a violation of the law and were severely punished." -Lamsa, *NT Commentary*, p.244)

     Cf.dif. vv. 4:1, 3-8, 13-14, 17-19;   5:1.

son should marry his father's wife. *

2 But instead of boasting as you have, rather had you sat down mourning that he who has done this deed has not been removed from among you.

3 For while I am far away from you in body, yet I am near you in spirit, and I have already judged, as though I were present, him who has done this deed.

4 In the name of our LORD Jesus Christ, gather together, and I will be with you in spirit and with the power of our LORD Jesus Christ;

5 So that you shall deliver this man to Satan for the destruction of his body, in order that the spirit may be saved in the day of our LORD Jesus Christ.

6 Your boasting is not good. Do you not know that a little leaven will leaven the whole lump?

7 Clean out therefore the old leaven, so that you may be a new lump, just as you are unleavened. For our passover is Christ who was sacrificed for our sake.

8 Therefore let us celebrate the festival, not with the old leaven, neither with the leaven of evil and bitterness, but with the leaven of purity and sanctity.

9 I wrote to you in an epistle not to associate with immoral persons.

10 I do not mean that you should separate completely from all the immoral people of this world, or from the fraudulent and extortioners, or from idolaters; otherwise you would be obliged to leave this world.

11 Now what I have written to you is this: you are not to associate with any person who is known as a brother and yet is immoral or fraudulent or an idolater or a railer or a drunkard or an extortioner; with such a person you must not break bread.

12 For what business have I to judge those who are outside the church? But you may

judge those who are within the church.

13 God will judge the outsiders. Therefore, put away from among yourselves those wicked persons.

CHAPTER 6

WOULD any of you, having a lawsuit against his brother, dare to go to trial before the wicked rather than before the saints?

2 Do you not know that the saints shall judge the world? and if the world is to be judged by you, are you not worthy to judge small affairs?

3 Do you not know that we are to judge angels? How much more then should we judge those who belong to this world?

4 You have worldly affairs to be settled, and yet you have put men of bad reputation in the church on the judgment seat.

5 I say this to you to make you feel ashamed. Is it so, that there is not a single wise man among you, who could settle a dispute between a brother and his brother?

6 But brother goes to court against brother, and at that before unbelievers.

7 Now therefore you are already at fault because you go to court one with another. Why not rather suffer wrong? Why not rather let yourselves be defrauded?

8 No, you yourselves do wrong, and defraud even your brethren.

9 ¶ Do you not know that the wicked shall not inherit the kingdom of God? Be not misled: neither the immoral, nor idolaters, nor adulterers, nor the corrupt, nor men who lie down with males,

10 Nor extortioners, nor thieves, nor drunkards, nor railers, nor grafters, shall inherit the kingdom of God.

11 And some of these evils were to be found in some of you, but you have been cleansed, and have been sanctified, and made righteous

Cf.dif. vv. 5:2-4, 8, 10;   6:1, 3-5, 9.

in the name of our LORD Jesus Christ, and through the Spirit of our God.

12 All things are lawful for me, but all things are not advisable for me: indeed all things are lawful for me but I will not be brought under the power of any.

13 Food is for the belly, and the belly for food: but God will do away with both of them. Now the body is not meant for fornication, but for our LORD; and our LORD for the body.

14 ¶ And as God has raised our LORD, so he will raise us also by his own power.

15 Do you not know that your bodies are the members of Christ? How then can one take a member of Christ and make it the member of a harlot? Far be it.

16 Or do you not know that he who joins his body to a harlot is one body with her? For it is said, The two shall become one body.

17 But he who unites himself with our LORD becomes one with him in spirit.

18 Keep away from fornication. Every sin that a man commits, is outside his body; but he who commits adultery sins against his own body.

19 Or do you not know that your body is the temple of the Holy Spirit that dwells within you, which you have of God, and you are not your own?

20 For you have been bought with a price: therefore glorify God in your body, and in your spirit, because they belong to God.

CHAPTER 7

*N*OW concerning the things which you wrote to me: It is proper for a husband not to have intimacy with his wife at times.

2 Nevertheless, because of the danger of immorality, let every man cling to his own wife, and let every woman cling to her own husband.

3 Let the husband give to his wife the love which he owes her; and likewise also the wife to her husband.

4 The wife has no authority over her own body, but her husband; and likewise also the husband has no authority over his own body, but his wife.

5 Therefore do not deprive one another except when both of you consent to do so, especially at the time when you devote yourselves to fasting and prayer; and then come together again, so that Satan may not tempt you because of your physical passion.

6 But I say this only to weak persons, for it is not part of the law.

7 For I would that all men were like myself in purity. But every man has his proper gift from God, one after this manner, and another after that.

8 I say this to those who have no wives and to widows, It is better for them to be as I am;

9 But if they cannot endure it, let them marry; for it is better to marry than to burn with passion.

10 But those who have wives, I command, yet not I, but my LORD, Let not the wife be separated from her husband;

11 But if she separate, let her remain single, or be reconciled to her husband; and let not the husband desert his wife.

12 But to the rest, I say this, not my LORD: If any brother has a wife who is not a convert, and she wishes to live with him, let him not leave her.

13 And the woman who has a husband who is not a convert but is content to live with her, let her not leave him.

14 For the husband who is not a convert is sanctified through the wife who is a convert, and the wife who is not a convert is sanctified through the husband who is a convert; otherwise, their children would be impure, but in such cases they are pure.

    Cf.dif. vv. 6:13, 15; 7:1-3, 5-7, 9, 11, 14.

15 But if the one who is not a convert wishes to separate, let him separate. In such cases, a convert man or woman is free; for God has called us to live in peace.

16 For how do you know, O wife, that you shall save your husband? Or how do you know, O husband, that you shall save your wife?

17 But every man, according as the LORD has distributed to him, and every man, as God has called him, so let him walk. And this I command also for all the churches.

18 If a man was circumcised when he was called, let him not adhere to the party of uncircumcision. And if he was uncircumcised, when he was called, let him not be circumcised.

19 For circumcision is nothing, and uncircumcision is nothing, but the keeping of the LORD's commandments is everything.

20 Let every man remain in the station of life in which he is called.

21 If you were a slave when you were called, do not feel concerned about it; but even though you can be made free, choose rather to serve.

22 For he who is called by our LORD, being a slave, is God's free man; likewise he who is called, being a freeman, is also Christ's servant.

23 You have been bought with a price; you must not therefore become slaves of men.

24 My brethren, let every man in whatever station of life he was called, remain therein, serving God.

25 ¶ Now concerning virginity, I have no command from God; yet I give my advice as one who has been favored by God to be trustworthy.

26 And I suppose that this is good for the present necessity, therefore I say, It is better for a man to remain as he is.

27 If you are married, do not seek divorce. If you are divorced from a wife, do not seek a wife.

28 But if you marry, you do not sin; and if a virgin marry, she does not sin. Nevertheless such shall have trouble in the flesh: but I spare you.

29 But this I do say, my brethren, the time is short; let those who have wives be as though they had none;

30 And those who weep, as though they had not wept; and those who rejoice, as though they had not rejoiced; and those who buy, as though they did not possess anything;

31 And those who make use of this world should not abuse it, for the fashion of this world is passing away.

32 Therefore I would that you were free from worldly cares. For he who is unmarried, is concerned in the things of his master, so as to please his master.

33 And he who is married is concerned with worldly things, in order to please his wife.

34 So there is a difference between a married woman and a virgin. She who is unmarried is concerned about the welfare of her father, and to be pure both in body and in spirit; but she who is married is concerned with worldly things, in order to please her husband.

35 I am saying this for your own benefit; I am not trying to snare or put a yoke on you, but I exhort you to be perfect before the LORD, and faithful without distraction.

36 If any man thinks that he is shamed by the behavior of his virgin daughter, because she has passed the marriage age, and he has not given her in marriage, and that he should give her, let him give her in marriage and he does not sin. Let her be married.

37 Nevertheless, he who has sincerely decided, and who is not forced by circumstances, but has determined and decreed in his heart to keep his virgin daughter single, he does well.

Cf.dif. vv. 7:15, 18, 20-28, 32, 34-37.

38 So then he who gives his virgin daughter in marriage does well; and he who does not give his virgin daughter in marriage does even better.

39 ¶ A wife is bound by the law, as long as her husband lives; but if her husband dies, she is free to marry whom she pleases, but only in our LORD.

40 But in my opinion, she is happier to remain as she is. And I think also that I have the Spirit of God.

CHAPTER 8

*N*OW as concerning sacrifices offered to idols, we know well, that we all have knowledge; knowledge makes for pride, but love ennobles.

2 And if any man thinks that, of himself, he knows any thing, he knows nothing yet as he ought to know it.

3 But if any man loves God, the same is known of him.

4 As concerning the eating of the food offered to idols, we know that an idol is nothing in the world, and that there is no other God but one.

5 For though there are those that are called gods, whether in heaven or earth, just as there are many gods and many lords,

6 To us there is one God, the Father, from whom comes every thing and by whom we live; and one LORD Jesus Christ, by whom are all things, and we by him.

7 Howbeit there is not in every man that knowledge: for some with clear conscience eat that which has been offered to idols as a sacrifice; and their conscience being weak is defiled.

8 But meat does not bring us closer to God: for neither, if we eat, are we the better; neither if we do not eat, are we the worse.

9 But be careful lest this liberty of yours become a stumbling block to the weak.

10 For if any one should see you, who has knowledge, at table in the temple of idols, shall not the conscience of him who is weak encourage him to eat that which is sacrificed to idols?

11 So the one who is weak and for whom Christ died will be lost through your indifference.

12 And if you offend your brothers, and so influence their weak conscience, you also offend Christ.

13 Therefore if meat causes my brother to stumble, I will eat no meat, so that I may not cause my brother to offend.

CHAPTER 9

*A*M I not a free man? am I not an apostle? have I not seen Jesus Christ our LORD? are you not my work in my LORD?

2 If I am not an apostle to others, yet to you I am: for you are the seal of my apostleship.

3 So my answer to those who criticize me is this,

4 Have we not the right to eat and to drink?

5 And have we not the right to travel with a Christian wife, just as the rest of the apostles, and as the brothers of our LORD, and as Cephas?

6 Or only I and Barnabas, have not we the right to live without working?

7 What officer commands an army at his own expense? or who plants a vineyard and does not eat of its fruits? or who feeds sheep, and does not eat of the milk of his flock?

8 I say these things as a man. Behold the law says them also.

9 For it is written in the law of Moses, Thou shalt not muzzle the ox that treadeth out the corn. Why? Is God concerned only for the ox?

10 No. It is known that he said it for our sakes and it was written for our sakes because

the ploughman must plough in hope, and he who threshes, threshes in hope of the crop.

11 Now if we have sown among you spiritual things, is it too much that we should reap material things from you?

12 If others have this authority over you, have we not the more right? Nevertheless we have not used this authority; but we have endured all things so that we would not hinder the gospel of Christ.

13 Do you not know that those who work in the holy place are maintained out of the temple? And those who minister at the altar share the offerings with the altar?

14 Even so has our LORD commanded that those who preach his gospel should live by his gospel.

15 But I have used none of these privileges: neither have I written these things that it should be so done to me: for it were better for me to die, than that any man should declare my pride in my teaching worthless.

16 For though I preach the gospel, I have nothing to glory of: for I am under obligation; yea, woe is unto me if I preach not the gospel!

17 For if I do this thing willingly, I have my reward: but if against my will, it is like a stewardship intrusted to me.

18 What then is my wage? This is it. When I preach the gospel of Jesus Christ, I do it without thought of recompense, and I have not abused the power given to me in the gospel.

19 Because I am free from all these things, I have served all men that I may gain many.

20 So with the Jews I became as a Jew, that I might win the Jews; and with those who are under the law, I became as one who is under the law, in order to win those who are under the law.

21 To those who are without law, I became like one who is without law, though I am not lawless before God because I am under the law of Christ, that I might win them who are without law.

22 With the weak I became as weak, that I might win the weak: I became everything to every man, that I might by all means save everyone.

23 And this I do for the gospel's sake, that I might be partaker of it.

24 Do you not know that the runners in a race, all run, but only one is victorious? So you must run, that you may obtain victory.

25 And every man who battles in the contest, frees his mind from every thing else. And yet they run to win a garland which is perishable; but we to win one which is everlasting.

26 I therefore so run, not for something that is uncertain; and I so fight, not as one who beats the air:

27 But I conquer and subdue my body so that, by no chance, when I have preached to others, will I despise myself.

CHAPTER 10

MOREOVER, brethren, I want you to know, that our fathers were all under the cloud, and all passed through the sea;

2 And all were baptized by Moses, both in the cloud and in the sea;

3 And all ate the same spiritual food;

4 And all drank the same spiritual drink: for they drank of that spiritual Rock that followed them: and that Rock was Christ.

5 But with many of them God was not well pleased; for they were smitten in the wilderness.

6 But they became an example to us, so that we should not covet evil things as they did covet.

7 Neither should we become idolaters as were some of them; as it is written, The

people sat down to eat and drink, and rose up to quarrel.

8 Neither should we commit adultery, as some of them committed, for in one day twenty-three thousand of them fell dead.

9 Neither should we tempt Christ, as some of them tempted; for they were destroyed by snakes.

10 Neither should you murmur, as some of them murmured; for they were destroyed by the hand of the destroyer.

11 Now all of these things which happened to them are an example for us: and they are written for our admonition, for the world will come to an end in our day.

12 Therefore, let him who thinks he can stand, take heed so that he may not fall.

13 No other temptation has overtaken you but that which is common to man: but God is faithful; he will not suffer you to be tempted beyond that you are able; but will make your temptation to have a way of escape, so that you may be able to bear it.

14 Therefore, my beloved, keep away from idolatry.

15 I speak as to wise men: you are able to judge what I say.

16 The cup of thanksgiving which we bless, is it not the communion of the blood of Christ? The bread which we break, is it not the communion of the body of Christ?

17 For just as the loaf of bread is one, so we are all one body; for we are all partakers of that one bread.

18 Behold Israel whose observance is after the flesh: do not those who eat the sacrifices become partakers of the altar?

19 What do I say then? that the idol is anything, or that the sacrifice to idols is anything? No.

20 But that which the pagans sacrifice, they sacrifice to devils and not to God: and I would not have you in fellowship with devils.

21 You cannot drink the cup of our LORD, and the cup of devils: you cannot be partakers of the table of our LORD and of the table of devils.

22 Are we trying to provoke our LORD to jealousy? are we stronger than he?

23 ¶ Everything is lawful for me, but not everything is expedient: everything is lawful for me, but everything does not edify.

24 But let no man seek for himself alone, but let every man seek for his neighbor also.

25 Anything for sale in the market place, that eat without question for conscience sake:

26 For the earth is the LORD's and the fulness thereof.

27 If any pagan invite you, and you wish to go, whatever is set before you eat, without question for conscience sake.

28 But if any man say to you, This meat has been offered as a sacrifice, then do not eat it for the sake of him who told you and for conscience sake.

29 But the conscience of which I speak, is not yours, but the conscience of him who told you: for why is my liberty judged by another man's conscience?

30 For if I by grace am made worthy why should I be reproached for that for which I give thanks?

31 Whether therefore you eat or drink, or whatsoever you do, do all to the glory of God.

32 Give no offence, neither to the Jews, nor to the Syrians, nor to the church of God;

33 Just as I please all men in all things, not seeking my own good, but the good of many, that they may be saved.

CHAPTER 11

*T*AKE example by me, even as I also follow Christ.

2 Now I praise you, my brethren, that you remember me in all things, and keep the ordinances as I delivered them to you.

3 But I would have you know, that the head of every man is Christ; and the head of the wife is her husband; and the head of Christ is God.

4 Every man who prays or prophesies, having his head covered, dishonors his head.

5 And every woman who prays or prophesies with her head uncovered, dishonors her head: for she is equal to her whose head is shaven.

6 For if a woman does not cover her head, let her also cut off her hair; but if it be a shame for a woman to be shorn or shaven, let her cover her head. *

7 For a man indeed ought not cover his head, because he is the image and glory of God, but the woman is the glory of the man.

8 For the man was not created from the woman; but the woman was created from the man.

9 Neither was the man created for the woman; but the woman for the man.

10 For this reason the woman ought to be modest and cover her head, as a mark of respect to the angels.

11 Nevertheless, in our LORD, there is no preference between man and woman, neither between woman and man.

12 For as the woman is of the man, even so is the man also by the woman; but all things of God.

13 Judge for yourselves, Is it comely for a woman to pray to God with uncovered head?

14 Does not even nature itself teach you, that if a man have long hair, it is a disgrace to him?

15 But if a woman have long hair, it is a glory to her: for her hair is given her for a covering.

16 But if any man dispute these things, we have no precedent, neither has the church of God.

17 ¶ Now I give you these commands, not to praise you, for you have not made progress but have become worse.

18 First of all, when you gather in the church, I hear that there are divisions among you; and I partly believe it.

19 For controversies are bound to be among you, that those who are approved may be made manifest among you.

20 When you gather together therefore, you do not eat and drink as is appropriate on the day of our LORD.

21 But some men eat their supper before others: and so it happens that one is hungry and another is drunken.

22 Why? Have you not houses to eat and drink in? or do you not respect the church of God, and want to shame those who have nothing? What shall I say to you? Shall I praise you? No, for this, I cannot praise you.#

23 For I myself received from our LORD that which I also delivered to you, That our LORD Jesus on that very night in which he was betrayed took bread:

24 And when he had given thanks, he broke it and said, Take, eat; this is my body, which is broken for you: this do in remembrance of me.

25 Likewise after supper, he gave also the cup, and said, This cup is the new testament in my blood: do this, as often as you drink it, in remembrance of me.

26 For whenever you eat this bread and drink this cup, you commemorate our LORD's

---

* 1 Co.11:5-6- "Covering of women's faces is an old established Eastern custom that is still observed in Palestine, Syria and other parts of the Near East where Moslem civilization predominates. " - Lamsa, NT Commentary, p.271.

1 Co.11:21-22 - "Paul warns the Corinthians against Christians eating excessively on such occasions...There were many men and women who ate to excess and became sick. This happened quite often when people were hungry and found abundant food to eat." - Ibid, p.275.

Cf.dif. vv. 11:5, 10-11, 17, 20.

death until he come.

27 Therefore whosoever shall eat of the LORD's bread, and drink of his cup unworthily, shall be guilty of the blood and body of the LORD.

28 For this reason, let a man examine himself, and so eat of this bread, and drink of this cup.

29 For he who eats and drinks unworthily, eats and drinks to his condemnation; for he does not discern the LORD's body.

30 This is the reason many are sick and ill among you, and many are dying.

31 For if we would judge ourselves, we would not be judged.

32 But when we are judged by our LORD, we are simply chastened, so that we may not be condemned with the world.

33 Hereafter, my brethren, when you come together to eat, wait for one another.

34 And if any man hunger, let him eat at home; so that you may not come together unto condemnation. As to the rest of the things I will instruct you when I come.

CHAPTER 12

*N*OW concerning spiritual gifts, my brethren, I want to remind you,

2 That once you were pagans, and without exception you were carried away by dumb idols.

3 Wherefore I want you to understand that no man, speaking by the Spirit of God, calls Jesus accursed: and that no man can say that Jesus is the LORD but by the Holy Spirit.

4 Now there are diversities of gifts, but there is only one Spirit.

5 And there are diversities of ministries, but there is only one LORD.

6 And there are diversities of powers, but it is the one God who works all things in all men.

7 But the manifestation of the Spirit is given to every man as help to him.

8 For to one is given by the Spirit the word of wisdom; to another the word of knowledge by the same Spirit.

9 To another faith by the same Spirit; to another gifts of healing by the same Spirit;

10 To another the working of miracles; to another prophecy; to another the means to distinguish the true Spirit; to another divers languages; to another the interpretation of languages.

11 But all of these gifts are wrought by that one and the same Spirit, dividing to every one severally as he will.

12 For as the body is one and has many members, and all the members of the body, even though many, are one body, so also is Christ.

13 For all of us are baptized by one Spirit into one body, whether Jews or Gentiles, whether bond or free; and we have all received through the one Spirit.

14 The body is not one member, but many.

15 For if the foot should say, Because I am not the hand, I am not a part of the body; is it therefore not a member of the body?

16 And if the ear should say, Because I am not the eye, I am not a part of the body; is it therefore not a member of the body?

17 If the whole body were eyes, where would hearing be? And if the whole were hearing, where would smelling be?

18 But now God has set every member in the body, as it has pleased him.

19 If they were all one member, where would the body be?

20 But now they are many members, yet but one body.

21 The eye cannot say to the hand, I have no need of you: nor can the head say to the feet, I have no need of you.

22 But rather those members of the body which are considered to be delicate are necessary.

23 And those members of the body, which we think to be less honorable, we bestow more abundant honor; and the parts that are uncomely, we dress with greater care.

24 For our comely parts have no need for attention: But God has so tempered the body together, and has given greater honor to the member which is inferior:

25 That there may be no discord in the body, but that they may care one for another, all members should be equal.

26 So when one member is in pain, all the members suffer with it; and if one member is honored, all the members will glory with it.

27 Now you are the body of Christ, and members in your respective places.

28 For God has set in his church, first apostles; after them, prophets; then teachers, then performers of miracles, then those who have the gift of healing, helpers, leaders, and speakers in diverse languages.

29 Are all apostles? Are all prophets? Are all teachers? Are all workers of miracles?

30 Have all the gifts of healing? Do all speak in diverse tongues? or do all interpret?

31 ¶ But if you are searching for the greater gifts, I will show you a more excellent way.

CHAPTER 13

THOUGH I speak with the tongues of men and of angels, and have not love in my heart, I am become as sounding brass, or a tinkling cymbal.

2 And though I have the gift of prophecy, and understand all mysteries, and all knowledge; and though I have all faith, so that I could remove mountains, and have not love in my heart, I am nothing.

3 And though I bestow all my goods to feed the poor, and though I give my body to be burned, and have not love in my heart, I gain nothing.

4 Love is long-suffering and is kind; love does not envy; love does not make a vain display of itself, and does not boast,

5 Does not behave itself unseemly, seeks not her own, is not easily provoked, thinks no evil;

6 Rejoices not over injustice, but rejoices in the truth;

7 Bears all things, believes all things, hopes all things, endures all things.

8 Love never fails: but whether there be prophecies, they shall fail; whether there be tongues, they shall cease; whether there be knowledge, it shall vanish away.

9 For we know in part, and we prophesy in part.

10 But when that which is perfect is come, then that which is imperfect shall be done away.

11 When I was a child, I spoke as a child, I understood as a child, I thought as a child: but when I became a man, I put away childish things.

12 For now we see through a glass, darkly; but then face to face: now I know in part; but then shall I know even as also I am known.

13 And now abides faith, hope, love, these three; but the greatest of these is love. *

CHAPTER 14

FOLLOW after love, and desire spiritual gifts, above all that you may prophesy.

2 For he who speaks in an unknown tongue speaks not to men, but to God; for no man understands what he says; however through the Spirit he speaks mysteries.

3 But he who prophesies speaks to men for

---

* 1 Co. 13:13 - Love/Charity: the universal love and good-will to the poor and suffering.

Cf.dif. vv. 12:24-26, 28, 31;   13:1, 4-6, 12;   14:1.

edification, encouragement, and comfort.

4 He who speaks in an unknown tongue edifies himself; but he who prophesies edifies the church.

5 I would that you all spoke various tongues, but I would rather that you prophesied: for he who prophesies is greater than he who speaks various tongues, unless he interpret; however, if he interpret it, he edifies the church.

6 Now, my brethren, if I should come to you and speak in diverse tongues, what would I profit you, except I speak to you either by means of revelation, or by knowledge, or by prophesying or by teaching?

7 For even when things without life, giving sound, whether flute or harp, except they make a distinction between one tone and another, how shall it be known what is sung or played?

8 For if the trumpet give an uncertain sound, who will prepare himself for the battle?

9 Even so you, except you utter by the tongue words easy to be understood, how shall it be known what you say? you shall speak as into the air.

10 For, behold, there are many kinds of speech in the world, yet none of them are without expression.

11 So if I do not understand the utterance, I shall be as a barbarian to the speaker, and the speaker shall be as a barbarian to me.

12 Likewise you, since you are zealous of spiritual gifts for the edification of the church, seek that you may excel in these gifts.

13 Thus he who speaks in an unknown tongue, pray that he may interpret it.

14 For if I pray in an unknown tongue, my spirit prays, but my knowledge is fruitless.

15 What then shall I do? I will pray with my spirit, and I will pray with my understanding also: I will sing with my spirit, and I will sing with my understanding also.

16 Otherwise, if you say a blessing with the spirit, how can one who occupies the place of the unlearned say Amen to your thanksgiving, since he does not understand what you say?

17 For indeed you bless well, but your fellow man is not enlightened.

18 I thank God, that I speak with tongues more than you all:

19 But in the church I had rather speak five words with my understanding, so that I might teach others also, than ten thousand words in an unknown tongue.

20 My brethren, be not like infants in your intelligence, only to evil things be like children, but in your understanding be mature.

21 In the law it is written, With a foreign speech, and in another tongue, I will speak to this people; yet for all that, they will not listen to me, says the LORD.

22 Thus, the gift of languages is instituted as a sign, not for believers, but for unbelievers: but prophesying is meant, not for those who do not believe, but for those who believe.

23 If therefore the whole church assembles together and all speak in different tongues and there enter unlearned people or unbelievers, will they not say, They are fanatical?

24 But if all prophesy, and an unlearned man or an unbeliever enter, he will be convinced by all, and he will be set right by all.

25 Thus the secrets of his heart will be revealed, and then he will fall on his face, and he will worship God and say, Truly God is among you.

26 Therefore I say to you, my brethren, when you gather together, whoever among you has a psalm to sing, has a doctrine, has a revelation, has the gift of tongues, or the gift of interpretation, let everything be done for edification.

27 And if any man should speak in an un-

known tongue, let two or at most three speak, and speak one by one; and let one interpret.
28 But if there is no one to interpret, let him who speaks in an unknown tongue keep silence in the church; and let him speak to himself and to God.
29 Let the prophets speak two or three in turn, and let the others discern what is said.
30 And if anything is revealed to another who is seated, let the first speaker hold his peace.
31 For you may all prophesy one by one, so that every one may learn, and every one be comforted.
32 For the spirits of the prophets are subject to the prophets.
33 For God is not a God of confusion but of peace, and he is in all churches of the saints.
34 ¶ Let your women keep silent in the church for they have no permission to speak; but they are to be under obedience as is said in the law.
35 And if they wish to learn anything, let them ask their husbands at home; for it is a shame for women to speak in the church.
36 What? Did the word of God come from you? or did it come for you only?
37 If any one among you thinks he is a prophet, or that he is inspired by the Spirit, let him acknowledge that these things that I write to you are the commandments of our LORD.
38 But if any man be ignorant, let him be ignorant.
39 Therefore, my brethren, desire earnestly to prophesy, and do not prohibit speaking in unknown tongues.
40 Let all things be done decently and in order.

CHAPTER 15

MOREOVER, my brethren, I declare to you the gospel which I preached to you, and which you have accepted, and for which you have stood firm;
2 By which also you are saved if you keep in remembrance that very word which I have preached to you, and if your conversion has not been in vain.
3 For I delivered to you first of all that which I had also received, that Christ died for our sins according to the scriptures;
4 And that he was buried, and that he rose again on the third day according to the scriptures:
5 And that he appeared to Cephas, then to the twelve:
6 After that, he appeared to more than five hundred brethren at once; of whom a great many are still living though some are dead.
7 And after that, he appeared to James; then to all the apostles.
8 And last of all he appeared to me also, ignorant and imperfectly developed as I was.
9 For I am the least of the apostles, and I am not worthy to be called an apostle, because I persecuted the church of God.
10 But by the grace of God I am what I am: and his grace that is in me has not been in vain; for I labored more abundantly than them all: yet not I, but God's grace that is within me.
11 Therefore whether it were I or they, so we preached and so you believed.
12 Now if it is preached that Christ rose from the dead, how can some say among you that there is no resurrection of the dead?
13 And if there is no resurrection of the dead, then Christ also has not risen:
14 And if Christ is not risen, then is our preaching in vain, and your faith is also in vain;
15 And we are also found false witnesses of God; because we have testified of God that he raised up Christ when he had not raised him.
16 For if the dead rise not, then neither did Christ rise:

Cf.dif. vv. 14:29, 34, 37-38;   15:2, 6, 8-9.

17 And if Christ did not rise, your belief is in vain; and you are yet in your sins.

18 And also, then, those who have died in Christ have perished.

19 If in this life only we have hope in Christ, then we are of all men most miserable.

20 But now we know Christ is risen from the dead and become the first-fruits of those who have died.

21 For since by man came death, by man came also the resurrection of the dead.

22 For as in Adam all die, even so in Christ shall all be made alive.

23 But every man in his own order: Christ the first-fruits; afterward they who belong to Christ at his coming.

24 Then will come the end, when he shall have delivered up the kingdom to God, even the Father; when he shall have put down all rule, and all authority, and power.

25 For he must reign till he has put all enemies under his feet.

26 And the last enemy that shall be destroyed is death.

27 For he has put all things under his feet. But when he said all things are put under him, it is clear that he, who put all things under him, is excepted.

28 And when all things shall be subdued unto him, then shall the Son also himself be subject unto him who put all things under him, so that God may be all in all.

29 Else, what shall they do who are baptized for the dead, if the dead rise not at all? Why are they then baptized for the dead?

30 And why do we continue to stand in danger every hour?

31 I swear by your pride, my brethren, which I have in our LORD Jesus Christ, I die daily.

32 If, after the manner of men, I were thrown to wild beasts at Eph'e-sus, what good would come to me, if the dead rise not? Let us eat and drink for tomorrow we die.

33 Do not be deceived: evil communications corrupt good manners.

34 Awake your hearts to righteousness and sin not; for some have not the knowledge of God: I say this to your shame.

35 ¶ But some of you will say, How are the dead raised up? And with what body do they come?

36 Thou fool, the seed which you sow, is not quickened, except it die.

37 And that which you sow is not the body that shall be, but the bare grain; it may chance to be of wheat or barley, or some other seed.

38 But God gives it a body as it has pleased him, and to every seed, its own natural body.

39 All flesh is not the same flesh: but there is one kind of flesh of men, another flesh of beasts, another of birds, and another of fishes.

40 There are also celestial bodies and bodies terrestrial: but the glory of the celestial is one, and the glory of the terrestrial is another.

41 There is one glory of the sun, and another glory of the moon, and another glory of the stars: for one star differs from another star in glory.

42 So also is the resurrection of the dead. It is sown in corruption; it is raised in incorruption:

43 It is sown in dishonor; it is raised in glory: it is sown in weakness; it is raised in power:

44 It is sown a natural body; it is raised a spiritual body. There is a natural body, and there is a spiritual body.

45 And so it is written, The first man Adam was made a living soul; the last Adam was made a quickening spirit.

46 Howbeit, that was not first which is spiritual, but that which is natural; and afterward that which is spiritual.

47 The first man is of the earth, earthy: the second man is the LORD from heaven.

48 As is the earthy, such are they also that are earthy: and as is the heavenly, such are

they also that are heavenly.

49 And as we have borne the image of the earthy we shall also bear the image of the heavenly.

50 Now this I say, my brethren, that flesh and blood cannot inherit the kingdom of God; neither does corruption inherit incorruption.

51 Behold, I tell you a mystery; We shall not all die, but we shall all be changed,

52 In a moment, in the twinkling of an eye, at the last trump: for the trumpet shall sound, and the dead shall be raised incorruptible, and we shall be changed.

53 For this corruptible must put on incorruption, and this mortal must put on immortality.

54 So when this corruptible shall have put on incorruption, and this mortal shall have put on immortality, then shall be brought to pass the saying that is written, Death is swallowed up in victory.

55 ¶ O death, where is your sting? O grave, where is your victory?

56 The sting of death is sin; and the strength of sin is the law.

57 But thanks be to God, who has given us the victory through our LORD Jesus Christ.

58 Therefore, my beloved brethren, be steadfast, unmoveable, always abounding in the work of the LORD, for as much as you know that your labor is not in vain in the LORD.

CHAPTER 16

NOW concerning the collection for the saints, as I have given order to the churches of Galatia, likewise do you also.

2 Upon the first day of every week, let each of you put aside and keep in his house whatever he can afford, so that there may be no collections when I come.

3 And when I come, whomsoever you may select, I will send with a letter, to carry your gracious gift to Jerusalem.

4 And if it is right that I go also, they shall go with me.

5 I will come to you, when I pass through Mac-e-do'ni-a ; for I do pass through Mac-e-do'ni-a .

6 And perhaps I will remain some time with you, or pass the winter with you, so that you may escort me withersoever I go.

7 For I do not want to see you now just as a wayfarer; because I trust to tarry for a time with you, if my LORD permit me.

8 But I will tarry at Eph'e-sus until Pentecost.

9 For a great door, full of opportunities, is opened to me, and adversaries are many.

10 ¶ Now if Ti-mo'the-us come, see that he may be with you without fear: for he is engaged in the LORD's work, just as I am.

11 Let no man therefore despise him: but escort him in peace, that he may come to me: for I wait for him with the brethren.

12 My brethren, as for Apollos, I have often begged him to visit you with the brethren: probably it was not intended that he should come to you; but he will come to you when he has an opportunity.

13 Watch, stand firm in the faith, quit you like men, be valiant, be strong.

14 Let all your deeds be done with love.

15 I beseech you, my brethren, concerning the household of Stephanas, for you know that they were the first converts from A-cha'ia and that they have devoted themselves to the ministry of the saints,

16 That you may listen to all those who are as they are, and to every one who labors with us and is of help.

17 I am glad of the coming of Stephanas and Fortunatus and Achaicus: for that which was lacking on your part, they have supplied.

18 For they have refreshed my spirit as well as yours: therefore recognize them who are

Cf.dif. vv. 15:49-50, 55;   16:1-4, 7, 9, 12-13, 15, 16.

similar.

19 ¶ All the churches of Asia Minor salute you. Aquila and Priscilla salute you much in our LORD, with the congregation that meets in their house.

20 All the brethren greet you. Greet one another with a holy kiss.

21 ¶ This salutation is from me, Paul, in my own handwriting.

22 Whoever does not love our LORD Jesus Christ, let him be accursed. Maranatha, that is to say, our LORD has come.

23 The grace of our LORD Jesus Christ be with you.

24 My love be with you all in Christ Jesus. Amen.

Here ends the first epistle to the Corinthians, written at Philippi of Macedonia and sent by Stephanas and Fortunatus and Achaicus and Ti-mo'the-us.

ܫܠܡܬ ܐܓܪܬܐ ܕܠܘܬ ܩܘܪܢܬܝܐ ܩܕܡܝܬܐ܀
ܕܐܬܟܬܒܬ ܡܢ ܦܝܠܝܦܘܣ܀

Cf.dif. vv. 16:22.

THE SECOND EPISTLE OF PAUL THE APOSTLE TO THE
CORINTHIANS

❖ ܦܘܠܘܣ ܕܠܘܬ ܩܘܪܝܢܬܝܐ ܕܬܪܬܝܢ ❖

CHAPTER 1

*P*AUL, an apostle of Jesus Christ by the will of God, and Ti-mo'the-us our brother, unto the church of God which is at Corinth, with all the saints who are in all A-cha'ia:

2 Grace be to you and peace from God our Father, and from our LORD Jesus Christ.

3 ¶ Blessed be God, even the Father of our LORD Jesus Christ, the Father of mercies and the God of all comfort;

4 Who comforts us in all our troubles, so that we also may be able to comfort those who are in any trouble, by the very comfort with which we ourselves are comforted by God.

5 For as the sufferings of Christ abound in us, so our consolation also abounds in Christ.

6 Even though we are oppressed, it is for the sake of your consolation and for the sake of your salvation that we are oppressed; and if we are comforted, it is so that you might be comforted also; to be strength in you that you may be able to bear these sufferings, the same which we also suffer.

7 And our hope concerning you is steadfast, for we know that if you are partakers of the sufferings, you are also partakers of the consolation.

8 For we would wish you to know, my brethren, about the trouble we had in Asia Minor, for we were greatly oppressed beyond our strength; insomuch that we despaired of our lives:

9 And we decided to die, not trusting in ourselves but in God who raises the dead:

10 Who delivered us from horrible deaths, and who will, we hope, again deliver us;

11 You also helping by your supplications for us, that for his gift bestowed upon us, by means of many persons, thanks may be given by many on our behalf.

12 ¶ For our joy is this, the testimony of our conscience, in sincerity and in purity with the grace of God, we have conducted ourselves in this world, and not through the wisdom of the flesh; and above all, we have so dealt with you.

13 For we write nothing to you except those things which you know and understand, and I trust you will understand them to the end;

14 Just as you have understood in part that we are your pride and joy, even as you also are ours in the day of our LORD Jesus Christ.

15 ¶ And in this confidence I wished to come to you before, that you might receive grace doubly;

16 And to pass by you on my way to Mac-e-do'ni-a , and again to come back to you from Mac-e-do'ni-a , so that you may wish me Godspeed on my way to Judæa.

17 When I, therefore, was considering this, did I consider it lightly or are the things which I am considering wholly worldly? Because they should have been either yes, yes, or no, no.

18 But as God is true, our word to you was not yes and no.

19 For the Son of God, Jesus Christ, who was preached among you by us, even by me and Silvanus and Ti-mo'the-us, was not yes and no, but with him always yes.

20 For all the promises of God were in Christ, yes; therefore by his hand, we are given Amen to the glory of God.

21 Now it is God who has confirmed us with you in Christ, and who has anointed us;

22 And who has sealed us, and pledged his spirit in our hearts.

23 Moreover I testify to God concerning myself, that it was because I wanted to spare you, that I did not come to Corinth.

24 Not that we are the masters of your faith, but we are helpers of your joy; for by faith you stand.

CHAPTER 2

BUT I determined this with myself, that I would not come again to you in sadness. 2 For if I make you sad, who can make me happy, but him whom I made sad?

3 And I wrote this same thing to you, so that when I come to you I may not be made sad by those who ought to make me joyful; having confidence in you all, that my joy is the joy of you all.

4 For out of great affliction and anguish of heart, I wrote you with many tears; not to make you feel distressed, but that you may know the abundant love I have for you.

5 ¶ But if anyone has caused grief, he has not grieved me only, but to a certain degree all of you, therefore the news will not be a shock to you.

6 The rebuke of many persons is sufficient for such a man.

7 So that from henceforth you ought rather to forgive and comfort him, lest perhaps such a one will be overcome with overmuch grief.

8 I beseech you therefore that you confirm your love toward him.

9 For that is why I wrote you, that I might know by your word whether you are obedient in all things.

10 To whom you forgive anything, I forgive also; for anything which I have forgiven, to whomever I forgave it, it is for your sakes I forgave it in the presence of Christ:

11 Lest Satan might take advantage of us: for we know his devices.

12 ¶ Furthermore, when I came to Troas with the gospel of Christ, and a door was opened to me of the LORD,

13 I could not rest in my spirit, because I did not find Titus my brother; hence I took leave of them, and left for Mac-e-do'ni-a .

14 ¶ Now thanks be to God, who has made us in the pattern of Christ, and makes manifest the savour of his knowledge through us in every place.

15 For we are a sweet savour to God through Christ, in those who are saved and in those who perish:

16 To the one the savour of death unto death; and to the other the savour of life unto life. And who is worthy of these things?

17 For we are not like those who corrupt the word of God: but according to the truth, and as men of God we speak through Christ in the sight of God.

CHAPTER 3

DO we begin again to commend ourselves? Or do we need, as some other people, epistles of commendation concerning us written to you, or that you should write commending us?

2 You are our epistle written in our hearts, well-known and read by all men:

3 For you are known to be the epistle of Christ ministered by us, written not with ink, but with the spirit of the Living God; not on tablets of stone, but on tablets of the living heart.

4 Such is the trust that we have through Christ toward God.

5 Not that we are sufficient of ourselves to think anything as of ourselves; but our

strength comes from God,

6 Who has made us worthy to be ministers of the new covenant; not of the letter, but the Spirit: for the letter of the law punishes with death, but the Spirit gives life.

7 Now if the ministration of death, as contained in the letter of the law and engraved on stones, was so glorious that the children of Israel could not look at the face of Moses because of the glory of his countenance; which glory was not lasting:

8 Why then shall not the ministration of the Spirit be more glorious?

9 For if there be glory in the ministration of condemnation, much more will the ministration of righteousness exceed in glory.

10 Just as that which was not glorious became glorified, in comparison with that, this excels in glory.

11 For if that which was not lasting was glorious, much more glorious will that be which endures.

12 Seeing therefore that we have such hope, we conduct ourselves bravely:

13 And not as Moses who put a veil over his face, so that the children of Israel might not look upon the fulness of the glory which was not lasting:

14 But their minds were blinded: for to this day, when the Old Testament is read, the same veil rests over them, and it is not known to them that the veil has been removed through Christ.

15 But even unto this day, whenever the books of Moses are read, the veil is upon their hearts.

16 Nevertheless whenever a man turns to the LORD, the veil is taken away.

17 Now the LORD is that very Spirit: and where the Spirit of the LORD is, there is liberty.

18 But we all, with open faces, see as in a mirror the glory of the LORD, and we shall be transformed into the same likeness, from one glory to another, just as the Spirit comes from the LORD.

CHAPTER 4

FOR this reason we are not weary of the ministry in which we are engaged, just as we are not weary of the mercies that have been upon us;

2 But we have renounced the hidden things of shame, and we do not practice cunning, nor do we handle the word of God deceitfully, but by manifestation of the truth we commend ourselves to every man's conscience before God.

3 If our gospel is hidden, it is hidden to those who are lost:

4 To those in this world whose minds have been blinded by God, because they did not believe, lest the light of the glorious gospel of Christ, who is the likeness of God, should shine on them.

5 For we do not preach about ourselves, but about Christ Jesus our LORD; and as to ourselves, we are your servants for Jesus' sake.

6 For God, who said, Let light shine out of darkness, has shone in our hearts, so that we may be enlightened with the knowledge of the glory of God in the person of Christ.

7 But we have this treasure in earthen vessels, that the excellency of power may be from God, and not of us.

8 We are distressed in every way, but not overwhelmed; we are harassed on all sides, but not conquered;

9 Persecuted, but not forsaken; cast down, but not destroyed;

10 For we always bear in our bodies the death of Jesus, that the life of Jesus might also be made manifest in our bodies.

11 For if we who live are delivered to death for Jesus' sake, so also will the life of Jesus be made manifest in our mortal bodies.

Cf.dif. vv. 3:6-7, 9-15, 18;　　4:1, 4, 6, 8, 11.

12 Thus death is close to us, but life is nigh to you.

13 We have the same spirit of faith, as it is written, I believed, and therefore have I spoken; we also believe, therefore we also speak;

14 Knowing that he who raised our LORD Jesus shall raise us also by Jesus, and shall present us with you.

15 For all things are for your sakes that the abundant grace might, through the thanksgiving of many, redound to the glory of God.

16 ¶ For this reason, we do not grow weary; for though our outward man perish, yet the inner man is renewed day by day.

17 For while the troubles of the present time are little and light, a great and limitless glory for ever and ever is prepared for us.

18 We do not rejoice in the things which are seen, but in the things which are not seen, for the things which are seen are temporal; but the things which are not seen are eternal.

CHAPTER 5

FOR we know that if our earthly house were destroyed, we still have a building made by God, a house not made with hands, eternal in heaven.

2 We also weary over this earthly house, earnestly longing to use our house which is in heaven.

3 If not so, even when we are clothed, we will still be naked.

4 While we are in this earthly house, we groan because of its weight: yet we are unwilling to leave it, but rather wish to add to it, so that death will be overcome by life.

5 Now he who has prepared us for this very thing is God, who also has given to us the pledge of his Spirit.

6 Therefore we know and are convinced, that so long as we dwell in the body, we are absent from our LORD.

7 For we walk by faith, and not by sight.

8 This is why we are confident, and anxious to be absent from the body, and to be present with our LORD.

9 Wherefore we endeavor, that, whether present or absent, we may be pleasing to him.

10 For we must all stand before the judgment seat of Christ; that every one may be rewarded according to that which he has done with his body, whether it be good or bad.

11 ¶ Knowing therefore the fear of our LORD, we try in a persuasive way to win men; so we are very well understood by God; and I trust we are also understood by you.

12 We are not boasting of ourselves to you, but we give you occasion to be proud of us, before those who glory as hypocrites but who are not sincere in heart.

13 For if we go wrong, we answer to God, and if we go straight, it is for you.

14 For the love of Christ compels us to reason thus, that if one died for all, then were all dead:

15 And that he died for all, that those who live may not henceforth live for themselves, but for him who died and rose for them.

16 And now from henceforth we do not know any one in the body: even though once we had known Christ in the body, we no longer know him now.

17 Whoever from now on is a follower of Christ, is a new creation: old things have passed away;

18 And all things have become new through God who has reconciled us to himself by Jesus Christ, and has given to us the ministry of reconciliation;

19 For God was in Christ, who has reconciled the world with his majesty, not counting their sins against them; and has committed to us the word of reconciliation.

20 Now then we are ambassadors for Christ, as though God did beseech you by us: we beseech you for Christ; be reconciled to God.

Cf.dif. vv. 4:12, 17-18;   5:1-4, 9-11, 13, 17-19.

21 For he who did not know sin, for your sakes he made him sin, that we may through him be made the righteousness of God.

CHAPTER 6

SO we beseech you, as helpers, that the grace of God which you have received may not be in vain among you.

2 For he said, I have answered you in an acceptable time, and I have helped you on the day of salvation: behold, now is the acceptable time; and behold now is the day of salvation.

3 Give no occasion for offence to any one in anything, so that there be no blemish in our ministry:

4 But in all things let us show ourselves, to be the ministers of God, in much patience, in tribulations, in necessities, in imprisonment,

5 In scourgings, in bonds, in tumults, in toilings, in vigils, in fastings;

6 By purity, by knowledge, by longsuffering, by kindness, by the Holy Spirit, by sincere love,

7 By the word of truth, by the power of God, by the armour of righteousness on the right hand and on the left,

8 By honour and dishonour, by praise and reproach, as deceivers, and yet true;

9 As unknown, and yet well known; as dying, and behold, we live; as chastened, and not dying;

10 As sorrowful, yet always rejoicing; as poor, yet enriching many; as having nothing, and yet possessing all things.

11 O Corinthians, we have told you everything, and our heart is relieved.

12 You are not constrained by us, but are urged by your affections.

13 I speak as to my children, render me my reward which is with you, increase your love toward me.

14 ¶ Do not unite in marriage with unbelievers, for what fellowship has righteousness with iniquity? Or what mingling has light with darkness?

15 Or what accord has Christ with Satan? Or what portion has a believer with an unbeliever?

16 Or what harmony has the temple of God with idols? For you are the temple of the living God; as it is said, I will dwell in them, and walk in them; and I will be their God, and they shall be my people.

17 Wherefore come out from among them, and be separate, said the LORD, and touch not the unclean thing; and I will receive you,

18 And will be a Father to you, and you shall be my sons and daughters, said the LORD Almighty.

CHAPTER 7

HAVING therefore these promises, my beloved, let us cleanse ourselves from all filthiness of the flesh and spirit, and let us serve in holiness in the fear of God.

2 ¶ Be patient; my brethren, we have wronged no man, we have corrupted no man, we have defrauded no man.

3 I do not say this to condemn you: for I have said before, that you are in our hearts, to die and live with you.

4 I am familiar enough to speak boldly with you, and I am very proud of you: and I am filled with satisfaction, and I am overwhelmed with joy in all our troubles.

5 For ever since we came to Mac-e-do'ni-a, our bodies have had no rest but have been troubled by everything; war without and fears within.

6 Nevertheless God, who comforts the meek, comforted us by the coming of Titus;

7 And not by his coming only, but also by the comfort with which he was comforted in you, for he brought us the good news con-

Cf.dif. vv. 5:21; 6:2-5, 11-14; 7:2, 4, 6-7.

cerning your love towards us, your mourning and your zeal on our behalf; and when I heard it, I rejoiced exceedingly.

8 For even though I made you feel sorry with the epistle, I do not regret, even though it has caused sorrow: for I can see that though that very epistle has made you feel sorry, the sorrow was only for an hour.

9 But it has made me exceedingly happy, not that you were sorry, but that your sorrow led to repentance: for you were sorry over the things of God, so that you lack nothing from us.

10 For sorrow over the things of God causes enduring repentance of the soul, and brings one to life: but sorrow over the things of the world causes death.

11 For behold that very thing which distressed you on account of God, has resulted much more in painstaking effort, in apology, anger, fear, love, zeal, and vengeance. In all things you have proven yourselves clear in this matter.

12 Be that as it may, though I wrote to you, I did not do it for the one who had done the wrong nor for the one who had suffered the wrong, but that your painstaking care for us might be known before God.

13 Therefore we were comforted and with our consolation we rejoiced exceedingly in the joy of Titus, for his spirit was refreshed by you all.

14 For I was not shamed in the things which I have boasted to him about you; but just as all the things about which we have spoken to you are true, even so our boasting to Titus is found to be true.

15 And his affections have increased more toward you, as he remembers the obedience of you all, how you received him in fear and trembling.

16 I rejoice therefore that I have confidence in you in all things.

CHAPTER 8

MOREOVER, our brethren, we want you to know that the grace of God has been bestowed on the churches of Mac-e-do'ni-a :

2 How that in a great trial of affliction, the abundance of their joy and their deep rooted poverty abounded unto the riches of their liberality.

3 For to their power, I can testify, yes, and beyond their power they have shared of their own accord.

4 And besought us most earnestly that they might be partakers in the gift for the ministration to the saints.

5 And this they did, not only as we expected, but first they gave themselves to our LORD, and then to us by the will of God.

6 Insomuch as we desired Titus, that as he had begun, so he would also finish this same gift among you.

7 Therefore, as you abound in every thing, in faith, in the word of God, in knowledge, in all perseverance, and by our love toward you, you should likewise excel in this gracious favor also.

8 I am not making a demand on you, but I am prompted by the devotion of your fellow believers to test the sincerity of your love.

9 For you know the gracious gift of our LORD Jesus Christ, that though he was rich, yet for your sakes he became poor, so that you, through his poverty, might be rich.

10 Herein I give you my advice: that it may help you to go forward and accomplish what you, of your own accord, began to do last year.

11 Now therefore perform the doing of that which you wished to do; and as you were eager to promise it, so fulfil from that which you have.

12 For if there is a willingness to give, every man can give according to that which he

has, and not according to that which he has not, and his gift will be acceptable.

13 This is not intended to relieve other men and add a burden to you;

14 But that there may be an equality at this particular time, that your abundance may be a supply for their want, that their abundance also may be a supply for your want, that there may be equality.

15 As it is written, He that had gathered much had nothing over; and he that had gathered little had no lack.

16 But thanks be to God, who put the same vigorous care into the heart of Titus for you.

17 For indeed he has accepted our appeal; and because he was very desirous, he went to you of his own accord.

18 And we have also sent with him our brother, who has received praise throughout all the churches for his preaching of the gospel;

19 So that he also has been chosen by the churches to travel with us for this relief which is administered by us to the very glory of God and for our own encouragement:

20 But we are careful in this, lest any one should blame us in connection with this generous help which is administered by us.

21 For we are very careful to do the right thing, not only in the presence of God, but also in the presence of men.

22 And we have sent with them also our brother, who has oftentimes been proven by us in many things, that he is earnest, and now is more earnest because of the abundant trust he has in you.

23 And as to Titus, he is my partner and helper among you: and as to our other brethren, they are the apostles of the churches to the glory of Christ.

24 Henceforth you can shew to them before all the churches the proof of your love and of our pride in you.

CHAPTER 9

CONCERNING the ministration to the saints, it is superfluous for me to write to you.

2 For I know that you have made up your minds, and that is why I boasted of you to the Macedonians stating that A-cha'ia was ready a year ago; and your zeal has stirred up a great many people.

3 Yet I have sent the brethren, so that our pride in you should not be in vain because of this question; for as I have said, you must be prepared:

4 Lest it happen some Macedonians come with me, and find you unprepared and we would be ashamed for, because of our pride in you, we would not say anything which would put the blame on you.

5 Therefore I thought it necessary to ask these, my brethren, to go before me to you, and make ready in advance the contribution, of which you have long ago been notified, that you might have it ready as a contribution and not as though it were forced on you.

6 But remember this, He who sows sparingly shall reap also sparingly; and he who sows generously shall reap also generously.

7 So let every man give according to what he has decided in his mind, not grudgingly or of necessity: for God loves a cheerful giver.

8 God is able to make all goodness abound to you, and may you always have enough of everything for yourselves, and may you abound in every good work:

9 As it is written, He has distributed liberally; and given to the poor; and his righteousness endures for ever.

10 Now he who gives seed to the sower, and bread for food, will supply and multiply your seed, and cause the fruits of your righteousness to grow;

11 That you may be enriched in everything,

in all liberality, for such generosity enables us to perfect thanksgiving to God.

12 For the administration of this service not only supplies the wants of the saints, but it also is made abundant by many thanksgivings to God.

13 By this experiment of charitable service they glorify God in that you have subjected yourselves to the faith of the gospel of Christ, and through your generosity you have become partakers with them and with all men,

14 And they offer prayer on your behalf with greater love, because of the abundance of the grace of God which has been on you.

15 Thanks be to God for his incomparable gift.

CHAPTER 10

*N*OW I, Paul, beseech you by the gentleness and meekness of Christ, even though I am humble when present among you, I have the assurance when I am far away,

2 I beseech you, that when I arrive, not to be troubled by the things which I hope to carry out, for it is my purpose to put to scorn those men who regard us as if we lived after the flesh.

3 For though we do live an earthly life, yet we do not serve worldly things.

4 For the weapons which we use are not earthly weapons, but of the might of God by which we conquer rebellious strongholds;

5 Casting down imaginations, and every false thing that exalts itself against the knowledge of God, and to capture every thought to the obedience of Christ;

6 And we are prepared to seek vengeance on those who are disobedient, when your obedience is fulfilled.

7 Do you judge by outward appearance? If any man thinks of himself that he belongs to Christ, let him know this of himself, that just as he belongs to Christ, so we also belong.

8 For if I should boast somewhat more of the authority which our LORD has given me, I should not be ashamed, for he has given it to us for your edification, and not for your destruction.

9 But I am hesitant, lest I seem as if I were trying to frighten you with my letter.

10 For there are men who say that his epistles are weighty and powerful; but his bodily appearance is weak, and his speech foolish.

11 But let him who supposes so consider this, that, just as we express ourselves in our epistles when we are away, so are we also in deed when we are present.

12 For we dare not count or compare ourselves with those who are proud of themselves; for it is because they measure themselves by themselves that they do not understand.

13 We do not boast beyond our measure, but according to the measure of the rule which God has distributed to us, a measure to reach even to you.

14 It is not because we are unable to climb where you are; nor are trying to misrepresent ourselves; for we have climbed where we are through the gospel of Christ:

15 And we do not boast of things beyond our measure; that is, by other men's labor, but we have the hope, that when your faith grows, our pride shall be justified according to our measure.

16 And we shall become strengthened so that we may preach the gospel in the regions beyond you, and not boast of the things already done by others.

17 But he who boasts, let him glory in the LORD.

18 For it is not the one who praises himself who is approved, but the one whom the LORD commends.

CHAPTER 11

I WISH you to be patient with me for a while, so that I may speak plainly, and I am sure you will be.

2 For I am zealous for you with the zealousness of God, for I have espoused you to a husband, that I may present you as a pure virgin to Christ.

3 But I am afraid, that just as the serpent through his deceitfulness misled Eve, so your minds should be corrupted from the sincerity that is in Christ.

4 For if he who has come to you preaches another Jesus, whom we have not preached, or if you have received another spirit, which you had not received, or another gospel which you had not accepted, you might well listen to him.

5 For I think that I am not in the least inferior to the most distinguished apostles.

6 But though I am a poor speaker, I am not poor in knowledge; but we have been thoroughly made manifest among you in all things.

7 Probably I have acted foolishly in humbling myself that you might be exalted, because I preached to you the gospel of God freely.

8 I deprived other churches, taking supplies from them, in order to minister to you.

9 And when I came to you and was in need, I did not burden any of you for my wants were supplied by the brethren who came from Mac-e-do'ni-a : I have taken care of myself in every way and I will so continue to keep myself that I will not be a burden to you.

10 As the truth of Christ is in me, no man shall stop me of this boasting in the regions of A-cha'ia.

11 Why? Because I do not love you? God knows I do love you.

12 But what I do, I will continue to do, so as to give no occasion to those who seek an occasion; and that, in whatever they boast, they may not be found equal to us;

13 For they are false apostles, and deceitful workers, posing as apostles of Christ.

14 There is no marvel in this; for if Satan disguises himself as the angel of light,

15 It is no great thing if his ministers also pose as the ministers of righteousness; whose end shall be according to their works.

16 I say again, let no man think me a fool; if otherwise, yet as a fool receive me, that I may boast myself a little.

17 What I now say, I speak not after our LORD, but as it were foolishly, on this occasion of boasting.

18 Because many boast on the things of the flesh, I boast also.

19 For you endure fools readily, knowing that you yourselves are wise.

20 For you endure the man who dominates you, and the man who lives at your expense, and the man who takes from you, and the man who exalts himself over you, and the man who smites you on the face.

21 I speak this as a reproach, as though we were weak. Now I speak foolishly; in whatsoever other men are bold, I venture also.

22 Now if they are Hebrews, so am I. If they are Israelites, so am I. If they are descendants of Abraham, so am I.

23 If they are ministers of Christ, I speak as a fool, I am greater than they; in labor more than they, in wounds more than they, in imprisonments more frequent than they, and in danger of death many times.

24 By the Jews I was scourged five times, each time forty stripes less one.

25 Three times I was beaten with rods, once I was stoned, three times I was in shipwreck, a day and a night I have been adrift in the sea in shipwreck.

26 On many journeys, I have been in perils from rivers, in perils of robbers, in perils from my own kinsmen, in perils from the Gen-

Cf.dif. vv. 11:1-2, 4, 9, 15, 16, 19-21, 23, 25-26.

tiles, in perils in the city, in perils in the wilderness, in perils in the sea, in perils from false brethren;

27 In toil and weariness, in sleepless nights, in hunger and thirst, through much fasting, in cold and nakedness.

28 Besides other things, and the many calling on me everyday, I have also the care of all the churches.

29 Who is sick that I do not feel the pain? Who stumbles that does not have my heartfelt sympathy?

30 If I must needs boast, I will boast of my sufferings.

31 The God and Father of our LORD Jesus Christ, who is blessed forever and ever, knows that I do not lie.

32 At Damascus the general of the army of King Aretas placed the city of the Damascenes under guard, in order to seize me:

33 And I was lowered in a basket from a window over the city wall, and thus I escaped from his hands.

CHAPTER 12

B OASTING is proper, but there is no advantage in it, and I prefer to relate the visions and revelations of our LORD.

2 ¶ I knew a man in Christ more than fourteen years ago, but whether I knew him in the body or without the body, I do not know: God knows; this very one was caught up to the third heaven.

3 And I still know this man, but whether in the body or whether without the body, I cannot tell; God knows;

4 How that he was caught up to paradise, and heard unspeakable words, which it is not lawful for a man to utter.

5 Of such a person, I will boast; but of myself, I will not boast, except in my weaknesses.

6 But even if I would desire to boast, I shall

not be a fool; for I will tell the truth: but now I refrain, lest any one should think more of me than what he sees me to be and what he hears from me.

7 And lest I should be exalted through the abundance of the revelations, there was delivered to me a thorn in my flesh, the angel of Satan to buffet me, lest I should be exalted.

8 Three times I besought my LORD concerning this thing, that it might depart from me.

9 And he said to me, My grace is sufficient for you: for my strength is made perfect in weakness. Most gladly therefore I would rather boast in my infirmities that the power of Christ may rest upon me.

10 Therefore I am content with infirmities, insults, hardships, persecutions, and imprisonments for Christ's sake: for when I am physically weak, then I am mentally strong.

11 Behold, I am foolish to boast but you have forced me: for you ought to have testified concerning me: for in no way am I less than those apostles who are highly honored, though I am nothing.

12 The miracles which the apostles have wrought I have wrought among you also in all patience, in signs, in wonders, and mighty deeds.

13 For what do you lack that other churches have, except it be that I myself was not burdensome to you? Forgive me this "fault"!

14 ¶ Behold, this is the third time I am prepared to come to you; and I will not burden you; for I seek nothing from you, but yourselves: for children are not under obligation to lay up treasure for the parents, but the parents for the children.

15 I will gladly pay my expenses, and I will even give myself for the sake of your souls; though the more I love you, the less you love me.

16 ¶ But be it so, I did not burden you: nevertheless as a shrewd man, I caught you with guile:

17 Why? Did I extort anything from you by any of the men whom I sent to you?

18 I requested Titus to visit you, and I sent brethren with him. Did Titus extort anything from you? Did we not walk in the same spirit, and did we not walk in the same steps?

19 ¶ Why? Do you still think we are apologizing? No! We speak before God in Christ: and we do all these things, my beloved, for your edification.

20 For I fear, lest when I come to you, I shall not find you such as I wish to find you, and that you also will not find me as you wish to find me: lest there be controversies, envyings, angers, stubbornness, accusations, slanderings, boastings and disorders.

21 Perhaps when I come to you, my God will humble me, and I will mourn over many who have sinned, and who have not repented of the impurity, immorality, and lasciviousness which they have committed.

CHAPTER 13

*T*HIS is the third time I am ready to come to you, for by the mouth of two or three witnesses every charge is sustained.

2 I have told you before, and again I tell you in advance, just as I have told you on my two previous visits; and now even while I am far away I write to those who have sinned, and to all others, that if I come again, I will not spare any one:

3 Since you seek a proof of Christ speaking in me, he has never been weak among you, but is mighty in you.

4 For though Jesus was crucified through weakness, yet he lives by the power of God. As we are weak with him, so we are alive with him by the power of God who is among you.

5 Examine yourselves, whether you are in the same faith; heal your souls. Do you not realize that Jesus Christ is among you? If this is not so, then you are rejected.

6 But I trust that you shall know that we are not rejected.

7 And I pray to God that our investigation will find nothing wrong with you; but that you may be found doing good things, even though we may appear as though we were rejected.

8 For we cannot do anything against the truth, but for the truth.

9 For we are glad, when we are weak, and you are strong: and this also we pray for, that you may be perfected.

10 Therefore I write these things while I am far away, so that when I come, I need not deal harshly with you, according to the authority which my LORD has given me, which is for your edification and not for your destruction.

11 ¶ Henceforth, my brethren, rejoice, be perfect, be of good comfort, be of one mind, live in peace; and the God of love and peace shall be with you.

12 Greet one another with a holy kiss.

13 All the saints salute you.

14 The peace of our LORD Jesus Christ, and the love of God, and the fellowship of the Holy Spirit, be with you all. Amen.

Here ends the second epistle to the Corinthians, written at Philippi,
of Macedonia, by Titus and Lycas.

ܦܠܝܦܘܣ ܡܢ ܦܬܒܬܗܕ ܆ܕܩܘܪܢܬܝܐ ܕܬܪܝܢ ܐܓܪܬܐ ܫܠܡܬ

Cf.dif. vv. 12:19;   13:2, 4-5, 7.

THE EPISTLE OF PAUL THE APOSTLE TO THE
GALATIANS

❖ ܪܩܠܛܝܐ ܕܠܘܬ ܕܦܘܠܘܣ ❖

CHAPTER 1

*P*AUL, an Apostle, not sent by men, nor appointed by man, but by Jesus Christ, and God the Father, who raised him from the dead;

2 And all the brethren who are with me, to the churches of Galatia:

3 Grace be to you and peace from God the Father, and from our LORD Jesus Christ,

4 Who gave himself for our sins, that he might deliver us from this present evil world, according to the will of God our Father:

5 To whom be glory for ever and ever. Amen.

6 ¶ I am surprised how soon you have turned to another gospel, away from Christ who has called you by his grace;

7 A gospel which does not exist; howbeit, there are men who have stirred you up, and want to pervert the gospel of Christ.

8 But though we, or an angel from heaven, preach any other gospel to you than that which we have preached to you, let him be accursed.

9 As I have said before, so say I now again, If any man preaches any other gospel to you than that you have received, let him be accursed.

10 Do I now persuade men or God? Or do I seek to please men? For if I tried to please men, I should not be a servant of Christ.

11 ¶ But I want you to know, my brethren, the gospel that I preached was not from men.

12 For I did not receive it nor learn it from man, but through the revelation of Jesus Christ.

13 You have heard of the manner of my life in time past in the Jews' religion, how beyond measure I persecuted the Church of God and tried to destroy it:

14 And how that I was far more advanced in the Jews' religion than many of my age among the people of my race for above all, I was especially zealous for the doctrines of my forefathers.

15 But when it pleased God, who had chosen me from my birth, and called me by his grace,

16 To reveal his Son to me, that I might preach him among the Gentiles, I did not immediately disclose it to any human being:

17 Neither did I go up to Jerusalem to them who had been apostles before me; but instead I went to Arabia and returned again to Damascus.

18 Then after three years I went up to Jerusalem to see Cephas Peter, and stayed with him fifteen days.

19 But I did not see any one of the other apostles, except James the brother of our LORD.

20 Now the things which I write to you, behold, I confess before God, I do not lie.

21 After that I went to the regions of Syria and Cilicia;

22 And I was unknown by face to the churches of Christ in Judæa.

23 For they had heard only this much; that he who had persecuted us before now preached the faith which previously he tried to destroy.

24 And they praised God because of me.

Cf.dif. vv. 1:6-7, 13-14, 16, 20.

CHAPTER 2

*T*HEN, fourteen years later, I went up again to Jerusalem with Barnabas, and took Titus with me also.

2 And I went up because of a revelation, and I declared to them the gospel which I preached among the Gentiles, and I privately explained to those who were considered leaders among us, lest by any means I had labored, or should labor in vain.

3 And Titus, also, who was with me, being Syrian, was not compelled to be circumcised,

4 But because of the false brethren who had been brought in unknown to us to spy out the freedom which we have in Jesus Christ, with the intention of enslaving us;

5 To those false brothers we did not submit, not even for an hour; that the truth of the gospel might remain with you.

6 Now those who were considered to be important (what they are makes no difference to me, for God does not discriminate among men), even these very persons did not contribute additional knowledge to me.

7 But on the contrary, when they saw that the gospel of the uncircumcision was entrusted to me, as the gospel of the circumcision was entrusted to Peter,

8 (For he who made Cephas vigorous in the apostleship of the circumcision, has also made me mighty in the apostleship of the Gentiles:)

9 And when they knew that the grace had been given to me, then James, Cephas, and John, who were considered to be pillars, gave to me and Barnabas the right hand of fellowship; that we might labor among the Gentiles, and they, among the people of circumcision.

10 Only they would that we should remember the poor; and that I have endeavored to do.

11 But when Cephas came to An'ti-och, I reproved him to his face, because he was to be blamed.

12 For before certain men came from James, Cephas ate with the Gentiles: but after they came, he withdrew and separated himself, because he was afraid of them who belonged to the circumcision.

13 And all the other Jewish converts cast their lots with him on this issue, insomuch that Barnabas also was carried away by their dissimulation.

14 But when I saw that they were not following uprightly according to the truth of the gospel, I said to Peter, in the presence of them all, If you being a Jew live after the manner of Gentiles and not as do the Jews, why do you compel the Gentile converts to live as do the Jews?

15 For if we who are of Jewish origin, and not sinners of the Gentiles,

16 Know that a man is not justified by the works of the law, but by the faith in Jesus Christ, even we have believed in Jesus Christ, that we might be justified by the faith in Christ and not by the works of the law: for by the works of the law shall no human being be justified.

17 But if, while we seek to be justified by Christ, we ourselves also are found sinners, is therefore our LORD Jesus Christ a minister of sin? Far be it.

18 For if I build again the things which I destroyed, I will prove myself to be a transgressor of the law.

19 For through the law I am dead to the law, that I might live unto God.

20 I am crucified with Christ: henceforth it is not I who live, but Christ who lives in me; and the life which now I live in the flesh I live by the faith of the Son of God, who loved me and gave himself for me.

21 I do not frustrate the grace of God: for if righteousness comes by means of the law, then Christ died in vain.

Cf.dif. vv. 2:2-6, 9, 11-12, 14.

CHAPTER 3

O FOOLISH Galatians, who has be witched you from your faith after Jesus Christ, crucified, has been pictured before your eyes?

2 This only I want to know from you, Did you receive the Spirit through the works of the law, or through obedience to faith?

3 Are you so foolish, after having begun with spiritual things to end now with things of the flesh?

4 Have you believed all these things at random? I hope that it is to no purpose.

5 He therefore who gives you the Spirit, and works miracles among you, does he do these things by the works of the law, or by obedience to faith?

6 Just as Abraham believed God, and it was accounted to him for righteousness,

7 You must know therefore, that those who trust on faith are the children of Abraham.

8 Because God knew in advance that the Gentiles would be declared righteous through faith, he first preached to Abraham, as it is said in the Holy Scripture, In you shall all the Gentiles be blessed.

9 So then, it is the believers who are blessed through Abraham the faithful.

10 For those who rely on the works of the law are still under the curse: for as it is written, Cursed is everyone who does not practice everything which is written in the book of the law.

11 But that no man is justified by the law before God, is evident: for, as it is written, The righteous shall live by faith.

12 Thus the law is not made by faith, but, Whosoever shall do the things which are written in it shall live in it.

13 Christ has redeemed us from the curse of the law, by becoming accursed for our sakes: for it is written, Cursed is everyone who hangs on a cross:

14 That the blessing of Abraham might come on the Gentiles through Jesus Christ; that we might receive the promise of the Spirit through faith.

15 My brethren, I speak as a man; Though it be but a man's covenant, yet if it be confirmed, no man can reject it or change anything in it.

16 Now the promises were made to Abraham and to his seed as a covenant. He did not say, To your seeds, as of many, but to your seed, as one, that is Christ.

17 And this I say, that the covenant which was previously confirmed of God in Christ cannot be repudiated and the promise nullified by the law which came four hundred and thirty years later. 18 For if the inheritance is by the law, then it would not be as the fulfillment of promise: but God gave it to Abraham by promise.

19 ¶ Then what is the use of the law? It was added because of transgression, till the coming of the heir to whom the promise was made; and the law was given by angels by the hand of a mediator;

20 Now a mediator does not represent one alone, but God is one.

21 Is the law then against the promises of God? Far be it: for if a law had been given, which could have wrought salvation, righteousness would truly have come as the result of the law.

22 But the scripture has included everything under sin, that the promise by the faith of Jesus Christ might be given to those who believe.

23 But before faith came, we were guided by the law, while we were waiting for the faith which was to be revealed.

24 The law then was our pathfinder to bring us to Christ that we might be justified by faith.

25 But since faith has come, we no longer are in need of the pathfinder.

Cf.dif. vv. 3:1, 3-4, 8, 12-13, 16, 21, 23-24.

26 For you are all the children of God by faith in Jesus Christ.

27 For those who have been baptized in the name of Christ have been clothed with Christ.

28 There is neither Jew nor Syrian, there is neither slave nor free, there is neither male nor female: for you are all one in Jesus Christ.

29 So if you belong to Christ, then you are descendants of Abraham, and his heirs according to the promise.

CHAPTER 4

NOW this I say, That the heir as long as he is young, cannot be distinguished from the servants, though he is the lord of them all.

2 But he is under guardians and stewards, until the time appointed by his father.

3 Even so we, when we were young, were subject to the principles of this world:

4 But when the fulness of the time was come, God sent forth his Son who, born of a woman, became subject to the law,

5 To redeem them who were under the law, that we might receive the adoption of sons.

6 And because you are sons, God has sent forth the Spirit of his Son into your hearts crying, Abba, Avon," O Father, our Father.

7 From now on you are not servants but sons; and if sons, then heirs of God through Jesus Christ.

8 Howbeit then, when you did not know God, you served those things which from their nature were not gods.

9 But now after you have known God, and, above all, are known of God, you turn again to those weak and poor principles, and you wish again to come under their bondage.

10 You still observe days and months and times and years.

11 I am afraid that perhaps I have labored among you in vain.

12 ¶ My brethren, I beseech you, put yourself in my place; just as once I put myself in your place: You have not offended me at all.

13 You know that I was sick and weak when I preached the gospel to you at the first.

14 And yet you did not despise me, nor reject me on account of my weakness; but you received me as an angel of God, even as Jesus Christ.

15 Where is then the blessedness you had? for I can testify concerning you, that if it had been possible, you would have plucked out your own eyes and have given them to me.

16 Am I therefore become your enemy, because I tell you the truth?

17 These men do not envy you for good, but they would dominate you, so that you might envy them.

18 But it is good that you should always envy after good things, and not only when I am present with you.

19 My little children, for whom I am in travail again, until Christ be a reality in you,

20 I wish I could be with you now, and could change the tone of my voice; because I am deeply concerned about you.

21 Tell me, you who desire to be under the law, do you not hear the law?

22 For it is written, that Abraham had two sons, one by a bondmaid, and one by a freewoman.

23 But he who was born of the bondmaid was born after the flesh; but he who was born of the freewoman was born by promise.

24 Now these things are a symbol of the two covenants; the one from Mount Sinai, give girls birth to bondage, which is Hagar.

25 For this Hagar is Mount Sinai in Arabia, and surrenders to Jerusalem which now is, and is in bondage with her children.

26 But the Jerusalem which is above is free, and is the mother of us all.

Cf. dif. vv. 3:28;   4:2, 4, 7, 9, 12-14, 17, 19-20, 22, 24-25.

27 For as it is written, Make merry, O you barren who bear not; rejoice and cry, O you who travail not; for the children of the forsaken are more numerous than the children of the one who is favored.

28 ¶ Now we, my brethren, are the children of promise, as was Isaac.

29 But as then he who was born after the flesh persecuted him who was born after the Spirit, even so it is now.

30 Nevertheless what does the scripture say? Cast out the bondmaid and her son; for the son of the maidservant shall not inherit with the son of the freewoman.

31 So then, my brethren, we are not children of the maidservant but children of the freewoman.

CHAPTER 5

STAND firm therefore in the liberty with which Christ has made us free, and be not harnessed again under the yoke of servitude.

2 Behold, I, Paul, tell you that if you be circumcised, then Christ is of no benefit to you.

3 For I testify again to every man who is circumcised, that he is under obligation to fulfill the whole law.

4 You have ceased to adhere to Christ, who seek justification by the law; you are fallen from grace.

5 For we through the Spirit wait for the hope of righteousness by faith.

6 For in Christ Jesus, neither is circumcision anything nor uncircumcision; but faith which is accomplished by love.

7 You were progressing well; who confused you that you should not obey the truth?

8 Your persuasion comes from him who called you.

9 A little leaven leavens the whole lump.

10 ¶ I have confidence in you through our LORD, that you will consider no other be-liefs: that he who troubles you shall bear his judgment, whosoever he is.

11 And I, my brethren, if I still preach circumcision, why should I be persecuted? Why? Has the cross ceased to be a stumblingblock?

12 I wish those who are troubling you would be expelled.

13 ¶ For, my brethren, you have been called unto liberty; only do not use your liberty for an occasion to the things of the flesh, but by love serve one another.

14 For the whole law is fulfilled in one saying, that is; Thou shall love thy neighbor as thyself.

15 But if you harm and plunder one another, take heed lest you be consumed one by another.

16 This I say then: Lead a spiritual life, and you shall never commit the lust of the flesh.

17 For the flesh craves that which is harmful to the Spirit, and the Spirit opposes the things of the flesh: and the two are contrary to one another, so that you are unable to do whatever you please.

18 But if you are led by the Spirit, you are not under the law.

19 For the works of the flesh are well-known, which are these: adultery, impurity, and lasciviousness,

20 Idolatry, witchcraft, enmity, strife, jealousy, anger, stubbornness, seditions, heresies,

21 Envyings, murders, drunkenness, revellings, and all like things: those who practice these things, as I have told you before and I say to you now, they shall not inherit the kingdom of God.

22 But the fruits of the Spirit are love, joy, peace, patience, gentleness, goodness, faith,

23 Meekness, self-control: there is no law against these.

24 And those who belong to Christ have

controlled their weaknesses and passions.

25 Let us therefore live in the Spirit, and surrender to the Spirit.

26 Let us not be desirous of vain glory, provoking one another, envying one another.

CHAPTER 6

*M*Y brethren, if any one be found at fault, you who are spiritual, restore him in a spirit of meekness; and be careful test you also be tempted.

2 Bear one another's burdens, and so fulfil the law of Christ.

3 For if man thinks himself to be something, when he is nothing, he deceives himself.

4 But let every man examine his own work, and then may he glory within himself alone, and not among others.

5 For every man shall bear his own burden.

6 Let him who is taught the word, become a partaker with him who teaches all good things.

7 Do not be deceived; God is not deceived: for whatsoever a man sows, that shall he also reap.

8 He who sows things of the flesh, from the flesh shall reap corruption; he who sows things of the Spirit, from the Spirit shall reap life everlasting.

9 Let us not be weary in welldoing: for in due season we shall reap, if we faint not.

10 Therefore, as we have opportunity, let us do good to all men, especially to those who belong to the household of faith.

11 ¶ You can see how long a letter I have written to you with my own hand.

12 Those who desire to boast in the things of the flesh, are the ones who compel you to be circumcised only lest they should suffer persecution for the cross of Christ.

13 For not even they who are circumcised obey the law; but they want you to be circumcised so that they may boast over your flesh.

14 But as for me, I have nothing on which to boast, except the cross of our LORD Jesus Christ, by whom the world is crucified unto me and I am crucified unto the world.

15 For in Christ Jesus neither circumcision is anything, nor uncircumcision, but it is a new creation that counts.

16 And upon those who follow this path be peace and mercy; and upon the Israel of God, be peace and mercy.

17 From henceforth let no man trouble me, for I bear in my body the marks of our LORD Jesus Christ.

18 My brethren, the grace of our LORD Jesus Christ be with your spirit. Amen.

Here ends the epistle to the Galatians; written from Rome.

ܐܓܪܬܐ ܕܠܘܬ ܓܠܛܝܐ ܫܠܡܬ܀
܀ܕܐܬܟܬܒܬ ܡܢ ܪܗܘܡܐ܀

Cf.dif. vv. 5:24;   6:1, 4, 6-8, 15-16.

THE EPISTLE OF PAUL THE APOSTLE TO THE

EPHESIANS

❖ ܐܓܪܬܐ ܕܠܘܬ ܐܦܣܝ̈ܐ ❖

CHAPTER 1

*P*AUL, an apostle of Jesus Christ by the will of God, to those who are in Eph'e-sus, saints and believers in Jesus Christ:

2 Peace be with you and grace from God our Father, and from our LORD Jesus Christ:

3 ¶ Blessed be the God, and Father of our LORD Jesus Christ, who has blessed us with all spiritual blessings in heaven through Christ:

4 Just as from the beginning he has chosen us through him, before the foundation of the world, that we may become holy and without blemish before him.

5 And he marked us with his love to be his from the beginning, and adopted us to be sons through Jesus Christ, as it pleased his will.

6 To the praise of the glory of his grace that he has poured upon us by his beloved one.

7 In him we have salvation, and in his blood, forgiveness of sins, according to the richness of his grace;

8 That that grace which has abounded in us, in all wisdom and spiritual understanding;

9 And because he has made known to us the mystery of his will, as he has ordained from the very beginning, to work through it;

10 As a dispensation of the fulness of times, that all things might be made new in heaven and on earth through Christ:

11 By whom we have been chosen, as he had marked us from the beginning so he wanted to carry out everything according to the good judgment of his will:

12 That we should become the first to trust in Christ, to his honor and his glory:

13 In whom, you also have heard the word of truth, which is the gospel for your salvation: in him you have believed, so you are sealed with the Holy Spirit that was promised,

14 Which is the pledge of our inheritance, for the salvation of those who are saved, and for the glory of his honour.

15 ¶ Wherefore I also, since I heard of your faith in our LORD Jesus Christ, and your love toward all the saints,

16 Never cease to give thanks for your sakes and to mention you in my prayers;

17 So that the God of our LORD Jesus Christ, the Father of glory, may give you the spirit of wisdom and revelation in the knowledge of him:

18 And so that the eyes of your understanding may be enlightened; that you may know what is the hope of his calling, and what are the glorious riches of his inheritance in the saints;

19 And what is the exceeding greatness of his power in us as the result of the things we believe, according to the skill of his mighty power,

20 Which he wrought through Christ, when he raised him from the dead and set him at his own right hand in heaven,

21 Far above all angels and power, and might, and dominion, and every name that is named, not only in this world but also in the world which is to come:

22 And has put all things under his feet, and made him, who is above all things, the head of the church,

Cf.dif. vv. 1:4-6, 9-14, 17-18, 22.

23 Which is his body, and confirmation of him who fulfills all things and every thing.

CHAPTER 2

AND he has quickened you also who were dead because of your sins and trespasses;

2 In which you previously walked according to the worldly course of this world, and according to the will of the supreme ruler of the air, the spirit which is active in the children of disobedience.

3 In those very deeds in which we were also corrupted from the very beginning through the lusts of the flesh, fulfilling the wills of the flesh and of the mind: thereby we became completely the children of wrath, even as others.

4 But God, who is rich in mercy, for his great love with which he loved us,

5 Even when we were dead in our sins, has made us live together with Christ, by whose grace we are saved;

6 And he has raised us up with him, and seated us with him in heaven, through Jesus Christ.

7 In the ages to come he might show the exceeding riches of his grace in his kindness toward us through Jesus Christ.

8 For it is by grace that you are saved through faith; not of your doing: it is the gift of God:

9 Not of works, lest any man should boast.

10 For we are his creation, created through Jesus Christ ultimately for good works, which God has before ordained that we should live in them.

11 ¶ Wherefore remember that you were Gentiles in the flesh from the beginning, and you were called Uncircumcision, differing from that which is called Circumcision, which is the work of the hands in the flesh.

12 At that time you were without Christ, being aliens to the customs of Israel, and strangers to the covenants of the promise, without hope, and without God in the world.

13 But now, through Jesus Christ, you who sometimes were far off are brought near by the blood of Christ.

14 For he is our peace, who has made both one, and has broken down the fence of separation between them;

15 And he has abolished by his precious body, the enmity between them, and he has abolished by his commandments, the ordinances of the law, that he may create, in his person, from the two, a new man, thus making peace;

16 And he reconciled both in one body with God, and with his cross he destroyed the enmity:

17 And he came and preached peace to you who are far away and to those who are near.

18 Through him we both are able to draw near by one Spirit to the Father.

19 Thus from henceforth you are neither strangers, nor foreigners, but fellow-citizens with the saints, and children of the household of God;

20 And you are built upon the foundation of the apostles and prophets, Jesus Christ himself being the corner-stone of the building:

21 And through him the whole building is fashioned and grows into a holy temple through the help of the LORD:

22 You also are builded by him for a habitation of God through the Spirit.

CHAPTER 3

FOR this cause I, Paul, am a prisoner of Jesus Christ for the sake of you Gentiles.

2 Have you ever heard of the dispensation of the grace of God which was given to me for you?

3 For the mystery was made known to me by a revelation; as I have briefly written you before,

4 So that when you read it you can understand my knowledge of the mystery of Christ,
5 Which in ages past was not made known to the sons of men, as it is now revealed to his holy apostles and prophets by the Spirit;
6 That the Gentiles should be fellow heirs and partakers of his body and of the promise which is given through him by the gospel,
7 Of that very gospel, I have been a minister, according to the gift of the grace of God given to me by the effectual working of his power.
8 Even to me, who am less than the least of all the saints, this grace was given, that I should preach among the Gentiles the unsearchable riches of Christ:
9 And that I may enlighten all men that they may see what is the dispensation of the mystery, which for ages had been hidden from the world by God who created all things:
10 To the intent that through the church the manifold wisdom of God may be made known to the angels and powers which are in heaven,
11 Which is the wisdom he prepared in ages past, and has carried out in Jesus Christ our LORD:
12 In whom we have freedom of access with confidence in his faith.
13 Therefore I ask that I may not grow weary in my afflictions for your sakes, which is for your happiness.
14 For this cause I bow my knees to the Father of our LORD Jesus Christ,
15 For whom all fatherhood in heaven and in earth is named,
16 To grant you, according to the riches of his glory, to be strengthened with might by his Spirit;
17 That Christ may dwell in you by faith, and in your hearts by love, strengthening your understanding and your foundation;

18 So that you may be able to comprehend with all the saints what is the height and depth and length and breadth;
19 And to know the love of Christ which surpasses all knowledge, that you may be filled with all the fulness of God.
20 Now to him who is able by power to do for us more than anyone else, and to do for us more than we ask or think, according to his mighty power that works in us,
21 Unto him be glory in his church by Jesus Christ throughout all ages, world without end: Amen.

CHAPTER 4

I THEREFORE, a prisoner of our LORD, beseech you to live as is worthy of the rank to which you are called,
2 With all humility and gentleness and with patience, forbearing one another in love,
3 Endeavoring to preserve the harmony of the Spirit in the bond of peace,
4 That you may become one body, and one Spirit, even as you are called in one hope of your calling;
5 There is one LORD, one faith, and one baptism;
6 One God and Father of all, who is above all, and through all, and in all of us.
7 But to every one of us is given grace according to the measure of the gift of Christ.
8 Wherefore it is said, He ascended on high, and took possession of heaven and gave good gifts to men.
9 Now that he ascended, what is it but that he also descended first into the inner parts of the earth?
10 So he that descended is the same also that ascended far above all heavens, that he might fulfil all things.
11 And he has assigned some, apostles, and some, prophets, and some, evangelists, and some, pastors, and some, teachers;

12 For the perfecting of the saints, for the work of the ministry, for the edifying of the body of Christ:

13 Until we all become one in faith, and in the knowledge of the Son of God, and become a perfect man according to the measure of the stature of the fulness of Christ:

14 That we henceforth be not as children easily stirred and carried away by every wind of false doctrines of men who through their craftiness are artful in deceiving the people;

15 But that we be sincere in our love, so that in everything we may progress through Christ, who is the head.

16 It is through him that the whole body is closely and firmly united at all joints, according to the measure of the gift which is given to every member, for the guidance and control of the body, in order to complete the edifying of the body in love.

17 ¶ This I say therefore and testify in the LORD: that you henceforth live not as other Gentiles, who live in the vanity of their mind,

18 And whose understanding is dark, and who are alienated from the life of God, because they have no knowledge, and because of the blindness of their hearts;

19 And who have given up their hope, and have surrendered themselves to wantonness, and to the practice of all uncleanness in their covetousness.

20 But that is not what you have been taught about Christ;

21 If you have truly heard him, and have been taught by him, as the truth is found in Jesus:

22 That you lay aside all your former practices, that is to say, the old man which is degenerated with deceitful lusts;

23 And be renewed in the spirit of your mind;

24 And that you put on the new man, who is created by God in righteousness and true holiness.

25 Wherefore you must put away from you lying, and speak the truth every man with his neighbor: for we are members one of another.

26 Be angry, but sin not: and let not the sun go down upon your anger;

27 And do not give the devil a chance.

28 From henceforth let him that stole steal no more: but rather let him labor with his hands and do good deeds, that he may have something to give to him who is in need.

29 Let no bad word proceed from your mouth, but words that are good and useful for edification, that they will impart blessing to those who hear them.

30 And do not grieve the Holy Spirit of God, whereby you are sealed unto the day of salvation.

31 Let all bitterness and wrath, and anger, and clamouring and blasphemy be put away from you, together with all malice:

32 And be kind one to another and tenderhearted, forgiving one another, even as God has forgiven us through Christ.

CHAPTER 5

B E therefore God-like, as beloved children.

2 And walk in love, as Christ also has loved us and has given himself for us an offering and a sacrifice to God for a sweet example.

3 ¶ But let not immorality or any uncleanness or covetousness be heard of among you, as becomes saints;

4 Neither cursing, nor foolish words, nor insults, nor words of flattery, none of which are necessary: but instead of these, let thanks be offered.

5 You should know this: that no one guilty of fornication, or unclean person, or covetous man who serves idols, has any inheritance in the kingdom of Christ and of God.

6 Let no man deceive you with vain words: for because of these things the anger of God comes on the children of disobedience.

7 Therefore do not be partakers with them.

8 For previously you were ignorant, but now you have been enlightened by our LORD, and should live therefore like children of light.

9 For the fruits of light are found in all goodness, and righteousness, and truth;

10 And so you must discern that which is acceptable before our LORD.

11 Have no part in the unfruitful works of darkness, but rather condemn them.

12 For it is a shame even to speak of the things that are done by them in secret.

13 For all things that are condemned are exposed by the light: and anything that is made manifest is light.

14 Therefore it is said: Awake thou that sleepest, and rise from the dead, and Christ shall give thee light.

15 ¶ Watch therefore, that you live a glorious life, not as foolish men, but as wise men,

16 Who take advantage of their opportunity, for these are difficult days.

17 Wherefore do not lack wisdom, but understand what the will of God is.

18 And do not become drunk with wine, wherein is intemperance; but be filled with the Spirit,

19 Speaking to your souls in psalms and hymns, and in spiritual songs, sing with your heart to the LORD;

20 Giving thanks always for all men to God the Father in the name of our LORD Jesus Christ.

21 ¶ Submit yourselves one to another in the love of Christ.

22 Wives submit yourselves to your husbands as to our LORD.

23 For the husband is the head of the wife, even as Christ is the head of the church: and

he is the saviour of its body.

24 Therefore as the church is subject to Christ, so let the wives be to their own husbands in every thing.

25 Husbands, love your wives, even as Christ loved his church, and gave himself for it;

26 That he might sanctify and cleanse it, by the washing of water and by the word,

27 In order to build for himself a glorious church, without stain or wrinkle, or any such thing; but that it should be holy and without blemish.

28 So should men love their wives as their own bodies. He who loves his wife loves himself.

29 For no man ever yet hated his own body; but nourishes it and cherishes it, even as Christ does for his church.

30 For we are members of his body, of his flesh, and of his bones.

31 For this reason shall a man leave his father and mother, and shall be joined to his wife, and they two shall be one flesh.

32 This is a great mystery; but I speak concerning Christ and his church.

33 Nevertheless, let every one of you so love his wife as himself, and the wife see that she reverence her husband.

CHAPTER 6

*C*HILDREN, obey your parents in our LORD, for this is right.

2 This is the first commandment with promise: Honour thy father and mother;

3 That it may be well with thee, and thou mayest live long on the earth.

4 And parents, do not provoke your children to anger; but bring them up in the discipline and teaching of our LORD.

5 Servants, be obedient to your masters according to the flesh, with reverence and trembling, and with a sincere heart, as to Christ;

6 Not with eyeservice, as men-pleasers, but

Cf.dif. vv. 5:8-9, 14, 16, 19-21, 27;   6:4, 6.

as the servants of Christ doing the will of God from the heart.

7 And serve well with your whole soul, with love, as to our LORD, and not to men:

8 Knowing that whatever good thing any man does, the same shall he receive from our LORD, whether he be a slave or a freeman.

9 Also, masters, do the same things for your servants, forgiving their faults, because you also have your own Master in heaven; and there is no respect of persons with him.

10 ¶ From henceforth, my brethren, be strong in our LORD, and in the power of his might.

11 Put on the whole armor of God, that you may be able to stand against the wiles of the devil.

12 For your conflict is not only with flesh and blood, but also with the angels, and with powers, with the rulers of this world of darkness, and with the evil spirits under the heavens.

13 Wherefore put you on the whole armor of God, that you may be able to meet the evil one, and being prepared you shall prevail.

14 Arise, therefore, gird your loins with truth, and put on the breastplate of righteousness;

15 And have your feet shod with the preparation of the gospel of peace;

16 Together with these, take for yourselves the shield of faith, for with it you shall be able to quench all the flaming darts of the wicked.

17 And put on the helmet of salvation, and take the sword of the Spirit, which is the word of God:

18 And pray always, with all prayer and supplication in the Spirit, and in that prayer be watchful at all times, praying constantly and supplicating for all the saints,

19 And for me also, that words may be given to me as soon as I open my mouth, so that I may boldly preach the mystery of the gospel,

20 For which I am a messenger in chains: that I may speak openly about it, as I ought to speak.

21 ¶ In order that you also may know my affairs, and what I do, Tychicus, a beloved brother and a faithful minister in our LORD, shall make known to you all things;

22 Him I have sent to you for the same purpose, that you may know how I am, and that he may comfort your hearts.

23 Peace be to our brethren, and love with faith, from God the Father, and from our LORD Jesus Christ.

24 Grace be with all them that love our LORD Jesus Christ in sincerity. Amen.

End of the epistle to the Ephesians; written from Rome and sent by Tychicus.

ܪܠܡܬ ܕܠܬ ܐܓܪܬܐ ܫܠܡܬ܀
܀ܐܦܣܝܐ ܡܢ ܪܗܘܡܝ܂

THE EPISTLE OF PAUL THE APOSTLE TO THE

PHILIPPIANS

❖ ܐܓܪܬܐ ܕܠܘܬ ܦܝܠܝܦܣܝܐ ❖

CHAPTER 1

*P*AUL and Ti-mo'the-us, servants of Jesus Christ, to all the saints in Jesus Christ who are at Philippi, together with the elders and deacons:

2 Grace be to you, and peace from God our Father, and from our LORD Jesus Christ.

3 ¶ I give thanks to my God for your steady remembrance of me.

4 In all my prayers for you, I make supplication with joy,

5 For your fellowship in the gospel, from the very first day until now,

6 Being confident of this very thing, that he who has begun the good work among you, the same will continue it until the day of our LORD Jesus Christ:

7 And this is the right way for me to think of you all, because I have you in my heart, because through all my imprisonment and my defense and confirmation of the truth of the gospel, you have been partakers with me of grace.

8 For God is my witness of how much I love you through the love of Jesus Christ.

9 And for this I pray, that your love may abound yet more and more in knowledge and in all spiritual understanding:

10 So that you may choose the things that are excellent; and that you may be pure and without offence in the day of Christ;

11 And be filled with the fruits of righteousness, which are by Jesus Christ, to the glory and the praise of God.

12 ¶ Now I would have you know this, my brethren, that my work has been greatly furthered by the gospel;

13 And the reasons for my imprisonments have been made manifest by Christ to all Cæsar's court, and to all men.

14 And many of the brethren in our LORD have grown confident by my imprisonment and, with increasing boldness, speak the word of God without fear.

15 While some of them preach only because of envy and strife; others preach Christ in good will and love:

16 For they know that I am appointed for the defence of the gospel:

17 But those who preach Christ out of contention, do it not sincerely, but do it expecting to increase the hardship of my imprisonment.

18 And I have rejoiced and still do rejoice in this: that in every way, whether in pretense or in truth, Christ is preached.

19 For I know that through your prayers and the gift of the Spirit of Jesus Christ, all these things will ultimately turn out for my salvation,

20 Just as it is my earnest hope and expectation that in nothing shall I be ashamed, but that openly as always, so also now will Christ be magnified through my body, whether in life or death.

21 For Christ is my life, and to die is gain.

22 Even if, in this life of the flesh, my labors bear fruits, I do not know what to choose.

23 For I am drawn between two desires, the one to depart, that I may be with Christ, which is far better:

24 Nevertheless, for me to remain in the flesh is more needful for you.

Cf.dif. vv. 1:1, 4, 7-10, 12-13, 16, 18, 20, 22.

25 And this I surely know, that I shall be spared and remain for your joy and for the furtherance of your faith;

26 So that when I come again to you, your rejoicing in Jesus Christ will abound through me.

27 ¶ Only conduct yourselves as becomes the gospel of Christ: so that whether I come and see you, or whether I am far away, I may hear of your good conduct, that you are standing firm in one spirit, and in one soul, and triumphing together through the faith of the gospel;

28 And that in nothing are you terrified by our adversaries, whose conduct is the sign of their own destruction, but your salvation, and this is from God.

29 For it has been given to you, not only to believe in Christ, but also to suffer for his sake.

30 And that you may endure such trials as those which you have seen me in, and such as you now hear that I am in.

CHAPTER 2

*I*F, therefore, you have found consola tion in Christ, or whole hearted love or fellowship of the Spirit or compassion and mercies,

2 Complete my joy by being in one accord and one love and one soul and one mind.

3 Do nothing through strife or vain glory; but in humility let each regard his neighbor better than himself.

4 Let no one be mindful only of his own things, but let every one be mindful of the things of his neighbor also.

5 Reason this within you which Jesus Christ also reasoned,

6 Who, being in the form of God, did not consider it robbery to be equal with God:

7 But made himself of no reputation and took upon himself the form of a servant, and was in the likeness of men:

8 And, being found in fashion as a man, he humbled himself, and became obedient to death, even the death of the cross.

9 Wherefore God also has highly exalted him, and given him a name which is above every name;

10 That at the name of Jesus every knee should bow, of those in heaven, of those on earth, and those under the earth,

11 And every tongue shall confess that Jesus Christ is the LORD, to the glory of God his Father.

12 From now on, my beloved, just as you have always been obedient, not only in my presence, but much more in my absence, work out your own salvation with fear and trembling.

13 For it is God who inspires you with the will to do the good things which you desire to do.

14 Do all things without disputing, and doubting:

15 That you may be sincere and blameless, like the innocent children of God, in the midst of a crooked and perverse generation, among whom you shine as lights in the world:

16 For you are to them the light of life; for my pride and glory in the day of Christ, for I have not run in vain nor labored in vain.

17 Yes, even if my blood be offered upon the sacrifice and the service of your faith, I am happy and rejoice with you all.

18 Likewise you also must be happy and rejoice with me.

19 ¶ But I trust in our LORD Jesus Christ to send Ti-mo'the-us to you soon, that I also may be at ease when I learn of your well being.

20 For I have no one here as interested as I am, who will sincerely care for your welfare;

21 For all seek their own, not the things which are Jesus Christ's.

                        Cf.dif. vv. 1:26, 29-30;   2:1, 3-5, 13, 15-16.

22 But you know his record, that as a son with his father, he has served with me in the gospel.

23 I hope to send him to you presently, as soon as I see how it will go with me.

24 But I trust in my LORD that I also myself shall come shortly.

25 But right now I am forced through circumstances to send to you Epaphroditus, a brother, and assistant and co-worker with me, but he is also your apostle and one who ministers to my wants.

26 For he has been longing to see you all, and has been depressed because he knew you had heard that he had been sick.

27 For indeed he was sick to the point of death but God had mercy on him; and not on him only, but on me also, lest I should have sorrow upon sorrow.

28 Therefore I have sent him quickly, so that, when you see him again, you may rejoice, and that I may be relieved from anxiety.

29 Welcome him, therefore, in the LORD with all joy; and honour those who are like him:

30 Because for the work of Christ he came near to death; and by his self denial, he made good your lack of service to me.

CHAPTER 3

HENCEFORTH, my brethren, rejoice in our LORD. It does not bother me to write the same things to you, because they enlighten you.

2 Beware of backbiters, beware of evil workers, beware of circumcising.

3 For we are the true people of circumcision, who worship God in Spirit, and glory in Jesus Christ, and yet do not rely on things of the flesh.

4 As for me, I once relied on things of the flesh. However, if a man thinks his hope is on things of the flesh, I have more hope than he has;

5 Because I was circumcised when I was eight days old, being an Israelite by race, of the tribe of Benjamin, a Hebrew son of Hebrews, and according to the law a Pharisee;

6 And because, concerning zeal, I was a persecutor of the church; and according to the standards of righteousness of the law, I was blameless.

7 But these things which once were a gain to me, I counted a loss for the sake of Christ.

8 And I still count them all a loss, for the sake of abundant knowledge of Jesus Christ my LORD: for whom I have lost everything, and I have considered all those things as refuse, so that I may increase in Christ

9 And be found in him, since I have no righteousness of my own gained from the law, but the righteousness which comes through the faith of Christ; that is, the righteousness which comes from God:

10 So that through this righteousness I may know Jesus and the power of his resurrection, and be a partaker of his sufferings, even to a death like his;

11 That I may by any means attain the resurrection from the dead.

12 Not as though I had already attained or were already perfect; but I am striving, that I may reach that for which Jesus Christ appointed me.

13 My brethren, I do not consider that I have reached the goal; but this one thing I do know, forgetting those things which are behind me, I strive for those things which are before me,

14 I press toward the goal to receive the prize of victory of God's highest calling through Jesus Christ.

15 Therefore let those of you who are perfect think these things over; and if you reason in any other way, God will reveal even that to you.

Cf.dif. vv. 2:25-26, 28, 30;   3:1-2, 4, 8-10, 12-15.

16 Nevertheless, whereto we have already attained, let us walk by the same path and with one accord.

17 My brethren, be followers like me, and observe those who walk such a path, and then you will be examples as we are.

18 For there are many who live otherwise, of whom I have often told you, and now I tell you with tears that they are the enemies of the cross of Christ;

19 Whose end is destruction, whose God is their belly, and whose glory is in their shame; whose thought is on earthly things.

20 But our labours are in heavenly things, from whence we look for our Saviour, our LORD Jesus Christ,

21 Who shall transform our poor body, to the likeness of his glorious body, according to his mighty power, whereby he is able even to subdue all things unto himself.

CHAPTER 4

*H*ENCEFORTH, my dearly beloved brethren, my joy and crown, in this manner stand firm in our LORD, my beloved.

2 I beseech Euodias and I beseech Syntyche to be of one accord in our LORD.

3 I beseech you also, my true yokefellow, help those women who laboured with me in the gospel, together with Clement, and with the rest of my fellowlabourers, whose names are written in the book of life.

4 Rejoice in our LORD alway; and again I say, Rejoice.

5 Let your humility be known to all men. Our LORD is at hand.

6 Do not worry over things; but always by prayer and supplication with thanksgiving let your requests be made known to God.

7 And the peace of God, which passes all understanding, shall keep your hearts and minds through Jesus Christ.

8 Finally, my brethren, whatsoever things are true, whatsoever things are honest, whatsoever things are just, whatsoever things are pure, whatsoever things are lovely, whatsoever things are of good report; if there be any virtue, and if there be any praise, think on these things.

9 Those things, which you have learned and received, and heard, and seen in me, do: and the God of peace shall be with you.

10 ¶ But I rejoiced in our LORD greatly, that you have continued to care for me, just as you have always cared, even though you yourselves have not had sufficient.

11 Nor am I saying this simply because I am in want; for I have learned to make what I have meet my needs.

12 I know what it is to be poor, and I know what it is to be rich: I have gone through many things and experienced many things, both to be full and to be hungry, both to have plenty and to be in want.

13 I can do all things through Christ who strengthens me.

14 But you have done well to share my difficulties.

15 Now you Philippians know also, that in the beginning of the gospel, when I departed from Mac-e-do'ni-a , no church shared with me, as concerning giving and receiving, but you only.

16 For even at Thessalonica you sent more than once to meet my needs.

17 I do not say this because I want a gift, but because I want to see the fruits of the gospel increased to you.

18 I have received everything I need, and it is more than enough: I am satisfied, having received everything you sent me by Epaphroditus, and it was welcome as a fragrant perfume and a sacrifice acceptable and well pleasing to God.

　　　　　　　　　　　Cf.dif. vv. 3:16-18, 20;　4:6, 10-12, 14, 18.

19 But my God will supply all your needs according to his riches in the glory of Jesus Christ.
20 Now unto God our Father be glory and honour, for ever and ever.
Amen.

21 ¶ Salute every saint in Jesus Christ. The brethren who are with me greet you.
22 All the saints salute you, especially those who are of Cæsar's household.
23 The grace of our LORD Jesus Christ be with you all.
Amen.

Here ends the Epistle to the Philippians; sent from Rome by Epaphroditus.

ܪܚܡܠܘ ܬܠܕܢ ܐܬܓܪܐ ܬܠܫܙ܀
܀ܐܡܘܡܪ ܝܐ ܬܬܬܬܐܢ

THE EPISTLE OF PAUL THE APOSTLE TO THE

COLOSSIANS

❖ ܟܬܒܐ ܕܠܘܬ ܩܘܠܣܝܐ ❖

CHAPTER 1

*P*AUL, an apostle of Jesus Christ by the will of God, and Ti-mo'the-us our brother,

2 To those who are at Colosse, holy brethren and believers in Jesus Christ: Peace be with you, and grace from God our Father and our LORD Jesus Christ.

3 ¶ Always we give thanks to God, the Father of our LORD Jesus Christ, and always we pray for you,

4 Since we heard of your faith in Jesus Christ, and of your love for all the saints,

5 For the hope which is preserved for you in heaven, of which you heard before in the true word of the gospel;

6 Which has been preached to you, just as it has been preached throughout the world; growing and bringing forth fruits, as it does also in you, since the day you heard of it, and knew the grace of God in truth;

7 Just as you have learned it from Ep'a-phras our beloved fellow-servant, who is for your sakes a faithful minister of Christ:

8 And who has made known to us your love for spiritual things.

9 ¶ For this cause we also, since the day we heard it, do not cease to pray for you, and to ask that you might be filled with the knowledge of the will of God in all wisdom and in all spiritual understanding;

10 That you might live a righteous life, please God with all good works, and bring forth good fruits, and grow in the knowledge of God;

11 And be strengthened with all might, according to the greatness of his glory, in all

patience and longsuffering,

12 So that you may joyfully give thanks to God the Father, who has enlightened us and made us worthy partakers of the inheritance of the saints;

13 And has delivered us from the power of darkness, and brought us to the kingdom of his beloved Son:

14 By whom we have obtained salvation and forgiveness of sins.

15 He is the image of the invisible God, and the first-born of every creature:

16 And through him were created all things that are in heaven, and on earth, visible and invisible; whether imperial thrones, or lordships, or angelic orders, or dominions, all things were in his hand and were created by him:

17 And he is before all things, and by him all things are sustained.

18 And he is the head of the body, the church: for he is the beginning, the firstfruits of the resurrection from the dead; that in all things he might be the first;

19 For it pleased God to complete all things in him;

20 And by his hand to reconcile everything to himself; and through his blood shed on the cross made peace both for those who dwell on earth and for those who dwell in heaven.

21 ¶ Even to you, who in times past were alienated and hostile in your minds because of your evil works, has been given peace,

22 Through the sacrifice of his body and his death, so that he may raise you before him, holy, and without reproach and blameless:

Cf.dif. vv. 1:2, 8-12, 14, 16, 18-20, 22.

23 If you continue in your faith and your foundation is firm, and if you are not moved from the hope of the gospel, which you have heard, and which has been preached to every creature which is under heaven and for which I, Paul, have become a minister;

24 And now rejoice in my sufferings for you, and make up that which is lacking of the sufferings of Christ in my flesh for his body's sake, which is the church:

25 For which I became a minister, according to the dispensation of God which has been given to me for you, fully to preach the word of God everywhere;

26 Even the mystery which has been hidden from ages and from generations, but now is revealed to his saints:

27 To whom God wanted to make known the riches of the glory of this mystery among the Gentiles; which is Christ among you, the hope of our glory;

28 Him we preach, and teach, and make known to every man in all wisdom, that we may bring up every man perfect through Jesus Christ;

29 And to this end, I labour and strive through the help of the power which is given to me.

CHAPTER 2

I WOULD that you knew how I struggled for your sakes and for the sake of those who are at

La-od-i-ce'a, and for the rest who have not seen me personally;

2 That their hearts may be comforted, and that they may be brought near by love to all the riches of the full assurance of understanding of the knowledge of the mystery of God, the Father, and of Christ,

3 In whom are hidden all the treasures of wisdom and knowledge.

4 And I say this, so that no man may beguile you with enticing words.

5 For though I am far away from you in the flesh, yet I am with you in spirit, and I rejoice to see your orderliness and the sincerity of your faith in Christ.

6 Just as you have therefore accepted Jesus Christ our LORD, so you must be led by him:

7 Rooted and built up in him, and established in the faith as you have been taught, abounding therein with thanksgiving.

8 Beware lest any man mislead you through philosophy and vain deceit, after the teaching of men, after the principles of the world, and not after Christ.

9 For in him is embodied all the fulness of the Godhead.

10 And it is through him that you also have been made complete, for he is the head of all angelic orders and powers:

11 In whom also you are circumcised with a circumcision made without hands, in putting off the sinful body by the circumcision of Christ:

12 And you were buried with him in baptism, and by him you were raised with him, for you believed in the power of God who raised him from the dead.

13 And you, who once were dead in your sins and the uncircumcision of your flesh, he has granted to live with him, and he has forgiven you all your sins;

14 And by his commandments he cancelled the written bond of our sins, which stood against us; and he took it out of the way, nailing it to his cross;

15 And by putting off his mortal body, he exposed the powers of evil, and through his person put them openly to shame.

16 Let no man therefore create a disturbance among you about eating and drinking, or about the division of the feast days, the beginning of the months and the day of the sabbath:

17 These are shadows of things to come; but the main objective is Christ.

     Cf.dif. vv. 1:25, 27-29;   2:2, 7, 12, 14-16.

18 Let no man, by pretense of sincerity, doom you, so that you worship angels; for he is bold about the things he has not seen, and foolishly he is proud of his intellectual powers.

19 That very person does not uphold the Head by which the whole body is constructed and stands with the joints and members; and grows through the discipline of God.

20 Therefore, if you have died with Christ and are apart from the principles of the world why then should you be doomed as though living in the world?

21 Do not touch; do not taste; do not follow;

22 For these things are customs which are changeable and they are the commandments and doctrines of men.

23 And it appears there is some word of wisdom in these things when presented by the humble person in fear of God; provided they disregard the things of the flesh, not those things which are honourable but only those things which satisfy the pleasure of the flesh.

CHAPTER 3

*I*F you then are risen with Christ, seek those things which are above, where Christ sits on the right hand of God.

2 Set your mind on things above, not on things on the earth,

3 For you are dead, and your life is hidden with Christ in God.

4 When Christ, who is our life, shall appear, then shall you also appear with him in glory.

5 ¶ Mortify therefore your earthly members: immorality, uncleanness, intemperate desires, evil lusts, and covetousness, for these are idolatry;

6 And it is because of these things that the wrath of God comes on the children of disobedience.

7 In the past you also lived among these things, and you were perverted by them.

8 But now put off from you all these: anger, wrath, malice, blasphemy, foul conversation.

9 Do not lie one to another, but put away the old life with all its practices;

10 And put on the new life which is renewed in knowledge after the pattern in which it was originally created:

11 Where there is neither Jew nor Syrian, circumcision nor uncircumcision, Greek nor barbarian, slave nor freeman; but Christ is all and in all men.

12 Therefore as the elect of God, holy and beloved, put on mercy, kindness, gentleness, humbleness of mind, meekness, patience;

13 Forbearing one another, and forgiving one another; and if any one has a complaint against his fellow man, just as Christ forgave you, so should you also forgive.

14 And with all these things have love, which is the bond of perfection.

15 And let the peace of Christ govern your hearts; for that end, you are called in one body; and be thankful to Christ;

16 And let his word dwell in you abundantly in all wisdom; teaching and admonishing one another in psalms, hymns, and spiritual songs, singing with grace in your hearts to God.

17 And whatever you do in word or deed, do it in the name of our LORD Jesus Christ, giving thanks through him to God the Father.

18 ¶ Wives, submit yourselves to your own husbands, as it is appropriate in Christ.

19 Husbands, love your wives, and be not bitter toward them.

20 Children, obey your parents in all things: for this is well pleasing unto our LORD.

21 Parents, do not provoke your children, that they may not be discouraged.

22 Servants, obey your human masters in

Cf.dif. vv. 2:17-20, 22-23;   3:7, 9-12, 15.

all things, not with eyeservice, as men pleasers; but with a sincere heart, in fear of the LORD.

23 And whatever you do, do it with your whole soul, as to our LORD and not unto men;

24 Knowing that from the LORD you shall receive the reward of the inheritance; for you serve the LORD Christ.

25 But the wrongdoer shall be rewarded according to the wrong which he has done: and there is no respect of persons.

CHAPTER 4

*M*ASTERS, do to your servants that which is just and fair; knowing that you also have a Master in heaven.

2 ¶ Continue in prayer, and watch in the same with thanksgiving;

3 And pray for us also, that God may open unto us a door for preaching, to speak the mystery of Christ for whose sake I am a prisoner:

4 So that I may make it manifest and speak about it as I should.

5 Live wisely in peace with those who are outside the church, and avoid offending.

6 Let your conversation be gracious, seasoned with salt, and you should know how to answer every man.

7 ¶ All things concerning me will be made known to you by Tych'i-cus, who is a beloved brother, and a faithful minister and fellowservant in the LORD:

8 Whom I send to you for this very purpose, that he may know the state of your affairs, and comfort your hearts;

9 Together with O-nes'i-mus, a faithful and beloved brother, who is one of you. They shall make known to you all the things which have happened to us.

10 Ar-is-tar'chus, my fellow-prisoner, salutes you, together with Mark, cousin to Barnabas, concerning whom you have been instructed: and if he comes, receive him;

11 And Jesus, who is called Justus. These are of the circumcision, and the only ones who have helped me toward the Kingdom of God; and have been a comfort to me.

12 Ep'a-phras, who is one of you, a servant of Christ, salutes you: always labouring for you in prayer, that you may stand perfect and complete in all the will of God.

13 For I can testify concerning him, that he has a great zeal for you, and for those who are in

La-od-i-ce'a and Hi-e-rap'o-lis.

14 Luke, the beloved physician, and Demas, greet you.

15 Salute the brethren in La-od-i-ce'a, and salute Nym-phas and his family and the congregation that meets at his house.

16 And when this epistle has been read to you, see that it is read also in the church of the

La-od-i-ce'ans; and likewise you read the epistle written from La-od-i-ce'a.

17 And say to Ar-chip'pus, Take heed to the ministry which you have received in our LORD and that you fulfill it.

18 This salutation is by the hand of me, Paul. Remember my imprisonment.
Grace be with you.
Amen.

Here ends the epistle to the Colossians, written from Rome, and sent by Tychicus and Onesimus.

❖ܪܟܘܡܝ ܝܠ ܐܬܕܬܐܕ ܩܠܨܪ ܕܠܚ ܐܪܝܓܐ ܠܡܫ❖

THE FIRST EPISTLE OF PAUL THE APOSTLE TO THE

THESSALONIANS

∻ ܪܬܐܘܠܘܢܝܩܝܐ ܠܘܬ ܕܦܘܠܘܣ ܩܕܡܝܬܐ ܐܓܪܬܐ ∻

CHAPTER 1

*P*AUL, and Sil-va'nus, and Ti-mo'the-us, unto the church of the Thes-sa-lo'ni-ans which is in God the Father and in our LORD Jesus Christ: Grace be unto you and peace, from God our Father, and the LORD Jesus Christ.

2 ¶ We give thanks to God always for you all, remembering you continually in our prayers;

3 Mentioning before God the Father the works of your faith and the labor of your love, and the patience of your hope in our LORD Jesus Christ.

4 For we know that you are the elected ones, my brethren, and beloved of God.

5 For our preaching to you was not in words only, but also in power, and with the Holy Spirit, and with sincere assurance; and you know also how we lived among you for your sakes.

6 And you became followers of us, and of our LORD, for you welcomed the word with much tribulation and with joy of the Holy Spirit:

7 Thus you have become examples to all the believers in Mac-e-do'ni-a and A-cha'ia.

8 Not only have you sounded out the word of our LORD in Mac-e-do'ni-a and A-cha'ia but also, in every place your faith in God has been heard so that we need not speak anything about you.

9 For these people themselves relate how we entered first among you, and how you turned to God from idols, to serve the living and true God;

10 To wait for his Son from heaven, even Jesus, whom he raised from the dead, for it is he who will deliver us from the wrath to come.

CHAPTER 2

*S*O you yourselves, my brethren, know that our entrance among you was not in vain:

2 But from the beginning we suffered and as you know were treated shamefully, at Phi-lip'pi; then with more struggle but with confidence in our God, we preached to you the gospel of Christ.

3 For our comfort did not spring from deception, nor from uncleanness, nor from enticing speech:

4 But just as we have been examined by God to be entrusted with his gospel, even so we speak, not to please men, but to please God who searches our hearts.

5 And we have never used flattering words, as you know, to conceal greed; God is witness:

6 And we have not sought support from men, neither from you, nor from others, when we could have been burdensome on you for our maintenance, as the apostles of Christ should be.

7 But we were meek when we were among you, and like a foster mother who loves her children: 8 Likewise, we are affectionately desirous to give you, not only the gospel of God, but even our lives, because you were dear to us.

Cf.dif. vv. 1:4-5, 8-10;   2:2, 4-7, 9.

9 For you remember, brethren, that we labored hard, working night and day, with our hands, so that we would not burden you.

10 You are witnesses, and God also, how we preached to you the gospel of God, purely and righteously, and we lived blamelessly among all the believers.

11 You know how we exhorted and encouraged and charged every one of you, as a father does his children,

12 And we bore the testimony to you, so that you may live a life worthy of God, who has called you to his kingdom and glory.

13 For this cause also we thank God continually, because, when you received the word of God which you heard from us you received it not as the word of men, but as it is in truth, the word of God, which works effectively in you who believe.

14 For you, my brethren, have taken the pattern of the churches of God in Judæa which are in Christ Jesus: for you also have suffered from the people of your own tribe, even as they have suffered from the Jews;

15 Who both killed the LORD Jesus Christ, and their own prophets, and have persecuted us; and they do not please God, and are against all men;

16 Forbidding us to speak to the Gentiles that they might be saved, adding this to their sins always; but the wrath of God is upon them to the uttermost.

17 ¶ But we, brethren, have been deprived of your affection for a little while, yet only in presence and not in heart, so we have with great love vigorously endeavored to see your faces.

18 And we have wanted to come to you; I, Paul, tried several times but Satan hindered me.

19 For what is our hope, our joy, or crown of our glorying? Is it not you in the presence of our LORD Jesus when he comes?

20 For you are our glory and our joy.

CHAPTER 3

AND because we could no longer withstand these obstacles, we decided to remain at Athens alone;

2 And send Ti-mo'the-us, our brother, a minister of God, and our helper in the gospel of Christ, to sustain you and comfort you concerning your faith:

3 So that no man among you might be disheartened by these tribulations: for you, yourselves, know that this is our destiny.

4 For verily when we were with you, we told you before, that we should suffer tribulations; even as it has come to pass, and as you know.

5 For this reason also, when I could no longer wait, I sent to know your faith, lest by some means the tempter had tempted you, and our labor was in vain.

6 But now since Ti-mo'the-us has returned to us from you, and brought us good tidings of your faith and love, and that you have good remembrance of us always, longing to see us, just as we also long to see you:

7 Therefore, our brethren, we have been comforted by you, in the midst of all our distress and tribulations because of your faith:

8 Now we can live happily, if you stand firm in our LORD.

9 What thanks can we offer to God for you, for all the joy with which we rejoice for your sakes,

10 Except, before God to abundantly offer supplication, night and day, to see your faces, and to complete that which is lacking in your faith?

11 Now may God, our Father, and our LORD Jesus Christ, direct our journey unto you,

12 And may the LORD increase and enrich your love toward one another and toward all men, even as we love you:

13 And may he strengthen your hearts to be without blemish in holiness before God our

Father, at the coming of our LORD Jesus Christ with all his saints.

CHAPTER 4

FROM this time then, my brethren, we beseech you and entreat you earnestly by our LORD Jesus, that as you have been taught by us how you ought to live and to please God, so you will increase more and more.

2 For you know what commandments we gave you by our LORD Jesus.

3 For this is the will of God, even your sanctification, that you should abstain from fornication:

4 That every one of you should know how to possess his vessel in sanctification and honour;

5 And not through the passion of lust, even as the rest of the Gentiles who know not God:

6 And that no man overreach to transgress and defraud his brother in this matter; because our LORD is the avenger of all such, as we have also forewarned you and testified.

7 For God has not called you unto uncleanness but unto holiness.

8 Therefore, he who does an injustice, does not wrong man but God who has also given unto you his Holy Spirit.

9 ¶ Now concerning brotherly love, you do not need me to write to you for you yourselves are taught by God to love one another.

10 And indeed you show it toward all the brethren who are in Mac-e-do'ni-a ; but I beseech you, my brethren, that you increase your love more and more;

11 And that you endeavor to be quiet, and to do your own business, and to work with your own hands, as we commanded you;

12 That you may lead a life of good example toward outsiders, so that you depend on no man.

13 ¶ Now I want you to know, my brethren, that you should not grieve over those who are dead, as those do who have no hope.

14 For if we believe that Jesus died and rose again, even so those who have died in Jesus, God will bring with him.

15 For this we say to you by the very word of our LORD, that we who are alive and remain unto the coming of our LORD shall not overtake those who are dead.

16 For our LORD himself shall descend from heaven with a shout and the voice of the archangel, and with the trumpet of God; and those who died in Christ will rise first.

17 Then we, who are alive, and remain shall be caught up together with them in the clouds, to meet our LORD in the air: and so shall we ever be with our LORD.

18 Wherefore comfort one another with these words.

CHAPTER 5

BUT of the times and seasons, my brethren, you have no need that I should write to you.

2 For you yourselves know perfectly well that the day of our LORD comes just like a thief in the night.

3 For when they shall say: Peace and tranquility; then sudden destruction will come upon them, as travail upon a woman with child; and they shall not escape.

4 But you, my brethren, are not in darkness that that day shall overtake you as a thief.

5 You are all the children of light, and the children of the day; and you are not the children of the night, nor the children of darkness.

6 Therefore let us not sleep, as do others, but let us watch and be sober.

7 For those who sleep, sleep in the night: and those who are drunken are drunken in the night.

Cf.dif. vv. 4:6, 8, 10, 12, 15-16.

8 But let us who are the children of the day, be alert, putting on the breastplate of faith and love and for a helmet put on the hope of salvation.

9 For God has not appointed us to wrath, but to obtain salvation through our LORD Jesus Christ,

10 Who died for us, that whether we awake or sleep, we shall live together with him.

11 Wherefore comfort one another and edify one another, even as also you do.

12 ¶ We beseech you, my brethren, to respect those who labor among you, and admonish you in our LORD and teach you;

13 That you esteem them very highly in love, and be at peace with them for their work's sake.

14 Now we beseech you, my brethren, correct those who offend, comfort those who lack courage, bear the burdens of the weak, and be patient toward all men.

15 See that none of you render evil for evil; but always follow that which is good, both among yourselves, and to all men.

16 Be joyful always.

17 Pray without ceasing.

18 In every thing give thanks: for this is the will of God in Jesus Christ concerning you.

19 Do not quench the Spirit.

20 Do not reject prophecies.

21 Prove all things, uphold that which is good.

22 Abstain from every sort of evil.

23 May the very God of peace sanctify you wholly; and may your spirit and soul and body be preserved without blemish to the coming of our LORD Jesus Christ.

24 Faithful is he who has called you and he will keep his word.

25 My brethren, pray for us.

26 Salute all our brethren with a holy kiss.

27 I adjure you by our LORD that this epistle be read unto all the holy brethren.

28 The grace of our LORD Jesus Christ be with you. Amen.

Here ends the first epistle to the Thessalonians, written from Athens.

ܪܬܘܪܐܘܪ ܪܝܘܩܠܘܬ ܬܐܠ܂ ܪܬܝܝܪ ܬܘܠܝ܂܂

܂ ܘܩܘܬܪ ܢ ܬܘܬܘܬܪ܂

Cf.dif. vv. 5:8, 12-14, 23-24.

THE SECOND EPISTLE OF PAUL THE APOSTLE TO THE

THESSALONIANS

❖ ܐܓܪܬܐ ܕܬܪܬܝܢ ܕܠܘܬ ܬܣܠܘܢܝܩܝܐ ❖

CHAPTER 1

*P*AUL, and Sil-va'nus, and Ti-mo'the-us, unto the Church of the Thes-sa-lo'ni-ans in God our Father and our LORD Jesus Christ:

2 Grace be with you, and peace, from God our Father, and from our LORD Jesus Christ.

3 ¶ We are bound to give thanks to God always for you, my brethren, as it is appropriate to do, because your faith grows exceedingly, and the love of all of you for one another increases;

4 So that even we ourselves boast of you in the churches of God over your faith and patience in all your persecutions and tribulations that you endure;

5 As an example of the righteous judgment of God, that you may be made worthy of his kingdom, for which you also suffer.

6 And if it seems a righteous thing, before the presence of God, he will recompense tribulation to those who oppress you;

7 And to you who are oppressed, he shall grant to be at peace with us, when our LORD Jesus Christ shall be revealed from heaven with the host of his angels,

8 At which time he will avenge, with flaming fire, those who know not God, and those who do not acknowledge the gospel of our LORD Jesus Christ;

9 For they, at the judgment day, shall be rewarded with everlasting destruction from the presence of our LORD, and from the glory of his power;

10 When he comes to be glorified by his saints and to perform his wonders among his faithful ones, so that our testimony, concern-ing you, may be believed in that day.

11 Therefore we always pray for you, that God will vouchsafe you worthy of your calling, and satisfy all your desires which are for goodness, and the works of faith with power:

12 That the name of our LORD Jesus Christ may be glorified in you, and you in him, according to the grace of our God and our LORD Jesus Christ.

CHAPTER 2

*N*OW we beseech you, my brethren, concerning the coming of our LORD Jesus Christ, and concerning our gathering together with him,

2 That you let not your minds be hastily excited or troubled, neither by word, nor by prophecy of the spirit, nor by an epistle, supposedly from us, stating that the day of our LORD is at hand.

3 Let no man deceive you by any means: for that day shall not come, unless it is preceded by a rebellion, and the man of sin be revealed as the son of perdition,

4 Who opposes and exalts himself above all that is called God or that is reverenced; so that even in the temple of God, he sits as a god, and shows himself, as though he were a god.

5 Do you not remember, that when I was with you I told you these things?

6 And now you know what has prevented him from being revealed in his time.

7 For the mystery of iniquity is already at work: until he who now is the obstacle be taken out of the way.

Cf.dif. vv. 1:8-11;   2:1, 3-4, 7.

8 Then shall the Wicked be exposed, that one whom our LORD Jesus shall consume with the spirit of his mouth, and shall destroy with the revelation of his coming:

9 Even him, whose coming is due to the working of Satan, with all power and signs and lying wonders,

10 And with all deceitfulness of unrighteousness in those who perish; because they received not the love of the truth, that they might be saved thereby.

11 For this cause God shall send them strong delusion that they should believe a lie.

12 That they all, who did not believe in the truth but preferred unrighteousness, might be damned.

13 ¶ But we are bound to give thanks always to God for you, my brethren beloved of our LORD, because God has from the beginning chosen you to salvation, through holiness of the Spirit and through a true faith:

14 And it is to these things that God called you by our preaching, to be the glory of our LORD Jesus Christ.

15 Henceforth, my brethren, stand fast, and hold to the commandments which you have been taught, either by word, or by our epistle.

16 Now our LORD Jesus Christ himself, and God even our Father, who has loved us, and has given us everlasting consolation and good hope through his grace,

17 Comfort your hearts, and strengthen you in every good word and work.

CHAPTER 3

FINALLY, brethren, pray for us, that the word of our LORD may spread freely, and be glorified in every place even as it is among you:

2 And that we may be delivered from evil and unreasonable men: for not every man has faith.

3 But the LORD is faithful; he will guide you and deliver you from evil.

4 We have confidence in you through our LORD, that the things we have commanded you to do, you have done and will continue to do.

5 And may our LORD direct your hearts into the love of God, and into the patience of Christ.

6 Now we command you, my brethren, in the name of our LORD Jesus Christ, to shun every brother who leads an evil life, and not in accord with the commandments which he received from us.

7 For you know well how you ought to imitate us; for our behaviour was not disorderly among you;

8 Neither did we eat bread for nothing from any of you, but worked with hard labor and toiled night and day so that we might not be a burden to any of you:

9 Not because we did not have the right, but to make ourselves an example to you to follow us.

10 For even when we were with you, we commanded this very thing to you, that whoever is unwilling to work should likewise not eat.

11 For we hear that there are some men among you who lead an evil life, and do not work at all, but are busybodies.

12 Now it is these people that we command and exhort by our LORD Jesus Christ, that they work quietly and eat their own bread.

13 But you, brethren, be not weary in well doing.

14 And if any man does not obey our word in this epistle, note that man, and do not associate with him, that he may be ashamed.

15 Yet do not consider him as an enemy, but admonish him as a brother.

16 Now the LORD of peace himself give you peace always in every thing you do. Our LORD be with you all.

Cf.dif. vv. 2:8, 14-15; 3:3-4, 6, 12.

17 ¶ This salutation is in my own handwriting; I, Paul, wrote it, and it is the seal of all my epistles. This is the way I write.

18 The grace of our LORD Jesus Christ be with you all. Amen.

Here ends the second epistle to the Thessalonians, written from Laodicea of Pisidia.

ܫܠܡ ܐܓܪܬܐ ܕܬܪܬܝܢ ܕܠܘܬ ܬܣܠܘܢܝܩܝܐ܄ ܕܐܬܟܬܒܬ ܡܢ ܠܐܘܕܝܩܝܐ ܕܦܝܣܝܕܝܐ܄

THE FIRST EPISTLE OF PAUL THE APOSTLE TO
TIMOTHY

❖ ܐܓܪܬܐ ܕܛܘܒܢܐ ܦܘܠܘܣ ܩܕܡܝܬܐ ❖

CHAPTER 1

*P*AUL, an apostle of Jesus Christ by the commandment of God our Saviour, and Christ Jesus, our hope;

2 To Ti-mo'the-us, a true son in the faith: Grace, mercy and peace from God, our Father, and Christ Jesus our LORD.

3 When I went to Mac-e-do'ni-a , I besought you to remain at Eph'e-sus, so that you might charge certain ones not to teach diverse doctrines,

4 And not to give heed to fables and stories of endless genealogies, which cause dispute, rather than build up the faith of God.

5 Now the fulfillment of the commandment is love out of a pure heart and of a good conscience and of a true faith:

6 From which some have gone astray and have turned aside to foolish words;

7 Desiring to be teachers of the law; not understanding what they speak, nor even whereof they argue.

8 But we know that the law is good, if a man use it lawfully;

9 Knowing this, that the law is not made for the righteous, but for the wicked and rebellious, for the ungodly, and for sinners, for the profane and unholy, for those who abuse their fathers and ill-treat their mothers, for murderers,

10 For whoremongers, for those who defile themselves with mankind, for kidnappers of well-born sons, for liars, for perjurers, and for whatever is contrary to sound doctrine;

11 According to the glorious gospel of the blessed God, which was entrusted to me.

12 And I thank our LORD Jesus Christ who has given me strength, and has counted me trustworthy, and has appointed me to his ministry;

13 Who was before a blasphemer and a persecutor and a reviler; but I obtained mercy, because I did it ignorantly in unbelief.

14 Now the grace of our LORD has become abundant in me, as well as my faith and love in Jesus Christ.

15 This is a trustworthy saying and worthy of all acceptation, that Jesus Christ came into the world to save sinners; of whom I am chief.

16 Howbeit for this cause he had mercy on me, that in me first Jesus Christ may shew forth all patience, for a pattern to those who should hereafter believe in him to life everlasting.

17 Now to the King eternal, immortal, invisible, the only God, be honor and glory for ever and ever. Amen.

18 This charge I commit to you, my son Ti-mo'the-us, in accordance with the prophecies given before about you, that you might fight a good fight;

19 In faith and good conscience; those who have rejected this charge have lost their faith:

20 Namely Hy-me-næ'us and Al-ex-an-der, whom I have delivered to Satan, to be disciplined so that they may no longer blaspheme.

CHAPTER 2

I BESEECH you, therefore, first of all to offer to God, petitions, prayers, supplications, and thanksgiving for all men,

2 For kings and for all in authority; that we may live a quiet and peaceable life, in all purity and Godliness.

3 For this is good and acceptable in the sight of God our Saviour:

4 Who desires all men to be saved and to return to the knowledge of the truth.

5 For there is one God, and one mediator between God and men, the man Christ Jesus;

6 Who gave himself a ransom for all, a testimony which came in due time.

7 For that testimony I was appointed a preacher and an apostle; I tell the truth and I lie not; and I became the teacher of the Gentiles in a true faith.

8 I wish, therefore, that men pray everywhere, lifting up their holy hands, without anger and doubting thoughts.

9 In like manner also, let the apparel of women be simple and their adornment be modest and refined; not with braided hair, or gold, or pearls, or costly array;

10 But let them be engaged in good works, as is becoming women who profess fear of God.

11 Let the woman learn in silence with all subjection.

12 I do not think it seemly for a woman to debate publicly or otherwise usurp the authority of men but should be silent.

13 For Adam was first formed, then Eve.

14 And Adam was not deceived, but the woman was deceived and she transgressed the law.

15 Nevertheless, if her posterity continue in faith and have holiness and chastity, she will live, through them.

CHAPTER 3

THIS is a true saying, If a man desires the office of a bishop, he aspires to a good work.

2 He who becomes an bishop must be blameless, the husband of one wife, have an alert mind, must be sober, of good behaviour, given to hospitality, and apt at teaching;

3 Not given to wine, not a striker, not greedy of filthy lucre; but meek, not a brawler;

4 One who rules well his own household, and keeps his children under submission to bring them up with all purity.

5 For if a man does not know how to rule well his own household, how shall he take care of the church of God?

6 He should not be a recent convert, lest he become proud and fall into the condemnation of the devil.

7 Moreover, he must have a good report from outsiders; lest he fall into reproach and the snares of the devil.

8 Likewise the deacons must be pure, not double-tongued, not given to much wine, not greedy of filthy lucre;

9 But they must uphold the divine mystery of faith with a pure conscience.

10 Let these first be examined, and then let them minister after they have been found blameless.

11 Likewise their wives must be chaste, have an alert mind, faithful in all things, and they must not be slanderers.

12 Let the deacons be appointed from those who have not been polygamous, ruling their children and their own households well.

13 For those who minister well earn good recognition for themselves and grow more familiar with the faith of Jesus Christ.

14 ¶ These things I write to you, although hoping to come to you shortly,

15 So that if I am delayed, you may know how you ought to conduct yourself in the house of God, which is the church of the living God, the pillar and foundation of the truth.

16 Truly great is this divine mystery of righteousness: it is revealed in the flesh, justi-

fied in the Spirit, seen by angels, preached to the Gentiles, believed on in the world, and received up into glory.

CHAPTER 4

*N*OW the Spirit speaks expressly, that in the latter times some shall depart from the faith, following after misleading spirits, and doctrines of devils.

2 Who with false appearance mislead and speak lies and are seared in their own conscience;

3 Who prohibit marriage, and demand abstinence from foods which God has created for use and thanksgiving of those who believe and know the truth.

4 For all things created by God are good, nothing is to be rejected if it is received with thanksgiving,

5 For it is sanctified by the word of God and prayer.

6 If you teach these things to the brethren, you will be a good minister of Jesus Christ, brought up by the words of faith and in the good doctrine which you have been taught.

7 Refuse foolish and old wives fables, and train yourself in righteousness.

8 For physical training profits only for a little while: but righteousness is profitable in all things, having promise of the life that now is, and of that which is to come.

9 This is a true saying and worthy to be accepted.

10 Because of this, we both toil and suffer reproach, because we trust in the living God, who is the Saviour of all men, especially of those who believe.

11 These things command and teach.

12 ¶ Let no man despise your youth; but you be an example to believers, in word, in behaviour, in love, in faith, and in purity.

13 And until I come, strive to study, and continue in prayer and teaching.

14 Do not neglect the gift that you have, which was given to you by prophecy, and by virtue of the laying on of the hands of the presbytery.

15 Meditate upon these things; give yourself wholly to them; so that it may be known to all that you are progressing.

16 Take heed to yourself and to your doctrine; and be firm in them: for in doing this, you shall both save yourself and those who hear you.

CHAPTER 5

*D*O not rebuke an elder, but treat him as a father, and the younger men as your brothers;

2 And the elder women treat as mothers, and the younger as your sisters, with all purity.

3 Honor widows who are widows indeed.

4 And if any of the widows have children, or grandchildren, let them know that aid should be first sought from those of their own household so that the children have the opportunity to repay their obligations to their parents: for this is acceptable before God.

5 Now she who is indeed a widow and destitute, trusts in God, and is constant in prayers and supplications both night and day.

6 But she who lives wholly for pleasure is dead while she lives.

7 Continually charge them with these things, so that they may be blameless.

8 But, if any man does not provide for his own, and especially for those who are of his own household who are of the faith, he has denied the faith, and is worse than an unbeliever.

9 When you select a worthy widow to help, select therefore one who is not less than three score years, who has been the wife of one man only,

10 And well spoken of for good works; if

she has brought up children, if she has lodged strangers, if she has washed the feet of the saints, if she has comforted the distressed, if she has been diligent in every good work.

11 But refuse the younger widows: for when they have begun to wax wanton against Christ, they will marry.

12 Their judgment awaits them because they have been untrue to their first faith.

13 And with it all, they learn to be idle, wandering about from house to house; and not only to be idle, but tattlers also, and busybodies, speaking things which they ought not.

14 I would, therefore, that the younger widows marry, bear children, manage their own households, and give no occasion to the adversary for disdain.

15 For, as conditions are now, some have already strayed after Satan.

16 If any believers, either man or woman, have widows in their families, let them feed them, and do not let them be a burden on the congregation, so that the church may have enough for those who are widows indeed.

17 Let the elders who minister well be esteemed worthy of double honor, especially those who labor in the word and doctrine.

18 For the scripture says: Thou shalt not muzzle the ox that thresheth. And again, The laborer is worthy of his hire.

19 Do not accept an accusation against an elder unless it is supported by the testimony of two or three witnesses.

20 Those who sin, rebuke in the presence of all men, that others also may fear.

21 I adjure you before God and our LORD Jesus Christ, and his elect angels, that you observe these things without prejudice, doing nothing by partiality.

22 Do not lay hands hastily on any man, neither be a partaker of other men's sins; keep yourself pure.

23 Do not drink water in excess, but use a little wine for your stomach's sake, and because of your frequent illnesses.

24 There are men whose crimes are well known and the notoriety of them precedes them to the house of judgment, and there are others, the notoriety of whose crimes follows after them.

25 Likewise also the fame of the good works of some is well known beforehand; and if their acts are otherwise, they cannot be hidden either.

CHAPTER 6

*L*ET all of those who are under the yoke of slavery honor and respect their masters in every way, so that the name of God and his doctrines may not be blasphemed.

2 Those who have masters who are believers, let them not despise them, because they are brethren; but rather serve them more zealously, because they are believers and beloved in whose service they find rest; These things teach and exhort.

3 ¶ If there is any man who teaches a different doctrine, and does not offer the wholesome words of our LORD Jesus Christ, and the doctrine of reverence to God;

4 He is proud, knowing nothing, and dotes on an argument and quarrels on the use of a word and this is the cause of envy and controversy and blasphemy and evil premeditation,

5 And strife among men whose minds are corrupt and who are cut off from the truth and who think worshipping God is for worldly gain; you keep away from such things.

6 ¶ But our gain is greater contentment, for it is the worship of God.

7 For we brought nothing into this world, and it is certain we can carry nothing out.

8 Therefore, let us be satisfied with food and clothing;

9 For those who desire to be rich, fall into temptations, and snares, and into many foolish and hurtful lusts, which drown men in degeneration and destruction.

10 For the love of money is the root of all evil: and there are some men who have coveted it and have thereby erred from the faith, they have brought to themselves many sorrows.

11 ¶ But you, O man of God, flee these things; and follow after righteousness, piety, faith, love, patience, and meekness.

12 Fight the good fight of faith, lay hold on eternal life to which you are called, having professed a true profession before many witnesses.

13 I charge you in the presence of God, the giver of life to all, and before Jesus Christ who gave a good testimony before Pontius Pilate;

14 That you obey this charge without spot and without stain, until the appearing of our LORD Jesus Christ:

15 Who is to be revealed in his due time, blessed and all mighty God, the King of kings, and Lord of lords,

16 Who alone has immortality, dwelling in the light which no man can approach, and whom no man has seen, nor can see: to him be honor and dominion for ever and ever. Amen.

17 ¶ Charge those who are rich in this world, that they be not proud, nor trust in the uncertainty of riches, but in the living God who gives us all things so abundantly for our comfort;

18 That they do good works, and become rich in good deeds, and be ready to give and willing to share,

19 Laying up in store for themselves a good foundation against the time to come, that they may lay hold on the true life.

20 O Timothy, be careful of that which is entrusted to you, flee from empty echoes and from the perversion of science:

21 For those professing this, have strayed from the faith. Grace be with you. Amen.

Here ends the first epistle to Timotheus; written from Laodicea of Pisidia.

ܟܬܒܬܐ ܩܕܡܝܬܐ ܕܠܘܬ ܛܝܡܬܐܘܣ܀
܀ [ܦܝܣܝܕܝܐ] ܠܐܘܕܝܩܝܐ ܡܢ ܐܬܟܬܒܬ܀

THE SECOND EPISTLE OF PAUL THE APOSTLE TO

TIMOTHY

❖ ܐܓܪܬܐ ܕܬܪܬܝܢ ܕܛܘܒܢܐ ܦܘܠܘܣ ❖

CHAPTER 1

*P*AUL, an apostle of Jesus Christ by the will of God and by the promise of life which is in Jesus Christ,

2 To Ti-mo'the-us, a dearly beloved son: Grace, mercy, and peace, from God the Father and Jesus Christ our LORD.

3 I thank God, whom I have served from boyhood with a pure conscience, that I have always remembered you in my prayers night and day.

4 I am anxious to see you; I still remember your tears; I am filled with joy,

5 Especially when I am reminded of your true faith, which dwelt first in your grandmother Lois, and your mother Eunice; and I am sure now in you also.

6 For this reason, I remind you to stir up the gift of God, which is in you by the laying on of my hand.

7 For God has not given us the spirit of fear but of power and of love and of good discipline.

8 Be not, therefore, ashamed of the testimony of our LORD, nor of me his prisoner; but bear the hardships that go along with the preaching of the gospel through the power of God;

9 Who has saved us, and called us with a holy calling, not according to our works, but according to his own will and his grace, which was given us in Jesus Christ before the world began,

10 And is now made manifest by the appearing of our Saviour Jesus Christ, who has abolished death, and has revealed life and immortality through the gospel;

11 To which I am appointed a preacher, and an apostle, and a teacher of the Gentiles.

12 For this cause I suffer these things: nevertheless I am not ashamed; for I know whom I have trusted, and I am sure he will take care of me until that day.

13 Let these bright and sound words which you have heard from me abide with you in the faith and love which is in Jesus Christ.

14 That good thing which was committed to you keep by the help of the Holy Spirit which dwells in us.

15 This you know: that all those in Asia Minor have turned away from me; of whom are Phy-gel'lus and Her-mog'e-nes.

16 Let our LORD grant mercy to the house of On-e-siph'o-rus; for he has often refreshed me, and he was not ashamed of the chains of my imprisonment:

17 But when he was in Rome, he searched for me diligently, and found me.

18 Let our LORD grant to him, that he may find mercy in heaven, where our LORD is, in that day: and of how he ministered to me at Eph'e-sus, you know very well.

CHAPTER 2

*Y*OU, therefore, my son, be strong in the grace that is in Christ Jesus.

2 And the things which you have heard from me by many witnesses, these entrust to faithful men, who shall be able to teach others also.

3 Therefore endure hardships, as a good soldier of Jesus Christ.

Cf.dif. vv. 1:2-3, 5, 7-9, 12-15;   2:2.

4 No man can be a soldier, and also entangle himself with the things of this life; if he would please him who has chosen him to be a soldier.

5 And if a man also strive for mastery in contest, he is not crowned except he compete lawfully. 6 The husbandman who labors should be the first to be sustained by the fruits.

7 Perceive these things: and may our LORD give you wisdom in all things.

8 Remember Jesus Christ who rose from the dead; he who was a descendant from David according to my gospel:

9 Because of him I suffer hardship, even to bonds like a malefactor; but the word of God is not restricted.

10 Therefore I endure all things for the sake of the elect, that they may also obtain the salvation which is in Jesus Christ, with eternal glory.

11 This is a true saying: For if we die with him, we shall also live with him:

12 If we suffer, we shall also reign with him: if we deny him, he also will deny us:

13 But if we believe not in him, yet he will still remain faithful; for he cannot deny himself.

14 You should keep these things in remembrance, as a testimony before our LORD, that the faithful should not argue over words in which there is no profit but which are destruction to those who listen to them.

15 Strive to conduct yourself perfectly before God, as a soldier without reproach and one who preaches straightforwardly the word of truth.

16 Shun empty and worthless words, for they only increase the ungodliness of those who argue over them.

17 And their word will be like a canker eating in many: such are Hy-me-næ'us, and Phi-le'tus,

18 Who have strayed from the truth, saying that the resurrection of the dead is already passed, thus destroying the faith of some.

19 Nevertheless the foundation of God stands firm, having this seal, The LORD knows those who are his, and he will save from iniquity every one who calls upon the name of the LORD.

20 But in a great house there are not only vessels of gold and of silver, but also of wood and of earth; some for formal use on occasions of honor and others for service.

21 If therefore a man purifies himself from these things, he will become like a vessel pure for honor, worthy of the master's use, and ready for every good work.

22 Keep away from all the lusts of youth: and follow after righteousness, faith, love, peace, with those who call on our LORD with a pure heart.

23 Keep away from foolish disputes which do not educate, you know they cause strife.

24 A servant of our LORD must not quarrel; but be gentle to all men, apt at teaching and patient,

25 So that he may discipline gently those who argue against him; and perhaps God will grant them repentance and they will know the truth:

26 And come to themselves, and be saved from the trap of Satan, by whom they have been trapped to his will.

CHAPTER 3

KNOW this: that in the last days disastrous times will come.

2 And men shall be lovers of themselves, and lovers of money, proud, conceited, blasphemers, disobedient to their own people, ungrateful, wicked,

3 False accusers, addicts to lust, brutal, haters of good things,

4 Traitors, hasty, boasters, lovers of plea-

sures more than lovers of God;

5 Having a form of godliness, but are far from the power of God: from such turn away.

6 For of this sort are those who creep into houses and captivate women sunken in sin, led away with divers lusts,

7 Ever striving to learn, and never able to come to the knowledge of the truth,

8 Now just as Jan'nes and Jam'bres stood up against Moses, so do these also resist the truth, men of corrupt minds and far off from the faith.

9 But they shall not progress, for their folly is well known to every man, as theirs also was.

10 But you have been a follower of my teaching, manner of life, purpose, faith, patience, charity, love, steadfastness,

11 Persecution and sorrows: you know the things which I endured at Antioch, and at I-co'ni-um, and at Lys'tra; how I was persecuted; and yet from all these my LORD delivered me.

12 Likewise, all those who wish to live a godly life in Jesus Christ shall suffer persecution.

13 But bad and deceptive men shall grow worse and worse, deceiving and being deceived.

14 But hold fast to the things which you have learned and have been assured of, knowing from whom you have learned them;

15 And knowing that you have learned from your childhood the holy scriptures which are able to make you wise unto salvation through faith in Jesus Christ.

16 All scripture, written by the inspiration of the Holy Spirit, is profitable for doctrine, for reproof, for correction and for instruction in righteousness:

17 So that God's people may become perfect, thoroughly perfected for every good work.

CHAPTER 4

I SOLEMNLY charge you before God, and our LORD Jesus Christ, who shall judge the quick and the dead when his kingdom is come;

2 Preach the word; and stand by it zealously in season and out of season, rebuke, reprove, through all patience and teaching.

3 For the time will come when men will not listen to sound doctrine; but they will add for themselves extra teachers according to their desires, being lured by enticing words;

4 And they will turn away their ears from the truth, and they will turn to fables.

5 But you must be awake to all things, endure hardships, do the work of a preacher, and fulfil your ministry.

6 From henceforth I am ready to die, and the time of my departure is at hand.

7 I have fought a good fight, I have finished my race, I have kept my faith:

8 Henceforth there is preserved for me a crown of righteousness, which my LORD, the righteous judge, will give me at that day: and not to me only but also to all those who eagerly await his appearance.

9 ¶ Make every effort to come to me soon:

10 For De'mas has forsaken me, having loved this world, and has gone to Thes-sa-lo-ni'ca; Cres'cens to Ga-la'tia; Titus to Dal-ma'tia.

11 Only Luke is with me. Take Mark, and bring him with you: for he is suitable to me for the ministry.

12 I have sent Tych'i-cus to Eph'e-sus.

13 The book-carrier which I left at Tro'as with Car'pus, bring it with you when you come, and the books, especially the parchment scrolls.

14 Alexander, the blacksmith, has done me much evil: our LORD reward him according to his works:

Cf.dif. vv. 3:7-8, 10-11, 16-17;   4:2-3, 6, 13.

15 You beware of him also; for he has greatly opposed our words.

16 When I first wrote you, there was no one with me, for all had forsaken me: Do not hold this against them.

17 Nevertheless, my LORD stood by me and strengthened me, that by me the preaching might be fulfilled, and that all the Gentiles might hear: and I was delivered out of the mouth of the lion.

18 And my LORD shall deliver me from every evil work, and will give me life in his heavenly Kingdom: To him be glory, for ever and ever. Amen.

19 Salute Pris-ca and A'qui-la, and their household, and On-e-siph'o-rus.

20 E-ras'tus has remained at Corinth: but I left Troph'i-mus sick at the city of Mi-le'tus.

21 Make every effort to come before winter. Eu-bu'lus greets you, and Pu'dens and Li'nus, and Clau'di-a, and all the brethren.

22 Our LORD Jesus Christ be with your spirit. Grace be with all of us. Amen.

The second epistle unto Timotheus, ordained the first bishop to the church of the Ephesians, was written from Rome, when Paul was brought before Nero the second time.

THE EPISTLE OF PAUL TO

TITUS

❖ ܩܠܛ ܬܘܠ ܐܝܟ ❖

CHAPTER 1

*P*AUL, a servant of God, and an apostle of Jesus Christ, in the faith of God's elect, and in the knowledge of true godliness;

2 In the hope of eternal life, which the true God promised ages ago;

3 And has in due time revealed his word by our preaching; which preaching has been intrusted to me by the command of God our Saviour;

4 To Titus, a true son in the common faith: Grace and peace from God the Father, and the LORD Jesus Christ our Saviour.

5 ¶ For this cause I left you in Crete, that you should set in order the things that are wanting and ordain elders in every city where there is a need as I had commanded you.

6 Appoint only an elder who is blameless, and the husband of one wife, and one who has faithful children who do not swear and who are not intemperate.

7 For an elder must be blameless, as a steward of God; and he must not be self-willed, not quick tempered, not excessive in the use of wine, not too ready to strike with his hand, not a lover of filthy lucre;

8 But a lover of hospitality, a lover of good things, sober, just, pious, and temperate of worldly desires;

9 Holding fast the doctrine of faith, so that he may be able to comfort by his sound doctrine, and to rebuke those who are proud.

10 For there are many unruly and vain talkers and deceivers of the people, especially those who belong to the circumcision:

11 Whose mouths must be stopped, for they corrupt many families, teaching things which they ought not, for the sake of filthy lucre.

12 One of them, even a prophet of their own, said, The Cre'tians are always liars, vicious beasts with empty bellies.

13 This testimony is true. Therefore rebuke them sharply, that they may be sound in the faith;

14 And not give heed to Jewish fables, and commandments of men who hate the truth.

15 To the pure, all things are pure: but nothing is pure to those who are defiled and faithless; even their mind and conscience is defiled.

16 They profess to know God, but in works they deny him, and they are abominable, and disobedient, condemning every kind of good work.

CHAPTER 2

*B*UT you must preach the things which are proper to sound doctrine.

2 Teach the older men to be vigilant, sober, pure, sound in faith, in love, charity and patience.

3 Teach the older women likewise, to behave as becomes the worship of God, not false accusers, not enslaved to much wine, but to become teachers of good things;

4 That they may teach the young women to be modest, to love their husbands and their children,

5 To be discreet, chaste, good home keepers, obedient to their own husbands, so that no one can reproach the word of God.

Cf.dif. vv. 1:5-6, 8-9, 12; 2:3, 5.

6 Likewise exhort the young to be modest.

7 In every thing show yourself an example in all good works, and in your teaching let your word be sound.

8 Choose sound words that are instructive so that no man can point the finger of scorn at us, and so that he who is against us may be shamed, when he can find nothing evil to say about us.

9 Exhort servants to be obedient to their own masters and to please them well in all things not contentious;

10 Not stealing but manifesting true sincerity that they may adorn the doctrine of God our Saviour in all things.

11 For the grace of God that brings salvation has been revealed to all men.

12 It teaches us to renounce ungodliness and worldly lusts, and to live in this world soberly, righteously, and in godliness;

13 Looking for that blessed hope, and the glorious appearing of the great God and our Saviour Jesus Christ;

14 Who gave himself for us, that he might redeem us from all iniquity, and might purify us to be his own, a new people, zealous of good works.

15 These things speak and exhort and rebuke with all authority. Let no man despise you.

CHAPTER 3

REMIND all to be obedient and submissive to princes and governors, and to be ready for every good work,

2 And not to speak evil against any man, and not to be quarrelsome, but to be meek, in every respect showing gentleness to all men.

3 For we ourselves also were sometimes foolish, disobedient, misled, and serving divers lusts and passions, living in malice and envy, hated, and also hating one another.

4 But after the goodness and kindness of God our Saviour was manifested,

5 Not so much by works of righteousness which we have done, but according to his mercy, he saved us by the washing of regeneration, and renewing of the Holy Spirit;

6 Which he shed on us abundantly, through Jesus Christ our Saviour,

7 That being justified by his grace, we should be made heirs to the hope of eternal life.

8 This is a true saying, and these things I want you to constantly affirm, so that those who believe in God may be careful to continually do good works. These things are good and profitable to men.

9 But avoid foolish questions, and genealogies, and contentions, and the theological arguments of the scribes, for they are unprofitable and vain.

10 After you have admonished the heretic once or twice shun him;

11 Knowing that he who is such is corrupt; he sins and condemns himself.

12 ¶ When I send Ar'te-mas or Tych'i-cus to you, endeavor to come to me at Ni-cop'o-lis: for I have decided to winter there.

13 See that Ze'nas, the scribe, and A-pol'los are given a good farewell on their journey, that they lack nothing.

14 And let our people be taught to do good works in times of emergency, that they be not unfruitful.

15 All who are with me salute you. Greet those who love us in the faith. Grace be with you all. Amen.

Here ends the epistle to Titus, ordained the first bishop of the church of Cretians, written from Nicopolis of Macedonia.

✢ ܐܠܗܐ ܕ ܟܠ ܐܬܟܬܒܬ ܐܪܝܫܝܐ ܟܠܗܝܢ ܕܝܠܗ ✢

     Cf.dif. vv. 2:7-9, 14;   3:5, 14.

THE EPISTLE OF PAUL TO

PHILEMON

❖ ܦܝܠܡܘܢ ܠܘܬ ܕܦܘܠܘܣ ❖

*P*AUL, a prisoner of Jesus Christ, and brother Ti-mo'the-us, unto Phi-le'mon our dearly beloved and our fellow-worker,

2 And to our beloved Ap'phi-a and Ar-chip'pus our fellow-labourer, and to the congregation in your house:

3 Grace be with you, and peace, from God our Father and our LORD Jesus Christ.

4 ¶ I thank my God, and always make mention of you in my prayers,

5 Since I have heard of your faith and love, which you have toward our LORD Jesus, and toward all saints;

6 That the participation of your faith may bear fruits in works, and in knowledge of everything that is good which you have in Jesus Christ.

7 For we have great joy and consolation in your love, and the hearts of the saints are refreshed.

8 For this reason, I have great boldness in Christ, to command of you those things which are right,

9 And for love's sake I earnestly beseech you; even I, Paul, an old man as you know, and now also a prisoner for the sake of Jesus Christ.

10 I beseech you on behalf of my son O-nes'i-mus, whom I converted during my imprisonment: 11 But of whom in the past you could not make use, but now he is very useful both to you and to me.

12 I send him to you again: welcome him as my own boy:

13 For I would have kept him with me to minister to me in your place during my imprisonment for the gospel:

14 But I did not wish to do anything without consulting you, that your good deeds might not be done as though by compulsion, but of your own desire.

15 Perhaps this was the reason why he left you for a while, that you can now engage him for ever;

16 Henceforth not as a servant, but more than a servant, a brother beloved, specially to me, and much more to you, both in the flesh and in our LORD.

17 Now, therefore, if you still count me a partner, welcome him as you would me.

18 And if he has caused you any loss, or if he owes you anything, put it on my account:

19 I, Paul, have written this with my own hand; I will repay it, not reminding you that you owe to me even your own life.

20 Indeed, my brother, let me have comfort through you in our LORD: refresh my heart in Christ.

21 Because I have confidence in your obedience, I wrote to you, knowing that you will also do more than I ask.

22 In addition to all this, prepare me a lodging; for I hope that through your prayers I shall be spared to come to you.

23 Ep'a-phras, my fellow prisoner in Jesus Christ, salutes you;

24 So do Mark, Ar-is-tar'chus, De'mas, and Luke, my fellow-workers.

25 The grace of our LORD Jesus Christ be with your spirit. Amen.

Here ends the epistle to Philemon, written from Rome
and sent by Onesimus a servant.

❖ ܫܠܡ ܦܝܠܡܘܢ ܠܘܬ ܕܦܘܠܘܣ ܕܐܬܟܬܒܬ ܡܢ ܪܗܘܡܐ ❖

Cf.dif. vv. 1-2, 6, 8-9, 11-12, 14-15.

329

THE EPISTLE OF PAUL THE APOSTLE TO THE

HEBREWS

❖ ܐܓܪܬܐ ܕܠܘܬ ܥܒ̈ܪܝܐ ❖

CHAPTER 1

FROM of old God spoke to our fathers by the prophets in every manner and in all ways; and in these latter days, he has spoken to us by his Son;

2 Whom he has appointed heir of all things, and by whom also he made the worlds;

3 For he is the brightness of his glory and the express image of his being, upholding all things by the power of his word; and when he had through his person, cleansed our sins, then he sat down on the right hand of the Majesty on high;

4 And he is altogether greater than the angels, just as the name he has inherited is a more excellent name than theirs.

5 For to which of the angels has God at any time, said You are my Son, this day have I begotten you? And again, I will be to him a Father, and he shall be to me a Son?

6 And again, when he brought the Firstbegotten into the world, he said, Let all the angels of God worship him.

7 And of the angels he said thus, Who makes his angels spirits; his ministers a flaming fire.

8 But of the Son he said, Thy throne, O God, is for ever and ever: the scepter of thy kingdom is a right scepter.

9 You have loved righteousness, and hated iniquity; therefore, God, even your God, has anointed you with the oil of gladness more than your fellows.

10 And from the very beginning you have laid the foundations of the earth; and the heavens are the works of your hands:

11 They shall pass away; but you shall endure; and they all shall wear out like a garment;

12 And as a cloak you shall fold them up, and they shall be changed: but you are the same, and your years shall never end.

13 For to which of the angels has he at any time said, Sit thou at my right hand, until I make thine enemies thy footstool under your feet?

14 Are they not all ministering spirits, sent forth in the service for those who shall inherit life everlasting?

CHAPTER 2

THEREFORE, we should give earnest heed to the things which we have heard, lest at any time they be lost.

2 For if the word spoken by the angels has been affirmed, and every one who has heard it and transgressed it has received a just reward,

3 How shall we escape, if we neglect the very things which are our salvation and which were first spoken by our LORD, and were proved to us by those who had heard him,

4 And to which God testified with signs and wonders and with divers miracles, and with the gift of the Holy Spirit, given according to his will.

5 ¶ For he has not put into subjection to the angels the world to come, whereof we speak.

6 But as the scripture testifies, saying, What is man that thou art mindful of him? and the son of man, that thou visitest him?

7 For thou hast made him a little lower than the angels: and have crowned him with glory and honor, and have set him ruler over the works of thy hands:

Cf.dif. vv. 1:1, 3-4, 8, 11-12, 14;   2:1-4, 6-7.

8 Thou hast put all things in subjection under his feet. By putting all things under his control, he left nothing that he did not put under subjection to him. But now we do not see yet that all things are in subjection to him.

9 We see that he is Jesus who humbled himself to be a little lower than the angels, through his suffering and his death, but now he is crowned with glory and honor; for he tasted death for the sake of every one but God.

10 ¶ And it was meet and proper for him, in whose hand is everything and for whom are all things, to bring many sons to glory, so that from the very beginning of their salvation, they are made perfect through sufferings.

11 For both he who sanctifies and those who are sanctified are all of one origin: for this reason he is not ashamed to call them brethren,

12 Saying, I will declare thy name to my brethren; in the midst of the congregation will I praise thee.

13 And again, I will put my trust in him. And again, Behold me and the children which God has given me.

14 Forasmuch then as the children are partakers of flesh and blood, he also likewise partook of the same; and by his death he has destroyed him who had the power of death, that is, the devil.

15 And has released them who, through fear of death all their lives, were subject to slavery.

16 For he did not take on him the pattern of angels; but he did take on him the seed of Abraham.

17 Therefore it was meet and proper that in every thing he should resemble his brethren, that he might be a merciful, and faithful high priest in the things of God, to make reconciliation for the sins of the people.

18 For in that he himself has suffered, being tempted, he is able to help those who are tempted.

CHAPTER 3

*F*ROM henceforth, O my holy brethren, called by a call from heaven, look to this Apostle and High Priest of our faith, Jesus Christ:

2 Who was faithful to him who appointed him, as also Moses was faithful to all his house.

3 The glory of Jesus is much greater than that of Moses, just as the honor of the builder of the house is greater than the house.

4 For every house is built by some man; but he who builds all things is God.

5 And Moses, as a servant, was faithful to all his house, and was a testimony of those things which were to be spoken after;

6 But Christ, as a son, over his own house, whose house we are, if to the end we hold fast with confidence to the glory of his hope.

7 ¶ Therefore, as the Holy Spirit said, Today if you will hear his voice,

8 Harden not your hearts to provoke him, as the murmurers did in the day of temptation in the wilderness:

9 Your fathers tempted me even though they examined and saw my works forty years.

10 Therefore I was not pleased with that generation, and said, These are a people whose hearts have been misled and they have not known my ways.

11 So I swore in my anger, They shall not enter into my rest.

12 ¶ Take heed therefore, my brethren, lest perhaps there is a man among you who has an evil heart and is not a believer, and you will be cut off from the living God.

13 But search your hearts daily, until the day which is called, The day; to the end that no man among you be hardened through the

deceitfulness of sin.

14 For we are made partakers of Christ, if from the beginning to the very end we hold steadfast to this true covenant,

15 As it is said, Today, if you hear even the echoes of his voice, do not harden your hearts to anger him.

16 Who are those who have heard and provoked him? Were they not those who came out of Egypt under Moses, although not all of them?

17 But with whom was he displeased for forty years? Was it not especially with those who had sinned and whose bones lay in the wilderness?

18 And against whom did he swear that they should not enter into his rest, except against those who did not listen?

19 So we see that they could not enter in because they did not believe.

CHAPTER 4

*L*ET us therefore fear, while the promise of entering into his rest remains, lest some amongst you find they are prevented from entering.

2 For the gospel was preached to us, as it was to them also, but the word they heard did not benefit them: because it was not mixed with faith in those who heard it.

3 But we who have believed will enter into rest, as he said, As I have sworn in my wrath, they shall not enter into my rest; for behold, the works of God were from the very foundation of the world.

4 For he said concerning the sabbath, God rested on the seventh day from all his works.

5 And here again he said, They shall not enter into my rest.

6 There was a chance for some to enter therein, but they to whom the gospel was first preached did not enter, because they would not listen:

7 And again, after a long time he appointed another day, as it is written above, for David said, Today if you hear his voice, harden not your hearts.

8 For if Joshua the son of Nun had given them rest, he would not afterward have spoken of another day.

9 It is therefore the duty of the people of God to keep the Sabbath.

10 For he who has entered into his rest, he also has ceased from his own works, as God did from his.

11 Let us strive therefore to enter into that rest, lest any man fall like those who were disobedient.

12 ¶ For the word of God is living and powerful and sharper than any twoedged sword, piercing even to the point of division between soul and spirit, and between the joints and marrow and bones, and is a discerner of the thoughts and intents of the heart.

13 And there is no creature which is hidden from his sight: but all things are naked and open before the eyes of him to whom we are to answer.

14 ¶ We have, therefore, a great high priest who has ascended into heaven, Jesus Christ, the Son of God; let us remain firm in his faith.

15 For we do not have a high priest who cannot share our infirmities, but we have one who was tempted with everything as we are, and yet without sin.

16 Let us, therefore, come openly to the throne of his grace, that we may obtain mercy, and find grace to help in time of need.

CHAPTER 5

*F*OR every high priest chosen from among men is ordained on behalf of men about things pertaining to God, that he may offer both gifts and sacrifices for sins:

2 He is one who can humble himself and have compassion on those who are ignorant

Cf.dif. vv. 3:13-16;　4:1, 3-8, 12-16.

and go astray: for he himself also is subject to weaknesses.

3 Because of these, he is obliged, just as he offers sacrifices for the people, likewise to offer for himself on account of his own sins.

4 And no man takes this honor unto himself, but only he who is called of God as was Aar'on.

5 So also Christ did not glorify himself by becoming a high priest, but he glorified him who said to him, Thou art my Son, Today have I begotten thee.

6 And he said also in another place, Thou art a priest for ever after the order of Mel-chis'e-dec.

7 Even when he was clothed in the flesh, he offered prayers and supplications, with vehement cries and tears, to him who was able to save him from death; and verily he was heard.

8 And though he were a good Son, because of fear and suffering which he endured, he learned obedience.

9 And he grew to be perfect, and became the author of life everlasting to all who obey him;

10 So he was called by God, a high priest after the order of Mel-chis'e-dec.

11 ¶ Now concerning this very Mel-chis'e-dec, we have much to say, but it is difficult to explain because you are dull of comprehension.

12 By now you should be teachers because you have been a long time in training: But even now you need to be taught the primary writings of the word of God; but you are still in need of milk, and not strong meat.

13 For every man whose food is milk, is unfamiliar with the word of righteousness: for he is a babe.

14 But strong meat belongs to those who are of full age, even those who by reason of use have their senses exercised to discern both good and evil.

CHAPTER 6

THEREFORE, let us leave the elementary word of Christ, and let us go on to perfection: Why do you again lay another foundation for the repentance from past deeds, and for faith in God?

2 And for the doctrine of baptisms, and for the laying on of hands, and for the resurrection of the dead and for eternal judgment?

3 If the LORD permits, this we will do.

4 But this is impossible for those who have once been baptised, and have tasted the gift from heaven, and have received the Holy Spirit,

5 And have tasted the good word of God, and the powers of the world to come,

6 For, for them to sin again, and be renewed again by repentance, they crucify the Son of God a second time, and put him to open shame.

7 For the earth which drinks in the rain that falls abundantly on it, and brings forth herbs useful to those for whom it is cultivated, receives blessing from God:

8 But if it should produce thorns and briers it is rejected and not far from being condemned; and at the end this crop will be used for fuel.

9 But beloved brethren, we expect from you the things that are good and that pertain to salvation, even though we speak in this manner.

10 For God is not unjust to forget your works and your labor of love which you have made known in his name, for you have ministered to the saints and still do minister.

11 ¶ We desire that every one of you show the same diligence toward the fulfillment of your hope, even unto the end,

12 And that you be not slothful, but be followers of those who through faith and patience have become heirs of the promise.

13 For when God made a promise to A'braham, because there was none greater than

himself by whom he could swear, he swore by himself,

14 Saying, Blessing, I will bless you, and multiplying, I will multiply you.

15 And so he was patient, and obtained the promise.

16 For men swear by one who is greater than themselves: and in every dispute among them, the true settlement is by oaths.

17 Therefore, because God wanted more abundantly to show to the heirs of promise that his agreement was unchangeable, he sealed it by an oath.

18 Thus, by the promise and by the oath which are unchangeable, and in neither of which could God lie, we find courage to hold fast to the hope that has been promised by him in whom we have taken refuge.

19 That promise is like an anchor to us; it upholds the soul so that it may not be shaken, and it penetrates beyond the veil of the temple;

20 Therein Jesus has previously entered for our sakes, and become the high priest for ever, after the order of Mel-chis'e-dec.

CHAPTER 7

FOR this Mel-chis'e-dec was king of Sa lem, the priest of the most high God, who met

A'bra-ham, returning from the slaughter of the kings, and blessed him;

2 And to whom A'bra-ham also set aside a tenth part from the choice things he had with him. His name is interpreted King of righteousness, and again, King of Salem, which means King of peace.

3 Neither his father nor his mother is recorded in the genealogies; and neither the beginning of his days nor the end of his life; but, like the Son of God, his priesthood abides for ever.

4 Now consider how great this man was, unto whom even the patriarch Abraham gave

tithes and paid head tax.

5 For those sons of Levi who received the office of the priesthood, were authorized by law to take tithes from the people; even from their own brethren who also had come out of the loins of Abraham.

6 But this man who is not recorded in their genealogies took tithes even from Abraham, and blessed him who had received the promises.

7 Beyond dispute: he who was less was blessed by him who was greater than himself.

8 And here mortal men receive tithes; but there he, of whom the scripture testifies that he lives, receives them.

9 Speaking as a man, through A'bra-ham, even Levi who received tithes, also gave tithes.

10 For he was yet in the loins of his forefather Abraham, when Mel-chis'e-dec met him.

11 If therefore perfection had been reached by the Le-vit'ic-al priesthood, by which the law was enacted for the people, what further need was there that another priest should rise after the order of Mel-chis'e-dec? Otherwise, the scriptures would have said, that he would be after the order of Aaron.

12 Since there was a change in the priesthood, so also there was a change in the law.

13 For he, concerning whom these things are spoken, was born of another tribe, from which no man ever ministered at the altar.

14 For it is evident that our LORD sprang out of Juda, of which tribe Moses said nothing concerning the priesthood.

15 And yet, it is far more evident because he said that another priest would rise after the order of Mel-chis'e-dec,

16 One who was not appointed after the law of carnal commandments, but after the power of life which abides for ever.

Cf.dif. vv. 6:13, 16-20; 7:2, 4, 6-7, 9-11, 13, 16.

17 For he testified concerning him, Thou art a priest for ever after the order of Mel-chis'e-dec.

18 For the change which took place in the former law, was made on account of its weaknesses, and because it had become useless.

19 For the law made nothing perfect, but there has come in its place a better hope, by which we draw near to God.

20 And he confirmed it for us by oath.

21 For they were made priests without oaths; but this one was made a priest with an oath, as it was said concerning him by David, The LORD has sworn, and will not lie, Thou art a priest for ever after the order of Mel-chis'e-dec.

22 All these things make a better covenant because Jesus is its surety.

23 And these priests were many, because they were mortal, and they were not permitted to continue because of death:

24 But this man, because he is immortal, has a priesthood which remains for ever.

25 Therefore he is able to forever save those who come to God by him because forever he lives to make intercession for them.

26 ¶ For this is the kind of high priest proper for us; pure, without evil, and undefiled, far away from sin, and made higher than the heavens;

27 And who needs not daily, as do those high priests, to offer up sacrifice, first for their own sins, and then for the people's, for this he did once when he offered up himself.

28 For the law appoints imperfect men priests; but the word of the oath which came after the law appoints the Son who is perfect for evermore.

CHAPTER 8

NOW above all we have a high priest, who is seated at the right hand of the throne of the Majesty in heaven;

2 And he has become the minister of the sanctuary, and of the true tabernacle, which God pitched and not man.

3 For every high priest is appointed to offer gifts and sacrifices, therefore it is necessary that this man have something to offer also.

4 For if he were on earth, he would not be a priest, because there are priests who offer gifts according to the law:

5 Who serve the semblance and shadow of heavenly things, just as it was commanded to Moses when he was about to make the tabernacle: See that you make all things according to the pattern showed to thee in the mount.

6 But now Jesus Christ has received a ministry which is greater than that; just as the covenant in which he was made a mediator, is greater, so are the promises greater than those given in the old covenant.

7 ¶ For if the first covenant had been faultless, then there would have been no need for the second.

8 For he found fault with them, and said, Behold, the day is coming, saith the LORD, when I will perfect a new covenant with the house of Israel and with the house of Judah:

9 Not according to the covenant that I made with their fathers in the day when I took them by the hand and led them out of the land of Egypt; and because they abode not in my covenant, I rejected them, saith the LORD.

10 For this shall be the covenant that I will make with the house of Israel; After those days, saith the LORD, I will put my law into their minds, and I will write it on their hearts: and I will be their God, and they shall be my people.

11 And no man shall teach his neighbor, neither his brother, saying, Know the LORD: for all shall know me, from the youngest to the oldest.

12 And I will forgive their wickedness, and

I will no longer remember their sins.

13 By that which he has said, With a new covenant, the first one has become old, and that which is old and obsolete is near destruction.

CHAPTER 9

*T*HEN verily the first covenant had also ordinances of divine service and a worldly sanctuary.

2 For the first tabernacle which was made, had in it the candlestick, and the table and the shewbread; and it was called the sanctuary.

3 But the inner tabernacle, which is within the veil of the second door, was called the Holy of Holies.

4 And there was in it the golden censer, and the ark of the covenant all overlaid with gold, and in it was the golden pot containing the manna, and Aaron's rod which sprouted, and the tablets of the covenant;

5 And over it the cherubim of glory, overshadowing the mercy seat; now is not the time to describe how these things were made.

6 The priests always entered into the outer tabernacle and performed their service of worship;

7 But into the inner tabernacle, the high priest entered alone, once every year, with the blood which he offered for himself, and for the faults of the people.

8 By this the Holy Spirit revealed that the way of the saints would not yet be made known, so long as the old tabernacle remained;

9 Which was the symbol for that time, now past, in which were offered both gifts and sacrifices, which could not make perfect the conscience of him who offered them,

10 But which served only for food and drink, and in divers ablutions, which are ordinances of the flesh and which were imposed until the time of reformation.

11 But Christ, who had come, became the high priest of the good things which he wrought; and he entered into a greater and more perfect tabernacle which was not made by hands, and was not of this world;

12 And he did not enter with the blood of goats and calves, but by his own blood, he entered in once into the holy place, and obtained for us everlasting redemption.

13 For if the blood of goats and calves, and the ashes of a heifer, sprinkled on those who were defiled, sanctified them even to the cleansing of their flesh;

14 How much more will the blood of Christ, who through the eternal Spirit offered himself without blemish to God, purify our conscience from dead works so that we may serve the living God?

15 ¶ For this cause he became the mediator of the new testament and by his death he became redemption for those who transgressed the old covenant, that those who are called may receive the promise of eternal inheritance.

16 For where a testament is, it is proved after the death of its maker.

17 For a testament is of force after men are dead, otherwise it is useless so long as its maker lives.

18 For this reason not even the first covenant was confirmed without blood.

19 For when Moses had given every precept to all the people according to the law, Moses took the blood of a heifer with water, and scarlet wool and hyssop, and sprinkled it on the books and on all the people,

20 Saying, This is the blood of the testament, which has been ordained for you by God.

21 That very blood he also sprinkled on the tabernacle and on all the vessels used for worship;

22 Because nearly everything, according to the law, is purified with the blood: and without shedding of blood there is no forgiveness.

23 It is necessary, therefore, that the patterns of things which are heavenly should be purified with these; but the heavenly things themselves, with sacrifices better than these.

24 For Christ has not entered into the holy place made with hands, which is the symbol of the true one; but he entered into heaven itself to appear before the presence of God for our sakes.

25 Not so that he should offer himself many times, as did the high priest who enters into the holy place every year with blood which is not his own;

26 And if not so, then he would have been obliged to suffer many times from the very beginning of the world: but now at the end of the world, only once, by his sacrifice, did he offer himself to abolish sin.

27 And just as it is appointed for men to die once, and after their death, the judgment;

28 So Christ was once offered to bear the sins of many; so that at his second coming, he shall appear without our sins for the salvation of those who look for him.

CHAPTER 10

*F*OR the law had in it a shadow of the good things to come, but was not the essence of the things themselves; hence although the same sacrifices were offered every year, they could not perfect those who offered them.

2 For if they had once been perfected, they would have ceased from their offerings; for, from henceforth their minds would not have driven them into the sins from which they had once been cleansed.

3 But in those sacrifices they remembered their sins every year.

4 For it is not possible that the blood of bulls and of goats could take away sins.

5 Therefore, when he entered into the world, he said: Sacrifices and offerings thou didst not desire, but a body thou hast prepared me:

6 Burnt offering and sin offering thou has not required.

7 Then said I, Lo, I come, in the beginning of the books, it is written of me, I delight to do thy will, O God.

8 Above when he said: Sacrifices and offerings and burnt offerings and offerings for sins, thou wouldst not, the very ones which were offered according to the law:

9 And after that he said, Lo, I come to do thy will, O God. Thus he put an end to the first in order to establish the second.

10 By this very will, we are sanctified through the offering of the body of Jesus Christ once for all.

11 For every high priest appointed ministered daily, offering the same sacrifices, which had never been able to cleanse sins:

12 But this man after he had offered one sacrifice for sins, sat down on the right hand of God for ever.

13 From henceforth there he will remain until his enemies are placed as a foot-stool under his feet.

14 For by one offering he has perfected for ever those who are sanctified.

15 The Holy Spirit is also a witness to us: for he had said before,

16 This is the covenant that I will make with them after those days, saith the LORD, I will put my law in their minds, and write it on their hearts.

17 And their iniquities and sins will I remember no more.

18 For where there is forgiveness of sins, there is no need for offering for sins.

Cf.dif. vv. 10:1-2, 5, 11, 13, 16, 18.

19 ¶ Having therefore, my brethren, boldness to enter into the holiest by the blood of Jesus,

20 By a new and living way, which he has made new for us, through the veil, that is to say, his flesh;

21 And having a great high priest over the house of God:

22 Let us draw near with a true heart in full assurance of faith, having our hearts sprinkled and cleansed of evil thought, and our bodies washed with pure water.

23 Let us remain firm in the profession of our faith without wavering: for he who has promised us is faithful.

24 And let us consider one another to arouse love and good works:

25 Not forsaking the assembling of ourselves together, as is customary for some; but exhorting one another: and so much the more when you see that day approaching.

26 For if any man sin willfully after he has received the knowledge of the truth, then there is no more sacrifice to be offered for sins,

27 But he is ready for the fearful judgment and the fiery indignation which shall consume the adversaries.

28 He who transgressed the law of Moses, on the word of two or three witnesses; died without mercy:

29 How much more punishment do you think he will receive who has trodden underfoot the Son of God, and has considered the blood of his covenant, through which he had been sanctified, as ordinary blood and has blasphemed the Spirit of Grace?

30 For we know him who said, Vengeance is mine, and I will repay, saith the LORD. And again, The LORD shall judge his people.

31 It is a fearful thing to fall into the hands of the living God.

32 ¶ Remember, therefore, the former days,

in which, after you received baptism, you endured a great fight of suffering.

33 By reproach and trouble, you were made an object of ridicule; and you have also become companions of those men who have also endured these things.

34 And you had pity on those who were prisoners, and you took the seizure of your property cheerfully, for you know in yourselves that you have a better and a more enduring possession in heaven.

35 Do not lose, therefore, the confidence that you have, for it has a great reward.

36 For you have need of patience in order that you may do the will of God and receive the promise.

37 For the time is all too short, and he who is to come will come, and will not delay.

38 But the righteous shall live by my faith: and if any draw back, my soul shall have no pleasure in him.

39 But we do not belong to those who draw back to perdition, but to the faith which restores our soul.

CHAPTER 11

*N*OW faith is the substance of things hoped for, just as it was the substance of things which have come to pass; and it is the evidence of things not seen,

2 And in this way it became a testimonial of the elders.

3 For it is through faith we understand that the worlds were framed by the word of God, so that the things which are seen came to be from those which are not seen.

4 It was by faith, Abel offered a more excellent sacrifice to God than Cain, and because of this, he received a testimonial that he was righteous, and God testified to his offering: therefore, even though he is dead, he speaks.

5 By faith Enoch departed and did not taste death, and he was not found, because God

transferred him: but before he took him away, there was a testimonial about him, that he pleased God.

6 Without faith, man cannot please God: for he who comes near to God must believe that he is, and that he is a rewarder of those who seek him.

7 By faith Noah, when he was warned concerning the things not seen, became fearful and he made an ark to save his household, and by it he condemned the world and he became heir of righteousness which is by faith.

8 By faith Abraham, when he was called to depart for the land which he was to receive for an inheritance, obeyed; and he went out, not knowing where he was going.

9 By faith he became a sojourner in the land which was promised him as in a strange country, and he dwelt in tents with Isaac and Jacob, the heirs with him of the same promise:

10 For he looked for a city which has foundations, whose builder and maker is God.

11 Through faith also Sarah who was barren, received strength to conceive seed, and was delivered of a child when she was past age, because she was sure that he who had promised her was faithful.

12 Therefore, there sprang from one who was as good as dead, as many as the stars of the sky in number, and as the sand which is on the sea shore innumerable.

13 These all died in faith not having received the promised land, but they saw it from afar off, and rejoiced in it; and they acknowledged that they were strangers and pilgrims on earth.

14 For they who speak so, declare plainly that they seek a country for themselves.

15 And if they had a desire for that very country from which they went out, they had time to return to it again.

16 But now it is evident, that they desire a better city, that city which is in heaven: therefore God is not ashamed to be called their God: for he has prepared for them a city.

17 By faith Abraham, when he was tested, offered up Isaac: he lifted upon the altar his only begotten son, even that very one who had been received in the promise.

18 Of whom it was said, In Isaac shall thy seed be called:

19 And he reasoned in himself, It is possible for God even to raise the dead, and because of this Isaac was given to him as a parable.

20 By faith in the things to come Isaac blessed Jacob and Esau.

21 By faith Jacob, when be was dying, blessed both of the sons of Joseph, and he worshipped, leaning upon the head of his staff.

22 By faith Joseph, when he died made mention of the departure of the children of Israel; and gave commandment concerning his bones.

23 By faith the parents of Moses, hid him for three months after his birth, because they saw that the infant boy was fair; and they were not afraid of the King's commandment.

24 By faith Moses, when he came to manhood, refused to be called the son of Pha'raoh's daughter.

25 Choosing rather to suffer affliction with the people of God, than to enjoy the pleasures of sin for a short while.

26 And he reasoned that the reproach of Christ was greater riches than the treasures of Egypt: for he looked forward to be paid the reward.

27 By faith he forsook Egypt, not fearing the wrath of the king; and he survived after he had seen God, who is invisible.

28 Through faith he instituted the passover, and sprinkled the blood, lest he who de-

Cf.dif. vv. 11:5, 7, 9, 11, 13-17, 19, 23, 26-27.

stroyed the first-born should touch them.

29 By faith they passed through the Red Sea as by dry land: but in it the Egyptians were drowned when they made the attempt.

30 By faith the walls of Jericho fell down, after they were being encompassed seven days.

31 By faith Rahab the harlot did not perish with those who were disobedient, for she had received the spies in peace.

32 And what more shall I say? for time would fail me to tell of Gideon, and of Barak, and of Samson, and of Jeph'tha-e, and of David also, and Samuel, and of the rest of the prophets:

33 Who through faith conquered kingdoms, wrought righteousness, obtained promises, stopped the mouths of lions,

34 Quenched the violence of fire, escaped the edge of the sword, out of weakness were made strong, and became valiant in battle, and routed the camps of enemies;

35 Restored to women their sons, raised from the dead: while others died through tortures, not hoping for deliverance; that they might have a better resurrection:

36 Others endured mockings and scourgings, still others were delivered to bonds and imprisonment:

37 Others were stoned, others were sawn apart, others died by the edge of the sword: others wandered about, wearing sheep skins and goat skins; destitute, afflicted and tormented;

38 Of whom the world was not worthy: they wandered as though lost in the desert, and in mountains, and in dens and in caves of the earth.

39 Thus these all, having obtained a testimonial through the faith, did not receive the promise:

40 Because God, from the beginning, provided for our help lest, without us, they should not be made perfect.

CHAPTER 12

*T*HEREFORE, seeing we also are surrounded with so great a cloud of witnesses, let us lay aside every weight, and the sin which does so easily beset us, and let us run with patience the race that is set before us;

2 And let us look to Jesus, who was the author and the perfecter of our faith; and who, instead of the joy which he could have had, endured the cross, suffered shame, and is now seated at the right hand of the throne of God.

3 See, therefore, how much he has suffered from the hands of sinners, from those who were a contradiction to themselves, lest you become weary and faint in your soul.

4 ¶ You have not yet come face to face with blood in your striving against sin.

5 And you have forgotten the teaching which has been told to you as to children, My son, despise not thou the chastening of the LORD, nor let your soul faint when thou art rebuked of him,

6 For whom the LORD loves, he chastens him, and disciplines the sons with whom he is pleased.

7 Now, therefore, endure discipline, because God acts toward you as towards sons; for where is the son whom the father does not discipline?

8 But if you are without discipline, that very discipline by which every man is trained, then you are strangers and not sons.

9 Furthermore if our fathers of the flesh corrected us and we respected them, how much more then should we willingly be under subjection to our Spiritual Father, and live?

10 For they only for a short while, disciplined us as seemed good to them; but God corrects us for our advantage, that we might become partakers of his holiness.

11 No discipline, at the time, is expected to be a thing of joy, but of sorrow; but in the end it produces the fruits of peace and righ-

Cf.dif. vv. 11:31, 36, 40;   12:3, 5-9.

teousness to those who are trained by it.

12 ¶ Therefore, be courageous and strong;

13 And make straight the paths for your feet, so that the weak do not go astray but are healed.

14 Follow peace with all men, and holiness, without which no man shall see our LORD.

15 Take heed lest any man among you be found short of the grace of God; or lest any root of bitterness spring forth and harm you, and thereby many be defiled;

16 Or lest any man among you be found immoral and weak like Esau, who sold his birthright for a morsel of meat.

17 For you know that afterward when he wished to inherit the blessing, he was rejected, and he had no chance of recovery, even though he sought it with tears.

18 For you have yet neither come near the roaring fire, nor the darkness nor the storm nor the tempest,

19 Nor to the sound of the trumpet and the voice of the word; which voice they heard but refused so that the word will not be spoken to them any more.

20 For they could not survive that which was commanded, for if even a beast drew near the mountain, it would be stoned.

21 And so terrible was the sight, that Moses said, I fear and quake.

22 But you have come near to Mount Zion, and to the city of the living God, the heavenly Jerusalem, and to the innumerable multitude of angels,

23 And to the congregation of the first converts who are enrolled in heaven, and to God the Judge of all, and to the spirits of pious men made perfect

24 And to Jesus, the mediator of the new covenant, and to the sprinkling of his blood, which speaks a better message than Abel did.

25 Beware, therefore, lest you refuse him who speaks to you. For if they were not de-livered who refused him who spoke with them on earth, much more can we not escape if we refuse him who speaks to us from heaven:

26 The one whose voice shook the earth; but now he has promised, saying, Once more I will shake not only the earth, but also heaven.

27 And this word, Once more, signifies the change of things which may be shaken, because they are made, in order that the things which can not be shaken may remain.

28 Therefore, we receiving a kingdom which cannot be shaken, let us hold fast that grace whereby we may serve and please God with reverence and godly fear:

29 For our God is a consuming fire.

CHAPTER 13

*L*ET brotherly love continue in you.

2 And forget not hospitality toward strangers: For thereby some were worthy to entertain angels unawares.

3 Remember those who are in prison, as though you were a prisoner with them; remember those who suffer adversity, for you are human also.

4 Marriage is honourable in all, and the bed undefiled; but God will judge those who practice vice and adultery;

5 Do not be carried away by the love of money; but be content with what you have: for the LORD himself has said, I will never leave thee, nor forsake thee.

6 So that we may boldly say, The LORD is my helper, and I will not fear what man shall do unto me.

7 Remember those who are your leaders, those who have spoken the word of God to you: mark the completeness of their works, and imitate their faith.

8 Jesus Christ the same yesterday, and today, and for ever.

9 Do not be carried away by strange and divers doctrines. For it is a good thing to strengthen our hearts with grace; not with food, because it did not help those who greatly sought after it.

10 We have an altar from which those who minister in the tabernacle have no right to eat.

11 For the flesh of the beasts, whose blood is brought into the sanctuary by the high priest for sin, is burned outside the camp.

12 Wherefore Jesus also, that he might sanctify his people with his own blood, suffered outside the city.

13 Let us go forth therefore to him outside the camp, bearing his reproach.

14 For here we have not a permanent city, but we seek one to come.

15 By him, therefore, let us always offer the sacrifice of praise to God, that is, the fruit of the lips giving thanks to his name.

16 And do not forget kindness and fellowship with the poor: for with such sacrifices God is well pleased.

17 Listen to your spiritual leaders, and obey them: for they are watchful guardians of your souls, as one who must give account, that they may do it with joy, and not with grief: for that is unprofitable for you.

18 Pray for us: for we trust we have a good conscience, in all things willing to live honestly.

19 But above all, I beseech you to do this that I may return to you sooner.

20 ¶ Now the God of peace, who brought again from the dead our LORD Jesus, that great shepherd of the sheep through the blood of the everlasting covenant,

21 Make you perfect in every good work to do his will, working in us that which is well-pleasing in his sight, through Jesus Christ; to whom be glory forever and ever. Amen.

22 ¶ And I beseech you, my brethren, to be patient in the word of comfort: for I have written you very briefly.

23 You should know our brother Timothy has been set at liberty; and if he should come shortly, I will see you together with him.

24 Salute all your spiritual leaders and all the saints. All of the brethren of Italy salute you.

25 Grace be with you all. Amen.

Here ends the epistle to the Hebrews written from Italy.

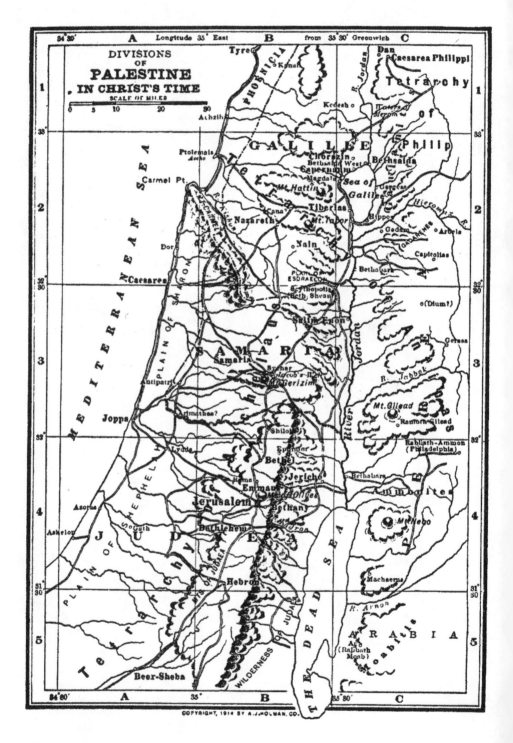

DIVISIONS
OF
PALESTINE
IN CHRIST'S TIME

SCALE OF MILES

0   5   10   20   30

Longitude 35° East   from 35° 30' Greenwich

Tyre

Kanah

PHOENICIA

Achzib

Ptolemais
Accho

Carmel Pt.

GALILEE

Kedesh

Chorazin
Bethsaida West
Capernaum
Magdala
Mt. Hattin
Cana
Tiberias

Dan
Caesarea Philippi

Waters of
Merom

Tetrarchy

of

Philip

Bethsaida
Gergesa

Sea of
Galilee

Hippos

Hieromax R.

Gadara
Arbela

Dor

Nazareth
Mt. Tabor

Nain

Caesarea

PLAIN OF
ESDRAELON
Scythopolis
Beth Shean

Salim Enon

SAMARIA

Samaria

Sychar
Jacob's Well
Mt. Gerizim

Antipatris

Arimathea?

Joppa

Shiloh

Ephraim

Bethel

Lydda

Jericho

Emmaus

Mt. of Olives
Jerusalem
Bethany

Bethlehem

Hebron

Azotus

Gath

Ashkelon

JUDEA

Beer-Sheba

MEDITERRANEAN SEA

PLAIN OF SHARON

PLAIN OF SHEPHELAH

Mt. Carmel

R. Jordan

Bethabara

o (Dium?)

Gerasa

R. Jabbok

Mt. Gilead
Ramoth-Gilead

Rabbath-Ammon
(Philadelphia)

Jordan River

Bethabara

Ammonites

Mt. Nebo

THE DEAD SEA

Machaerus

R. Arnon

ARABIA

Ar
(Rabbath Moab)

Moabites

Tetrarchy of

PLAIN OF JUDAEA

WILDERNESS OF JUDAEA

346

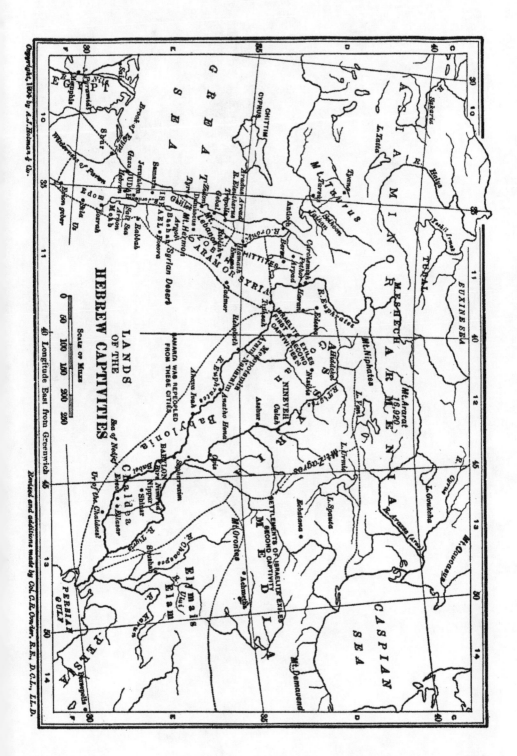

LANDS OF THE HEBREW CAPTIVITIES

348

Printed in the USA
CPSIA information can be obtained
at www.ICGtesting.com
CBHW021011290824
13869CB00027B/86